Miracle on
Second Avenue

Miracle on
Second Avenue

Hare Krishna Arrives in the West
NEW YORK, SAN FRANCISCO, AND LONDON: 1966-1969

MUKUNDA GOSWAMI
with Mandira Dasi

TORCHLIGHT PUBLISHING, INC.
shifting the paradigm

Jacket and text design and production by Mayapriya Long, Bookwrights

Jacket photo © The Bhaktivedanta Book Trust. Used with permission.

Printed in India

Published simultaneously in the United States of America and Canada
by Torchlight Publishing.

Library of Congress Cataloging-in-Publication Data
Goswami, Mukunda, 1942-
  Miracle on Second Avenue : Hare Krishna arrives in the west : New York,
San Francisco, and London, 1966–1969 / by Mukunda Goswami with
Mandira Dasi.
    p. cm.
  ISBN 978-0-9817273-4-9
1. International Society for Krishna Consciousness–United States–
New York. 2. International Society for Krishna Consciousness–England–
London. 3. International Society for Krishna Consciousness–History.
I. Mandira Dasi. II. Title.
  BL1285.835.U62N49 2011
  294.5'512–dc22

                            2010044609

www.miracleonsecondavenue.com

TORCHLIGHT PUBLISHING, INC.
shifting the paradigm

P.O. Box 52 Badger CA 93603 • Phone: (559) 337-2200 • Fax (559) 337-2354
torchlightpublishing@yahoo.com   www.torchlight.com

To His Divine Grace, A.C. Bhaktivedanta Swami,
my spiritual master

Author's Note

This is a true story. However, some of the names were changed for a variety of reasons.

Satsvarupa Das Goswami's *Srila Prabhupada Lilamrita* is, by my estimation, a fine document that portrays Shrila Prabhupada's founding of the Hare Krishna Movement. In this book, the reader will see through my eyes. I do not think that my account is perfectly objective, but histories and biographies must always be as accurate as possible. My story in some minor ways differs from what Satsvarupa Das Goswami has so expertly written. However, my purpose is to tell a true story.

Acknowledgement

I wish to thank everyone who helped bring this book into existence.

Mukunda Goswami
November 2010

"Of all forms of evidence for establishing the truth, experience from one's own life is the strongest."

—Sanatana Goswami

Contents

Introduction

From afar again you've called, from the land of Oz – what is it now, nearly 50 years since first we met? Even then, Reed College in 1960, you were my hero, my touchstone, the mysterious Michael Grant always turning our small group of friends onto something new and COOL; Lenny Bruce, Thelonius Monk, hanging out in late-night coffee-houses while you jazzed the crowd with your keyboards, in shades and black beret.

Then your odyssey to New York City in '65, this swami you wrote back to us about; many of us too, in those drug-laced days, were looking for a Teacher, a guide to higher reality. Then suddenly, me and Melody, horse, dog and chicken, amazed from our mountaintop Oregon fire-lookout to see this dusty VW grind to a stop at the base of the tower in autumn of '66 and you and Joanie and her sister Jan – then your wife! – piled out non-stop from New York City to rave about him: the swami! Ecstatic, smiling, declining a coke, a smoke, a bloody steak, all the things that had so far bound us. For days we watched you, Melody and I. Hey, if Michael and Joan are always so happy, chanting something about "Krishna" on those big red beads, maybe we should give it a shot...

You who had always seemed so detached from everyone and everything around you, suddenly so attached – devoted! – to a Teacher, a Yogi, wow, someone who could show us the Truth! You said you were on your way to San Francisco where the swami had asked you to start a Krishna temple; the next day it snowed, my boss radioed we could leave (and as we lived for magic in those days), we eventually followed you down the mountain and off to the greatest adventure of our lives; now named Mukunda, but still my touchstone.

Walking through Haight-Ashbury in recent years I see you everywhere. Sweet-talking Allen Cohen into an article for the Oracle: "The New Science"; pre-dawn raids spray-painting Hare Krishna on empty Haight sidewalks; quietly orchestrating one of the great rock concerts in history; and then the swami came! His physical appearance, his words, his actions, they had us in total awe. He seemed from another planet. And you were the swami's favorite, living down the hall from him in those apartments on Frederick Street, how we envied your fortunate intimacy. And here it was that your deep inner humility and unselfish nature was so freely displayed. You would say to us, "Go up and see the swami, he really wants to meet you." And slowly we warmed to him, sat at his side, and in a short time became his familiar children. Mukunda the touchstone.

Swamiji; the most beautiful person we'd ever met, who knew everything, the master magician, the most bold of all adventurers, our dearest well-wisher, who so smoothly vibrated with his words and music all the complex dissonance of our lives into one simple harmony.

The swami was always saying, "Become yourselves Krishna conscious and spread Krishna Consciousness." Action! Well, we quickly learned from your example that spreading the Krishna consciousness movement in a big way not only made us more Krishna conscious but especially that big service caught the attention of the swami. "So Shyamasundar, you have made $2000 from that program last night? You must come each day and I will teach you to keep the books."

So to please our wonderful Spiritual Master we went out, you and I and our godbrothers and godsisters, and spent our furious young energies spreading Krishna's name all over the world. You transferred to the rest of us the swami's mood that nothing was impossible; everything was Krishna's magic, and so it was. We struggled and celebrated as all obstacles melted away and Krishna became a global household word. In these adventurous times, you were our rock, our quiet anchor, unmoved when cyclonic winds of change threatened to blow us away. You are the most un-judgmental person I have ever met, Mukunda, before or since those days, always seeing the good in everyone, never critical, and your seldom-said but right-on-time "Don't worry, Krishna will help us" endeared us ever stronger to the swami.

Thinking back, Mukunda, anytime there was some great accomplishment when we were together, even if someone else took the credit, I felt then and still do, that it was you somehow that had made it happen so nicely.

Miracle on Second Avenue is the best description yet of those fine days of endless horizons, when everything was possible, when Krishna consciousness would become a worldwide religion.

Your incredible sense of mimicry – the heart and soul of a great musician – has endowed this book with the immediacy of dialogue, puts the reader right into the event. Mukunda the musician, the humorist, the guy who always had us cracking up at his impersonations: the full-on hippy ("Yeah man, groovy") with Bill Graham or Jerry Garcia; the mannered Lincoln's Inn solicitor with Mr. Savage and Mr. Black, who had come to condemn our London temple, calmly appealing ("Oh I say there...") to the laws of religious tolerance and the deep-grained British sense of fair play; the cool musician with George Harrison and John Lennon ("I think we should go into an E-minor on this bit") – we laughed till we cried when you did your take-offs on Mr. Balfour, our British banker, or when you lovingly mimicked Panditji, our music guru, or our sweet new British devotees, or the Anglicized Indians who invited us to programs or into their homes for heavy meals...

Miracle on Second Avenue is the logical extension of your lifelong devotion to Shrila Prabhupada and his injunction to "spread Krishna consciousness," a duty you have never left, steadfastly spreading Krishna consciousness during our times together in San Francisco and London, and then with your ISKCON Communications programs, and still with your ISKCON News weekly website – which still inspires thousands of people daily. I have no doubt whatsoever that this perfectly written book will inspire millions to the wonders of our dearly beloved Spiritual Master, the one and only A.C. Bhaktivedanta Swami Prabhupada.

– Shyamasundar Das Adhikari

PART I

NEW YORK

The Bowery Swami

A Wonderful Town

East Side, West Side,
All around the town
The tots sang "ring-around-rosie,"
"London Bridge is falling down"
Boys and girls together,
Me and Mamie O'Rourke
Tripped the light fantastic
On the sidewalks of New York

—James W. Blake & Charles B. Lawlor

CHAPTER 1

A Gesture of Friendship

August 1966

The phone was ringing. It had been eerily silent for the past two days.

"Hello?" I said.

"Mr. Michael, there has been some trouble?" It was the swami's voice – raspy, but concerned, warm and paternal.

I had met the swami only a few months ago. There *had* been some trouble.

"I read the article in the *New York Times*," he said.

I cringed, thinking of the swami reading the article: *"Michael Grant, 24, was charged with offering narcotics to a minor. Accused of statutory rape, possession with the intent to sell narcotics and contributing to the delinquency of a minor."*

"No, I think it's all under control now," I blurted into the phone. "Some lawyers are working on it, and they tell me it'll be over in a few weeks. Nothing to worry about." I was trying to sound optimistic even though my nightmare was far from over.

"Can you come here for lunch?"

"I … I think so. When?"

"We have lunch every day at one. Can you come today?"

"Yes, I think so. Yes. I'll come. See you then. G'bye."

The week before the swami's phone call I'd been arrested in Hurleyville, New York, and jailed for five days. After the *New York*

Times article appeared, my piano tuner didn't answer my phone calls. Neither did my work contacts or my friends. My social circle crumbled overnight. Everyone hated me, or so it seemed – the FBI, the Hurleyville police, the New York State troopers, the *New York Times*, the musicians' union, and apparently even my small cluster of friends. Where were they? Why didn't they care, or at least phone? I could explain that the charges were false. I hadn't done anything wrong. I wasn't caught in bed with Henry's fifteen-year-old girlfriend like the state cop told his pals; and she wasn't my companion, like the *New York Times* said. Although I was far from a saint at twenty-four, I wasn't *that* bad.

As I was being arrested, it occurred to me that this event had the potential to turn my musical career into a complete shambles. Publicity like this scared people. Although I was well-known and slightly idolized by a few people in the jazz underworld, and although I had made the grade in that world with a kind of twisted fame, my bubble had burst. Now I felt it was me and my partner Jan alone against the rest of the world.

"Who was that?" asked Jan when I hung up the phone.

"It was the swami. Jeez, I never thought *he'd* call. You know, maybe this whole arrest thing is a sign. Maybe we should just chuck the whole thing and live more simply, you know, move out to the country or to somewhere else in the world, someplace like India. What do you think? I don't want to hang around for the court case."

"Oh, I don't know," she sighed. "If you don't show up for the hearing and they catch you then you'll really be in trouble."

Things were changing in my life … fast. Within the past two years both my parents had died and with a modest inheritance in hand and an obliging, fun partner, I could really see myself leaving New York for good – maybe for some exotic destination. Now, in the midst of my legal quagmire, I felt I should have left the city long ago.

A few hours later, I headed over to the swami's new location on Second Avenue, about a half-hour walk from my place in the Bowery. It was hot and muggy. The corner garbage cans overflowed. As usual, the Bowery smelled like a mixture of urine and beer, an unmistakable odor that always hung in the summer air in that part of Manhattan. I'd gotten used to the non-stop rumble of cars and trucks along the Bowery. Most of the people on the wide sidewalk were drunks, but there were a few deliverymen and Chinese on

ay | **24 SEIZED IN RAIDS**
Seen | **IN THE CATSKILLS**
re

Narcotics Crackdown Called
nade | **Sullivan County's Biggest**
nver
elec-
the | *Special to The New York Times*
the | LIBERTY, N. Y., Aug. 8—
was | Twenty-four persons were ar-
ther | rested today in a series of raids
iga- | described by the police as the
arti- | biggest narcotics crackdown in
imes | the history of Sullivan County.
ada, | The raids, in the Catskill
andy | resort villages of Liberty, Falls-
own | burgh and Thompson, began at
wide | 5 A.M. and continued for 12
nflu- | hours. All the suspects, 12 of
y | whom gave New York City
the | addresses, were held in Sullivan
or- | County Jail at Monticello.
e in- | Sullivan County District At-
date | torney Robert C. Williams said
a bid | at least three well-known
n on | "Borsch Belt" hotels employed
nded | many of the suspects, but he re-
Clos- | fused to name the hotels on the
pail | ground that they were "not tied
very- | in" with the arrests or the nar-
urist | cotics-pushing activities of the
for | employes.
Pike. | Police records in Liberty,
aban- | however, show that one of the
gs to | suspects, David Joseph Rivera,
rther | 27 years old, of Monticello, was
who | arrested at Grossinger's.
andi- | The police said Rivera had
mber, | tried to stab arresting officers.
rings | He was charged with two
cause | counts of assault, resisting
arrest, possession of dangerous
weapons and sale and possession of heroin and marijuana.
Capt. Edgar Croswell, head of
ares | the state police Bureau of
nded | Criminal Investigation at Sid-
ney, said two of the persons
Reu- | arrested were teen-aged girls,
of Ni- | one a 15-year-old whose male
new | companion, Michael Grant, 24,
bolish | of 110 Bowery, New York City,
gov- | was charged with offering nar-
y by | cotics to a minor.
gulyi- | Captain Croswell, who as a
sergeant led the 1957 raid on
owon | the Apalachin gangland conven-
dcast | tion, said yesterday's raids had
would | resulted from a 40-day investi-
an as- | gation in which state police,
con- | New York City detectives and
tions, | the Federal Narcotics Bureau
ed to | had cooperated. Sullivan County
m. | and local police also took part.
Captain Croswell said the
raiders had picked up "several

thousand dollars" worth of
heroin, marijuana and ampheta-
mines, plus needles and syringes
commonly used in the taking of
heroin.
The District Attorney said
most of those arrested were
narcotics "pushers" or peddlers
who over a period of more than
a month had sold drugs to some
of the 100 undercover agents
who had worked on the case.
A Federal Narcotics Bureau
spokesman said undercover
agents had posed as hotel room
clerks and had arranged to buy
narcotics from the alleged
pushers. One official said "the
Hotel Association interests up
here are raising hell about the
bad publicity."
There was no indication, police officials said, that an
organized ring was operating in
the Catskills, although some of
the suspects "obviously had contact with one another." They
said a number of the suspects
had arrest records.

TWO ROBBERS SLAIN
IN SUFFOLK DRIVE-IN

SMITHTOWN, L. I., Aug. 8
(AP)—Two Suffolk County detectives, acting on an anony-
mous tip that a drive-in theater would be robbed near here
early today, shot and killed
two Smithtown men they found
in the act of breaking into the
theater's safe.
John L. Barry, Suffolk Police Commissioner, said the two
detectives were Sgt. Frank
Barylski and Nick Cutrone. Mr.
Barry said he believed the two
men caught robbing the theater office in Nesconset had
been in the audience at the
time the detectives arrived.
After the movie had ended,
he said, Sergeant Barylski
found the suspects in the office, one with an acetylene
torch turned on the safe.
"This is the police," they announced. "The place is surrounded. Don't move."
But the man at the safe,
Frank Dohman, 23 years old,
turned the torch toward the
detectives and moved toward
them, the police said. Both detectives fired, killing the man.
The second man, identified
as Henry Arns, 25, appeared
with what Mr. Barry said
seemed to be a weapon, which
turned out later to be a metal
tool. The detectives fired again,
killing him.
Mr. Barry said both men had
long police records.

The New York Times *August 9, 1966 misreported in paragraph six that I was
the "companion" of a 15-year-old girl. I was 24 at the time.*

their way to or from Chinatown on the other side of Canal Street.

There was a large black felt announcement board propped up in the front window of the small storefront I'd helped the swami secure six weeks earlier. Inch-high white letters were stuck into the grooves of the board.

Classes on *Bhagavad-gita*

Monday, Wednesday and Friday, 7 p.m.

Chant *Hare Krishna Hare Krishna Krishna Krishna Hare Hare Hare Rama Hare Rama Rama Rama Hare Hare*

... and your life will be sublime!

Sign in the window shelf at 26 Second Avenue

Glancing inside the storefront as I passed, I saw that the bare place had been transformed into a tiny Indian temple. An expensive-looking oriental-patterned rug stretched from the front of the room all the way down to the back windows that looked out onto the courtyard and were cloaked with heavy drapes. Decorations hung from the ceiling, including a large cymbal that I had once seen a guy named Howard playing. There was a low platform covered in maroon velvet and hung with tassels, from which I'd seen the swami lecture, and behind it an enormous circular painting of Lord Krishna and his consort Radha. The smell of incense and crushed rose petals drifted from the room. The *tamboura* I had brought for the swami some months ago sat in one corner.

I went through a dim hallway into a small leafy courtyard and then up the twelve stairs to his second-floor apartment. My heart was beating fast from the climb. The door was slightly ajar, and through it wafted the fresh and alluring aroma of sandalwood and jasmine, mixed with the rich smell of Indian cooking spices. I pushed open the door. Seven men were sitting on the floor with their backs against the walls of a small living room that had no furniture, carpets or rugs. They were eating off wax paper and from plastic and glass bowls and an unusual assortment of drinking glasses. Sunlight flooded through the curtain-less windows, spreading in warm pools on the clean, wooden slat floor.

The swami smiled up at me from the cushion where he sat on the floor.

"Mr. Michael, come, come. Sit. Eat. You are OK?" His hospitality encouraged me; I felt like an invited special guest.

The swami watched his visitors eat the lunch he had prepared for them, monitoring their progress through their meals and replenishing the preparations as they disappeared from their plates. I took my place beside one of the other guests on the floor, and Janis, the guy helping the swami serve the meal, gave me a plate piled high with food. I'd drifted into vegetarianism several years ago, but this looked a lot better than the food I usually ate. I'd been experimenting with macrobiotic food and often ate at a restaurant called The Paradox on the Lower East Side, a place that I learned a few years later was frequented by Yoko Ono. Macrobiotic food was not particularly inspiring for me, and the swami's vegetarian food looked appetizing and exotic: instead of bland brown rice and zucchinis, sesame seeds and beans, the spread before me consisted of hot *dahl* made with lentils and vegetables and fresh herbs, steaming fluffy rice, warm whole meal *chapattis* brushed with a little butter, lightly spiced potatoes and warm milk with bananas. Suddenly I was hungry.

"Yeah, I'm fine, Swami," I said. "How do you like your new place?" It was the first time I had sat with him to talk for some time.

"Very nice, very nice. And the temple is nice also."

He turned his attention to the man sitting to his left. "Stanley, Stanley. Take. Take." He kept handing Stanley warm *chapattis*. Stanley was nearly six feet tall, gaunt and emaciated looking, with short black hair, stubble, and sharp, angular features. After eleven *chapattis,* the swami laughed heartily and said, "My spiritual master, he didn't like fat disciples." Stanley just shrugged off the swami's comment and kept eating, but I thought I saw a slight smile on his face and sensed that he was laughing internally with the swami.

CHAPTER 2

The Seeker

Although I'd known the swami for what amounted to only a matter of months when I joined his guests for lunch that day, I felt that my meeting him had been a long time coming, that it was the latest episode in a string of events throughout my life.

I had come from a conservative Jewish background, but I had a distinct rebellious streak that I nurtured from an early age. Social clubs, sports and playing in bands were the main things about school that interested me, although I was keen on music and literature. As a teenager, I enthusiastically consumed "good writing": Shakespeare's *Julius Caesar*, Billy Wilder's *Stalag 17*, Somerset Maugham's *The Razor's Edge*, Conrad's *Heart of Darkness*, Faulkner's *As I Lay Dying*, Graham Greene's *The Third Man*, Saul Bellow's *The Adventures of Augie March*, Hemingway's *The Old Man and the Sea*, Lawrence Ferlinghetti's *Pictures of the Gone World* and lots of Dylan Thomas.

When I was sixteen, I started drinking rather heavily, smoking pot and hanging out with musicians, many of whom were older than I was. Some wore goatees, and some were pimps. My parents seemed oblivious to it all, including the fact that I was smoking, and not just cigarettes.

During this time, I became friends with Dick Miller, who was the most rebellious but academically brilliant guy in school. Although he was in all the high academic classes, he was everything the older generation hated: he cut class, came to school drunk, worked as a male prostitute and had affairs with female members of staff who were twice his age. He exposed me to the underworld of dope, prostitution and jazz. I admired his outspokenness and his rejection of the system in which we had been raised; I laughed at the world with him and in some ways even emulated his behavior.

Then, when Dick and I were seventeen, the car he was driving was involved in a head-on collision with a truck. The other members of his family in the car were not seriously injured, but he was killed.

His funeral was held in Seattle, a two-hour drive from my home in Portland. I rode up to the service with a teacher of mine, Wayne Altree, and a friend named Craig. The funeral parlor was full of flowers and loud, dreary organ music and blinding sunlight from the clerestory windows. Dick's ex-girlfriend Linda was there, dressed in white, her cheeks stained black with tears and mascara. She looked gray.

I filed past the coffin with the other mourners. When I saw Dick's face bruised black and blue in the open casket, I felt sick. It was the first time I'd come face to face with death, and I couldn't process what had happened to this person who was the same age as me. I was overcome with grief and rode back to Portland in complete silence while Craig whimpered in the back seat.

Barely able to function, I ran into Altree some days later as I drifted between classes.

"How are you doing?" he asked.

"Not so good."

"You know," he said, "bad things are going to happen in life, even to extraordinary people like Dick."

"But why?" I asked, not really expecting an answer.

"I don't really know." He paused. "You need a teacher," he said.

"You're my teacher."

"I mean a teacher who can explain this stuff, someone who has some answers."

I didn't take Altree's advice very seriously, but I did become interested in philosophy in my early twenties. I easily accommodated the Eastern and oriental variety and was attracted to the works of Aldous Huxley, especially books such as *Doors of Perception* which leaned eastward and touted the "here and now" philosophy. Despite being something of a spiritual seeker, I was an agnostic. I had witnessed a great deal of hypocrisy in the people of God in my childhood. My parents considered religion more or less an add-on to a happy, successful life. Their Judaism seemed to me to be based more on social intercourse than on spirituality. There was a lot of discrimination and condescension toward other faiths. Shortly after my Bar Mitzvah, I mentally renounced identification with Judaism.

When I was nineteen, I moved to New York to seek a career as a musician. I lived in the center of the city and began working to establish myself in the underground world of jazz. In 1962, when I was twenty, I married Beverly, a small woman with dark brown hair, brown eyes and a round face. We'd been friends through most of high school, but I had known her since age seven. Due to our mutual infidelity throughout our four-year marriage, she moved out and I was left on my own.

After Beverly and I separated, I returned to Portland, Oregon, for a brief family visit. While I was there, I met Jan. She was quiet and petite and struck me as glamorous, with her striking blue eyes and long black hair.

My first words to her were, "What do you think of getting high?"

"If you have to ask, you couldn't possibly know," she answered coolly.

We both took LSD that day. It was her first time, and her older sister Joan thought she shouldn't have. That night in an old rented house on the southeast side of town, Jan and I paired off, and the two other couples there thought it was great, if a bit abrupt. The next day we watched an art film at Reed College and began our private dialogue. We were both at loose ends with nothing much to do, except that I wanted to go back to New York and she wanted to do something different and new.

We drove to New York the week after we met in a 1957 Chevrolet I'd bought from my brother. Joan thought Jan was being impulsive and that New York City was too dangerous for her. Since it was winter, we decided to drive from Portland via the southern route to New York. When we got into northern California it was snowing hard, and we almost ran out of gas. But we coasted a lot in neutral with the engine off and managed to make it to the next gas station without freezing to death on the remote mountain road covered with deep snow on both sides.

Once in New York, we moved into a loft on the top floor of 110 Bowery. Our loft was an AIR (Artists in Residence) apartment that, like so many building top floors at the time, was undecorated and functioned as both a studio and a home. The place was huge – nearly two thousand square feet – and the rent was cheap, only fifty-five dollars a month. We didn't care about the lousy neighborhood. We just wanted our own place with space and privacy and the ability to make as much noise as we wanted any time of the day or night. We made lots of music with the alternative people we met, and we made sure that books like the *Kama Sutra* weren't lost on us.

We began to explore various spiritual and religious experiences, which were as prevalent and easy to come by in New York as drugs. A couple of months into our stay in New York, I visited an "uptown" swami in Manhattan's chic East 50s. It was an informal lecture in what looked like a converted apartment. The plush well-decorated room was redolent with white pipe smoke. Portly, gray men and women sat motionless in over-stuffed leather chairs. The Indian swami's squeaky voice grated on my nerves; no cohesive message emerged.

Some time later, I attended New York's First Zen Institute. The first floor of the Manhattan brownstone apartment front room had been made into a sparsely decorated and immaculately clean temple room with folding chairs, white curtains and a dark sickly green carpet. About ten followers in their middle to late thirties – older people, I thought – were seated, waiting in apparent expectation. A small, shaven-headed oriental monk dressed in black came from the rear, down the middle aisle, to take his place at the front of the room. He stood before what appeared to be a small altar, a table draped in white cloth upon which sat a green glass bowl of bananas, oranges, apples and peaches.

Someone passed out a small song sheet. We all read and chanted together, following the monk. "*O ro mo so, do lo jo po, may, fay, say, day, ray, ee, lee, mee, jee, kee, ree.*" The song was about twenty lines long, and it took about ten minutes to sing, repetitions included. The monk's voice rang out above the others.

After the chant, he exited as fast as he'd entered, disappearing through a door at the back of the room, which banged shut after him. About six of the American Buddhist members of the audience invited me to another room upstairs for an informal chat, which turned out to be a conversation at a round table centered on fasting. The main message from what I could gather was "don't break a fast with orange juice." I was unimpressed. How was this spiritual? "God," I thought, "I'll never go back there."

A few weeks later, on the recommendation of a friend, I talked with an elderly Christian priest. This monumental four-minute meeting took place after a one-hour wait in the foyer of a huge New York church in upper Manhattan. I was annoyed at being made to stand and wait; I felt like I was waiting in line to get a driver's license.

The priest finally showed up wearing an overcoat and walked briskly toward me. He was tall and gray-haired, and wore a suit and smiled a lot.

"Are you the one waiting to see me?" he asked.

"Yes."

"And what can I do for you today?"

I thought quickly. "What's the most important teaching to concentrate on?"

"Once I visited Mother Vivian," he said.

"What?"

He suddenly became very still and got a far-off look in his eyes. "She was living in a convent in a small village in southern Italy. When I looked into her eyes, I knew she knew something I didn't know. Her eyes were clear; they were limpid. I knew she was wise."

"What did she say?"

"She didn't say anything. I expected her to say a little bit, but she didn't say a word. She just *looked* at me. And I knew what I had to know. She was in another world. That was enough for me. I have a meeting to go to now." And in a friendly, paternal way, he touched my shoulder and added, "I hope you don't mind."

Discouraged by the results of these various spiritual explorations, I decided to go it alone. I began reading Tao, Zen, various types of Buddhism, Confucianism and the *Bhagavad-gita* – Juan Mascero's translation. All of these scriptures made me curious but skeptical. The *Bhagavad-gita*, which I'd heard a lot about, was a very short book and made me particularly uncomfortable. As a "peacenik" of sorts, I couldn't figure out why this scriptural conversation between Krishna and Arjuna took place on a battlefield. Why was a war fought after a deep spiritual discourse? The contradiction bothered me. I asked Surya Kumari, an acquaintance of mine from Madras who was trained in classical Indian music. She said the book was a symbolic discourse that meant we had to "fight out our own lives." That made some sense, but her off-hand answer didn't really quell my doubts about the book.

Several weeks later, I ran into an associate on a cross-town bus. Mickey was an African-American jazz drummer with whom I'd worked. His face was wrinkled and he had short brown hair that formed a cap over a long pointed head. I had come to his rescue some months earlier on the Staten Island Ferry when a drunken white Vietnam vet had been trying to pick a fight with him. After I had managed to calm the fat, obnoxious drunk, Mickey and I had stood and talked at the rail of the ferry as the boat churned through the icy Atlantic waters forty feet below.

On that hot afternoon in 1966, we exchanged news during the few blocks that we shared the bus.

"You know," said Mickey in his gravelly, ancient-sounding voice, "there's a swami who's living at 94 Bowery. You really ought to check him out."

"Really? 94 Bowery? That's just a few doors down from me!"

"Yeah. It's every Monday, Wednesday and Friday at seven. He has a chanting session. Just walk in. Nobody cares. It's on the top floor."

"I'll have to check that out. I can't believe it. Are you sure he's living there?"

"Sure as shit. He's living there, all right. He's written a lot of books. He's an old guy from India."

An Indian swami living on the Bowery! It seemed totally incongruous to me. I'd been going uptown for my spiritual experiences. With its flophouses, bums and bars, the Bowery was skid row, the antithesis of my idea of "spiritual."

Mickey was scribbling the address on a wrinkled piece of paper with a half-chewed pencil as the bus swerved and bounced: "94 Bowery." He handed it to me.

"Here."

"I won't forget where it is. It's just a few places down from my loft."

"Take it," he said.

CHAPTER 3

Encounter in the Loft

A few days later on a warm late May night, I decided to visit the swami's loft. Jan wanted to stay home, so I walked alone through the fading evening light to the building.

Sitting on the stoop outside the door, two noisy drunks talked unintelligibly and animatedly. The glass transom showed a little light inside. The drunks belligerently blocked the entrance and muttered curses at me when I pushed my way past them. Their profanities were muffled when I closed the door behind me.

Slowly my eyes grew accustomed to the dank, dark hallway. With the faint light that filtered through above the door, I could just make out a long stairway that led up and back to the opposite end of the building. Even inside, the place smelled of beer, urine and vomit.

I waited a minute, acclimatizing and deciding if I wanted to continue. As I stood there I could make out a faint sound that sounded like bells or cymbals, ringing together in groups of three: "ching-ching-ching, ching-ching-ching." Using the right-hand wall as my guide, I carefully climbed the stairway. The sounds of the cymbals got louder as I climbed. At the top platform to my right was a door that was ajar, beaming a chink of light. The sound of the cymbals was now loud and distinct. I heard voices singing.

I cautiously pulled open the door and shuffled quietly inside. The place was dirty and dingy, and the smell of incense barely covered the mustiness. At the other end of the dimly lit room I could make out a few chanters sitting cross-legged on a rug with their backs to me.

Directly in front of them was a wooden platform upon which the elderly Indian swami sat. His skin was smooth and brown, and he sat cross-legged and erect. He was shaven-headed with a few long white and black hairs protruding from his long Buddha-like ears. He wore a beige turtleneck sweater and red horn-rimmed glasses; his eyes were closed. His expression was intense, brows knitted together in concentration as he chanted a mantra repeatedly: "*Hare Krishna Hare Krishna Krishna Krishna Hare Hare, Hare Rama Hare Rama Rama Rama Hare Hare.*" Singing in a deep, baritone voice, he led the chanting while the group responded. He played on a small African drum that was tucked under his left arm.

I moved toward the bizarre spectacle before me. I recognized a guy named Jimmy whom I knew among the chanters, although neither he nor anyone else noticed or acknowledged me. Despite the lack of welcome, the atmosphere was friendly and intimate, so I sat down and tried to join in without knowing the exact words of the chant. As I struggled to keep pace with the chanting, I glanced around the loft. Like mine, it was undecorated, but it was barer, dirtier and seedier than mine; it looked distinctly unlived-in. The bare light bulb hanging above the swami's sitting place cast a weak light throughout the place, revealing naked ceiling beams luxuriously swathed in webs by what must have been a very industrious team of spiders.

After fifteen minutes of chanting, the swami began to speak in a thick accent. In front of him sat a tome that looked like a three-hundred-year-old guestbook. He spoke with his eyes closed in an authoritative yet plaintive voice. His tone was strong. I'd heard powerful speakers before, but never in this kind of setting, and never with closed eyes.

"Krishna, this sound, is transcendental," he said. "Freedom from suffering is achieved when we are constantly in touch with the supreme spirit Krishna. All of us are suffering the pangs of *janma-mrityu-jara-vyadhi* – birth, death, old age, and disease. An intelligent man can stop this process, this repetition of birth and death. He can get his real, actual spiritual form again, and be blissful, full of knowledge and eternal life. That is the whole process. So we should not miss this. And the whole thing begins with just what we have begun now, this chanting and hearing. I want to point out that this chanting and hearing is as good as actual association with God, Krishna."

This discourse was a little too much for me to compute, but his Sanskrit-laced English fascinated me. "There are eighty-four *lakhs* species of life," he continued. "That means eight million and four hundred thousand forms of different varieties of life. The purpose of human life is to get out of these species."

One phrase of the swami's that stuck in my mind was, "I am not this body." He said it many times and in many different ways and with such conviction that I began to assimilate the phrase.

"So," I thought, "the swami isn't his body."

As I listened, I observed that there was something elegant, stately, and immaculate about him. He looked like someone important and scholarly. The fact that he was located in the Bowery amid such plain surroundings fascinated me. How did he get here and why? Why would a person of his apparent distinction and erudition set up shop in the Bowery? Would he disappear behind a curtain like the Zen monk? Would people talk with each other? Was he going to take part in a discussion here in this grungy-looking place?

"Material nature consists of three modes," the swami was saying. "Goodness, passion and ignorance. Ignorance is hopeless life. Passion is too much materialistic; passion means one wants false, material enjoyment. Then, when you are in goodness, what is your attitude? *Prasanna-manasah.* You will find yourself joyful in every circumstance. You will never feel morose. In that stage we understand, at least theoretically, what I am, what is this world, what is God, what is our interrelation."

The swami opened his eyes. "Any questions?"

I raised my hand. He looked at me curiously and nodded.

Pronouncing each word slowly and articulately, I asked, "Say a good man who has passed the states of being passionate and ignorant is walking down the street, say in Istanbul or Delhi or any city, and he sees a young man beating an old man for no reason at all, and the old man is crying out for help. And being a good man, he feels the whip on this other human being's back. As a good man, should he take sides or should he just accept it and walk on? Should he give in to what might be a passionate desire to try to interrupt and stop injustice?"

The swami closed his eyes again. "The whole idea is that whatever the action, it should be done from the spiritual consciousness platform," he said. "From the material point of view, stopping the violence is all right. From the material point of view. But even if you do good work, you still have to accept the reaction. That is the problem. If we act on the material platform, even in the mode of goodness, that is also not the solution to my life. We have simply to see whether I'm acting under the direction of the supreme consciousness. That is the thing to be seen. Then we are free. Then our life becomes free."

I had no idea what the "spiritual consciousness platform" or "supreme consciousness" might be. His answer seemed indefinite and evasive to me; I was looking for a "yes" or "no" answer.

"Paul," said the swami. He motioned with his head by raising it a little for a young man in the group to come forward. Getting up from the cross-legged position, the man awkwardly teetered and then edged over to the swami. He was thin and tall with sandy brown hair; he looked very adolescent with his pimply complexion and plaid shirt.

"Water," said the swami, handing him an old bronze chalice. Paul almost ran to the back of the loft, and then came back and gently placed the drinking vessel back on the swami's platform. The swami lifted the cup with his right hand, tilted his head way back, and lifting the cup above his mouth, tipped it forward letting a thin silvery stream pour into his wide-open mouth. He swallowed. I could hear the water dripping in his throat, and the swallow ring out in the quiet room. I had never heard such a sound before, especially not attached to the act of drinking; it reminded me of the sound my pet cocker spaniel had made once when it shook its head violently.

Paul stood there throughout, waiting and watching. Then he picked up the empty glass, turned around, walked a few steps back to his sitting place, and sat back down cross-legged. He was still holding the glass upright in front of him, as if it were too sacred for it to touch his body or the floor.

"Any further questions?" the swami asked.

I raised my hand again. "I really need to know if a good person would interfere if they saw something bad happening to someone else. I kind of feel like you didn't really answer my question."

"Yes. They would interfere," he said.

The session ended and people began to disperse. I expected the swami to quickly disappear, but he stayed sitting on the dais; I thought I might be able to speak to him personally, see what he was like. But first, out of curiosity I walked over to Paul and sat on the floor next to him.

"Is this your place?" I asked, almost whispering, keeping my eyes on the motionless swami.

"Yeah," he said. "Except I'm actually subletting from a guy named Harvey Corbett."

"So Harvey's not around? And you share with the swami?"

"Yeah."

"How old are you?"

"Seventeen."

"Can I talk to the swami?"

"Sure. He doesn't mind."

I took stock of all I had seen and heard that evening. I couldn't really make out what the swami was getting at when he spoke, but his strident tone – his urgency –convinced me that he had something important to say. At times his speech had actually accelerated in speed, so desperate did he appear to impart his message to his audience. And his humble surroundings intrigued me. Unlike the other "spiritual" people I'd met so far, the swami obviously wasn't after pursuing his share of wealth or followers or the American Dream. If that seventeen-year-old boy was his main companion, he must not have known very many people or have many contacts. He seemed very alone and dependent to me; I felt sorry for him, like I wanted to help him if I could.

I added it all up, trying to fit together the pieces of this unusual puzzle – his tone, his scholarly appearance, his age, his surroundings.

"He's got to be here on some sort of mission," I thought. "Why else would he speak the way he does? Why else would someone his age choose to come here of all places?"

I approached the swami; he had to tilt his head upward to look at me. I later learned that this is a *faux pas* within Indian culture – it is disrespectful to stand so that a swami or teacher must look up at you. The swami, however, gave no hint of disapproval; the wide grin with which he greeted me was surprisingly disarming. Whatever I'd thought I'd say evaporated on the spot.

"I have a *tamboura*," I blurted out.

Without losing a beat, still smiling and lifting his right hand and drawing it dramatically toward him in a "come here" kind of gesture, he said, "Then bring it."

"I will," I said.

As a musician, I anticipated that the most rewarding part of getting to know an Indian swami would be the music we would make together. For me, making music was the most intimate way to associate with another person, more satisfying than getting at the truth about life, whatever that might be. It was more enjoyable than a good movie, more interesting than philosophy and even better than sex.

As I hurried back to my place, I thought that the short walk up the dark smelly stairs to 94 Bowery had been worth the trouble. I didn't know quite why, but my future now didn't seem as onerous and uphill. I wondered why the swami was so inviting, so accessible. Maybe he felt sorry for me. Maybe he saw me as a potential follower or just as an inquisitive, misguided member of American society. Whatever the case, he seemed to have all the time in the world for me.

Village Voice *article about the swami in the loft in New York*

CHAPTER 4

Getting Acquainted

June 1966

A few days after my first experience at the swami's evening program, I decided to try to see the swami during the daytime, when there wouldn't be a crowd of other people there. When I stopped outside the entrance to 94 Bowery at three o'clock in the afternoon, the place was locked. There was no bell or buzzer. I started to call out to the young boy Paul I had met the other day, but the Bowery's four lanes of traffic made such a clatter that I would have needed to shout to be heard even if he were standing right next to me.

Imitating what I'd seen New Yorkers do sometimes to get attention, I fished through my pockets and then started throwing pennies up at the fourth-story window, hoping Paul would hear me.

A hand raised the sash window. To my surprise, it was the swami who stuck out his head. When he saw me he nodded and raised one finger as if to say, "I'll be right down." I felt embarrassed and ashamed about making such an elderly man come downstairs to open the door for me. Where was Paul? Wasn't he the swami's assistant or disciple or something?

Momentarily the swami appeared and opened the door for me. I started with profuse apologies for making him come all the way down. He just shook his head.

"This is my dyooti," he said. "Come on." Turning quickly and holding the front of his saffron robe with one hand, he bolted up the stairs two at a time. It was the first time I had seen him standing. He was short and thin, but with a modestly rounded belly, and he walked with the quick steps of someone half his age. Right behind him, I clambered up the long staircase. The stairway got darker near the top as we moved away from the Bowery.

He led me across the dusty sandal-scented loft to a small office situated behind a makeshift curtain of ocher cloth that he'd draped over baling wire. A few of the swami's robes of the same color also hung over wire, drying in the hot, humid air. An ancient-looking Underwood typewriter sat next to a foot-high stack of typed pages that occupied most of his workspace. Furnished with only a small dark brown wooden table and two chairs, this workspace's windows overlooked the Bowery, admitting an incessant orchestral background of automobile horns, thundering trucks and swishing cars. Despite being in one of the busiest and noisiest parts of New York, the atmosphere of the loft was peaceful and serene, almost like a small pocket of countryside in the midst of the city.

"Please sit," the swami said, gesturing toward the chair opposite him.

"I really enjoyed your program the other night, Swami," I said.

"Veddy nice," he said, smiling. "You must come again."

"Yes, I hope to," I said. I paused, not sure of what to say next. The swami gazed steadily back at me.

"How long have you been in America?" I asked at last.

"Now I think it is almost one year," he replied. "I am not sure how long I will stay. I have return ticket."

"You mean an airplane ticket?"

"Airplane? No, I came by boat. I was given free passage through Indian steam navigation company."

"You came on a boat? Wow! What was that like?"

"It was veddy difficult. Rough seas. Twice I thought I would not get here because of my heart."

"Your heart?"

"Yes. I was attacked with two heart attacks. I thought 'I am dying now.'"

"Man! Why bother coming all that way though? I thought a swami would want to stay in a spiritual place like India."

"My spiritual master wanted me to preach in the Western

countries. In 1922 he asked me. I was married then, working, busy with family affairs. So now, forty-three years later, I am here." He laughed. "So, better late than never. I thought I should come to America. If American people take seriously my mission, then others will also."

"So you have a spiritual master? I thought *you* were some kind of spiritual master."

"I am not master. I am servant preaching what my spiritual master has told me. I am not making up anything new, any new philosophy. Everyone serious in spiritual life must have a spiritual master, a guru."

"Hmmm. I've been looking for a guru for a while. What's your guru's name?"

"Bhaktisiddhanta Saraswati Thakur."

"What did he ask you to preach?" I asked, intrigued that this elderly Indian man had come to a foreign country on the strength of someone else's suggestion.

"He asked me to spread Krishna consciousness," he replied.

"What's that?"

"Krishna consciousness, God consciousness. In this world, we are trying to forget God; we are embracing so many miseries of life. We are suffering. So my mission is to help people remember God. Only then will this suffering stop. We are seeking after so many material things, but our real aim of life should be to understand our spiritual identification and search out our relationship with God, Krishna. Have you heard of Chaitanya Mahaprabhu?"

"Um, no, I don't think so."

"He is an incarnation of Krishna who lived five hundred years ago. Actually, my mission is His mission. He predicted that Krishna's name would be chanted in every town, every village of the world. He gave instruction that those born in India should work to benefit others by spreading His mission, by spreading the name of God."

"No, I haven't heard of Chaitanya. But I'm really interested in India and its history and philosophy. Gandhi freed India from the British, didn't he?"

"Gandhi was a rascal."

"What do you mean?"

"Bose freed India."

"Who's Bose?"

"Bose. Subash Bose. He organized the Indian National Army. He brought the Indian fighters back from Japan and Germany and Burma. The Gurkhas. Didn't you know?"

"No. Where was he from, Bose?"

"Bengal. The British used to pat Gandhi. It was Bose who said he'd fight the British. So they decided to leave."

"I have a picture of Nehru which my friend Surya Kumari gave me," I said, producing a black and white photo. "Wasn't he instrumental in freeing India?"

"He was trained in England to be a barrister. He was practically British. Another nonsense."

I was a bit dumbstruck, hearing the swami so abruptly shoot down the people I'd been taught were the heroes of Indian independence. He seemed very sure about what he was saying. The history books I'd read apparently weren't giving the full picture.

"I was a follower of Gandhi once," he said. "But the Britishers thought his mood could be – how do you say? – accommodated. They patted him. It was Bose who frightened the Britishers. He was prepared to fight, to turn the whole Indian people against the Britishers. So they withdrew. I think it was in nineteen and I think forty-seven."

"I am planning to go to India," I said. "A friend of mine is staying in a little room in Delhi and is learning Indian flute. He says everyone there is obnoxious, but I still kind of want to go. I'm just not sure what I'd do. Maybe I could study Indian flute playing myself."

"Oh, Indian flute-players. They spit up blood."

"What?"

"Yes. They spit up blood. Do you play music?"

"I play the piano."

"I can teach you how to play the piano for Krishna."

Now I was stumped. Play the piano for the god from the *Bhagavad-gita*? I liked the prospect of playing music with the swami, but I couldn't imagine that playing a few *ragas* or Indian-type scales on the piano would be terribly interesting.

Despite the somewhat bewildering quality of this conversation, my first daytime meeting with the swami meant more to me than the lecture a few days earlier. For me the fact that he was so approachable was important, an absolute contrast with the other spiritual people I had met so far. I felt that I could go and see him any time I wanted.

A few days later on a Thursday afternoon, I meandered over to the swami's loft again. This time the front door was unlocked. At 1:00 PM there were no drunks obstructing my passage; I felt relaxed as I climbed the dark stairs and knocked on the door.

"Come," called out the swami in a loud voice.

I walked to the front end of the loft, past the lecture platform, and dipped behind the hanging brown-saffron curtain, where I pulled up the visitor's chair.

"So, how are you, Mr. Michael?" the swami asked.

"Fine, fine. I just thought I'd come over to see you. What are you doing?"

"Most of the time I type."

He indicated the stack of paper next to his typewriter on the rickety-looking table.

"What is that? What do you type?"

"That is my *Bhagavad-gita*. Someday it will be a book."

"The *Bhagavad-gita*'s in Sanskrit, right?"

"Yes."

"Would you be able to give a class in Sanskrit?"

"You want Sanskrit?"

"Yeah. I think a lot of people would come."

He looked out the window pensively. "The thing is I'm speaking three nights a week and people already come."

"What about another day?"

"Maybe Saturday ..."

"Saturday morning?"

"If you could organize ..."

"I think I could get people to come."

"So try." He was clearly tentative about this project. Still, I felt encouraged and wanted to do something to help him, because he was so friendly, and because it seemed such an amazing coincidence – or significant convergence – that he would be here in the Bowery of all places at the same time as me.

I thought it was too late in the week to organize a Sanskrit class for the coming Saturday, so I started phoning around the people I knew, inviting them to come the following weekend. I bought a book by Judith Tyberg called *First Lessons in Sanskrit Grammar*, which showed how to make Sanskrit letters with a special pen that had to be dipped into ink. I also bought the special pen that made wide swaths so I could write the Sanskrit letters as they were shown in the book. I practiced the order and method of making the letters in preparation for the swami's class.

Saturday morning rolled around and four people showed up, people I'd phoned almost demanding that they come. I didn't know any of them very well except for Carl Yeargens, a bearded African-American Princeton graduate who was a regular at the swami's programs and who always seemed to have high-quality Moroccan hashish on hand. The swami had acquired a blackboard that looked like it came from a Bowery garbage can. This he set upon an unsteady three-legged wooden easel in the lecture area of his loft. The five of us sat on the floor in front of the blackboard, looking up at him expectantly.

The swami took up a short piece of white chalk which crumbled as he wrote across the blackboard:

ईश्वरः परमः कृष्णः सच्चिदानन्दविग्रहः ।
अनादिरादिर्गोविन्दः सर्वकारणकारणम् ॥

Under this, in Roman letters with diacritics, he wrote:

īśvaraḥ paramaḥ kṛṣṇah
sac-cid-ānanda-vigrahaḥ
anādir ādir govindaḥ
sarva-kāraṇa-kāraṇam

"I will explain the meaning of each word, as well as the whole phrase," he said. He pointed to the first word with his piece of chalk. "*Ishvarah* means 'the controller' – the supreme controller. God – Krishna – is the supreme controller." He walked over to a small book that was sitting on his lectern and read aloud:

"He has an eternal blissful spiritual body. He is the origin of all. He has no other origin."

As the swami translated the verse word-for-word, I began to suspect that the Sanskrit lesson was something of a ruse that he had decided to use to present us with his philosophical and religious perspectives. Even though this indicated proselytizing of some sort to me, I didn't mind; the Sanskrit interested me, and I was beginning to be intrigued about the philosophy that inspired the swami's mission.

"And *karanam* means 'cause,'" the swami said with a note of conclusion in his voice. "Krishna is the prime cause of all causes. Now you should all copy the Devanagari alphabets."

With concentration, we began to reproduce the swami's Devanagari script into our books. The swami moved quietly around the room, standing behind each of us and observing our work.

After an hour or so, the swami said, "That is enough for today."

"Shall we have another class next Saturday, Swami?" I asked on my way out.

"Perhaps," he said diplomatically.

Carl and I walked up the street back to my loft.

"I got the feeling the swami wasn't really that into teaching Sanskrit," Carl said, dropping onto the couch. "He really just wanted to talk about the meaning of that passage."

"Yeah, I thought that too," I said. "I didn't really get the verse, though. The swami talked to me a little bit about his mission, but I don't really understand or get the whole philosophical point of what he's doing here. What is it that he believes? What's he into?"

"There's a whole lot about it in the books he brought from India with him," Carl said. "You should check them out. He'll sell them to you. I think it's about all he brought from India. There's a lot of Sanskrit in them too."

"How many books did he bring?"

"A trunk-full, I think. He'll sell you the first three as a set."

"He's selling them himself? Doesn't he have a publisher or a sales rep or something?"

"Nope, I don't think so. He just sold them to me himself. I got them the other day. They're really intense. I mean deep. Know what I mean?"

Carl pulled out a quantity of Moroccan mud and held it at eye level.

"This is pretty good stuff," he said. "You want to try some?"

"Sure. Hey, what does the swami think about drugs?"

"He's not into them. But …" Carl smiled confidentially, "he admitted to me that he used to deal drugs in India when he was younger."

I wasn't sure what to make of this new information. I shook my head. "I can't really imagine that," I said. "The swami dealing drugs? It just doesn't sound right."

Carl shrugged. "That's what he told me."

Two nights later after the swami's chant and lecture I asked him if I could buy his books.

"Paul! Bring the first three volumes," the swami said.

Paul jumped up and got the books from a small wooden shelf. Increasingly Paul's behavior around the swami alarmed me. He seemed like a robot that would do whatever the swami asked, almost as if he had no mind of his own. Presumably he was the swami's follower and would be his disciple eventually. Was that what happened when you became someone's follower?

The swami handed the books to me. They were tawny hardbacks, with colorful dust jackets covered in floating globes. Each book was about an inch and a half thick.

"They're fifteen dollars," the swami told me.

I fumbled in my wallet and found one five dollar bill. I held it out.

"This is all I have."

"That's all right. You can bring the rest next time."

"I'm sorry, I just didn't think …"

"That's all right." He wobbled his head from side to side with eyes closed.

When I got home that evening, I opened the first of the three volumes. It smelled like it had been in an attic for years. The title page read in large letters "*First Canto of Srimad-Bhagavatam.*" I turned to the contents page. The chapter headings intrigued me: "The Cause of All Causes," "The Lord in the Heart," "Scheduled Incarnations with Specific Functions," "Description of the Kingdom of God" and "The Glories of Devotional Service."

I flicked past the preface, foreword and introduction to the first chapter. The book followed the same format the swami had used in the Sanskrit class two days earlier. Each numbered verse was written in Devanagari letters – something I hadn't seen before in books – followed by an English transliteration with diacritical marks, a word-for-word translation, and an English translation of the whole verse. Finally, there was something called a purport, which seemed to be the swami's commentary on the verses. Most of the verses included purports.

"Chapter One. 'Questions by the Sages,'" I read to myself. The first chapter seemed mainly to detail the words of a group of sages who were asking someone called Suta Goswami to explain knowledge of the Supreme Lord – Krishna – to them. I read that in the present "age of quarrel," people were "lazy, misguided, unlucky and always disturbed." The word "unfortunate" appeared a lot. I thought that was a good way of describing the state of the people I knew in the Bowery, and elsewhere too for that matter. It wasn't that they were bad people; it was that they were just plain "unfortunate." That seemed a wise and non-judgmental thing to say. It was the influence of the age of quarrel.

The sages in the book thought that Suta was the right person to explain spiritual knowledge to them not only because he was learned, but because he was "free from vice." The swami said in his purport that "vice" included animal slaughter, intoxication, illicit sex and gambling, and that anyone who wanted to be spiritually advanced must refrain from these things. Suta was also qualified to be a spiritual teacher because he was a "gentle disciple" of his spiritual master. "The secret of success in spiritual life is in satisfying the spiritual master and thereby getting his sincere blessings," I read. I thought of the swami and his spiritual master who had inspired him to come here. He seemed to be a pretty committed disciple himself, and according to this book, at least, that was an important part of being able to impart spiritual wisdom.

The translations and commentaries in the books were quaintly Indian. I noticed an occasional upside-down "e," which suggested that the typesetter probably didn't know English. But I read on anyway, intrigued by the breadth and depth of the philosophy and by the unusual poetic way the swami wrote.

"It is natural," I read, "that a philosophical mind wants to know about the origin of creation. At night he sees the stars in the sky and he speculates ..."

"Yes," I thought, reviewing my spiritual and philosophical explorations. "It *is* natural."

I read about how the "material cosmic manifestation" is like a mirage, how everything in "the material sky" is relative truth. Real truth and reality, the book said, were to be found in "the spiritual world," where the Supreme exists eternally.

Although this seemed kind of cosmic and otherworldly, the swami also wrote about the world in which I lived. The first chapter described the "distorted values" of present-day society more accurately than the works I'd read before. I'd read about the ills of society in lots of books, but in most writings these maladies were expressed in sociological terms. The swami's approach was both sociological and *personal*. He approached the problems of existence in a direct and personal way, stating the things the individual could do to get him- or herself onto a "spiritual platform" where they could perceive God. Sometimes the things the individual could do were very practically presented – things like getting up early to perform spiritual practices and accepting a spiritual teacher. The book said that getting onto the spiritual platform – becoming "self realized" – was the very purpose of human life.

I'd never read anything quite like this, and I found the reading experience unusual and transforming. Although much of it was over my head and at times a bit morbid and fatalistic, I found the swami's words hopeful as well, like he had the answers I was looking for. Behind my reading, there was always the thought of the swami himself. I began to see that he wasn't just a nice, friendly Indian swami, but that he himself was practicing a serious form of discipline and spirituality.

The books didn't suggest that I should abandon or change my present lifestyle. They didn't imply I should give up my planned adventure to India or my musical career. What they did do was inspire me to think beyond the cynicism and skepticism that usually colored my spiritual pursuits. My thinking changed, almost imperceptibly, and with it, my personal practices. I began to lose my zest for what I used to enjoy – the good things in life like music, wealth, fame, sex, food. I gave up my agnosticism and began to think that God did exist, and maybe He was Krishna. I became a committed vegetarian and began to bathe every morning, since the books said cleanliness was part of being in the "mode of goodness."

I read on and on, and the more I read, the more I wanted to read. I took the book everywhere with me and read it whenever I got a spare minute – on the bus or waiting for friends or standing in line at Safeway. When I finished the first volume, I immediately opened the second one, because the books seemed to be answering many complex questions about life, the universe and our place in it. My philosophical and spiritual journeys and spiritual convolutions had, I thought, finally reached a resting place. Maybe the swami was the teacher I had sought for so long.

The Storefront Temple

July 1966

One evening a few of us were sitting and talking with the swami, when he said, "I was thinking of having a Love Feast with singing, dancing and eating. No one will refuse such a function. What do you think?"

No one spoke. A few nodded and made expressions of approval, but I was thinking, "Where did he get the words *Love Feast*? That sounds like counterculture jargon, not our erudite Indian swami." I was surprised by his assimilation of American hippy vernacular.

The word "feast" sounded bacchantic to me, like something social and self-congratulatory. I expected that it would be a party of some kind where the swami would treat everyone to the delights of Indian cuisine and would shore up his success. It wasn't that I didn't want to go; it was more that the philosophy in his books was a serious matter for me, and I wasn't interested in what I considered to be the social aspects of his mission. I wasn't very gregarious or people-centered; I thought spiritual life was more or less a private affair. And I really couldn't figure out how dancing fit into it all. Eating, yes. Singing or chanting, sure. But dancing? That didn't seem to go with the chanting. The swami said that chanting was a spiritual sound and was for getting in touch with the Supreme, Krishna. How could you dance and do that at the same time? *Our* chanting was always done in meditation posture, sitting on the rug, cross-legged. There didn't seem to be any place for dancing. The only kind of dancing I could think of was ballroom-style or square dancing.

A couple of nights later at the end of the evening chanting session, he made his announcement.

"So, on Sunday afternoon we will be having a Love Feast here. You please all come." As he spoke I looked around the dismal loft and failed to imagine how any kind of festive atmosphere could be achieved in such a place.

Even though I wasn't very enthusiastic, I decided to go because he was so insistent and because I wanted to be courteous. He hadn't given us much notice, but I lived in the here and now, and long-term planning wasn't part of my agenda.

On Sunday afternoon, several people showed up at the swami's loft. The lecture platform was out of sight and had been replaced by a big round wooden table that someone had dragged to the end of the lecture area. The table was covered with food of all kinds, some on trays and some in large strange pots without handles that were pocked on the outside with what appeared to be random hammer marks.

The swami circulated around the room, smiling and talking in an animated manner with everyone. I stood to one side, unsure that I would be able to come up with any small talk. Moving through the small groups of people, he was no longer the sage, the wise man from India; he was an affable, indefatigable host. Not used to seeing him standing up, I was struck once again by how small he looked in comparison to the other people in the room.

The smells coming from the pots were intriguing. I edged over to the table to see what the food looked like. The pots were full of various vegetable and bean dishes: a dark brown chickpea stew, creamed spinach with pieces of milk curd, yellow rice studded with peas, and an eggplant and tomato curry with chunks of fried golden potato. On a tray to my left were pastry fritters accompanied by a dish of rich-looking tamarind chutney. Beside it were a tray of pale brown sweets and a deep bowl of creamy dessert with strands of saffron floating in it.

Carl came up behind me, followed by his live-in girlfriend Carol. Both she and Jan had come to a few of the swami's programs, but neither of them was really into the philosophical or spiritual side of things. They had sat at the back of the gatherings, not nearly as moved by the swami as me.

"It all looks pretty good, huh?" I said.

"Yeah. The swami cooked everything himself," Carl said.

"And I helped him," Carol added. "I loaned him some of our pots because he doesn't have a lot of stuff himself. It's really amazing watching him cook. He doesn't taste anything at all when he's cooking because he says the food has to be offered to Krishna first. He told me that everything should be cooked with love."

"With love?"

"That's what he said. Like if you love your boyfriend or girlfriend or your child and you cook with care thinking about pleasing them, your cooking will be full of love. So I guess he cooks thinking about Krishna, almost like a meditation. He's really focused, you know? At the end when everything was finished he said some prayers over the food. That's the offering part. He called the food *prasadam* after he offered it."

The swami suddenly appeared next to us, handing us each a china plate. Rather than leaving it up to us to help ourselves to what we wanted, he served us each preparation. Throughout the evening, he moved energetically around the room with a pot under his left arm and a serving spoon in his right hand.

"Take, take," he said, grinning and piling more and more portions onto our plates without waiting for us to say yes. "You'll like it. You will." I cautiously tried two bites of the chickpea stew when all of sudden he was in front of me with another ladleful. "Take more!" he insisted.

Nobody refused. Carl looked up and nodded his head each time, mumbling through mouthfuls of food, "OK, OK."

"You like?" the swami asked me.

I could only nod, chewing and swallowing. The whole event seemed to mean a great deal to the swami, and I didn't know why. I wasn't sure where any of this was going to lead. What follows a Love Feast? At least there was no dancing, thank god!

———

The ringing of the telephone tore me out of a deep sleep. Carl's voice was loud in my ear.

"The swami and I were just going for a little walk and we thought we'd come up and see you."

I looked at my watch: 7:00 AM. I'd recently gotten a job in a Staten Island nightclub on the weekends and I'd been asleep for only two hours.

"Carl, you've got to be kidding me! I just got home and I'm sound asleep!"

"The swami wanted to come up and see you."

"Where are you?" I asked.

"We're at a pay phone on the corner."

The pay phone was fifty feet from my front door.

"But we're in bed."

"Well, the swami really wants to see you."

I sat up in bed. "You've got to give me at least five minutes. I have to get up."

Jan rolled over, turning toward the wall away from me and the phone.

"OK," he said. "We'll be there."

I dragged myself out of bed and tried to pull myself together. Just as I was buttoning my shirt, the doorbell rang. The downstairs door must have been open, because they were suddenly already up the two flights of stairs and at our front door. Jan slept on.

Half-dressed, I opened the front door.

"Come in, Swami," I said. "Here. You can sit on the couch."

The swami sat in the middle of the couch, while Carl and I sat at either end.

"So, this is your home?" the swami asked me.

"Yes it is, Swami. We rent it for really cheap; it's a good place to make music."

The swami nodded and looked up as Jan staggered in looking sleepy in her nightgown and a bathrobe. She rubbed her eyes and looked like she was trying very hard to focus on the unexpected guests in her living room.

"Oh, hi Swami," she said. "I'm Jan. We haven't met properly, but I was at your Love Feast last week."

"Yes, I saw you there. You are Michael's wife?" he asked.

"Wife?" She glanced at me and gave a short laugh that came out sounding like a yelp. "Not exactly, no. We just live together." I thought I saw a flash of disapproval in the swami's eyes, but it quickly dissolved.

The television was still on from the day before. There was no sound, but cartoons were playing one after another. It was a black and white TV with a rainbow-tinted glass in front of the picture tube, which was supposed to give the impression of color. I didn't even notice it was on, but the swami did.

"This is nonsense," he said, gesturing toward the TV.

Looking over at the animation, I said, "Oh yes, this *is* nonsense." I quickly turned it off.

As we engaged in small talk, Jan brought some peeled and separated orange sections in a dish, which she offered to the swami. *"That's* a nice touch," I thought, smiling at her. Jan knew I was pretty into the swami's philosophy; she thought it was a good thing, but it was definitely *my* thing.

Scuzzlebrunzer, our black cat, suddenly jumped up on the swami's lap. I thought it quaint that he had perceived such peace in a stranger. But the swami pushed him away. Later, when I finally visited India, I thought back to this incident and realized the vast cultural differences between Western and Eastern perceptions of animals. In India, while most people respect animals as spiritual equals, they do not intimately associate with them. Dogs and cats, in particular, are street animals that are considered dirty and generally are not allowed to enter homes or temples. Scuzzlebrunzer was friendly, but there was a sense that he had been overly familiar with the swami. Later I understood this incident from the swami's cultural standpoint, but for now, I felt his rejection of the cat was a little out of character for a holy man.

"So how long have you been here in this loft?" Carl asked.

"About one year," I answered. "Why?"

"The swami needs a better place to live, because Paul's getting out of hand."

"What do you mean?"

"He's just getting hard to live with. You know, he swears, acts weird, disappears for hours on end. And he's rude, loud and unpredictable. You know, he's just *weird*." He shrugged his shoulders. "Weird to live with anyway, at least for the swami."

Paul had always struck me as immature and without direction. Still, he didn't seem particularly difficult to me; a bit odd, maybe, but everyone was in some way.

"So, how can we help the swami?" Carl asked me.

I was silent. The swami, perhaps sensing my lack of concern, began to tell me about Paul's unusual behavior.

"Paul left the soap on the floor of the shower," he said. "This is dangerous. When I asked him to pick it up, he started ill-naming me."

I was tired. A bar of soap and a little bit of swearing didn't seem like such a big deal to me.

"In India," the swami continued, "we have a saying: *guru-mara-vidya*. You sit opposite a guru, learn from him everything, then you kill him, move his dead body aside, and sit in his place, and then you become the guru." He paused. "Paul is a very dangerous man."

As the swami said this he looked right through me. I felt a shiver down my spine. Paul seemed utterly subservient to the swami, almost like a slave who lacked a mind of his own. But as the words left the swami's mouth, I began to think that maybe Paul's peculiar mindless demeanor was his own problem, part of his psychological state, whatever that was, and not part of his being a follower of the swami's. He certainly seemed unbalanced, and if he was taking heavy doses of drugs, maybe he could be capable of violence. It occurred to me that Paul *was* quite possibly a dangerous man, especially for a small, elderly Indian swami.

I looked up. "So you need a new place, right?"

"That's it," said Carl.

I felt a little guilty and very uneasy. Was the swami asking me indirectly if he could appropriate *my* place, turn it into a temple and me into a Paul replacement? I wasn't ready for that!

"People play drums here, sometimes late at night," I said hastily. "There are always musicians hanging around here. But maybe I can help."

Carl said, "Well, for now, the swami can stay at my place."

They stood up, and Scuzzlebrunzer zoomed from his perch near us to a corner of the room.

"Thank you," the swami said, looking me up and down.

"OK. Bye."

"Hare Krishna," they said quietly in unison. As they left, I realized that the swami was carrying a small suitcase. I wondered if he had already moved out of Paul's loft, if the suitcase contained all his belongings.

When the swami and Carl left, I felt strangely alone. I felt I had to do something for the swami, but not just because I told him I would. I realized suddenly that during the past few weeks I had begun to feel I was a part of his mission. He had come to America for the purpose of spreading his mission, and to do that he needed somewhere to live. All he needed was a decent apartment of some kind, preferably on the ground floor of a building in a better neighborhood.

Experience in loft-hunting had taught me that the *Village Voice*, a weekly newspaper, was the best resource. I browsed the "For Rent" section and then, from the nearest pay phone, called a telephone number for a storefront located at 26 Second Avenue, about a half-hour walk from the Bowery. I got the first available appointment with a Mr. Gardiner and telephoned the swami and Carl to meet me and Gardiner at the premises at ten o'clock the next morning.

It was already sunny and hot for a Manhattan morning in late June. I rode my bike up the Bowery, turned right on Houston and then left onto Second Avenue. I wheeled to number twenty-six and chained my bike to a *No Parking* sign. I was early. The ride over had taken only ten minutes, so I checked out the place while I waited for the others to arrive. It had obviously been a store; the whole front was glass – a large glass window and a door with a single glass pane. The name painted at the top of the glass windows was *Matchless Gifts*.

In the distance, a short, slim, bouncy man who looked to be about forty-five, with close-cropped silvery hair, was approaching. He wore a short-sleeved yellow sports shirt, blue denim pegged pants and white cut-down tennis shoes. He looked up and down the buildings, jangling a big ring of keys, and checking me out as he neared me. Gardiner, I guessed. He was early too.

Matchless Gifts storefront

"Hi," I said, when he stopped at number twenty-six, "My name's Michael. I talked with you on the phone yesterday."

We shook hands.

"Right. Paul Gardiner," he said in a business-like voice. "So what's up?"

"Well, the storefront's not for me. It's for an Indian swami who wants to lecture here three nights a week. He's a writer, and he wants to have some yoga classes here. He's a pretty respected scholar; he gave some of his books to the Prime Minister of India. He should be here any minute. My friend Carl Yeargens is coming over with him. Carl graduated from Princeton in philosophy. He's been working with the swami for several weeks and … Actually, that looks like them now, see, down the street?"

"Oh yeah. I see them."

"Yeah. So can we have a look at the place when they get here?"

"That's what I brought the keys for."

"So, yeah, I think he'll want to have the classes Monday, Wednesday and Friday nights around seven."

"Sounds OK. What'll he be doing?"

"Well, the classes usually start out with some chanting, then he lectures, people ask questions and then there's some chanting again."

"And what do *you* do?"

"Well, I'm just trying to help the swami out. I'm a musician, but I'm learning Sanskrit and reading some of his books and learning a lot. About Indian philosophy, I mean."

"I see."

"Oh, here's the swami now. Swami, this is Mr. Gardiner. Mr. Gardiner, this is the swami, and this is Carl Yeargens."

They all shook hands. Carl was carrying a set of the swami's books.

"Your friend here's been telling me about you," Gardiner said, squinting and looking at the swami. "Come on in. I'll show you the place."

Gardiner selected one of his numerous keys and unlocked the front door. It was a rectangular-shaped room, about eighty feet by twenty-five feet. It was bare, but reasonably clean. A few long cylindrical fluorescent lights were twisted into white flanges that projected from a ceiling about twelve feet above the floor. The white ceiling was made of painted metal sheets, some bulging. A large white pewter basin stuck out from the left wall at the back end of the store next to a back door. There were bars over the two back windows, which looked into a little courtyard.

"Well, this is it," Gardiner said, motioning us to sit down on the small ledge that ran along the store's front windows.

"How much is the rent?" I asked.

"A hundred a month."

The swami said, "Mr. Michael and Mr. Carl are members of our society, and they pay a subscription of twenty-one dollars a month."

"That's not true," I thought. I wondered why the swami said this. I wasn't a member of anything, and I certainly hadn't given any money to join. The only money I'd parted with was the fifteen dollars for the books.

"So, I'd like you also to be a member of our society."

He held out his three hardcover books to Gardiner. The agent smiled and took them.

"Thanks," he said, starting to page through them.

"Please take these books. You can be a member. It's twenty-one dollars a month, and we can pay you seventy-nine dollars a month rent. You won't have to pay anything now." I began to see that the swami was striking a deal with Gardiner, and that his claiming we were already members was a part of this. I remembered him telling me that he had been a businessman back in India.

"It looks like these books were a lot of work," Gardiner said, looking genuinely pleased. "OK. Thank you. By the way, I also have an apartment in this building for rent."

The three of us looked at each other, surprised.

"How much is it?" I asked.

"You can have it for eighty-five dollars a month."

"Where is it?" asked Carl.

"It's just a flight up, in the back. I'll have to paint it if you want it."

"Can we see it?" asked the swami.

"Sure. We can look right now if you want."

We followed him to the back of the store, as he flicked through his keys, looking for the right one to open the door. Unlocking it, he led us through a darkened hallway until we found ourselves in the little cement courtyard that could be seen from the store's back windows. It had a small camellia bush and a scanty birch tree in the middle. On the other side of the courtyard was a door that opened onto a stairway. We headed up its dim flight of stairs.

The apartment was a little old looking, but it was airy and bright. We walked around, inspecting the two rooms, the kitchen and the bathroom. Carl and I thumped on the walls, looked outside, checked out the steam radiators, flicked on the dead light switches and flushed the toilet. I counted the number of electrical outlets. It seemed to be in reasonably good condition.

"What color will you paint it?' I asked.

"White."

"Eighty-five dollars including utilities?"

"No, they're separate."

Looking official and scratching his head, Carl said, "Maybe we can go back down to the store."

We went back down and sat on the ledge.

"I think we should do it. Get the store *and* the apartment," Carl said decisively.

"That's one hundred and sixty-four dollars a month," I said to Carl.

"Between us and the others, we can do it. I'm sure," Carl said, nodding his head confidently.

The swami looked at Carl and me, poker-faced, then at Gardiner.

"You'll have to give me a week to paint the apartment." Gardiner smiled and added, "You can have 'em both with no deposit."

"Great," Carl said. "We'll take them both."

I unlocked my bike, and the three of us walked back to the Bowery.

"I can stay at Dr. Mishra's for the week," the swami said. "He is a friend I stayed with for some time when I first came to New York. He won't mind."

"That's a good idea," Carl said.

"Mr. Michael, you can have the electricity turned on in the new store. Tell them it is for non-profit and they will not charge for deposit."

"OK," I said, wondering how "they" would react.

The next day I sat before a fat gray-suited bureaucrat at his desk in the Con Edison building.

"Um, I'd like to have the electricity turned on at 26 Second Avenue and at apartment 114 at the same address."

"How much is the rent per month in the apartment?"

"Eighty-five dollars."

"OK. You'll just need to pay a deposit of eighty-five dollars to us to get the electricity put on there."

"The thing is, the place is going to be used for a non-profit organization. I thought non-profit organizations didn't have to pay the deposit."

"Do you have an already existing account?"

"No."

"Do you have a guarantor or corporation papers?"

"No, but ..."

"Then you'll have to pay the deposit the same as everybody else, buddy."

"Just as I expected," I thought.

I headed back to Carl's place, hoping to catch the swami before he left for Dr. Mishra's. I knocked and Carl let me in.

"Is the swami still here?"

"Yep, he's not leaving until tomorrow. Just go through," he said, pointing to the living room.

The swami looked up as I entered.

"I went to the electricity company, Swami," I said.

"What did they say?" he asked.

"That I'd have to pay, despite it being a non-profit organization."

"Then?"

"I just thought, 'OK. I'll have to pay.'"

He seemed disappointed and annoyed. There was a distinct glimmer of dissatisfaction in his expression.

The next day, the swami went to the Con Edison office himself and had the deposit requirement waived. I was amazed he did this, as well as dismayed that he had to go, that I hadn't managed to complete the thing he'd ask me to do.

———

Moving day. It was a warm and sticky Manhattan afternoon when the small crew of the swami's friends gathered to transport his belongings from Paul's loft to the new storefront. The move to Second Avenue resembled a safari. The expedition snaked along the Bowery, avoiding drunks lying on the sidewalk, everyone carrying something.

The seventy-year-old swami carried two suitcases, one in each hand, as we trudged the mile-long walk to Second Avenue. I couldn't imagine how he was managing to carry them; it was so hot, and after his heart attacks on the way to America, this kind of exertion couldn't have been good for him.

I was struggling with my own burden, a Roberts seven-inch reel-to-reel tape recorder. One of the regulars at the swami's evening programs had begun to use the heavy machine to record the lectures in the Bowery. I carried it on my right shoulder but had to switch it back to the left shoulder and then back again several times. My arm and shoulder were sore for days afterward.

When we finally arrived at the storefront, Carl rummaged through his pocket for the key to the front door. The rest of us, sweating and tired, rested our loads on the sidewalk and leaned on parking meters and the store window, trying to catch our breath. Carl held the door open for the swami. Picking up his two suitcases, he stepped into the bare, musty storefront and looked around. The rest of us followed him in, relieved to be out of the heat. Some kicked off their shoes and sat against the walls; others found seats on the window ledge. I put the tape recorder in the corner so it wouldn't get damaged or kicked, and headed back home, satisfied that I'd done my part in helping the swami to find his place and move his stuff.

Soon after moving into the storefront, the swami decided to incorporate his fledgling movement.

"We will call it the International Society for Krishna Consciousness. ISKCON for short," he said one day.

"Why don't you call it the International Society for *God* Consciousness?" someone suggested.

"No," the swami said. "*Krishna* Consciousness."

A lawyer named Steven Goldsmith oversaw the proceedings. As part of the process, the swami drew up a document, which he entitled "Seven Purposes of the International Society for Krishna Consciousness." These purposes included:

1. To systematically propagate spiritual knowledge to society at large and to educate all peoples in the techniques of spiritual life in order to check the imbalance of values in life and to achieve real unity and peace in the world.

2. To propagate a consciousness of Krishna, as it is revealed in the *Bhagavad-gita* and *Srimad-Bhagavatam*.

3. To bring the members of the Society together with each other and nearer to Krishna, the prime entity, thus to develop the idea within the members, and humanity at large,

that each soul is part and parcel of the quality of Godhead (Krishna).

4. To teach and encourage the *sankirtan* movement, congregational chanting of the holy name of God as revealed in the teachings of Lord Shri Chaitanya Mahaprabhu.

5. To erect for the members and for society at large, a holy place of transcendental pastimes, dedicated to the Personality of Krishna.

6. To bring the members closer together for the purpose of teaching a simpler and more natural way of life.

7. With a view towards achieving the aforementioned purposes, to publish and distribute periodicals, magazines, books and other writings.

The swami asked Jan and me if we would act as signatories of this document that would establish his movement as a legal entity. In our early twenties, we were almost the oldest people frequenting the swami's chanting evenings, so it made sense to us that he would ask us over the teenagers and less-responsible visitors who drifted in and out of the scene. We agreed to his proposal, even though the legality of it all seemed a bit excessive given that the "movement" consisted of nothing more than a handful of alternatives and a rented storefront.

CHAPTER 6

Two Schools
of Thought

July 1966

Not long after the swami moved into his new storefront and apartment, he asked some of us if we'd like to accompany him to visit a friend of his. It would be a weekend trip to Ananda Ashram in Monroe, upstate New York. The *ashram* was run by Dr. Mishra, the friend with whom the swami had stayed during his first few months in the city.

So, one hot day in July of 1966, seven of us, including Jan and me, piled into the back of a panel truck for our first field trip with the swami. He rode in a separate car. A small, thin young man named Charlie was part of the party. He was a flute-player, and I'd jammed with him at a friend's house a few months before. We recognized one another, and exchanged a few words.

"How you doing?" I asked.

"Yeah, OK. I thought I'd check out Monroe with the swami."

"Bring your flute?"

"Always. Right here." He patted the small flute case.

The rest of the way we didn't talk very much; we mostly chanted Hare Krishna.

Ananda Ashram was a large colonial-style house situated in a picturesque setting with big green lawns and a beautiful lake with ducks and geese. We were greeted by about twenty young people, with whom we made friends. There were many hippie types there,

Charlie the flute-player at 26 Second Avenue

with long hair and tie-dyed clothes. Apart from them, there was also a large group of very conventional, conservative people who looked like the social opposites of us and the other alternative people.

We – the swami's people – sat down outside for lunch with them – Mishra's people – at long tables covered with white tablecloths. The seven of us flanked the swami on both sides. It was the first time I'd seen the swami hold a fork. He held it in his right hand with his middle finger and thumb, European-style. As he ate, I saw him begin to carefully pick things out of the salad and put them aside. When I looked closer, I saw that they were little onions. I glanced at the people on either side of me, and I saw that they had noticed too; we all dutifully followed him, picking out the onions as he did.

That evening the swami led a roof-raising chanting session in the main meeting room of the ashram, which probably had once been the home's living room. Decorated in conservative earth tones, the room had French windows that looked out onto the ashram's expansive lawns. One of the members of our party played an electric organ, while an experienced black musician played a large standup string bass. The bass sounds took the event to a higher ground. Suddenly, in the midst of the chanting, the swami stood up. Raising his arms above his head, he alternately crossed one leg in front of the other in a graceful swaying motion.

"So that's what he meant by 'dancing,'" I thought, remembering his suggestion that there might be dancing at the Love Feast. As the swami swayed, he began to move forward in a clockwise circle around the room, gesturing for us to follow. We gamboled behind him, forming a single conga-like line. The swami continued to chant for well over an hour, and we responded, dancing to the quickening pace of the music.

Several of Mishra's students stood along two walls and chanted with us. A few swayed to the beat, but they didn't dance – not the middle-aged suited men, and not the younger hippy crowd either. Only two of Mishra's followers joined in – an Indian man and his American girlfriend. They clasped each other tightly and became increasingly animated, whirling around ballroom style. I caught a whiff of liquor. I looked at them and then at the swami, trying to gauge his reaction to their behavior, trying to make out what he was thinking. He was watching them with an expression that could be taken either as a smile or a smirk.

After the chanting and dancing ended, most of Mishra's followers, including the dancing couple, drifted out of the room. One or two of the younger ones hung back to hear the swami speak, joining us crossed-legged on the floor.

"Krishna's name is not different from Krishna Himself," the swami said. "Therefore, as soon as my tongue touches the holy name of Krishna, I am immediately associating with Krishna. So if you constantly keep yourself associated with Krishna by chanting this mantra, then just imagine how you are being easily purified from material existence. Lord Chaitanya distributed this chanting freely. Freely. But don't neglect it. Take it. Don't minimize the value because we are distributing free. It is the most valuable thing of your life, chanting Hare Krishna. And if you chant regularly, you'll practically find the result."

In the midst of his talk, the swami opened his eyes. He looked toward the adjoining room and, almost inaudibly, he said, "Just see.

We are chanting God's name, and he is taking it as a ball-dance."
We glanced at each other, our suspicions of the couple's inappropriateness confirmed.

The evening program concluded and we all retired for the evening. Since Jan and I were the only couple in our party, the swami had arranged for us to stay in a large room upstairs next to his. The room was like a log cabin, with wooden walls, floor and ceiling and a few small windows overlooking the lake and a forested hill.

Some hours after we had fallen asleep, I awoke to the sound of a loud voice.

"What is that?" I was foggy from sleep.

"It's the swami chanting," Jan said. "I've been lying here listening to him for a while now."

I groped around in the dark for my alarm clock -- 2:30 AM. We listened to his voice repeating the Hare Krishna mantra in a meditative monotone. We were amazed that anyone would choose to meditate at this hour of the day. Gradually, we slipped into sleep, almost lulled to rest by the swami's distinctive voice.

We rose early the next morning to take part in a *hatha-yoga* class led by a thirty-year-old woman, a follower of Mishra's. Most of the other students were middle-aged, overweight women who looked like they were using yoga as part of an exercise regime in the hope of shedding some excess fat.

At nine that morning, we gathered to hear the swami speak in the main room of Mishra's complex. The swami was seated cross-legged on a maroon sofa at the rear of the room. It was a bright summer morning, and the sunlight was streaming through the large windows behind him. We all sat on a large carpet in the sun facing the swami, while two men in their late twenties or early thirties sat in the middle of the room, just beyond the fall of the sunrays. Like the men who watched the chanting the previous evening, these guys were dressed in corporate-looking business suits.

The swami's talk was short and to the point.

"Krishna is *adi purusa*, the original person," he said. "Every one of us – humans, animals, demigods, even plants and trees – we are all individuals. So if every living entity is an individual, how can the origin of every living entity not be a person himself? Therefore

Lord Brahma prays, 'govindam adi-purusam tam aham bhajami – I worship Govinda, that original person from whom everything emanates.'

"But because He is a person and I am a person, I should not think that He is like me. No. The Vedas inform us that although Krishna is a person, He is maintaining all other persons. One person maintaining millions and trillions of other living entities. He is a person like us, but He is different. He is sac-cid-ananda-vigraha. He is a person who is eternal, who is full of bliss, and who possesses all knowledge. We die; He does not die. Our bodies are full of suffering, but His is full of bliss.

"So although He is a singular person, He is providing all the necessities to the different plural persons. That is the distinction between God and us."

I glanced at Mishra's followers and saw them whispering to each other. I sensed a tension in the air between them and the swami.

One of them raised his hand. The swami nodded at him, indicating he could speak. He began to read a passage from one of Mishra's books. The passage suggested that liberation was achieved when the individual merged into God, just as a drop of water merges with the sea.

A short way into the passage, the swami interrupted.

"Just try to understand," he said in a loud, forceful voice. "The gold ring and gold mine are of the same substance, but the gold ring can never be the gold mine. We have the same qualities as God, but He has them in unlimited quantity, whereas we have only a minute portion. Do you understand?"

"But Dr. Mishra says ..."

"Just answer. Can the gold ring ever become the gold mine?"

"Well, Dr. Mishra says here that ..."

"Never mind. Just answer this question, 'Can the gold ring ever become the gold mine?'"

"No, but ..."

"So if the gold ring can never become the gold mine, how can you ever lose your individuality?"

"The goal is to lose the ego."

"The false ego, yes, but your real ego, your real identity, that can never be lost. Our real identity is that we are servants of God. That ego, that identity, we don't want to lose. It is our eternal position."

"I thought that the goal was to lose one's ego."

"No, you have misunderstood," said the swami. "It is only my false sense of identity that must be lost. We are thinking 'I am American. I am Indian. I am man. I am woman. I am black. I am white.' This is skin disease. I am actually servant of God and that can never be taken away."

"But can't we serve Him as liberated beings merged into infinite existence?"

"How is that service? Can you serve your mother by returning to the womb?"

"Of course not, but …"

"Well, how can you serve if you merge?"

"What I mean is that there is a form of service in oneness."

"That is nonsense. How can you serve someone if you are one with him?"

There was silence. I felt uncomfortable that such a heated debate was going on, that the swami was challenging Mishra's teachings. The two men excused themselves. They said they had a meeting to get to, and left us alone in the large room with the swami.

"So what do you think of Dr. Mishra's viewpoint, anyway?" asked Charlie.

The swami replied, "Once Dr. Mishra asked me, 'Swamiji, can God become a snake?' I answered, 'Why not? God can become anything. If He wants to become a snake, who can stop Him? Certainly He can become a snake.' Then Dr. Mishra said, 'Then you are my guru.'"

We all stood and left the room.

"I think it's time to head back to the city," I said to Jan.

"Yeah," she agreed. "I feel close to the swami out here in this place, but the atmosphere somehow doesn't feel right. It's not like at the temple. I mean, it's beautiful here, but it's so isolated. What are you supposed to do out here?"

On the way back to town I talked to Charlie about the weekend.

"The swami really pushed his point on those guys," I said to him. "He's not just a teacher; he's a fighter. He really didn't like Mishra's philosophy, did he?"

"Maybe, but I heard that the swami and Mishra are actually good friends," Charlie said. "They disagree on philosophy and they argue like that a lot, but they are still good friends."

"Yeah, but that scene out there was just plain weird," I said.

"They represent two different schools of thought. Mishra's an impersonalist who thinks we should merge into God, but the swami is a personalist. For him, God is a person and so are we, and our purpose is to serve Him." Charlie seemed very knowledgeable. "The swami told me it's an age-old debate," he said knowingly.

Then and there I rejected impersonalism as a philosophy for my life. And I realized I needed to read more to increase my knowledge about the swami's teachings so I could really know what it was all about and talk to others about it knowledgeably.

CHAPTER 7

My Nightmare:
The Cabins, Hurleyville,
New York

August 1966

After a month or so in the new temple, the swami was acquiring a more regular following. A core group – Janis, Raymond, Keith, Stanley, Howard and Wally – hung around the place all the time. Wally, Keith and Howard lived in an apartment on nearby Mott Street, and a few of them actually slept on the floor of the temple. With them around so much, the swami began holding a program each morning, during which he would lecture and chant with whoever was there.

I heard about the morning programs and started to walk over to the storefront occasionally in the early hours of the morning. The hours before seven were the only time of the day when lower Manhattan was relatively quiet. Usually the area was noisy, smelly and choking with refuse, overflowing garbage cans festering in the heat on every street corner. Almost totally devoid of trees, shrubs or plants, the streets' only living inhabitants besides humans appeared to be mosquitoes and rats. During the early morning hours, though, things took on a dreamlike quality. Without all the cars, the air was less toxic; it was warm but not hot yet, so the garbage stank less; and with only a few people around, the atmosphere changed from metropolis to quiet neighborhood. I really liked being up at that hour. Some mornings I could even hear birds singing in Sara Roosevelt Park as the sun rose.

Although I was attending the swami's programs and reading his books a lot, I wasn't part of his core group. That crowd didn't do a whole lot for me, and I wasn't interested in just hanging around. One afternoon I dropped by the swami's apartment and found about eight men sitting cross-legged on the floor, leaning against the wall of his small unfurnished bedroom. An intense philosophical discussion was underway, mostly fuelled, I thought, by the fact they had nothing else to do. Patiently listening to their comments, the swami sat opposite them on a sponge-rubber mattress covered by a white sheet.

"So, the mode of goodness is called *sattva*, right?" one of them asked.

"Yes, that's right," the swami answered.

"And does *sattva* lead to the mode of pure goodness?"

"Yes, but according to the Vedic understanding, the modes of *raja* and *tamas* – passion and ignorance – are always attacking *sattva*," the swami said.

I wasn't in a hurry, so I sat and listened for a while, trying to look inconspicuous. The boys talked on, and eventually the swami lay down on his side and drifted off to sleep. The group went silent.

"The swami takes short naps," one of them whispered to me. "We shouldn't talk until he wakes up."

I thought about leaving but stayed sitting against the wall. Twenty minutes later, the swami sat up and the conversation resumed exactly where it had left off. I was surprised that he seemed so fully alert and could remember what was being discussed before he went to sleep.

The conversation seemed endlessly conjectural and rather speculative to me. I liked the swami's teachings, but this type of discussion seemed a bit pointless; I had a partner, a career and a life to get on with. I quietly slipped away to meet up with a friend named Henry Salmon, who that afternoon had invited Jan and me to accompany him and his girlfriend, Julie, for a week away in rural Hurleyville, New York.

We liked the idea of getting out of the city for a week or so, so we agreed to go away with Henry. I hadn't known him for long, but we had really good rapport. His girlfriend seemed quite young but fun and sweet enough. The four of us drove up to Hurleyville the following afternoon.

"There's four cabins," Henry said as we headed out of the city on the freeway. "My family owns them. We'll have two, and they've rented the other two out to other people. It's really nice up there. Clean and secluded."

At six o'clock on the first morning, I discovered that the water tap in our cabin wasn't working. So much for rural life! I left Jan sleeping and went next door to Henry's cabin to get a drink. Henry wasn't in, but the door was unlocked, so I let myself in to get some water from the kitchen.

Unknown to me, Julie was asleep in the adjacent bedroom. I also didn't know that she was only fifteen years old – three years younger than Henry – and that she had sold marijuana to a local undercover agent the previous afternoon when we arrived in Hurleyville.

I gazed absently out Henry's kitchen window as I drank my glass of water. The sun's rays were just beginning to rise above the pine trees, and I could hear a stream flowing somewhere nearby.

"We'll have to check that out later today," I thought.

I rinsed the glass and turned the tap off tight so it wouldn't drip like it had been before I turned it on. Was that sirens I could hear in the distance? They seemed to be getting louder and louder. Suddenly they were screaming right outside the door, cars lurching and skidding onto the grass, red lights flashing in the windows.

"What's going on?" I heard myself say.

I rushed through the cabin's open front door. Police crouched behind their cars, guns drawn. One cop, halfway up the stairs of the cabin, lunged at me with his pistol drawn.

"You're under arrest!" he shouted. "Put your hands in the air!"

Bewildered, I slowly raised my hands above my head. It was hard to take seriously. I felt like I was watching a TV drama in which things like that occurred regularly, except this was all unfolding in slow motion. This was a dream; it couldn't have been happening.

The officer shoved his cocked Smith & Wesson .45 into my stomach and waved a piece of paper in my face.

"Henry Salmon, this is your arrest warrant. You have the right to remain silent. Whatever you say may be used as evidence against you in a court of law."

I was relieved. This was one drama I wasn't going to be a part of.

"There's been a mistake, officer," I said. "I'm not Henry. My name's Michael Grant, and I just came over here for some water. Our faucet next door isn't working."

"Doesn't matter," shouted another cop, overruling me. "You were in the house." To his colleague, the one with the gun, he said, "Take him in as well."

The officer with the gun forced my hands behind my back. I felt the cold steel of handcuffs around my wrists and his hands forcing me down into a chair. The reality of the situation hit me. This wasn't a movie – this was for real.

The policemen fanned out through the house, marching with heavy steps into the kitchen and the bathroom. They went through my pockets. Empty.

Suddenly Jan was there, fear and confusion in her eyes. Two burly policemen stood in the doorway, just in case I'd make a run for it. They blocked her from entering.

"What's all this about?" She sounded panicky.

"They think I'm Henry!" I shouted. "Just tell them that I'm not! This is *ridiculous*. I have my ID next door."

"We *are* staying next door," she said. "And he's *not* Henry. Can you let him go, please? We have things to do today."

"Shut up," snapped one of the cops by the door. "This is none of your business."

"But Michael's my fiancé," she insisted. We exchanged a look. *Fiancé*? It was worth a try. "We're just up here for a week. You made a mistake!"

Without looking at her, the policeman said rudely, "Why don't you go home, lady? We got a job to do. And keep your mouth shut or you're going downtown too."

Jan backed away but hovered outside the doorway. More cars pulled up, and the state and federal police swarmed into the small cabin. An officer in a blue uniform, his gun in a holster, emptied the kitchen cabinets and pulled out silverware drawers, rifling through their contents. He looked in boxes under the sink, opened Handy Andy bottles, Ajax cans, bags of flour. He flung open the fridge and freezer doors and even ripped into bags of frozen vegetables.

I could see an officer going into the small bathroom. He lifted the lid on the water tank behind the toilet, peering inside. Another patrolman stood at the door.

"Anything there?"

"Nope."

More policemen combed the cupboards, looked under the table, inside the light fixtures, on the shelves, at the back of the curtains, inside colored flower vases, beneath the cupboard linings and behind pictures on the wall.

So far, no one had gone into the bedroom. The door was shut, and I assumed Henry and Julie were out somewhere. Finally, four policemen stormed the room. Seconds later, Julie staggered out in a pale-green thigh-length nightgown, rubbing the sleep out of her eyes.

"Boy," I thought, "she's a deep sleeper. Or maybe she's taken something?"

A policeman clutched one of her upper arms as he escorted her out. He cuffed her hands behind her back. I wasn't surprised to see her shaking; she'd awakened to four uniformed men ransacking her bedroom. She sunk onto a kitchen chair near mine.

I heard voices shouting in the bedroom, furniture moving, drawers opening, shoes scuffing the floor, window shades opening, jewelry rattling, cosmetic bottles clanging.

"Look between the mattresses."

"Hey! Look what daddy found!" someone said in a loud bass voice.

White shafts of sunlight streamed through the window in the front room, piercing the air in the small kitchenette. Particles of flour rose slowly to the ceiling. Peas rolled languidly on the floor. Jan had inched her way inside and was talking diplomatically to a plainclothes detective, but both of them stopped talking when they heard the exclamation from inside the cabin. The policeman emerged from the bedroom holding a small plastic bag between his thumb and forefinger.

He clomped into the kitchen. "It was in one of those drawers."

"Lemme see that!" the sergeant-in-charge demanded, grabbing the clear plastic bag and scrutinizing it. "Yep, this looks like it." He held it to his nose, sniffed it, nodded his head, and the others came in for a closer look.

Another black and white Ford screeched to a stop outside, red light still revolving.

"I got him! He's here in my car," I heard the driver shout. The door slammed and a flushed-looking officer appeared in the cabin doorway.

"It's Henry," he said. "I found him."

Satisfied now, the officers prepared to leave the scene. One grabbed me and another grabbed Julie. They led us down the front stairs; my arm felt bruised beneath the hard clamp of the officer's grip. Henry was alone in the back seat. He looked small and frightened sitting in that police car. His goatee, stubble, mustache and hair made him look like a criminal. He peered at us through the car window.

As we came down the steps, I felt his anguish, but I was relieved. *He* was the person named on the warrant, not me. They'd gotten their man.

"Can I go now?" I asked demandingly, to no one in particular.

"No way, buddy. You're coming with us."

"What?"

The policeman holding me pushed me into the car, his hand on my head, just like on TV. Julie was pushed into the back seat from the other side of the car. Henry sat in the middle between us.

For half a minute we were alone while local, state and federal police planned their next move.

"The best thing," I whispered, not looking at them, "is if you don't say anything at all." I tried to sound resolute and wise. I was six years older than Henry, and I knew I could pull a little rank on him. "We'll get our lawyers to talk to them." Then I looked straight at them. "Whatever we say, they'll use it against us. It's best not to say anything. OK? I'm sorry you guys are in this situation, but I don't want to be involved in this. It's nothing to do with me."

Out of the corner of my eye I saw the policemen coming toward us. A bad-tempered New York State patrolman slammed the driver's door and drove us away fast. We headed toward the freeway in silence. The car's clean seats, floor, panels and dust-free dashboard looked and smelled like the inside of a hospital.

"Why did you arrest me when you didn't have a warrant for me?" I asked.

"I don't talk to idiots," he hissed, looking at me in the rear-view mirror, not turning his head. He drove faster.

"This is so unjust," I thought. "I don't have any weed on me."

As we approached the station, my mind was racing. I'd heard many stories about false arrests, erroneous convictions and even wrongful executions. I had visions of a long prison sentence ahead. For the police, having marijuana was the same as having narcotics, and it amounted to a serious misdemeanor, almost a felony. And even though I wasn't in possession of any drugs, I was with Henry, and that seemed to be enough for them.

The car pulled up outside the station, and I was taken immediately for an initial hearing before a judge. The judge looked me up and down as I entered the room flanked by two police officers. I was bearded and dressed shabbily. The judge looked pointedly at my gold earring.

I heard him mutter under his breath, "If my kid ever looked like that I'd beat the crap out of him." The police briefed him on the arrest. I was charged with possession of narcotics with intent to sell, statutory rape and contributing to the delinquency of a minor. I was put in prison on five thousand dollars bail, with a formal trial scheduled to take place in two weeks.

Twenty minutes later I was booked, photographed and fingerprinted.

As I stood before the cameras, the state policeman who had driven us to the station said to the police photographer, "We caught him in bed with Henry's girlfriend."

"That's a lie," I snapped. He strolled over and kicked my leg as hard as he could.

"Can't stand the truth?" I shouted.

He kicked me again and glared. It hurt too much for me to say anything but "Ouch!"

The Hurleyville and state police treated me like a hardened criminal. They hardly talked to me, and when they did, they shouted and cursed at me. They shoved me around and pushed me from room to room.

I spent five days at the Hurleyville City Prison. I was in a cell with a toilet that had no seat on it. I wrote a letter to a relative asking him if he would pay my bail; I began to doubt if the letter even got out of the prison. I fasted, protesting a "false arrest," but no one seemed to notice.

Finally, on the fourth day, I succumbed to hunger. I told the guards I was vegetarian.

"You think this is a restaurant where you can order whatever you want to eat?" they sneered.

I was given three pieces of white bread and a hot dog that I dumped into the toilet. To remind myself how little nutrition I was getting, I squished each slice of bread into a cube the size of dice.

I repeatedly requested a phone call and after four days managed to speak to Jan for thirty seconds.

"You've got to get me out of here!"

"Don't worry, I will," she said. "I'm doing everything I can. I'm coming up to see you soon."

"I've already been here four days!" I whispered. "Why hasn't anyone visited me? Do you think maybe Henry and his friends are setting me up?"

The guard standing near me said, "Time's up."

"OK," I said, glancing at him. I felt the urgency of the situation in the pit of my stomach. "When're you coming up?"

"Tomorrow. I'll try tomorrow," she said.

The only things to read in jail were worn paperbacks, mostly Zane Grey cowboy stories. There were no newspapers or radios allowed. Everyone else in the cellblock was playing solitaire. Time dragged on. Judging from the stories other inmates told, I thought I could be inside forever. I was scared, angry and felt completely helpless.

Then I remembered Krishna and the swami.

I remembered what I had read in the books, and I remembered the swami saying that chanting helped a person transcend material suffering. The swami had written specifically about that in a section I had read just before leaving for Hurleyville: "Those entangled in the complicated meshes of birth and death can be freed immediately by even unconsciously chanting the holy name of the Lord." I began to chant Hare Krishna, and it made things a little easier. Although I was uneasy about the injustice of my situation and the possibility of prolonged incarceration, my newfound affiliation with the swami gave me a philosophical perspective that helped me to somewhat transcend this horrible experience. I chanted and chanted, and I calmed down a little bit.

The·next day, a prison guard came to my cell, his keys rattling as he swaggered.

"Grant! You have a visitor."

He opened the door and led me out. I followed him down a narrow stairway to the visiting cubicles.

Jan was on the other side of the wired glass, looking earnest and cheerful.

"You'll get out today." I could tell she was trying to look bright. "Don't worry. I got the best lawyers in New York."

A tall, clean-shaven guard appeared behind me, smirking. "We're going back. Come on."

"Hey, I haven't even been here for one minute," I exclaimed.

"Tough." He looked impassive as he took me by the upper arm, literally yanking me away. "Back upstairs," he said, nodding to the right.

I looked back at Jan. Her mouth was open wide in astonishment, but she quickly shut it and nodded reassuringly.

That night, the same tall guard marched up to my cell. "Grant! Get your stuff and come with me."

He opened the door, and I followed him. I was getting out! At last! Jan was there waiting for me. She looked overwhelmed.

She briefed me on my situation on the drive back to New York.

"I got one of your uncles in Oregon to pay the bail," she said.

"I'm really freaked out by the trial. How am I going to wait two weeks to find out what's going to happen to me?"

"Don't worry," she said. "I've been in touch with Maurice Barret, and he's got really great lawyers to represent you. And he's going to front the money for your trial."

Yeah, I thought. If anyone could get good lawyers, it'd be him.

Maurice was a graduate of Columbia University, a good friend of mine. He liked Eastern culture like I did and was keen on LSD, but he was also clean-cut and had numerous contacts in the professional world. His mother, Ophelia Mendoza, worked for the United Nations.

With the help of his mother, he'd managed to secure the services of two lawyers named Dominic Straski and Morris Novak. They were older, experienced attorneys; Novak had worked as a judge for many years in Brooklyn and had been involved in many high-profile cases. Jan, Maurice and Ophelia thought they were the best people to help me.

I met with the lawyers several times over the next two weeks. Apart from Maurice and Jan, the rest of my friends and acquaintances seemed to have dissolved. Only the swami made the effort to call me a few days after I arrived home, and his care and thoughtfulness impressed me and touched me deeply.

On the evening of my trial, the lawyers arrived at my loft to drive Jan and me up to Hurleyville. I had shaved my beard off and had my hair cut for the hearing. I wore a dark blue suit and tie. As I followed them down our front steps, I saw a brand new Buick parked at the curb; slipping into the back seat, I felt reassured to be supported by such affluent men. The car smelled like new shoes.

Mostly we rode in silence. Then I saw Novak watching me in the rear-view mirror.

"If the judge asks you if you've ever used marijuana, you have to say no. Don't even say you've tried it once. The more indignant you act about being asked the question the better."

I nodded.

It was dark by the time we arrived in Hurleyville. We were escorted into a big court room that was packed with people. The judge that had presided over my first hearing sat at the front of the room. He looked up as we entered, and rose.

"Good evening, Judge Novak," he said.

Novak nodded to acknowledge him and motioned for me to sit down in the rows of seats at the back of the room. It was then that I realized that all the people in the room were there for their own trials.

After endless child support, rent arrears and traffic cases, the judge rose and walked down the aisle. He paused when he reached us.

"Please come with me for a moment," he said to my lawyers.

The three of them disappeared into a back room. A few minutes later, my lawyers returned and took their places, one on either side of me.

"You don't need to worry," Novak whispered. "It's going to be OK."

"Case number 7523," a clerk read out. "The State of New York versus Michael Grant on charges of statutory rape, contributing to the delinquency of a minor and possession of narcotics with intent to sell. Case dismissed for lack of evidence."

The relief coursed through me. Jan was beaming next me. With sedate smiles and a final nod to the judge, my lawyers led us from the room.

The lawyers were almost completely silent on the ride back to the city. Jan and I also exchanged only a few words.

"I'm going to see the swami tomorrow," I said quietly to her. "I want to tell him what's happened with all this."

She nodded.

"I mean, I don't want him to think I was dealing drugs." I paused, and a thought suddenly occurred to me. "Actually, Carl says that *he* used to deal drugs. Did you know that? Maybe he wouldn't care that much if I was selling, but I want to clear it up anyway."

Jan laughed. "The swami wasn't a drug dealer!" she exclaimed. "He was a *pharmacist!* In Allahabad! That was his job when he was younger!"

"Really?"

"Yes. Carol told me. And he told her. Carl obviously misunderstood him. Imagine that – the swami a drug dealer!"

The thought of it mixed with the relief we felt, and we laughed the rest of the way back to New York.

CHAPTER 8

Becoming a Regular

My trial and time in jail had a life-changing impact on me. I returned to my "normal" life, only to find that I could no longer embrace it wholeheartedly. The prospect of spending years in jail made me seriously rethink my priorities. I became a strict vegetarian, gave up all drugs and began to doubt whether happiness could be found in fame and success in the music industry. I resolved to get out of New York as soon as possible to live a simpler, more natural way of life. My city ways had never influenced Jan's love for country life, and I realized I was now ready for a more rural existence. I thought a lot about going to India.

More than anything, I was disappointed in the lack of response from the people I thought were my friends. In my time of need, it was the swami who cared enough to contact me and ask about my welfare. That gesture – the phone call that summer morning – changed my life. After the trial, I quickly became a regular at 26 Second Avenue and began to devote more of my time to study and spiritual pursuits. I wanted to seriously embrace the philosophy the swami was teaching and to learn everything about it that I could.

I increased my attendance at the swami's morning programs. Soon it became part of my daily schedule to rise early and to chant as I walked over to the temple to hear the swami lecture at seven o'clock.

One morning when I was heading back to my Bowery loft from the temple, I was offered drugs by a member of the late night/early morning crowd that hung out on the Lower East Side. I was on Chrystie Street chanting quietly when I heard a baritone voice behind.

"Nickel bag?" asked the bearded figure, reaching into the pocket of his World War II leather jacket. He produced a quantity of marijuana –five dollars worth – and held it out to me.

With a shock, I realized how much I had changed. A few months ago this would have been an opportune moment, a fortuitous contact with the New York underworld. I might have bought the dope from the dealer, and we might have even shared a joint right then and there on the street, eyes darting furtively this way and that, looking out for the usual police cars patrolling the streets in the early New York morning. But today, this casual proposition from a street-wise comrade seemed horribly wrong. To me he now represented a devilish specter from a past life.

"Nickel bag, brothuh?"

He moved a little closer and pronounced the phrase more distinctly as if I hadn't heard him the first time. I looked at him straight in the face. Then I closed my eyes for a few seconds, took a deep breath and shook my head. I walked faster, hoping I'd made it clear that I wasn't interested either in his nickel bag or in talking.

As I made my way home, I thought of a stanza from Shakespeare's *Julius Caesar*, which I'd memorized when I was fifteen:

… 'Tis a common proof,
That lowliness is young ambition's ladder,
Whereto the climber-upward turns his face;
But when he once attains the upmost round.
He then unto the ladder turns his back,
Looks in the clouds, scorning the base degrees
By which he did ascend.

It was an uncomfortable thing to admit, but I knew that I felt myself to be on a higher rung of the ladder than I used to be. I also knew that I was scorning the position I'd come from, turning my back on an earnest weed seller, even though I myself had been in that "base degree" only a few months earlier. I counted myself fortunate to have met the swami and to have left that world, but in order to avoid temptation, I somehow had a need to reject and despise that world I'd once embraced.

"I could have talked to him," I thought as I walked. After all, he was a soul in this world too; I could have told him about what I'd found in Krishna consciousness and the swami. But despite, or perhaps because of my past, I was anxious to be pure and to remain aloof from it.

That evening, I joined a crowd of fifty people who crammed into the swami's storefront to hear his lectures. The swami's three evening programs had grown in popularity since he had been at his new premises. Most of his guests sat cross-legged on the thick oriental carpet, peering at the swami through clouds of incense and chanting with him to the rhythm of his cymbals before and after each talk. Some chanted, some clapped, and some just stared. Most were teenagers and people in their twenties. The Sunday Love Feasts had also become a regular weekly feature.

Most of the time, the swami was open, friendly and tolerant of all the various kinds of people that passed through his little storefront. He was welcoming to everyone. One mid-summer evening, a short middle-aged drunk man staggered into the temple, his black hair disheveled under a bent checked fedora, his eyes rolling wildly. Apparently oblivious to the oppressive New York heat, the man wore a heavy black overcoat with dirty brown pants that bagged at the ankles. Behind his weeklong stubble, a silly grin was plastered on his face. The strong smell of cheap wine, musty clothes, and body odor spewed from every part of him.

The swami was speaking from the fourth chapter of the *Bhagavad-gita* and talking about *dharma*, which he translated as "duty" or "law."

"*Dharma* means 'the essential nature of a thing' – its ethos," the swami said. "Liquidity is the *dharma* of water. Heat is the *dharma* of fire. So what is the *dharma* of humanity? Humanity's *dharma* is service. The nature of the living entity is to serve someone else, perhaps family, nation, government. But always the living entity is rendering some service." He was gradually losing his Indian accent.

I was sitting with everyone else on the rug, trying to listen attentively. I noticed the drunk come in out of the corner of my eye. His stench hit me, and I exchanged glances with the other regulars. I didn't want to interrupt the swami and make a scene by throwing him out. Also, I didn't think it would be very kind or loving or spiritual to remove him, even though I found his presence offensive. I couldn't be certain if the swami was bothered by him or if he even noticed.

The unwelcome visitor stumbled resolutely toward the swami's sitting place. We all just sat there as if suspended in time, anxiously watching the odd and potentially dangerous situation unfold. The drunk reached the lectern, groping inside his coat for something. What would it be – a rock, a knife, a gun? I was ready to spring forward if anything untoward happened. After a few seconds that seemed like eons, the man withdrew his hand and pulled out a roll of packaged toilet paper. He plunked it down on the lectern in front of the swami.

"What is this?" the swami asked.

The drunk spun around, and teetered away to the center of the room where he fell into a cross-legged position on the rug.

The swami smiled at his strange guest. "Thank you very much," he said. "Thank you. Thank you."

Then he looked out at his audience. "Just see," he said. "It is a natural tendency – to give some service. Just see. He's not in order, but he thought, 'Here is something. Let me give some service.' That is *dharma*."

The swami picked up his small drum and began to lead the chant: "*Hare Krishna Hare Krishna Krishna Krishna Hare Hare, Hare Rama Hare Rama Rama Rama Hare Hare.*" As the tempo picked up, we stood one by one and began to dance in the way the swami had showed us, putting weight on one foot and then the other, as if we were nervous or urgently needed to use the toilet.

The drunk stood up too. He extended his arms and began to spin around, eyes closed with the silly smile widening on his face. As the pace increased, he twirled around faster and faster, staggering and barely keeping his balance. The chant, aided by the swami's drum, reached a crescendo and then suddenly stopped. The visitor collapsed on the floor and lay on his back, arms and legs spread-eagled, his eyelids closed, the delirious smile still on his lips.

Two nights later, he turned up at the temple, but this time he was sober and respectably dressed, his hair combed, his trousers pressed, his face cleanly shaved. He sat through most of the swami's lecture, and I thought that the swami's kindness and gratitude must have won him over.

As well as the homeless and the very young, the swami's programs were occasionally frequented by respectable people, and even the odd famous person. One night I arrived at the program a little bit late. The room was packed with singing people who were seated and swaying from side to side. I spotted a small gap in the center of the room; I picked my way through the crowd, tapping people on the back to ask them to let me through. The little opening was really too tight for me to sit, but the guy next to me moved over a little bit so I'd have enough room to sit down.

Apart from a sideways nod to thank him for accommodating me, I didn't pay very much attention to the man at that moment. Then I looked again, and realized I was sitting next to Allen Ginsberg, celebrity poet of the Beat generation. He was unmistakable with his bald head and bushy black beard, and I wondered how I'd failed to recognize him immediately. I began to think that maybe that little gap I'd noticed in the crowd was there because everyone else had tried to make him comfortable by giving him a bit of extra breathing room.

Ginsberg was a revolutionary figure whose poems decried materialism and praised non-compliance. In the 1950s, at the height of US prosperity and conformity, he wrote about drug use, psychiatric illness and homosexuality, and his best-known poem, "Howl," landed him on trial for obscenity. He was friends with a group of individuals – William Burroughs, Jack Kerouac, Gregory Corso and Gary Snyder, to name a few – that had inspired an entire generation of young people with their conviction in the free expression of spirituality, drugs and sex. And now here he was, sitting in the swami's temple next to me.

I expected the swami to acknowledge Ginsberg in some way, but the lecture proceeded as usual. "According to Vedic conception there are four divisions of spiritual order," the swami said. "This is called *varna-ashrama dharma*. The four divisions of spiritual order are *sannyasa*, *vanaprastha*, *grihasta* and *brahmachari*. *Bramachari* means student life, to be trained up in spiritual understanding,

Krishna consciousness, fully trained up. Then, after full training, the student gets married and lives with family and children. That is called *grihasta*. There is no boyfriend, girlfriend in Vedic society; one is either celibate or is nicely married. Then, after fifty years, husband and wife leave the children alone and travel in the holy places. That is called *vanaprastha*, retired life. And at last one gives up the family entirely and remains alone. And that is called renounced order of life. *Sannyasa* means that all energy and work is for Krishna; nothing is for me."

Ginsberg sat still, listening attentively to the swami for the entire lecture. I was impressed that someone as famous as him would be humble enough to sit on the floor. After the question-and-answer session, the swami began to chant, and Ginsberg stayed. It was only after another hour of chanting that he rose to leave, the eyes of the room following him as he departed.

Another professional who would sometimes attend the evening programs was Steven Goldsmith, the lawyer who had incorporated the swami's society. One evening, after the lecture when the swami asked for questions, Steven stood up. He loudly asked – indirectly on behalf of millions of peaceniks – "If God is so kind, why is He allowing so many of our American boys to be killed in Vietnam?"

This question changed the polite, usually philosophic question-and-answer period. Looking right at Steven, the swami immediately answered, "You are daily killing so many animals, so God is saying, 'send your *sons* to the slaughterhouse.'" As the word "sons" escaped his lips, his eyes opened wide and with his right hand raised and close to his face, he pointed to the left wall with his index finger. It was at that point that I realized the swami wasn't ever going to compromise.

Steven Goldsmith's question was symptomatic of the concern gripping millions of Americans. Anti-Vietnam war demonstrations, flag and draft-card burnings, and many types of protests were going on all the time. The possibility of being drafted for Vietnam constantly lurked at the back of my mind as well. So when word got out that the swami was going to conduct a "peace vigil" at the United Nations headquarters in Manhattan, it was an exciting proposal for me and the other men in the swami's group. I thought it would be a fun summer outing with the swami, a kind of spiritual protest, and a way for us all to get out and do something a little bit different.

At 6:30 AM on August 31ˢᵗ, twelve of us assembled with the swami on First Avenue near Forty-second Street. It was the first time Jan and I had seen the swami engage in what seemed like social protest or a demonstration of any kind. He didn't seem to be into the "peace movement" per se, but he knew we were young, available for conscription, and that most of us thought it was morally wrong for our country to be in Vietnam.

We began to chant opposite the United Nations Secretariat, the towering glass and steel structure near Forty-sixth Street in Manhattan. At 10:30 AM, after four hours, several officials in suits emerged from the building and politely told us that we were allowed only to engage in silent prayer. We looked at each other and sat down on the sidewalk to quietly chant.

The swami stayed on his feet, handing out leaflets to the early morning commuters and tourists. The leaflet was entitled "Peace Formula:"

"The earth is the property of God, but we, the living entities, especially the so-called civilized human beings, are claiming God's property as our own, under both an individual and collective false conception. If you want peace, you have to remove this false conception from your mind and from the world. This false claim of proprietorship by the human race on earth is partly or wholly the cause of all disturbances of peace on earth.

"Foolish and so-called civilized men are claiming proprietary rights on the property of God because they have now become godless. You cannot be happy and peaceful in a godless society. In the *Bhagavad-gita* Lord Krishna says that He is the factual enjoyer of all activities of the living entities, that He is the Supreme Lord of all universes, and that He is the well-wishing friend of all beings. When the people of the world know this as the formula for peace, it is then and there that peace will prevail.

"You can change your consciousness into Krishna consciousness, both individually and collectively, by the simple process of chanting the holy name of God. This is a standard and recognized process for achieving peace in the world.

"We therefore recommend that everyone become Krishna conscious by chanting *Hare Krishna Hare Krishna Krishna Krishna Hare Hare, Hare Rama Hare Rama Rama Rama Hare Hare.*

"This is practical, simple and sublime. Four hundred and eighty years ago this formula was introduced in India by Lord Shri Chaitanya, and now it is available in your country. Take to this simple process of chanting as above mentioned, realize your factual position by reading the *Bhagavad-gita As It Is*, and reestablish your lost relationship with Krishna, God. Peace and prosperity will be the immediate worldwide result."

After some time, the swami sat down to rest for a few moments. Then he rose and spoke aloud, even though there was hardly anyone there. After a while a few people stopped to listen.

"If we want peace," he said, "we have to worship God. Not just with words or rituals, but with sincerity and devotion, otherwise there will be no chance for peace. So please take up this chanting of *Hare Krishna Hare Krishna Krishna Krishna Hare Hare, Hare Rama Hare Rama Rama Rama Hare Hare*. Chant and be happy."

The following day, the *New York Post* published an article on our peace protest. It included a large photograph of the twelve of us sitting on the pavement around the swami. All of us, including the swami, were happy to see our efforts had been noticed.

The New York Post *shows how devotees and the swami promote "spiritual peace" outside the UN Secretariat building on New York's 1ˢᵗ Avenue.*

I thought a lot about the swami's position on celibacy and marriage in respect to my and Jan's relationship. Apart from one sharp look the first time he visited our loft, he never directly indicated any disapproval of our live-in status. Nevertheless, now that I was attending his lectures more regularly, it was becoming more and more apparent to me that our living together out of wedlock didn't fit with the culture the swami embodied.

Finally, the day after the peace vigil, I got up the nerve to ask Jan to marry me.

She looked shocked and then pleased. "This is so unexpected," she said. "Why are you asking me now? I thought things were going OK just the way they are."

"Well, sure. But you know, we've been together for a while, and it seems like the right thing to do now if we're going to live by what the swami's saying. It kind of seems from his lectures that you either have to be married or be celibate."

"Yeah. I guess I hadn't really thought about it like that."

"We could ask the swami to marry us."

"Yeah, we could. That would be far out."

"Yeah. I thought that if he married us our marriage would be kind of like blessed or something. Like I thought having him do it would make it lasting and permanent."

"Look, Michael, this is all kind of sudden. I can see where you're coming from, but I need a bit of time to think. I kind of like the way things are now, and I think I'd like it to stay the same as it has been the last year or so."

I wasn't overly encouraged by this initial response, but the following day she said yes. "The more I thought about it, the more I realized that I actually wanted to get married," she said. "If it's what you still want, that is."

"It is! That's great, Jan!" I exclaimed.

That afternoon I asked the swami if he would consider performing our ceremony, even though I had no idea what a Vedic wedding ceremony included.

He looked pleased when I told him Jan and I wanted to get married. "Yes, I will do," he said. "We will have it here." He gestured around the main room of his apartment which had remained almost empty despite his having lived there for several weeks. "Maybe in two weeks?" he asked.

"That sounds fine. What do I need to do for the wedding? Should I invite people?"

"Yes, of course. Your families. And friends."

"What should we wear? Does the bride wear white?"

"No, bridegroom should wear white. Bride wears red."

"Red?"

"Yes, red sari. Maybe you can purchase somewhere in New York. I don't know. But she should wear red."

After trawling through the yellow pages, I managed to locate an Indian store named Sona – The Golden One in Manhattan's East 50s. There I was able to purchase Jan a Benarsi sari of rich deep silk, its borders embroidered with gold thread. When the store proprietor figured out the sari was for a wedding he tried to sell me a set of heavy gold jewelry – hair ornaments, hand chains with rings for every finger, red and gold bangles, ornate earrings with shiny red stones – but knowing Jan's understated taste I settled on a small pair of gold earrings. On the way home, I bought myself a simple white dress shirt and pair of white slacks.

———

The swami's programs continued to grow in popularity. More people began attending the morning sessions as well, and I began to think that the swami really was managing to acquire a "society" of some sort after all. Then one morning, out of the blue, he made an announcement at the end of his class.

"I'm going back to India in two weeks," he said, rather casually.

Jaws dropped. People glanced at each other and whispered. How could he just be "going back to India?" What about his temple? What about all of us?

The swami rose and retired to his apartment. Several of us hung back in the temple to have an urgent impromptu discussion.

"I can't believe it," Jan said. "Did anyone have any idea this was coming?"

"I kind of did," admitted Wally. He was a good-natured twenty-one year old who I thought of as the temple's resident scribe because he always walked around with a little book in which he seemed to be writing down everything the swami said. He was one of the people who hung around the temple during the day, and therefore spent more time with the swami than the rest of us. "I knew he was on a visitor's visa," he said, "and I knew that it was coming up for renewal. But I didn't know that meant he was going to have to leave. He's renewed it before, and I just figured he'd renew it again."

"Well, someone's going to need to look into the details of this," I said. "We should try to see if it can be renewed without him having to leave the States."

That evening we met again to see if anyone had found out more. Bruce, a husky wrestler in his early twenties, had called immigration and discovered that visitors from India could renew their visitor visas only once. And we couldn't get him onto another kind of visa, because the law didn't permit a change of status for Indians unless they first returned to their native land. We knew the swami was a law-abiding type, and that we wouldn't be able to convince him to overstay. The only option was to try to renew the visitor visa again.

"Allen Ginsberg's been here!" Wally said, suddenly lighting up. "Maybe he'll help. We should *ask* him, at least."

The next morning, at Wally's urgent request, Ginsberg came to the temple to discuss the matter with all of us after the swami's class.

We all gathered on the oriental carpet in front of the swami, who sat on his small dais. We knew we wanted the swami to stay, and Ginsberg knew we wanted him to stay, but he didn't seem sure about the swami's intentions.

"Swamiji, do *you* want to stay in America?" he asked rather matter-of-factly.

The swami knew from us that Ginsberg was famous, and though he never treated him any differently than the rest of us, he didn't seem to want to come right out and ask him for a favor. He slowly looked around at us one by one. I had never seen such a sad expression on his face before. He seemed forlorn, like a father looking at sick children that he now had to leave alone to fend for themselves.

The swami cleared his throat and said in a whispery, hoarse, almost imploring way, "Well, I have my *students* here."

Ginsberg seemed convinced. "I know a Congressman," he said. "I can have a bill put in the House. He'll be able to extend, I'm sure. No problem. US immigration can be arbitrary at times. But I've got some good connections. We need a lawyer." He looked at us. "You guys got any money?"

We looked at each other. "Maybe a little."

"OK. Look, I'll donate a few hundred bucks for a start, and that'll get things rolling. But I want it back."

Two days later, he turned up at the temple with good news: he'd been able to get the swami another six-month extension on his visitor's visa. Bruce had gone round all the regulars at the swami's evening program to get donations to cover the legal fees, and we gave Ginsberg back his three hundred dollars, so grateful that he had given us a little bit longer with the swami. Bruce had even been to Central Park and approached strangers, mostly tourists, begging for money so his "father" could stay in America.

New Indian Religion Sends You Higher Than LSD!

The Secrets Of Krishna Consciousness

A New York tabloid called Midnight *printed this article in September, 1966.*

CHAPTER 9

Celebrations
with the Swami

September 1966

September was an unseasonably warm month in 1966. Hungarian and Polish immigrants in T-shirts were sweating and cursing about the heat as Raymond Marias and I made our way up Second Avenue early one Tuesday afternoon. Twenty-one-year-old Ray was one of the swami's "in" crowd, one of the people who saw him every day. Unlike me, Ray spent most of his time at the temple, chanting, cleaning the place or talking to the swami. He had been a comic book illustrator and had some experience in the world of publishing, but now he was mainly interested in pursuing the swami's philosophy. The swami had been talking about starting up a magazine called *Back to Godhead*, and he was pleased when he heard that Ray had publishing experience. Back in India before he came to the States, the swami had written, produced and distributed the *Back to Godhead* magazine all on his own, but now he was saying that Ray could be the editor, since he had a background in the profession.

"Hey, you know, the swami's going to have an initiation on Friday," Ray said to me. "You wanna be initiated?"

The invitation sounded a bit half-hearted, extended out of courtesy to a wannabe. I was in a different space than the other guys. For one thing, I wasn't single, while they all were. For another, I had wanted to retain my own space and time, and I was a bit older than most of them. I was still working as a musician on the weekends,

"Ray" (Raymond Marias) in New York near 26 Second Avenue, Manhattan

and I was kind of on the outside; I spent my days doing my own thing and I turned up at the temple for the morning and evening programs. Increasingly, though, I was feeling like I wanted to be part of the inner circle that seemed to be forming around the swami.

I wasn't privy to all the discussions that went on in the swami's room on a daily basis, so I had never heard of "initiation." I had no idea that the swami "initiated" people, and still less idea of what that might involve. The word "initiation" sounded kind of like a bid to join a secret society. Of course, the swami was far from being a secretive person. If anything, he was just the opposite. Still, "initiation" sounded like a mystical rite of passage and had daunting connotations for me.

"What *is* 'initiation'?" I asked Ray.

"Well, the swami said it means that he formally accepts you as his student and you accept him as your spiritual master. Also he said that as a student you accept your spiritual master as God." Ray was soft-spoken, but his bright blue eyes shone with enthusiasm.

"What do you mean 'as God'?"

"I dunno. That's just what he said."

We walked a little further, saying nothing. He seemed to be waiting for that to sink in.

"That can't be right," I thought to myself. Other people had told me that the swami *refused* to be called God. He always said he was the servant of God. "Ray must have gotten something wrong," I thought. "There's no way the swami could have said that."

Ray looked like he was holding back a smile. "What do you think?" he asked. "A bunch of us are going to do it. The swami said we should get some beads and string them up to use as chanting beads. He said chanting on beads is called *japa*. So they'll be *japa* beads I guess. There's a place called Wall Bead that's got lots to choose from. We're going to go down there and pick some out later today."

I was silent. Initiation was the next logical step. If the swami was offering, I didn't feel that I could or should miss out on the opportunity. And if it didn't work out, nothing would really be lost.

"I think I'd like to," I said to Ray.

"Well, do you want us to get you some beads?"

"Sure. And I'll ask Jan what she thinks about getting initiated. So maybe get some for her too, just in case."

— • —

"Today is Janmashtami, the birth of Lord Krishna," the swami said on Thursday morning. "This day is important for all devotees of Krishna. In India, Janmashtami is like Christmas in the West."

The twenty-five people present for the morning program glanced at each other in anticipation. I had no idea that the day was the equivalent of Christmas in India, and judging from the looks of the others, they hadn't known either.

"To celebrate Janmashtami," the swami continued, "devotees dedicate the whole day to Krishna. We will have *kirtan* all day. *Kirtan* sometimes means chanting with instruments, sometimes speaking, sometimes reading *Srimad-Bhagavatam*. *Kirtan* means glorifying the Lord, so all of this is *kirtan*. So we will sing for half an hour, Hare Krishna, then I shall speak half an hour, and then we will all chant on beads half an hour. In this way we continue whole day. Also we shall fast whole day, up till midnight, and at midnight we can eat. In this way we will minimize our bodily needs so we have more time for *kirtan*."

I suddenly felt apprehensive. It was only seven o'clock in the morning.

"I don't know if I can do that," I whispered to Jan. "That's almost eighteen hours away. I'm going to have to eat something today."

"You can't. He said we have to fast all day."

"I don't care. I'm eating."

And so the day began. The swami gave a lecture about the significance of the day.

"Today is the most auspicious day," he said. "On this day Lord Krishna appeared five thousand years ago in Mathura. Mathura is about ninety miles south of Delhi; it is still there, eternally existing. You can still visit there today. Krishna appeared in the home of His maternal uncle, Kamsa, in very precarious situation. He was born in prison cell. Kamsa had imprisoned Krishna's mother and father because their child was prophesized to kill him.

"God's birth in this world is not like our birth. No. As long as we are in this material world, we must cycle through all the various species of life according to our *karma*. So Krishna's birth is not like that. Krishna does not require mother and father to appear. He is within your heart, He is everywhere, so He can appear from everywhere. Just like the sun rises from the eastern side. It does not mean that eastern side is the mother of sun. We simply see that sun is rising from the eastern side. So, Krishna appears within this material world due to His kindness to His devotees. Nobody is real father and mother of Krishna, because Krishna is the original father of everyone. But when Krishna comes here, advents, He accepts some devotees as His father, as His mother.

"So why does Krishna advent? In *Bhagavad-gita* He tells Arjuna, 'yada-yada hi dharmasya glanir bhavati bharata – My dear Arjuna, I come when there is discrepancy in the processes of religion.' What process of religion does Krishna recommend? Simply surrender unto Him. Krishna advents to teach us this lesson: 'you are immortal by nature. As spirit soul you are part and parcel of Me. I am also immortal. So you are immortal but you are unnecessarily trying to be happy in this material world.' Krishna is the original person. We should try to understand Him, why He advents, why He comes to this material world, what is His business, what are His activities.

If we try to understand Him, then what is the result? The result is that we achieve liberation from this material world. That is the aim of this life."

After the swami's class, we chanted with instruments, then listened to the swami again, then chanted on our beads. The time passed quickly, but by noon I was getting restless.

"My legs hurt," I complained to Jan. "I've been sitting cross-legged for five hours now."

"Then get up," she said.

I stood up at the back of the room and listened to the swami speak. He had been talking about Krishna, but about 12:30 PM he started to talk about his own guru. I'd heard him talk only very briefly about his spiritual master before, and I'd never heard how he had met him.

"In 1874 my spiritual master, Shrila Bhaktisiddhanta Saraswati, was born," the swami said. "And then, in 1918, my Guru Maharaja started with his mission; he called it Gaudiya Math. And he was trying to spread it. I was taken to Bhaktisiddhanta Saraswati by one of my friends. I did not want to go there, but he forcibly took me there. Yes. And Bhaktisiddhanta Saraswati ordered me, 'You preach the mission of Chaitanya Mahaprabhu in English language. This is very much essential.' So, on the first meeting he told me like that. At that time I was in favor of Gandhi's movement. So I said that 'We are not independent – we are subjugated. Who will hear about our message?' But he refuted my argument. 'This so-called nationalism,' he said, 'or any ism, they are all temporary. Real need is the self-realization.'

"So I was convinced. But at that time, although he wanted me to immediately join him and spread this movement, at that time I was a married man, a young man. I was married in 1918. And I also had a son also at that time, 1921. I met my Guru Maharaja in 1922. At that time I was a manager in a big chemical factory. So I thought that 'I am a married man. I have so many responsibilities. How I can join immediately? It is not my duty.' Of course, that was my mistake. I should have joined immediately. I should have taken the opportunity immediately.

"Then in 1954, when I was fifty-eight years, I left home and I was living alone. Then, that year, I accepted the renounced order, *sannyasa*, and I decided to take up the responsibility of my

Guru Maharaja. Then when I was seventy years old I decided, 'Now I must do and execute the order of my Guru Maharaja to preach Krishna consciousness in the English language.' So I came here to New York one year ago.

"I was not very much hopeful, because it is very difficult task, because this culture is so opposed to the European and Western culture. I used to walk on Forty-Second Street, near the cinema houses. When I first came, I had no money. I came by ship. So when I was on the ship seeing New York for the first time, I was thinking, 'Why have I come here?' I do not know what is the purpose, because how will the people accept this movement? They are differently educated, and as soon as I will say, 'So, my dear sir, you have to give up meat-eating and illicit sex and no intoxication and gambling,' they will say, 'Please go home.' But I thought, 'let me try.'

"I was practically just like a homeless man. But I had full faith that my Guru Maharaja was with me. I never lost this faith. If you accept *Bhagavad-gita* as it is, then you should know that Krishna is present before you in His words in the *Bhagavad-gita*. This is called spiritual realization. It is not mundane historical incidences.

"Now I am trying my level best to execute the order of my *guru maharaja*. Similarly, if you will also try your level best on the same principle, then it will go on. Same principle. It doesn't matter whether one is born in India or outside India. No. Chaitanya Mahaprabhu said, '*prithivite ache yata nagaradi-gram* – As many towns and cities and villages are there, My name will be sung.' He did not say it to make a farce. He is the Supreme Personality of Godhead.

"So, sometimes I am very much criticized that I have foreigners as followers. The caste *brahmins* in India, they are very much against me. But you may be a very learned scholar or you may be a fool. It doesn't matter. You are under the laws of material nature. We have got this human form of life. It will be finished, as the cats and dogs' life is also finished. But if we try through the guru and Vaishnavas – the followers of Visnu, that is, Krishna – then we can achieve in this life full success, not failure, like cats and dogs' life. That is the opportunity."

The swami looked out at his audience. "If you can't fast all day, then you can eat some sugar candy," he said, and he picked up his small African drum and began to chant. Jan looked over her shoulder at me and got up and came to the back of the room.

"How are you feeling?" she asked me.

"Pretty terrible," I answered. "I don't think I can make it."

"What the hell is sugar candy?" asked Charlie the flute-player, who was leaning against the wall next to me.

"Damned if I know," I said. "Maybe he means rock candy. Does it matter? Anything'll do. The swami said if we can't fast all day ..."

"Let's get some," he interrupted. "I can't make it till midnight either. I feel sick."

"I'll go," Jan said. "I don't feel that bad. I'll get it. I need some air anyway."

"OK. You got money? OK, go. But don't be long. We're dying in here."

It was an hour and a half later when she came back with three packets of Life Savers.

"*That's* sugar candy?" I asked. Charlie looked skeptical too.

"Well, it's sugar and it's candy," she shot back. "They'd never heard of rock candy. That's the clear crystal sugary stuff, I think. They said I'd have to go to midtown and look around. They thought a place called Stovers on Fifty-third Street might have it. But I'm too weak to hunt for it, and a bus to midtown is just too much today. It's *hot* out. Here you go."

Sitting cross-legged on the rug, I quietly broke open one of the Life Saver packs. I hoped the person sitting in front of me obscured me from the swami's view. I pretended I was scratching my face and eased a yellow lemon-flavored one into my mouth as inconspicuously as possible. I passed a red one to Charlie, who did the same.

The "sugar candy" perked us up a bit, and before I knew it, the afternoon had passed and it was seven o'clock. The heat had become bearable, and it was starting to get dark. We had been in the temple with the swami for twelve hours straight.

About 8:30 two Indian couples in their thirties arrived at the temple. They opened the door without knocking and sat down cross-legged on the floor as if they had been invited and were supposed to be there. The men were dressed in Western clothing – black pants and sports jackets – but the women wore brightly colored saris.

From his seat at the head of the temple, the swami smiled and nodded to them. They nodded back. The swami said something loud to them in Hindi, and one of the men replied in an equally loud voice.

Then, unexpectedly, the swami turned to us. "So, I would like to invite the young devotees of Krishna present here to speak some of their realizations of Krishna consciousness. Ray, can you speak something about Krishna consciousness? What you have realized."

Ray looked surprised, and his face went white. After about half a minute and three loud throat clears he said, "Well, I like the philosophy ... and I like the atmosphere too. I think I'd like to dedicate myself more to Krishna. I'm not the body, and heat and cold can't affect me like they used to. This chanting is a way of life. We're not the body, and materialism is not good for us. I think anyone who wants to get high can do it without drugs by chanting ... well it makes you feel good, and it's legal. That's what I like about it. Also, it doesn't cost anything. Uh ... That's another good thing about it."

He nodded his head looking straight at the swami, signaling that his speech was over. Then the swami looked at Charlie.

"Mr. Charlie, speak something about your realizations of Krishna consciousness."

After a long silence, Charlie swallowed and closed his eyes like the swami did. He said, "Well, I'm not a very good speaker. But anyway ... Krishna consciousness is, you know, a way to be peaceful inside. You don't have to look for a place, I mean, outside yourself. You're not the body, so that's it, yeah. You can be ... uh ... satisfied ... yeah, satisfied ... to know you don't have to get, you know, all worked up ... I mean to do anything."

He opened his eyes, looked around at the audience, then at the swami and then at the round picture of Radha and Krishna on the wall and then back to the swami. Then he closed his eyes again.

"It's like being peaceful all the time. So, chanting, you know, does it. I think it'll work OK for anyone, I mean anyone who tries. So, we're not these bodies; that's what it is, you know. So, if everyone tries it, you know, it works. You have to try it, though. I mean, don't be afraid; just try and you'll see, you know? It really works. And I think ... well that's it."

He put his head down and looked at the floor.

"Miss Denise, you can speak something about Krishna consciousness."

"Me?" Denise was about sixteen and had been coming to the swami's evening programs for the past week or so. She looked over her left shoulder at the Indian guests sitting on the rug. They were expressionless. "Well, if you chant, it's hard to stop. I mean, you shouldn't stop. It makes your thinking clearer, and you can even see better, I think. So, I mean, if your heart is in it, you can chant every day and have anything you want. Inside, I mean. I guess it's hard at first, you know. But you have to hear the swami speak. You'll feel better, more at ease, slowly. I mean, more comfortable, you know. It's a nice way to spend free time instead of trying to do things when you don't know what's really going to happen. You know, like drugs and stuff."

The swami smiled at her. "Thank you very much," he said.

"Please don't pick me, please not me," I thought.

"I would request our guests to speak," he said.

One of the Indian men smoothed his mustache and spoke in English with a thick Indian accent. "We were walking down street and looked in window and thought I was in India. So we walked in. We're in Indian Merchant Marines. I am captain. Our ship is *Golkunda*. We have ship in New York." He paused. "I can say some *Gita shlokas*," he said, like he was making a suggestion.

The swami raised his chin and said, "So recite."

Staring at the swami, the man waited for a few seconds, looked at the ceiling and then started singing verses. "*Dharmakshetray koo-rooshetray ...*" he sang, and he continued for several minutes, chanting what I thought was an impressive number of verses by heart. He sang the same melody for each verse. Being a musician, I took note of the melody; it was a tetra chord, the first four notes of a major scale. I thought of it as a part of the tradition I should be learning.

His singing was melodious and heartfelt. It seemed to me as though a piece of India had suddenly been brought into our midst and was right here in the room between the swami and these people. I realized for the first time how the philosophy the swami was teaching was not just a philosophy but was a culture. Krishna consciousness was not just the ideas of one person – the swami – but was something greater; it wasn't just about God and the spiritual world. It was a way of life that was embraced by an entire civilization.

As I listened to the man sing, India seemed less mysterious and less unknown, and at that moment, I knew that I would go there.

The man paused and looked at the swami. Some of the devotees had turned around to stare at him. He resumed his chanting and after about five more minutes he nodded at the swami and stopped.

"Thank you very much," said the swami, beaming at his visitors. I had forgotten all about my gnawing hunger and knew I would make it through the last few hours till midnight!

————

The following day, Friday September 9th, the swami performed our initiation ceremony. Jan had decided she would get initiated too, so the two of us turned up together at the temple that evening. We were directed upstairs to the swami's small apartment, where we were told the ceremony was to take place.

The main room of the apartment where the swami and his followers took their meals was already full of people. The swami sat in the middle of the room in front of a small rectangular mound of soil taken from the apartment building's small courtyard. Pieces of an orange crate had been cut into kindling and were piled up next to him. A small pot of melted golden *ghee* was on the floor by his side. To his right was a small altar – a box draped with a red and blue velvet cloth – upon which sat an El Greco-like picture, a photo of a painting. The figure in the picture looked like a Christian saint, complete with halo. I wasn't sure who he was.

The swami motioned for the two of us to sit in front of him along with several of his core group and a few who were less involved like we were. I counted the number of initiates: eleven – ten men and Jan. I sat on the floor with Jan on my left and Carl on my right. Ray passed us each a string of large red beads, the *japa* beads he had bought for us the other day.

"Begin chanting," the swami requested, and the sound of the Hare Krishna mantra filled the small room.

After a few moments, the swami indicated we should stop.

"Repeat the following mantra after me," he said. "*Om* ..."

"*Om*," we responded.

"*Apavitra* ..."

"*Apavitra ...*"

"*Pavitro-va ...*"

"*Pavitro-va ...*"

The swami continued with the word-for-word chant for about one minute and then explained its meaning.

"*Apavitra* means 'unclean' and *pavitra* means 'clean.' So anyone who may be unclean or clean, it doesn't matter. In whatever condition one may be, either unclean or clean, if that person remembers Krishna, who has lotus eyes, that person immediately becomes cleansed, internally and externally.

"Now I will explain the meaning of this initiation ceremony. This initiation means purification. We are all impure in this material world, and therefore birth, death, old age and disease have overcome us. So in order to overcome these miseries, we must voluntarily accept some *tapasya*, some sacrifice, some rules and regulations.

"Why do we need to accept a spiritual master? To accept a spiritual master is not a hobby. One who is interested in hearing about the transcendental subject matter, *ramante yoginah anante*, the unlimited, infinite subject matter, for him a spiritual master is needed. Not for all. So we must accept a spiritual master who can teach us about God. And who is such a person? That also is stated in the *Upanishads* it is said, *shrotriyam brahma-nishtham*, the spiritual master must come down in disciplic succession and as a result of such authorized succession must be fully, firmly convinced in Brahman.

"And the student must surrender himself to the spiritual master for instruction. Why? Because spiritual master is representative of God. A spiritual master is supposed to spread God consciousness, Krishna consciousness, make everyone Krishna conscious. The disciple should respect the spiritual master as much as God Himself, because he is the most confidential servant of God. Not that the spiritual master is God; no. But he is to be respected as such because he gives us the words of the disciplic succession, the words of God."

"I knew Ray had gotten things a bit wrong," I thought, reassured that my understanding of the swami's role had been correct. "So this initiation is called *harinam* initiation – first initiation. The spiritual master gives the disciple *harinam* – the Hare Krishna mantra – to chant and thus be purified. Later some of you may receive second initiation, Brahmin initiation, and another mantra is given then. So, along with chanting Hare Krishna, you must follow some rules and regulations. If we want to purify ourselves, then four principles must be followed. The principles are no illicit sex life, no intoxication, no meat-eating, and no gambling. These four things are very prominent everywhere in *kali yuga*, the age of quarrel. Anyone indulging in these four things, they cannot imagine where they are, who is God and how they will be free from this conditional life. So this is purificatory process. Initiation means beginning of your purificatory process, and if we are serious about purification, then we must follow these four principles."

The swami paused for a moment, eyeing us all carefully to let us absorb his instructions. "Now," he said, "I will give spiritual names, Sanskrit names. When we give some spiritual name, that name is the name of Krishna, and it is followed by *Das* or *Dasi* – man and woman. *Das* means 'servant of.' So you please take your beads – you all have 108 beads?"

Jan and I shot a look over at Ray, who we assumed had strung up our beads. He nodded at us. We looked back at the swami and nodded to him.

"Good. So we should chant the whole Hare Krishna mantra on each bead: *Hare Krishna Hare Krishna Krishna Krishna Hare Hare, Hare Rama Hare Rama Rama Rama Hare Hare.* That is one round. And you must chant sixteen rounds of Hare Krishna mantra on beads every day. Yes? Each of you now please pass beads to me one at a time."

Ray was sitting closest to the swami. He took his beads off from around his neck and gave them to the swami.

"Now we will all chant one round," the swami said.

When we finished one round, the swami said, "So, Ray, your spiritual name is Rayarama Das." Smiling, he handed Ray back his set of large red beads. "Next beads." Carl gave his set to the swami and we chanted another round. "Carl, your new name is Karlapati Das."

One by one, each initiate passed their beads to the swami, who chanted on them and then gave the new name. Finally it was my turn. I handed my string of beads to the swami and we began chant-ing again. The swami fingered each bead as he chanted the mantra.

"So, Mr. Michael," he said when we had finished another round. "Your spiritual name is Mukunda Das Adhikari. 'Mukunda' is a name of Krishna meaning 'giver of liberation.' Jan, you please now give me your beads."

We chanted another round and the swami gave Jan her name.

"Your spiritual name is Janaki Devi Dasi. This is the name of Lord Rama's consort Sita, the daughter of one King Janaka." He handed Jan her beads. "Now you please each touch your beads to the feet of Lord Chaitanya."

I remembered the swami mentioning Chaitanya before, but I couldn't remember exactly in what context. Ray gestured toward the small altar. I followed the others and touched my large red beads to the feet of the figure in the picture and then took my seat once again.

The swami lit a whole handful of incense sticks and placed them at regular intervals around the earthen mound. As the fragrant smoke wafted through the small room, he took small pinches of colored powder and made criss-cross lines over the mound. Then, arranging the smallest of the wooden sticks in a little pyramid on top of the mound, he lit a fire into which he fed larger and larger pieces of the orange crate. He began to chant mantras word by word in a loud, deep voice, and we repeated each word after him:

> om ajnana-timirandhasya
>
> jnananjana-salakaya
>
> caksur unmilitam yena
>
> tasmai sri-gurave namah

After each verse, the swami poured a ladle-full of *ghee* onto the fire. It got bigger and bigger until the flames reached up almost to the ceiling.

This was unlike any sacrament I'd ever been part of. I remem-bered the rituals in the synagogue and how hollow, inexplicable and pointless I found them. No one had ever tried to explain to me the meaning behind them; they didn't seem to know why they were taking part either. This wasn't that much different in the sense that I still didn't know very much about what was going on. What was different was that I knew the swami knew. This somehow made the

The swami at 26 Second Avenue

ceremony seem more genuine.

The room's one window was closed, and the room was gradually filling with smoke. Although my eyes were watering, I was mesmerized by the ceremony. It was more than just the enthralling spectacle of having a fire burning on the floor in the middle of the apartment. This ritual felt sacred. I'd gone into the initiation casually, but this had become more than an informal, relaxed event. It was more like a change from one life to another, an oath to follow a philosophy, to accept a particular person as my teacher for life. I had crossed the Rubicon.

My guide on the journey was the swami, this person who had become a friend, but was still a teacher. I liked him and I trusted him because unlike the other people of the cloth I had met, he lived his life by the philosophy he spoke. I felt that the ceremony was between him and each of the initiates on a personal level. Unlike the Western religious rituals I had attended, this one was not a big affair; there was no ornate high ceiling, pews, organs, stained glass, choirs or large congregation made up of family and friends. Here in this modest, austere setting, the ceremony was about the agreement made between him and me, the sealing of a commitment and sacrament that was not dependent on anyone or anything else. I felt happy that I was now officially part of the swami's mission, and although he looked solemn as he concluded the ceremony, I could sense that he, too, was happy.

—·

The day after our initiation, Janaki's sister Joan flew in from Oregon for our wedding. She was the only member of either of our families to attend. On the day of the wedding, Janaki and a handful of others decorated the swami's apartment with ornaments made of leaves, which were strung from the upper corners of the room. As they decorated, the swami moved around the kitchen preparing our wedding feast; he had Joan – his sole assistant – busily engaged in rolling and folding potato pastries.

Finally, Janaki and I were sitting before the swami for the second time that week, this time dressed in our wedding clothes and garlanded with fresh flowers. Crammed into the small room were the eighteen friends we had invited. In front of the swami were a now familiar mound of soil and a bowl of *ghee*. Janaki looked dazzling in her red sari.

"So, I am very happy that Mukunda and Janaki are today being married," the swami said. "Actually, I am *sannyasi*, retired from married life; it is not the business of *sannyasi* to take part in marriage ceremony, but in this country, just to save my students from sinful activities, I am personally taking interest. I see that here in New York most of the boys and girls, they are keeping the boyfriend and girlfriend. So I am requesting all my students that if you want to make progress in spiritual life, you have to refrain from four kinds of sinful activities: illicit sex life, first; second, non-vegetarian diet; third, intoxication; fourth, gambling. Unless one is free from these four principal activities, one cannot make progress in spiritual life. According to our Vaishnava principles, marriage is allowed because there is male, there is female. Why they should not unite? This is proper."

The swami turned his attention from the audience toward us. "I request that you live happily together," he said. "Please do everything in relationship with Krishna, live a pure life, and be happy in this life and next life. Now you all please chant Hare Krishna."

The room once again filled with the sound of the mantra while the swami lit the fire. Once it had begun to crackle, he said, "Janaki, please repeat: 'Mukunda, I agree to serve you throughout my life.'"

"Mukunda, I agree to serve you throughout my life," she said.

"Mukunda, you say, 'Janaki, I accept you as my wife and will take charge of your life in all conditions.'"

"Janaki, I accept you as my wife and will take charge of your life in all conditions."

"Now you each exchange garlands. Yes. Now Mukunda you cover her head with her sari. And now you change places – you come to this side, you go to that side. Good. Now you are husband and wife."

The swami began chanting mantras and ladling *ghee* into the fire as he had at our initiation. For Janaki and me this was an exciting way to formally begin our married life, without the materialistic trappings that were usually part of Western weddings. Getting married sitting in front of a blazing fire on the floor of a New York apartment with only a few friends and without our families felt alternative, unique and counter-cultural and, well … just right.

The feast the swami had prepared was awe-inspiring – spicy rice with chunks of homemade cheese and red peppers, sweet and sour *dahl*, richly spiced chickpea stew, curried potatoes with peas and eggplant, dumplings in yogurt sauce sprinkled with coriander leaves and freshly ground spices, whole wheat fried flat breads, deep-fried cauliflower fritters, flaky potato pastries, chunky tomato chutney, spongy *panir* globes floating in a sauce of condensed milk, squares of milk fudge. We sat with our guests in rows on the floor of his apartment, amazed as dish after dish emerged from the kitchen. Several of our macrobiotic guests threw caution to the wind and abandoned themselves to the swami's culinary delights.

"This stuff is just too good to resist!" an old friend from my musical past exclaimed as the swami appeared with a bowl of sweet condensed saffron yogurt. I had to agree. Jan and I had never seen or tasted anything like this before, and we felt immensely grateful to the swami for going to so much trouble for us.

After the feast, we headed back to our loft to continue the fes-
tivities with about ten people who had attended the ceremony.
The newly initiated Hayagriva – formerly Howard – loudly sang
Indian mantras interspersed with recitations of Wordsworth and
Longfellow, the poets he taught when he was an English professor
in Ohio. Joan told us about her cooking experience with the swami.

"He's very friendly, isn't he?" she said. "When I arrived to help
him cook, he gave me these lemony crackers and a chilled yogurt
drink. And he kept telling me to wash my hands."

"Yeah, the swami's always very clean," I said. "He says being
clean is part of being a devotee of Krishna."

"Well, he kept noticing I was touching my mouth and he'd ask
me to wash my hands every time. I didn't even realize I was doing
it. He did so many things at once, and all so quickly."

We turned on the TV and watched Allen Ginsberg being interviewed by an uptight-looking reporter. To our amazement, after a
few minutes of questions, he sat down and began chanting the Hare
Krishna mantra to the accompaniment of a small harmonium. It
seemed an auspicious conclusion to our day.

Despite the memorable quality of our wedding and the swami's
insistence that we never separate, there was a nagging feeling of

Hayagriva at the 26 Second Avenue temple, New York

impermanence about our marriage. Janaki was troubled by the swami's suggestion that devotees should ultimately renounce their marriage partners and dedicate themselves one hundred percent to God. She raised the issue with me one afternoon a few days after the wedding as we walked down Columbia Street toward the Delancey Street Bridge.

"This morning I asked the swami if you would have to become a *sannyasi* one day," she said. "He renounced his wife and grown-up children to become a man of God, so I wanted to know if he thought you would have to do that too."

"What did he say?"

"He just laughed and said yes. It seemed like he was joking with me."

"You don't look very happy about it," I said.

"Well, how could I be? I don't think it's a laughing matter, actually. I mean, if we've made a vow not to ever separate, how am I supposed to understand that one day you're supposed to become a monk? What will happen to me? Does the swami think that our marriage won't work out, or what?"

"I don't really know very much about all that *sannyasa* stuff," I admitted. "Parts of the Vedic philosophy seem kind of contradictory to me too."

"That's not very helpful. I mean, this Krishna thing was your thing to begin with, and I want to know how it's going to affect me in the future."

"I just don't know, Janaki," I said. "The whole idea of becoming a renunciate is pretty hard to figure out however I look at it. But we're together in this now. We're married and initiated, and you've been so supportive, even when I was going to have to go to jail for being a drug dealer! I think Krishna consciousness is changing our lives, but renunciation isn't part of anything that I can see."

Dodging Vietnam

Mid-September 1966

Being drafted for the war in Vietnam was a constant threat, a muted anxiety that followed me wherever I went. I'd been called up many times, but I had procrastinated repeatedly, throwing away the third and fourth draft notices and hoping the whole thing would just quietly fade away. Finally, right after our wedding, I was summoned to an FBI office and told I must appear at an army induction center in New York. It was confirmed by letter two days later that if I failed to make an appearance I would go to jail.

I thought about the best way to deal with the situation. I wasn't ready for another term in prison, so not turning up was no longer an option. A high school friend of mine named Jim Snyder had been called up a few years before, and he'd avoided being drafted by taking a whole tube of Benzedrine tablets. He'd stayed up for three days, didn't shave and got drunk right before he went so he couldn't act coherent even if he had wanted to. To crown it all, when he'd turned up at the induction center in Portland, Oregon, he'd wet his pants. He said that if it worked for him, it would work for me.

There were numerous cases like Jim's but I didn't think I had the courage to pull such a risky stunt. Also, now that I was an initiated devotee, I wasn't taking any drugs.

"I'm just dreading this," I said to Janaki. "What should I do?"

"Don't worry – it'll be OK." She sounded more confident than I felt. "Krishna will get you out of there. He will! Surely, anyone who doesn't take intoxicants or eat meat or have illicit sex or gamble won't be taken by the US Army! The swami says Krishna protects devotees."

"That's true," I thought. "The swami *does* say that. It's all well and good saying 'Krishna will protect you,' but I'm still going to have to put myself at the mercy of the draft board."

I thought about it over the next few days. On the one hand, I was scared and didn't have much faith that Krishna would help me. But on the other, I felt that maybe it was time to put an end to my years of draft dodging. Now that I had met the swami, I had some understanding that the things going on in this world were part of a bigger picture. After all, Krishna, or at least the swami's philosophy, had helped me when I was in jail.

"I'll just have to go and face it," I thought. "I don't know what I'll do or how I'll handle it all, but it's out of my control now. I'll just have to leave my fate in Krishna's hands."

It was with that rather fatalistic attitude that I decided to forego the option of taking drugs. The night before the induction we slept in the New York temple room; I thought that if I was going to be relying on Krishna to protect me, it would be a good idea to be there in His temple the night before my day of reckoning.

The following morning dawned bright and sunny, a sharp contrast to my dark and nervous mood. Although I wasn't prepared to take drugs, I didn't want them thinking I was keen to be a soldier, so I didn't shave and I wore untidy, unclean clothes. As I climbed the long, wide stairs of the induction offices in lower Manhattan, I chanted softly to myself and thought that if worse came to worse I could just lie down and not co-operate, à la Mahatma Gandhi.

I made my way to a long counter at the far end of a room full of inductees, mostly African-Americans. "Blacks fighting Buddhists in the blistering Vietnamese jungles?" I asked myself. "It doesn't make any sense. Even though we might not be our bodies, life is still so body-based in this country, and probably the rest of the world too."

Strangely to me, most of the men there seemed to want to be drafted. I overheard an excited conversation between two black guys who were hoping they would be shipped out that same day to Virginia for their basic military training. I handed my crumpled

FBI papers to the official behind the counter. He eyed my dirty clothes as he smoothed out the wadded piece of paper.

"Let's see. Grant, eh?" he said. He turned to a filing cabinet behind him and pulled open a drawer. As he rifled through the files I chanted softly, mumbling the mantra to calm myself. He looked up from the cabinet and gave me a long stare. Finally, he found my file, but he read only the first page before pointing to a room to my left.

"OK. You need to go into that room," he said.

I felt panicky. Why hadn't I just taken a large dose of bennies like Jim had suggested, and failed the physical examination? It would have been so easy. I would have been sick for only a day or two, but getting out of going to Vietnam would have made it worth the trouble. Now here I was without any preparation.

In the tiny gray office a man sat behind a metal desk observing four teenagers who all seemed to be in various states of derangement. It was then that I realized I'd been assigned to the "irregular category," probably on account of my mumbling at the main desk. I decided then and there that I was going to make the most of this. I chanted the Hare Krishna mantra audibly, purposely not making eye contact with anyone in the room. I knew I was creating a spectacle, but that was the whole point.

Another uniformed official came in and deposited a pile of files. I overheard the man at the desk say to his newly arrived colleague, "These kinds of people aren't good timber for the army." He nodded in my direction and didn't appear to care whether or not I heard him. It seemed like a good sign to me.

Finally, after thirty agonizing minutes, the man at the desk stood and walked over to me and waved a slip of paper in my face. "Go upstairs to see the psychiatrist," he said.

I stumbled into the top-floor office which was flooded by sunlight pouring in through a huge ribbed skylight. Behind a lone big desk sat an elderly man whose name badge said "N.H. Gerhardt, MD."

He looked friendly enough as he sized me up through his thick glasses, half smiling. His thick German accent broke the silence of the office.

"You are afraid to go into zee army? Yah?" he asked.

I thought this was a loaded question. "I don't know," I muttered, determined to come off as neurotic, psychotic or at least uncommunicative and unable to follow basic instructions. "I haven't been out for a few months. I don't want to see anybody." I watched him writing in my file. He paused and looked up at me.

"I'm gonna classify you 1-Y," he said. "You vould go only in national emergency, OK?"

I felt a surge of relief and thought, "Why isn't the Vietnam War already considered a national emergency?"

The doctor watched me closely as he delivered this news. My heart was hammering with joy, but I acted impassive as if I didn't care or didn't understand. I wasn't sure if the doctor knew I was faking. What I was sure of was that 1-Y meant I was effectively free. 4-F would have been better. That would have meant I could never be called up under any circumstances, but I was happy with 1-Y.

"You go back home now," he said, handing me a piece of paper. "Be careful."

I headed to the door and didn't say good-bye.

After years of postponement, my dreaded ordeal was over quickly and easily. "Thank you, Krishna," I thought, and I walked back to the temple to tell Janaki, the swami and the devotees that Krishna had saved me after all.

On the Way
to India?

October 1966

Janaki and I finally decided to make the break from New York and head to India. We felt that everything was pushing us in that direction – our meeting the swami, our initiation and marriage, my arrest and my freedom from the threat of Vietnam. So one warm autumn afternoon I went over to the swami's apartment to tell him that we were going to leave.

"Janaki and I are going to go to India for a while, Swami."

"Oh?" He opened his eyes wide. "When you will leave?"

"Not tomorrow but the next day."

"So soon?"

"Yes."

"Will you fly from here?"

"No, we're going to head over to the West Coast to Oregon, which is where I'm from, and then we'll go to India from there."

He nodded.

"We're ready for India," I said, trying to explain. "We want to experience its atmosphere and spirituality. Do you know anyone in India we could see? Like someone we could contact?"

"There is a man named Chandra Shekar Sharma," he said.

"Is there an address or phone number?"

"I can give you." He reached into a *faux*-leather maroon bag at the end of his sitting mat and pulled out a small book.

"His address is three stroke fifty-one Horsey Road. You can note down."

I fumbled for a pen and wrote on the back of a small piece of paper that was in my wallet.

"Three *stroke* fifty-one? What is stroke?" I asked.

"Like this."

He pointed to the book. I scooted over to him.

"Oh, you mean slash," I said.

"Yes. Slash."

"OK. And a phone number?"

"Here it is: four one six nine seven one."

"What city?"

"Delhi. Old Delhi."

There was a long pause. I wasn't sure how to say goodbye to him.

"California would be a good place for you to start a temple," I said at last. "There's lots of interest in India and spirituality in that part of the country, especially in Los Angeles. There's lots of open-minded people there. Some even understand Sanskrit, like '*isvarah paramah krishnah sac-cid-ananda-vigrahah anadir adir govindah sarva-karana-karanam.*'"

The swami's face lit up like a light bulb when I recited the one and only Sanskrit verse I'd memorized, the verse he'd taught us in the Saturday Sanskrit class. A huge grin appeared on his face.

"Oh! Very good!" he exclaimed. "So you remember the *Brahma-samhita* verse?"

"Yes, Swami. I thought I should try to memorize it."

He nodded, obviously very pleased. Somehow the Sanskrit words seemed to mean more to him than the entire English conversation.

"Well, I guess I'll go then," I said. "Hare Krishna." I bowed down on the floor before him as I'd seen others do.

I heard the swami's voice behind me as I reached the door.

"Mukunda." I turned around. "Just see if you can start one center on the West Coast. It would be a very great service."

I smiled and gave a half-nod. "OK," I mumbled.

As I walked down the stairs to the swami's courtyard, I could smell the garbage wafting from the street. I made my way back to our loft, wondering why the swami had mentioned opening a center *after* all the good-byes. When I mentioned opening a temple in California to the swami, I had no intention of volunteering myself for the task. I only meant that I could really imagine a temple taking off there in the future.

The next day, I hired a new drive-away Volkswagen station wagon and Janaki and I packed up our few belongings. It didn't take us long to clean out the loft, and by the following morning we were ready to drive to Oregon. We set off on the three-thousand-mile journey with our cat Scuzzlebrunzer, Joan, and my friend Maurice, who had been so helpful when I was arrested. It was a warm autumn, so we slept each night under the stars in army surplus "mummy bags." We ate macrobiotic food and did a lot of chanting as we drove.

We planned to go to Klamath Falls to see Janaki and Joan's aunt and uncle, but first we took a small detour to a tiny city in Oregon called Bend, where an old college friend of mine named Dustin lived with his girlfriend Melody. Dustin, Melody, Joan and I had all gone to Reed College together in Oregon, and we'd all been inspired by a professor named Lloyd Reynolds, who was an art lover and suspected communist. I hadn't seen Dustin for years, but we always kept in touch. He had a Masters degree in philosophy and was intensely into exploring alternative religious and spiritual perspectives. He'd also been at the cutting edge of the West Coast alternative scene – he'd lived for a while in San Francisco's Haight-Ashbury, he was at Ken Kesey's LSD happenings (the Cool-Aid Acid Tests), and he identified with the growing crusade of young people committed to stopping the war in Vietnam, lowering the voting age, legalizing marijuana and distributing the new consciousness-expanding drug LSD.

Dustin had a position with the US Forest Service. He was a lookout whose job it was to spot forest fires and to report them to the National Park Service. He and Melody had been provided with a small cabin for as long as he had the job; it was way out in the woods on a hilltop near a 100-foot lookout tower. He and Melody were thrilled to see us.

That night over dinner, we began to tell them about our last few months in New York – my arrest, our wedding and especially the swami.

"So, yeah, I discovered this swami was living right there in the Bowery," I said, trying to fill them in on how we'd found the swami in the first place. "You guys would really like him."

"Is he going to stay put in New York?" Melody asked.

"Yeah, I think so for now," I answered. "He has dreams of starting up a worldwide movement. He says that there's a prediction in one of the ancient Indian scriptures that Krishna's name will be chanted all over the world."

"What's the chanting all about?" Dustin asked.

"The swami says that God and His name are the same," Janaki said, "So that by chanting the names of God you get direct access to Him. When he initiated us he asked us to chant every day. Mukunda, show them your beads."

"My beads broke," I said. "I have to restring them. Get yours."

She went into the small room where we were staying and returned with her string of large red *japa* beads.

"So you have to chant the mantra on each bead," she said, demonstrating for everyone. "We're meant to go round them sixteen times a day, but sometimes we don't finish. It takes at least a couple of hours."

"The swami's into changing the world, the same way we are," I said. "But his vision is to change it spiritually. He told me that he used to be part of Gandhi's movement in India, you know, to try to get independence from England. But his spiritual master told him that Krishna consciousness transcends any material conditions. It gets to the root of all things. So we're trying to follow his teachings. Things like civil rights and opposing the Vietnam War are OK, but once they're solved there'll be something else, you know. The swami says the only way to solve all this is to get out of this material world altogether. He says real peace will only come from a spiritual source."

"Wow!" said Dustin. "That's really exciting. Where did he come up with all this?"

"Oh, no. No, no," Janaki said. "The swami hasn't come up with it himself. He's just repeating what his spiritual master told him. He's part of something he calls the disciplic succession, which goes all the way back to Krishna Himself." She pronounced the word "dis-sip-lick" the way the swami did. "So the idea is that there's nothing made up, nothing new added. It's just one teacher repeating the words of his own teacher. He's really, really knowledgeable; he's a real scholar who's written books and everything. You should hear him quote Sanskrit."

"So it's not like a personality cult or something," I said. "The swami *is* an amazing person, but he represents something older, you know, a whole culture and tradition of knowledge. He's in touch with something sacred."

"He really practices what he preaches," Janaki said. "Like, he says all living entities are spiritual equals and you see him interact with all kinds of people, even like drunks or bums. And Allen Ginsberg came to the temple for a while, and he didn't treat him any different than any of us."

"Allen Ginsberg came to the swami's temple?" Melody asked incredulously.

"Yeah! He did!" I said.

"Wow."

"I know. The temple's a really spiritual place, and I guess Ginsberg could feel that," I said.

"Mukunda helped the swami find the temple," Janaki said. "He had nowhere to go, so Mukunda found the storefront for him and the little apartment where he lives now. It feels like another world in the temple, especially when the chanting's going on."

"I've been reading *Autobiography of a Yogi* by Paramahansa Yogananda," Dustin said. "I really liked some of the stuff he's saying, and I feel like I'm moving in that direction myself. I'd like to have a look at the swami's writings."

"I can loan you my books while we're here," I said.

"You know, you guys are different," he said eyeing us. "It's like you're naturally high, you know, without drugs. You're happy. That's what we're all after, right? I mean, that's why we try to expand our consciousness, right? I want to try what you're doing. And I want to meet the swami."

"Well, you could go to New York to see him, I guess," I said. "But he said he'd like to start a temple on the West Coast next, so you could go down and see him after that's open. Actually, he asked me if we would open one for him."

Dustin and Melody looked at each other.

"Really? He asked you to do that?"

"Yeah. But Janaki and I are going to India."

The following day, Dustin took me up to the little room at the top of the lookout tower. Looking out over an ocean of Douglas fir trees, we saw a blizzard in the distance blowing toward us. He picked up the phone and reported it to the NPS.

He hung up the phone. "You better get going unless you want to get stuck up here in the mountains," he said.

"Yeah, I was thinking that too," I said. "I'll go and tell Janaki."

"Listen, Michael, I mean, Mukunda," he said. "Melody and I were talking last night after you all went to bed. We're really interested in what you and Janaki were saying about the swami and the philosophy he's teaching. We're seekers, you know, and it sounds like you found the right thing."

"Yeah, he's really changed my and Janaki's life," I said.

"The thing is, my job here at the tower is about over and we don't have any plans after that. So we were thinking ... why don't we all go to San Francisco and start that temple the swami asked you to open?"

"But we're going to India," I said. I felt like I'd been repeating that sentence a lot over the past few days.

"Sure, I know," Dustin said. "It's just that the swami asked you to help him, and now I'm saying Melody and I will help you. I've got lots of contacts in San Francisco. I don't think it'd be hard. The place to open a temple would be Haight-Ashbury. We were down there a few months ago and things are really taking off."

"OK, we'll think about it," I said. "We're heading over to Janaki's aunt's place, and we'll stay there a while before we go to India. We don't go for another couple of months, so I'll keep in touch."

Janaki and I headed out of the forest alone; Joan and Maurice had decided they liked the vibes of Dustin and Melody's place, and they thought they'd hang out there for a while before heading to their respective destinations in Oregon. By the time we were on the winding road leading down the mountain, huge snowflakes started flying everywhere. The road turned white and we had no chains or snow tires, so we drove down to sea level as fast as possible. There the snow turned to sleet and then rain that lashed at the windscreen with such fury that we had to pull over a couple of times. Klamath Falls was only a couple of hours away.

"Dustin offered to help us open a temple in San Francisco," I said to Janaki as soon as the weather eased up enough to give us a chance to talk.

"But you told him we're going to India, right?" she asked.

"Yeah."

"They were pretty into what we told them about the swami," she said. "Maybe we should take them up on their offer."

"But that would mean not going to India!" I said. I'd had the idea of traveling abroad suggested to me a couple of times before, and each time I'd turned down the offer. The first one came when I was in college and a friend of mine named Roberto suddenly suggested in the midst of a dorm party that we go to India. Then, a few years ago, I'd turned down an all-expense-paid trip to Mallorca off the coast of Spain, where a plush nightclub needed a band to play for four weeks. Each time, something had held me back from leaving the States and taking the leap into the unknown. I was determined not to let it happen again.

"Why do you want to go to India?" Jan asked.

"Well, because it's exotic, and because it'll be like an adventure or something," I said.

"Staying in the States and opening a temple for the swami would be a different kind of adventure," she said. She was obviously losing her enthusiasm for the India plan.

I silently agreed with her. I was unwilling to admit it, but Dustin and Melody's enthusiasm about opening a temple had affected me too.

We arrived at the home of Janaki's Aunt Edna and Uncle Dean Howell an hour or so later. Waiting for me on their kitchen table was a letter. I flipped it over and saw the sender's name: "A.C. Bhaktivedanta Swami." A letter from the swami! I had completely forgotten that I'd given him this address, and I tore open the enve-

THE NEW YORK TIMES, MONDAY, OCTOBER 10, 1966.

Swami's Flock Chants in Park to Find Ecstasy

50 Followers Clap and Sway to Hypnotic Music at East Side Ceremony

By JAMES R. SIKES

Sitting under a tree in a Lower East Side park and occasionally dancing, 50 followers of a Hindu swami repeated a 16-word chant for two hours yesterday afternoon to the accompaniment of cymbals, tambourines, sticks, drums, bells and a small reed organ.

Repetition of the chant, Swami A. C. Bhaktivedanta says, is the best way to achieve self-realization in an age of destruction.

While children played on Hoving's Hill—a pile of dirt in the middle of Tompkins Square Park—or bicycled along the sunny walks, many in the crowd of about 100 persons standing around the chanters found themselves swaying or clapping hands in time to the hypnotic, rhythmic music.

"It brings a state of ecstasy," said Allen Ginsberg, the poet, who was one of the celebrants. "For one thing, the syllables force yoga breath control; that's one physiological explanation."

The ecstasy of the chant, or mantra — "Hare Krishna, Hare Krishna, Krishna Krishna, Hare Hare, Hare Rama, Hare Rama, Rama, Rama, Hare Hare"—has replaced LSD and other drugs for many of the swami's followers, Mr. Ginsberg said.

Drugs Are Replaced

He explained that Hare, pronounced HAH-ray, is the name for Vishnu, a Hindu god, as the "bringer of delight." Rama, pronounced RAH-mah, is the incarnation of Vishnu as the prince of responsibility. Krishna is the God-narrator of the Bhagavad-Gita, one of the chief Hindu religious books. The chant therefore names different aspects of God, Mr. Ginsberg said.

Another celebrant, 26-year-old Howard M. Wheeler, who described himself as a former English instructor at Ohio State University now devoting his full time to the swami, said: "I myself took 50 doses of LSD and a dozen of peyote in two years, and now, nothing."

The swami orders his followers to give up "all intoxicants, including coffee, tea and cigarettes," he said in an interview after the ceremony. "In this sense, we are helping your Government," he added.

However, he indicated, the Government apparently has not appreciated this help sufficiently, for the Department of Immigration recently told Swami Bhaktivedanta that his one-year visitor's visa had expired and that he must leave, he said. The case is being appealed.

The swami, a swarthy man with short-cropped grayish hair who was clad in a salmon-colored robe over a pink sweater, said that when he first met his own teacher, or guru, in 1922, he was told to spread the cult of Krishna to the Western countries through the English language. "Therefore, in this old age [71], I have

The New York Times (by Allyn Baum)

Two youths are stirred to dance at concert presided over by Swami A. C. Bhaktivedanta in Tompkins Square Park.

taken so much risk," he said. He arrived in the United States in September, 1965.

The swami, whose title is equivalent to the reverend, conducts chanting and gives lectures at his International Society for Krishna Consciousness, Inc., a storefront at 26 Second Avenue, between First and Second Streets, on Mondays, Wednesdays and Fridays from 7 to 9 P. M. and every morning at 7 A. M. He has scheduled another session in the park at Seventh Street and Avenue A on Sunday at 2 P. M.

His followers were said to include a lawyer, a mathematics professor and several teachers and social workers, as well as full-time devotees.

The New York Times October, 1966 issue included this article headlined, "Swami's Flock Chants in Park to Find Ecstasy," and was the first major newspaper coverage about ISKCON.

lope like it was a notice of an unexpected lottery win. There was a single sheet of paper and a newspaper clipping with the headline "Swami's Flock Chants in Park to Find Ecstasy."

I unfolded the letter. It read as if it was from an old friend.

"We are having some success," the swami wrote. "I have enclosed a clipping from the *New York Times*. Many people are coming, and now the place has been decorated more than before."

I scrutinized the grainy newspaper photo. I recognized several faces in the photo, including those who were dancing with their arms raised in the way the swami had first shown us at Dr. Mishra's *ashram*. The swami was in the photo too, leading the chanting with his drum. We had only ever chanted in the temple, and I was surprised that the swami would take everyone out in public. In the article, Allen Ginsberg was interviewed; I knew he'd helped us all a lot, but being quoted in the *New York Times* was another thing.

As I regarded the photo, I thought, "The swami *has* started a movement, just like he said he would." I remembered the word "movement" appearing in the incorporating document I had signed, but I never took it very seriously. Now I could see things were actually happening in New York; the swami's society was moving forward. *A movement!* I was so happy for him, and happy for myself that I was part of it.

Janaki and I spent a night with her aunt and uncle and then headed out to a small cabin that they owned on Klamath Lake. On our first night there, Scuzzlebrunzer's feral instincts got the better of him and he escaped into the woods. Years later, Janaki's aunt said she saw him in his new habitat, wild as any tiger.

Throughout the next week I was constantly weighing India and San Francisco. I read and re-read the swami's letter and the article he had sent me. One afternoon I sat restringing my *japa* beads on the rickety Klamath Lake dock near our cabin. I had learned that there should be a knot between each bead so that they didn't touch. The hot autumn sun beat down on my neck as I knotted and threaded the smooth red beads. The swami's parting words to me echoed in my head: "Just see if you can start one center on the West Coast. It would be a very great service."

I looked out over the lake. Autumn was slow in arriving that year. The trees at the lake's margin were ostentatious shades of red and yellow, but this was the only sign that winter was approaching.

The air was fragrant with pollen, the sky unblemished by clouds.

There was a small row boat nestled in the river weeds under the dock. When I finished stringing my beads, I flung them around my neck and leaned over the edge of the dock to drag the boat through water flora so that I could clamber into it. With the small oar I maneuvered my vessel through the pale pink lilies that rose out of the lake. Droplets of water sat as pearl-like thoughts on the flat green lily pads.

Once I was out on the lake and in clear water, I laid back and closed my eyes. I could hear little streams of air bubbling up from the Tuli plants growing many feet below on the lake's silt floor. I opened my lids a crack and saw single silver strands of spider filaments drifting from the lake surface and ending somewhere in the blue sky above.

"What should we do?" I wondered to myself. I had dreamed for years of visiting exotic India, smelling its smells, eating its food, meeting its spiritual people and visiting its architectural wonders. But we didn't really know anyone there and we didn't really have a plan about where we'd go or what we'd do when we arrived. Was I just looking for an excuse not to travel and take risks like I had in the past? I had been so sure that it was the right time for Janaki and me to go to India, but now I wasn't so sure. Dustin and Melody's interest in the swami had affected me a lot. Unexpectedly, it seemed that they wanted to be teammates as well as friends.

"Perhaps we should just abandon our India trip and all go to San Francisco after all," I thought. "That would be simpler, and we'd be helping the swami in his mission."

I drifted off to sleep and dreamed I was floating in a magenta-colored outer space. I saw things growing and swerving over the surface of Earth, Jupiter and the moon. Then I dreamed I was in the middle of a place where thousands of people my age and younger were gathering, arriving from all over the globe, congregating in a mass street-gathering complete with bands and giant banks of loudspeakers. They were smoking grass in large pipes right out in the open in broad daylight with nobody trying to stop them. Loud music throbbed in my head. I was standing on the sidewalk of Haight Street. I was inhaling lots of pot, coughing and getting a "contact high." People were crowding in on me. I started to suffocate.

I woke with a start and sat up, rubbing my eyes.

It was all quiet on the lake. "Weird dream," I thought, and I lay back down and drifted off again. The Taj Mahal and the Ajanta Caves appeared in my dream. It was mysterious, exotic, but it soon became crowded, dark and menacing. The gurgling bubbles coming up from the lake floor got louder and louder. The bubbles amplified until they became deafening in my dream, the sound of large mallets that frightening half-naked Indians were banging on big log drums in a tropical twilight near a beach in south India. I couldn't read their faces, couldn't understand what they were doing and thinking. I started to panic, hoping they couldn't see me. I woke again and felt the sun on my face.

I floated in the small rowboat on Klamath Lake for six hours with nothing to do, nowhere to go, my mind in turmoil about our destination.

A week later I sent our India tickets back and got a refund. We headed for San Francisco.

PART 2

SAN FRANCISCO

Flowers in Their Hair

If you're going to San Francisco
Be sure to wear some flowers in your hair
If you're going to San Francisco
You're gonna meet some gentle people there
For those who come to San Francisco
Summertime will be a love-in there
In the streets of San Francisco
Gentle people with flowers in their hair

— *Scott McKenzie*

Breaking
New Ground

November 1966

Janaki and I arrived in San Francisco at the end of 1966, and after a brief stay at a friend's in Berkeley, we headed straight for the Haight-Ashbury district on Dustin's recommendation. The area was fast becoming a Mecca for alternative thinking and living, and we thought it would be the most fertile soil in which to plant a new temple for the swami.

At the beginning of the twentieth century, Haight-Ashbury had been an upper-middle class neighborhood, one of the few areas of San Francisco that was spared by the post-earthquake fires of 1906. In the 1930s, the Depression stripped many of the Haight's affluent residents of their wealth, and in the 1940s large homes that had previously been occupied by a single rich family were converted into small apartments to house war workers. In the 1950s, anyone who had a choice moved out of the Haight district; numerous dilapidated buildings provided cheap housing for those who were down and out, while other buildings were simply left to decay.

By the 1960s, the area looked like an ordinary San Francisco neighborhood with a lot of immigrants. The cheap accommodation also appealed to drug users and dealers and those who had little material means. In November 1966 it was still six months or so before the Summer of Love, but from our perspective as new residents of the area, hippy culture was already underway. Clusters of exotically dressed young people in their teens and twenties hung out in

113

Haight-Ashbury

the streets and in doorways. Although the manufacture, possession, sale and use of LSD had all been made illegal in October, just
a few weeks before we arrived, there was plenty of evidence that
drugs were readily available. Pot was everywhere, its smoke part of
the distinctive smell of the region. The danger factor of consuming
illegal drugs made it more exciting.

Haight-Ashbury was the colorful underbelly of the American
Dream. Some of the young people arriving in San Francisco were
college and high-school dropouts; others were educated members
of affluent families. All were looking for an alternative to the way
of life that typified the Dream, including having a family, getting a
good education and making lots of money.

The act of opposing norms was the norm in the Haight. Young
people there embraced a philosophy that rejected capitalism, US
military intervention in Vietnam, Christianity, authority, conformity of all kinds. Some had torn up or burned their draft cards and
other forms of ID in the hope of achieving total anonymity; one of
the local heroes, Gary Snyder, predicted group marriage and the end
of capitalism. Many looked toward Native American Indian culture
as the essence of true Americanism. They lamented that the indig-
enous inhabitants of the country had been exploited, slaughtered

and dispossessed of their land by European conquerors. As a symbol of their solidarity with Indian culture, many carried what came to be known as "God's Eyes" – diamond-shaped webs of yarn strung between two sticks and carried aloft like medieval standards. The God's Eye became a symbol for the young Haight-Ashbury migrants. Conventional clothing was replaced by long hair and beards, beads, head bands, feathers, miniskirts, leather jackets and magicians' robes. Anything went. Middle-aged tourists from Iowa, New York, Georgia, Canada, England and Germany would routinely drive up and down Haight Street on sunny days to gape at the spectacle of the flower people up-close in real life. Many women and some men wore flowers in their hair, and Scott McKenzie's song sold millions of copies and got played on radio stations all over the world.

It was an anti-community that was searching for a new reality. The tools of the search were drugs, sex, music and alternative spirituality. The architects of the newly minted hippy movement preached and believed that music and drugs – particularly LSD – opened new avenues of perception by which people could expand their consciousness. The "new music" included The Byrds, The Beatles and The Grateful Dead; it was thought that their music heralded a radical change in consciousness. One of the Haight's enthusiastic visionaries, Chester Anderson, said:

"Rock is evolving formal homo-gestalt configurations – the groups themselves living together. Superfamilies. Pre-initiate tribal groups. Rock is regenerative revolutionary art, not degenerative or decadent. Rock principles are not limited to music. Rock is an intensively synthesizing music, able to absorb all of society into itself. Rock has reinstated the ancient truth that art is fun. Rock is a way of life, internal and universal. Not even the dead are completely immune. In the land of the dark, the ship of the sun is driven by The Grateful Dead."

The music was best appreciated when the mind was expanded through drug use. The forty-something former Harvard

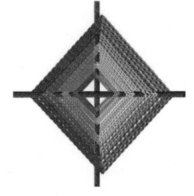

God's Eye

The Grateful Dead

professor and much sought-after Haight-Ashbury guru of sorts, Timothy Leary, was central to the philosophy of drug-aided consciousness expansion. Soon after coining the phrase "turn on, tune in, drop out," Leary advised middle class parents not to be afraid of their children's drug experiments. "My advice is to sit down with your kids," he said. "Ask them what they're learning, why they take it and learn from your children and perhaps eventually, when you're spiritually ready, you'll turn on with your children, if you feel that's the right thing to do."

Allen Ginsberg was also vocal in his advocacy of LSD. "How can we change America?" he asked. "I will make a first proposal: that everybody who hears my voice try the chemical LSD at least once – every man, woman and child over fourteen in good health. Then I prophesize we will have seen some ray of glory or vastness beyond our social selves, beyond our government, beyond America even, that will unite us into a peaceful community. America's political need is orgies in the park, on Boston Commons, with naked bacchantes in the national forest. I am already acknowledging what is happening among the young in fact and fantasy. I am in effect setting up standards which include drugs, orgies, music and primitive magic as worship ritual."

Ginsberg was not alone in his interest in non-Western religion. Many popular leaders of the time had a philosophy of freedom that was often expressed in the Eastern metaphysical terms of Buddhist and Zen thought. Alternative religion was in, Christianity was out – the new pilgrims considered Christianity archaic, corrupt and out of sync. The Haight had an underground newspaper called *The Oracle*, which printed articles like "Flower from the Street," "Bon Bon Mahadev," "Renaissance or Die," "Psychedelic Yoga" and "Environment for Expanded Awareness." One essay challenged the beliefs of Christianity with the words "We were suspicious of your god who never failed you – always loving, a Christ with no human faults. The terrible truth was that your Christ carried hell with him, and that each of you had a hell, a darkness."

Haight Street, San Francisco, 1967

The lifestyle and philosophy of The Scene was a bit too radical for me, but I thought we could make the most of it. Although the swami didn't back a lot of the main tenets of the hippy philosophy – especially not the drug use and free love – the popular interest in spirituality gave me hope that a new temple might thrive in this neighborhood of seekers.

———

The first thing I did when we arrived in San Francisco was find a phone booth to call Dustin and Melody. They were excited that we'd changed our minds about India, and they arrived in Haight-Ashbury a few days after us along with their collie Ralph, Joan, and her new partner Jim.

During our first week in San Francisco I cut out a couple of newspaper articles about India: "Pool of Goddess in India Dried Up" and "Rioting Over Cow Slaughter Leaves Seven Indians Dead." The first article was about the annual Dussehra festival, which involved bathing a goddess in a special pool. It had to be cancelled because a drought meant there was no water in the pool. The second one detailed how some holy men had stormed the gates of parliament in Delhi protesting the slaughter of cows taking place there. According to the article, there were about one hundred and seventy-five million cows in India and about thirty thousand were slaughtered every day by non-Hindus. Although the report said they arrived in "a relaxed almost festive mood," it had ended in rioting and police retaliation. Both articles seemed to confirm our decision not to go to India. There was trouble even there – rioting, slaughter, drought. I made a mental note to ask the swami what the Dussehra festival was all about (which I never did).

After about a week in San Francisco, we managed to rent a "railroad" apartment in the city's Mission district. Its three bedrooms were all in a row off a dim hallway, and there was a grungy kitchen and bathroom at the back. The street name was Lucky Alley, a good omen, we thought, despite the quality of accommodation.

As we moved in and got settled, we discussed what we would do in the Haight.

"The main thing is to get the swami to come here," I said. "But we need to get a temple set up first. That's what he asked us to do – to start a center."

"Sure. That's the plan," Dustin said. "The only catch is that we don't have any money."

"So maybe the first thing we need to think about is how to make some money," Janaki said. "But how can we do that? I mean, it'll take a lot of money, and it's not like we're professionals or anything."

"Well, there's one thing I know that'll sell fast around here and bring in a lot of money," Dustin said. "But I don't think the swami would be into it."

"Yeah, selling drugs just doesn't feel right," Melody said. "I guess we'll just have to think of other things to sell. I could start an essential-oils business – you know, selling oils in all those head shops around the Haight. I've checked them out. They sell stuff like pipes, posters, decals, jewelry, wooden flutes ... you know the kind of things. Essential oils would sell fast; I know they would."

"That'd be good steady money long-term," I said. "But we need to do something to bring in a big amount fast. You know, to get the temple set up."

"We also need to get the swami's message out to a lot of people fast," Janaki said. "So what if we had some kind of event that people paid for? Like a spiritual rock concert or something?"

We looked at each other. "That's not a bad idea," Dustin said.

"There's so many bands in the Haight," Melody said. "I'm sure we could get some really good ones to play."

"Hey, do you remember my buddy Rock Scully?" Dustin asked.

"I never met him," I said. "But I remember you talking about him."

"Well anyway, he's The Grateful Dead's co-manager now along with Danny Riskin! Wouldn't it be great if we could get *them* to play? It'd be huge!"

"We could call it Koncert for Krishna," I suggested.

"Or TranscenDance," said Jim.

Dustin grimaced. "I think we need to think about a name a bit longer."

"Maybe we could ask Allen Ginsberg to come," Joan suggested.

"And the swami," Janaki said.

"Of course the swami!"

"Imagine the swami on stage at a rock concert," Janaki said. "Thousands of people would hear him."

"He could speak at the concert," Dustin said. "And he could lead a chant. That'd be a pretty major event here!"

Over the next few weeks, we started to get to know our new neighborhood. Our days at Lucky Alley began to have shape and run to a routine. Every morning the six of us would chant together and eat a freshly cooked vegetarian breakfast offered to Krishna in the way the swami had shown us. Then everyone went their respective ways to earn whatever they could to get the center started. The only one who wasn't working was me. I had my small bequest, and someone needed to be working full-time on the concert, so I was the one who did it.

I spent my days looking for premises for the temple and meeting people along the way. Sometimes I drove, but mostly I walked, because it was a better way to meet people. Being in the Haight was a thrill for me, but unlike India it had the added bonus of being familiar territory. I made a point of meeting the gang who put out *The Oracle*; I knew having friends on a newspaper would be an advantage. *The Oracle* published an article by George Harrison in which he said that one can use mantras to get to the essence of music. I wrote a letter to him, certain he'd never read it, saying that the opposite was true: that one could use music to get to the essence of a mantra. It was a small step, but it felt good to write a letter to such a famous musician; maybe he'd notice us and help us with getting the swami's mission established. Meanwhile, Dustin got in touch with The Grateful Dead's manager and got them to agree to play at our concert, and they put him in touch with some other bands. Getting things done there seemed easy, almost magical.

One afternoon on Haight Street I was peering into a tiny vacant storefront – far too small for the temple, I realized as soon as I got there – when a voice called out to me.

"Hey! Are you with Bhaktivedanta?"

I turned. A tall portly guy with long brown hair waved to me from a few doors down.

"I saw your beads," he said to me, pointing to the chanting beads around my neck.

"Oh yeah, I am. But we just call him 'Swami,' " I said.

"You got a temple here?"

"No, not yet, but we wanna open one."

"I'll help you," he said. "I'll help you get one. I've heard lots about Bhaktivedanta and I'd like to do something to help him get started out here."

"Yeah? Have you met him?"

"Uh-uh. But I know a lot of people. Friend of a friend met him in New York. C'mon over to my place tonight. We'll talk about how to find a good place for him."

"I can't come tonight. How about tomorrow?" I wasn't sure what to make of this encounter and I didn't want to act impulsively.

"Yeah, that sounds good. Hey, were you at the temple in New York?"

"Yeah, I *was*. I helped the swami to find his temple there. We got here just a couple of weeks back. The swami said he'd like it if we could start a center over here on the West Coast."

"Well, I'm into good causes, and from what I hear, you guys are one of them. Come on over and we'll smoke to that. OK?"

"Tomorrow afternoon?"

"Any time. We're there all day. 351 Cole Street. By the way, my name's Wolf.

The next afternoon, five of us – me, Janaki, Dustin, Joan and Jim – headed over to Wolf's place. We all agreed that we might as well check out his scene and what he had to offer. So we piled into Dustin's green 1952 Chevrolet and drove the short distance from Lucky Alley to Cole Street.

"Hey, you know what?" Dustin said to us as we drove along. "I had a dream about the swami last night."

"Even though you never met him?" I said.

"Well, I can still dream about him, can't I? I dreamed I was chauffeuring the swami somewhere in this car."

"Oh god, I really wouldn't want the swami to have to ride in this car!" Janaki exclaimed.

"After a while, the swami asked if he could drive," Dustin said. "So we traded places and I let him take the wheel. He drove swimmingly."

"What a great dream!"

"I know."

"It was almost like Dustin trusted the swami without even having met him," I thought to myself as we pulled up outside Wolf's place. "And it really shows that it's the swami driving this whole project!"

Wolf answered the door wearing a brightly striped short-sleeved shirt and a pair of denim shorts that looked like they'd been tied to the bumper of a car and driven across a desert.

"Come on in," he said. He led us up a flight of stairs, through a door and into the living room of his apartment. There were intricately patterned Madras tapestries and paintings of Tibetan mandalas hanging on the walls. Brightly colored bottles sat on the windowsills, some holding hibiscus flowers, single daffodils or carnations. They cast colored shapes on the floor. In the center of the room sat an exotically carved hookah with smoke already billowing from its ceramic crucible. Three other people dressed in tie-dye clothes sat around it lounging on thick throw pillows covered with pink, blue, yellow and orange satin. The room smelled like burning hay, but I knew it was Moroccan hashish. It was warm in there, cozy and tempting.

"Sit down," he said gesturing toward the cushions. The floor was covered by a patterned Afghan carpet. It was pretty opulent and surprisingly clean for a Haight-Ashbury pad. We took our seats around the three-foot tall pipe. I knew straight off it was high-quality smoke. I found myself musing on its origin. Maybe it wasn't from Morocco. Perhaps it was from Lebanon, or Panama, or Iran.

"This is Cassandra, Ollie and Mike," he said. "And these are … uh … Krishnas, from … uh … New York, I think. Right?"

We nodded. He sat down with us and said, "So what's the scoop?"

"Well," I said, "we want to open a temple here in San Francisco. Um, the chanting's the main thing that the swami does at the temple." I was nervous. "You want to try it?"

"Sure," Wolf said.

"We can do it together. I brought these cymbals. It's a mantra. I wrote the words down for you."

I handed him a sheet of letter paper on which I'd printed the words to the mantra in large capital letters.

"OK, but first take a drag. Here," he said, handing me the water-pipe hose. "Welcome to Kali-fornia." He pronounced it "kah-lee."

I smiled at his joke. Dustin looked confused. "Kali – he means the age of Kali," I explained. "The age of quarrel that we're in now." I thought it was a good sign that he knew some of the Sanskrit words.

"Have a drag, man!" he insisted.

I picked up my cymbals. "Let's chant first," I suggested as tactfully as I could. Dustin, Jim and Joan started clapping in sets of three, and Janaki and I played the cymbals. I sang the lead: "*Hare Krishna Hare Krishna Krishna Krishna Hare Hare, Hare Rama Hare Rama Rama Rama Hare Hare.*"

The others joined in. Wolf and his friends were enthusiastic about the chanting and got the words quickly. They obviously knew something about Indian mantras and understood the sequence. I could tell they really liked the sound. They sang loudly and clapped along, pausing only to take a few deep tokes on the pipe. After a while they leaned back, smiled and closed their eyes, abandoning themselves to our chanting. Half an hour passed like a minute.

"Wow. That mantra's *powerful*," Wolf said when we finished. He shook his head back and forth fast. "I was meditating on India! Here," he said, thrusting the saliva-soaked water pipe hose at me, "have a hit now."

"No thanks," I said, trying not to sound too ungracious. "Not right now."

"OK, I get it," Wolf said. "So, you guys don't need grass to get high. OK. *OK!*"

Everyone laughed and they all sat back for a minute, silent.

I interrupted their reverie. "So what we're hoping to do is raise some money for the swami's new West Coast temple by having some bands play a benefit, maybe at the Avalon Ballroom or somewhere. And the swami will chant. Dustin knows The Grateful Dead's manager, and they already said they'd do it. And they got us in touch with Big Brother and the Holding Company – you know Janis Joplin's band?"

"Sounds great to me. But you need someone else," Wolf said.

"Whaddya mean?" I asked.

"Someone famous – a personality – well, you know, someone like Timothy Leary or someone. You've got to have someone famous, you know." He sounded excited.

Big Brother and the Holding Company

"Allen Ginsberg used to come to our temple in New York," I said. "He helped the swami get a longer visa. He went to the park in New York too and chanted. He likes the chant a lot. He even did it on television in New York once. Janaki and I saw it on TV."

"Ginsberg met the swami?" Wolf seemed incredulous. "That's a good thing, a really good thing, man. Guess what? I know him too. I *know* Allen; he's a good friend. I'll call him and ask him if he wants to be part of your concert. We wanted to get him out here anyway to show him what's going on."

We were excited on the way home. We knew that a celebrity like Ginsberg would draw the crowds in. I felt like a band manager

– the guy who did all the background work: the setting up, the tours, the publication.

A few days later, Wolf came over to Lucky Alley. I opened the door, and his beaming face greeted me. "Allen's coming."

———

By December I still hadn't found a location for the temple, but a few people were starting to notice us and take a bit of interest in what we were doing. The author Joan Didion made an extemporary visit to our place. Her article was published in *The Saturday Evening Post*. It was called "Slouching Toward Bethlehem." She wrote:

"I pay a visit to Michael Grant, the swami A.C. Bhaktivedanta's leading disciple in San Francisco. Michael Grant is at home with his wife, a pretty girl wearing a cashmere pullover, a jumper, and a red caste mark on her forehead.

"'I've been associated with the swami since about last July,' Michael says. 'See, the swami came here from India and he was at this *ashram* in upstate New York and he just kept to himself and chanted a lot. For a couple of months. Pretty soon I helped him get his storefront in New York. Now it's an international movement, which we spread by teaching this chant.' Michael is fingering his red wooden beads and I notice that I am the only person in the room with shoes on. 'It's catching on like wildfire.' Michael walks across the room and straightens a picture of Krishna as a baby. 'Too bad you can't meet the swami,' he adds. 'The swami's in New York now.' "

In addition to the *Post* article, *The Oracle* published a kind of raucous, hippy-jargon-filled essay I sent them, by-lined with the name "Mukundah Das Adhikary." They ran it with my suggested title, "The New Science." In order to tell people about the new temple, we also printed thousands of handbills, which we passed out to people whenever we went anywhere. Each handbill had a photograph of the swami in Tompkins Square Park taken by a photographer from New York's *East Village*. In the photos, the swami was seated cross-legged, leaning back against a large tree with his left hand atop his head and smiling from ear to ear. Across the upper part of the photo it said, "Bring Krishna Consciousness West." The handbill was framed with the Hare Krishna mantra written in Joan's calligraphy.

Leaflet distributed in the Haight-Ashbury prior to the swami's arrival

With all the publicity, we felt people would definitely get to know about us and would come to the concert. We talked a lot about what we should call the concert and finally, after much debate, decided on the name Mantra-Rock Dance. As for where we should have it, there were two venues that we thought would be big enough for us – the Avalon Ballroom on Sutter Street, which was run by Chet Helms, and the Fillmore Auditorium on the corner of Fillmore Street and Geary Boulevard, which was operated by Bill Graham, who was quite a bit more conservative than Chet. Eventually we decided on the Avalon because we thought Chet would be more sympathetic to the spirit of our concert. I finally managed to meet with him in the middle of December.

"Sure," he said. He was wearing a green suit, his long hair hanging in his eyes. "You can have the Avalon. Who you got lined up to play?"

"So far The Grateful Dead and Big Brother and the Holding Company. They said they'd do it for charity."

"That's OK, but you'll still need to pay each band two hundred and fifty dollars. That's the musicians' union minimum."

"Oh, OK. We didn't know that," I said. "Allen Ginsberg'll be there to speak."

"Sounds good, but you'll need another band to round it out."

"You think so?"

"Definitely," he said. "When do you want it for?"

"Well, we told the bands January."

"January's pretty tight," he said. "All the Fridays and Saturdays are booked."

I thought fast. "Could we have it on a Sunday night?"

"Sunday?" Chet looked skeptical. "Well, sure, but I'm not sure how many people would come. The crowds come out on Fridays and Saturdays. We haven't ever really had a rock concert in the Avalon on a Sunday before."

"We're really committed for January, so I guess we'll just have to risk it," I said, hoping the others would agree. "I was also thinking it'd be good if we could organize a light show for the concert. Do you know someone who does that kind of thing?"

"Yeah, you need Ben van Meter and Roger Hillyard. They do a lot of the shows at the Avalon – colored oils, strobe lights, projectors, that kind of thing. You want their number?"

"Yeah, that'd be great. That's just what we're looking for," I said.

"OK, so I'm going to book you in for Sunday, January 29th."

That evening I told the others that Chet thought we still needed another band.

"Who should we get?" Melody asked.

"I guess I can get back in touch with Rock to see if he knows of anyone else who'd like to be a part of it," Dustin said.

"There's one other thing I've been thinking about," Joan said. "How are we going to publicize this? We can't just expect people to find out about this through word of mouth."

Chet Helms, 1967

"We'll have to get some posters done," Jim said. "And we could get some handbills done to pass out to people."

"So, who will do the designing?"

"What about Harvey Corbett?" I said, the idea suddenly occurring to me.

"Who?"

"Harvey, the artist. He's the guy whose loft the swami first stayed in when he came to New York – you know, before he got the temple. The loft he was staying in with that weird kid Paul? Harvey knew the swami, and he liked him. He helped him get set up when he had nowhere to go."

"So you think he'll come out here from New York?"

"He had a studio on Madison Avenue in New York, but someone told me the other day that he's moved to Mendocino to work on his art there. That's only three hours away!"

"That sounds great!" Dustin said. "You think he'd do it?"

"Worth a try," I said.

The hip set in San Francisco was pretty tight, and I managed to track down Harvey's phone number without difficulty the following day. I called him from a pay phone on the corner of Lucky Alley and Twenty-fourth Street.

"Hello," said a sleepy voice at the other end.

"Hey, Harvey, hi," I said. "My name's Mukunda. I'm a disciple of the swami's." I realized I was talking fast.

"Who?"

"The swami. He's coming to San Francisco."

"Really?" He was waking up now. "When?"

"Some time next month," I said. "A bunch of us are here in San Francisco trying to open another temple for him."

"Yeah? That's good."

"And we're organizing a rock concert to try to raise money for it. That's going to be in January, and the swami will come out here for it. It'll be the first time he's ever flown."

"You're kidding."

"Uh-uh," I said. "We've got The Grateful Dead and Big Brother and Allen Ginsberg all coming."

"Sounds great."

"Yeah. What're you doing?"

"Me?" He sounded evasive. "Painting. I rented a place on the beach."

"Must be a great place to paint."

"It's perfect." I thought I heard a smile in his voice.

"Anyway, I'm calling because I wondered if you could come down and help us. We need a poster. All the concerts have posters. They're all over the place."

"I don't think so. Grateful Dead and Big Brother, huh? Wow!" He paused. "I don't know. This is a perfect spot on the beach. I'd like to think about it."

"You can go back to Mendocino. We just want to get this concert off the ground."

"It'd take me at least a week to get down there and maybe a week to do it."

"Well, that'd be OK," I said. "It's not until January 29th."

"OK, maybe I can do it … Can you call me back, like, later today?"

"Sure," I said. I hung up and went to meet with Ben van Meter and Roger Hillyard, the light show guys from the Avalon.

That evening I was able to report to the others that Harvey had agreed to come. Ben and Roger had also agreed to do the light show, and Sunday would be OK for them, if a bit risky. They said they would use colored oils to project shapes that would morph into one another in time with the music. They had strobe lights and a spotlight that they would beam into a revolving mirrored sphere that hung from the Avalon ceiling. It had hundreds of facets so that myriad incandescent coins would race across the walls as it turned. We also discussed the possibility of a slideshow; they decided in the end that they liked the idea, but I would have to put it together. So my next project was to make some slides of whatever Indian posters of Krishna I could find. I would also make a slide of the Hare Krishna mantra, which they would project on a wall during the chanting part of the show. They were enthusiastic about the whole thing and said they were confident they could put together a special Krishna light show. I imagined their special effects seen through clouds of billowing incense smoke, and I knew it would produce an effective otherworldly mood.

Melody had some news of her own.

"I found our other band!"

"Who are they?" I asked.

"They're called Moby Grape. There's five of them: three guitars, drums and a singer. They're all about eighteen."

"Melody, hang on," I said. I couldn't believe this. "We haven't even heard them. We don't even know who they are."

"*I've* heard them," she said. "I listened to them practicing for about fifteen minutes over on Twenty-fourth Street. They're really good; their music is loud – like so loud it hurts – but it was great."

"You can't just book a band without the rest of us," I said. "Especially a band no one knows."

Melody looked earnest. "They're incredible. Honest, you'll like them! They loved the sound of our concert. And they said they'd do it for free."

"Well sure," I said sarcastically. "They will be getting to play with the Dead at the Avalon, after all."

"Anyway, I gave our address to the lead singer Skip, and I said we'd keep in touch. They've said a definite yes already, though. It'll be like their debut."

I rolled my eyes. "Jesus, Melody, you can't just do things like this."

She smiled. "You'll see," she said.

CHAPTER 13

The Swami's Second Temple

It was Monday again. I was still looking for a temple, and time was running out. We wanted the temple to be as close to the intersection of Haight and Ashbury as possible so that it would be within reach of the thousands of people with packs on their backs that were coming to San Francisco every day. I was beginning to feel despondent. With only just over a month until the rock concert, we needed to get the swami out there and we couldn't do that until we had a location for a temple.

The morning was gray and dank, not the sunshine-drenched California of popular imagination. I was scuffing down Frederick Street close to Kezar Stadium when a *For Rent* sign caught my eye in the front window of number 518. It was an empty ground-level store in a big building marked 512. The storefront had a big plate-glass window, a front door and a small ledge inside the main window. It looked almost exactly like the 26 Second Avenue storefront in New York, except that it was a little bigger and a lot cleaner. I read the small print on the sign: "Contact Wilfred and Maddox, 412 Geary Street." I thought for a few minutes. It wasn't in Haight-Ashbury, but it was within walking distance of it. Not exactly what I was looking for, but still the best storefront I'd seen for rent the whole time we'd been in San Francisco. It was close to the middle of things, and the stadium would attract a lot of people; it was used for the San Francisco Forty-niners pro football games and held thirty thousand spectators. I decided to check it out.

"I'm interested in renting 518 Frederick Street," I said to the blonde, heavy-set woman behind the desk at the Geary Street office.

"You need to talk to Mr. Goodman. Just a minute." She swiveled in her chair and scanned the office. The other desks were empty. She looked back at me, a tired expression on her face.

"Can you come back?" she asked. "He's not here and …"

A tall balding man in a light brown suit came through a door-way at the back of the office.

"That's him," she said, indicating with her head, then raising her voice, "Ruby, he wants to rent Frederick Street."

"You want to rent Frederick? 518?" he yelled as he approached me.

"Yeah. How much is it?"

"One twenty-five a month plus utilities. What do you want it for?" Now he was looking me up and down. I was sockless in brown Indian sandals and an off-white jump suit with *NASA* written above the breast pocket. I hoped he wouldn't mind my beard and un-combed hair.

"I have a friend from India who wants to teach yoga three nights a week and maybe give some lectures in the morning."

"What part of India?" He seemed intrigued.

"Calcutta."

"How old is he?"

"Oh, about seventy."

"Sounds OK. There's a one-week deposit and a one-year lease."

"That's OK. When's it available?"

"It's vacant now," he said. "You pay the deposit and first month's rent, you can have it whenever you want it." I thought he seemed eager to rent the place out.

"So I need to bring the money here and sign today?" I wondered if we'd be able to scrape together the deposit between us.

He nodded, "That's right."

Suddenly I realized the swami would need a place to stay too.

"Are there any apartments for rent in that building? 518 is the storefront in the big 512 building, right?"

"Yeah, that's right. Let's see," he said thinking. "In 512, I have two apartments: 33 and 37."

"How much?"

"They're one hundred and ten dollars each," he answered. "You want 'em?"

"I think so. Same deal?"

"Yep, you'd have to pay today."

"Can I see 'em?" I asked.

"Sure," he replied. "We can go right now if you want."

We drove over to Frederick Street in our separate cars. Goodman let me into the storefront to have a look around and knocked on the walls to show that they were solid. It was perfect for a temple. There was a sink and bathroom at the back, and a large main space that would seat a lot of guests.

"I'll see if the Dethridges are in," Goodman said. "They manage the whole building and can let you in to see the apartments.

We took the elevator up to the fourth floor to the Dethridges' apartment. There was loud barking when we knocked, and a red-faced man with pitted cheeks opened the door. Lunging forward on their leashes were two Great Danes who were almost as tall as I was. Mr. Dethridge had short brown hair and wore corduroy pants. His face was square and his eyes bloodshot. He was of medium build, but short and muscular, and sort of rugged-looking. He was wearing a tight white T-shirt with rolled-up sleeves.

"What's up?"

"I woke you?" ventured Goodman.

"Yeah." He blinked his eyes rapidly. "I worked graveyard last night."

"Sorry," said Goodman. To me he said, "This is Dale Dethridge."

I warily held out my hand. The dogs were emitting a low grating rumble at the bottom of their throats. They looked vicious, but Dethridge looked OK – tired and kind of wiry-looking in his wrinkled corduroy pants.

"This guy wants to rent 518 and a couple of apartments on this floor," Goodman said. "Can we see 'em?"

"Yeah, I'll get Marianne to show them to you," he said. He yelled, "Hey, Mary, c'mere. Can you show a guy the apartments?"

Mrs. Dethridge appeared carrying a bunch of keys. She was dark, thin and frail-looking in her yellow dress.

"There's no furniture in 'em," she said to me. "But I have a rocker you can have for one of 'em if you want."

We walked down the hall to number 33. The apartment had a dim hallway, a small bathroom on the right as you entered, an unfurnished bedroom with a large flat window, and a narrow kitchen with sink and gas stove. The main room's three curved windows faced south over Frederick Street. I could see the green pines above the houses across the street and the California University Medical Center at the top of the hill two blocks away. Everything was sunny and airy – "just what the swami needed," I thought.

"Looks great to me."

"You want to see 37?"

"Sure."

Apartment 37 was much the same as 33 except there was a large window in the kitchen that overlooked Kezar Stadium. Since the apartment was on the fourth floor, you could actually see into the stadium.

"You can watch the NFL for free from this window," Goodman joked, oblivious to the fact that most bearded alternatives generally weren't into pro football.

"We'll take them both," I said. Internally I was engaged in a frenzy of planning. Janaki and I could take this apartment, because it would be the coldest and noisiest, and the swami could have 33. It would be just like New York, except here we'd live right down the hall from the swami. It was too good to be true.

"So you want the rocker?" Mrs. Dethridge asked. "I hope you got other furniture."

"Yeah, we do," I said, knowing that between us we'd come up with something.

———

Dustin and I crammed into the phone booth on the corner of Twenty-fourth and Lucky.

A bored voice cut in. "Please insert three seventy-five for the first three minutes."

I pulled a handful of quarters out of my pocket and started sticking them in – one, two, three … When I put in the fifteenth one, there was a clang and the same bored voice said, "Thank you."

It rang once, twice, three times, four – my heart was jumping out of my chest. It was stuffy and hot with the two of us in that phone booth, but I didn't care.

"Hello." It was him! I nodded excitedly to Dustin.

"Swami, I'm in San Francisco," I said. Dustin smiled and raised his eyebrows.

"Oh, yes?" he said. "This is Mukunda?"

"Yes."

"You are far away?"

"Yes, but only San Francisco. I wondered if you would come here. We decided not to go to India. We're opening a temple here, and we're going to have a benefit concert to raise the money we need. Allen Ginsberg is coming. It's on the 29th of January."

"I'm knowing Mr. Jinsberg. Yes, I can come."

It was that easy. We had thought it was going to be difficult to convince him, and now it seemed like it was over before it began.

"It's on the 29th of January," I repeated. "Many people will come. We just got the temple the other day, but we're going to set it up just like New York before you come. It's the same size and looks just like it." I held my breath. There was a long pause.

"So I should come on 29th?" he asked.

"I was thinking it's better if you could come earlier, like on the 17th."

"Yes, I can come."

He sounded almost too eager. Dustin seemed ready to burst with joy, rubbing his hands together and beaming.

"OK, great, we'll see you then, Swami," I said, about to hang up the phone.

"So how will I come?" the swami asked.

Whoops! We hadn't even talked about that.

"Um, the best thing is for you to … take an airplane." I was improvising. I looked at Dustin who was nodding fervently.

"So you will send me ticket?"

"Just a minute."

I put my right hand over the mouthpiece and twisted so Dustin and I could have a private mini-conference. We quickly agreed to pay.

"Yes, Swami," I said. "We'll pay for the ticket here, and you can take the airplane."

That same female-sounding voice cut in again. "Please insert one dollar for the next one minute."

The phone was dead. I fumbled for four more quarters, hoping the swami wouldn't hang up. I stuck in the money. One, two, three, four. A bell rang and the phone cut back in. He was still there.

"... will send it? How will I come there?"

"What did you say?"

"So you will send it by post? How will I get ticket?"

"No," I was talking slowly now, remembering that the swami had never flown before. "You go to United Airlines at the airport in New York and give your name, and it will all be arranged. We'll pay for it here in San Francisco."

"So they will know my name? Is it?"

"Yes, that's right. We'll pay United Airlines here, then they will telex the New York office, and they will expect you. It's called a prepaid ticket. That is how they do it. I've done this before. It's a standard thing."

"So I will not pay?"

"No. Just give your name. You may have to show them your passport. I will telephone again to give you the exact time." The line was sounding fuzzy.

"But it will be on 17th January?" he asked.

"Yes."

"Thank you very much."

"Hare Krishna, Swami."

"Hare Krishna." He hung up and no further sound came through the receiver. We were elated. The whole point of the concert, the new temple, our being in San Francisco in the first place was now fulfilled. He was coming.

— —

We had only a few weeks to get the storefront looking like a temple before the swami arrived, so we were working day and night on a seemingly endless number of tasks. Fortunately, now that we had the temple we were beginning to have a presence in

Haight-Ashbury. The first thing we did after I signed the lease was put up a sign in the front window like the one in the New York temple: "Radha-Krishna Temple, Classes by Bhaktivedanta Swami Mondays, Wednesdays and Fridays 7:00 PM, starting January 17th 1967." This was a little conjectural on our part, but we couldn't imagine the swami coming and not having his programs, so we felt it was probably OK.

We gradually acquired a team of volunteers who were eager to help us get the place into shape. Some were people we had met through work or through trying to get the concert off the ground. Others just walked through the storefront door, curious about what we were doing. It quickly became apparent to the six of us that a lot of other people thought that it was important for the swami to come to San Francisco to be part of the blossoming alternative world there. We knew people's acceptance of us was at least partly because we weren't like the Bible-pounding preachers who turned up in Haight-Ashbury periodically to save the heathens. We were part of the scene and yet not wholly of it.

A friend of ours – a guy named Brother David – donated his gray 1950 Ford to help us out. Using a stencil we spray-painted the words "Hare Krishna" in big, bright psychedelic letters in orange, yellow and red in the style of the Haight graphic artist Stanley Mouse. We used the same stencil to spray-paint buildings, fences and even the pavement as was the fash-

A Stanley Mouse 1960s-era psychedelic poster

ion in Haight-Ashbury. We increasingly noticed people calling us "Hare Krishnas" or just plain "Krishnas."

With a bit of effort, the store began to feel like a temple. We found an oriental carpet – the blood brother of the one at the New York temple – and spread it over the wooden floor. Dustin, our resident carpenter, crafted a small plywood seat with redwood legs at the back of the room, where we thought the swami could lecture from. I found some exotic-looking emerald brocade cushions and a bolster with black tassels to make the swami's seat comfortable. Next to it, Dustin made a small altar on which we placed the few pictures we had – one of Lord Chaitanya, one of Radha and Krishna and one of Krishna as a baby with butter in His hand.

We used the week between Christmas and New Year to do most of the work. The day after Christmas I took a break from cleaning the walls to go and pick up Harvey from the bus station. It was getting dark out.

"Hey, Dustin," I yelled over the vibrations of his drill. "I'm taking the Krishna car to get Harvey!"

He waved to me. As I was leaving a couple in their early thirties – older people I thought – poked their heads through the front door.

A Stanley Mouse psychedelic poster

"Hi," the guy said. "My name's James, and this is Charlotte. You guys need any help?"

"Ah, well, sure," I said. "I'm just on my way to pick up a friend from the bus station, but you could talk to Dustin down the back there, or Janaki." I pointed her out to them. "What do you guys do?"

"We're both artists," Charlotte said.

"Well, hey, you know what we really need is a sign for above the window," I said. "Could you do something like that?"

"Yeah, probably," James said.

"OK, that'd be great!" I exclaimed. "Dustin's a carpenter, so talk to him about it."

"OK."

I arrived at the Greyhound station just as the bus pulled in. I'd never seen Harvey before, and I'd forgotten to ask him what he looked like or what he'd be wearing, but I hoped we'd be able to recognize each other. My attire was pretty mellow by Haight-Ashbury standards, but outlandish for me. I was dressed in a Merlin-the-Magician cream-colored robe with brown paisley prints all over it; an outfit that I thought would be pretty noticeable. At the very least, the Krishna car was hard to miss, so I figured we'd find each other one way or another. A young woman in a mauve jacket emerged from the bus, followed by fifteen tired-looking other passengers who went straight to the side of the coach to get their luggage. None of them looked like they could be Harvey.

A guy in a green suede jacket wearing desert boots and jeans then stepped energetically off the bus. He was a little chunky with a neatly trimmed black beard and carrying a sleeping bag. He looked a bit like a lost dog who hoped someone would find him soon and feed him. I took a chance.

"Harvey," I yelled. He looked up immediately, smiled and waved.

Harvey embraced me like he was my elder brother.

"Mukunda! It's good to be here, you know," he said, sounding very New York. "Thanks for coming to get me!"

"No problem," I said. "It's great to meet you."

"Hey, I gotta get my stuff," he said. "From the bus, you know, before it leaves." He scanned the remaining suitcases beside the bus and selected a small blue one. "OK. Got it." He smiled. "Let's go."

I'd arranged for Harvey to stay at the new apartment Dustin and Melody had just moved into on the corner of Haight and Lyon streets opposite Buena Vista Park. It was a big high-ceiling apartment one flight up in a building known as "the shooting gallery" because it was a pad mainly for junkies. The rent was dirt cheap, and even if the neighbors weren't the best, the apartment itself was clean and fresh.

I showed Harvey to his room in Dustin's apartment. He lay down on the mattress and sighed. Dustin came in, and we filled Harvey in on the current scene and how things were going with the temple and the rock concert. He was half-smiling and we talked on excitedly but soon realized he was asleep.

"Hey, you know that couple, the artists?" Dustin whispered as we slipped out.

"James and Charlotte. Yeah, what about them?"

"They're going to do the front sign. They've got some great ideas, and they're going to donate the wood and all the materials they'll need! They think they can get it done in just a couple of days."

True to their word, the artists had completed the sign before the end of December. It stood out over the big plate glass window, resplendent in large golden letters against a deep red background: "Radha Krishna Temple."

Harvey, meanwhile, finished the Mantra-Rock Dance poster within a week. Stimulated by the spirit of Haight-Ashbury, he produced a Stanley Mouse-inspired poster featuring the photograph of the swami we'd used on the handbill. Harvey positioned the swami in the top half of the poster with small pastel blue circles rippling out from his chest. The effect was hip, the swami looking like he was sitting on top of the world, but the overall effect was more conservative than the Mouse posters. The poster had a Madison Avenue look to it, but at the same time it was psychedelic. The information about the concert filled the bottom half of the poster. Admission would be two-fifty, we would only have door sales, all proceeds would go to the San Francisco Hare Krishna temple, and so on.

I checked out other posters and was proud of Harvey's. We put them up everywhere, especially around our new premises and around the Avalon. Everything was ready. Now all we needed was the crowd and the swami.

Mantra-Rock Dance poster

Krishna Consciousness Comes West

As the day of the swami's arrival neared, we hurried to organize a big reception for him. We wanted as many people as possible to be there, so we advertised his arrival on bulletin boards all over the Haight:

SWAMI BHAKTIVEDANTA
ARRIVES 2.30 PM, TUESDAY, JANUARY 17
UNITED AIRLINES FLIGHT 21
AT 1 PM, JANUARY 17
CAR CARAVAN FROM PANHANDLE TO AIRPORT
BRING MUSICAL INSTRUMENTS, BELLS,
CYMBALS, INCENSE & FLOWERS

We weren't sure how many people would come, but we were hopeful given the sheer numbers of people in Haight-Ashbury that month. Just three days before the swami arrived, thirty thousand people gathered in Golden Gate Park for the Human Be-In "gathering of the tribes" event, which was inspired by the new law banning the use of LSD. Posters everywhere advertised the free event, suggesting that people bring incense, candles, flags, animals, drums and flutes. Timothy Leary spoke in his first-ever San Francisco appearance and Gary Snyder and Richard Alpert (Ram Dass) turned up to speak. Allen Ginsberg also came to chant mantras, his presence bringing a Hindu *mela* effect to the whole event. There were numerous bands playing, including Santana, Jefferson Airplane and The Grateful Dead, and in the midst of the concert, Stanley Augustus Owsley II – the millionaire synthesizer of LSD – parachuted into the sea of people.

The day after the Human Be-In event, I was buying milk in the local store, so I looked briefly at the papers to see if Owsley had made the headlines, parachuting out of an airplane and all. There was a lot on the escalation of the Vietnam conflict and the continuing "hamlet pacification" program there, but nothing about Owsley and his audacious parachute jump. Not a word.

At 12:30 PM on the day of the swami's arrival, about twenty people turned up in the Panhandle – a thin strip of bushes, trees and lawn that sticks out east from Golden Gate Park between Fell and Oak streets. Most were dressed in full hippy regalia – men with long hair, multi-colored shirts and pants, and women with long Indian patterned skirts and lots of turquoise and silver colored costume jewelry. Everyone brought at least one flower on a long stem, mostly roses and carnations. We knew very few of those who turned up.

As soon as we had a small gathering assembled, we started chanting. It was a sunny day, and we were on the grass among tall trees in the open air. Chanting seemed the right thing to do with this group of complete strangers. Almost everyone was holding a burning incense stick; it was like the temple had been transported outside to the Panhandle. We started singing, accompanied by the strangers' finger cymbals and guitars, and then, after a while, we stood up and danced as we had at Dr. Mishra's with the swami, and as the swami's followers looked like they were doing in the newspaper article he'd sent to me. It was the first time I'd stood up and danced without the swami being present. At first I felt self-conscious, but I realized that I wanted to be more honest, more forthcoming about my convictions in Krishna consciousness, and this was a way to do it.

Gradually more people assembled. By 1:00 PM – the time scheduled for us to leave for the airport – fifty people were dancing and chanting with us. We piled into a motley assortment of cars and drove to the airport in a convoy.

The fifty of us squeezed into a tiny boarding area and sat on the floor at United Airlines Gate 22 to wait for the swami's plane to arrive from New York. We created quite a spectacle with our exotic colorful costumes, flowers, musical instruments and burning incense. Our chanting resounded down the hallways, and passengers and airport workers stopped to watch as we swayed back and forth to the rhythm of the chanting. Some seemed mildly amused, and many others appeared genuinely curious about what was going to happen.

Suddenly Allen Ginsberg appeared out of nowhere carrying a huge bouquet of yellow roses wrapped in green tissue paper. It had been impossible to miss the Human Be-In posters advertising the fact that he would be in Haight-Ashbury, so I knew he was in town, but I hadn't anticipated that he might come to the airport to greet the swami. People began talking excitedly to each other when he appeared. He was unmistakable with his bushy beard and horn-rimmed glasses, and everyone knew who he was. His presence added significance to the event, at least for those observing; for us the fact the swami was arriving made the day about as significant as it could get.

I greeted Ginsberg and offered him a chair. He sat down and chanted along with everyone else.

The United Airlines plane touched down, and the volume of our chanting rose with our anticipation. We all got to our feet and spontaneously formed an aisle. Passengers, mostly businessmen, began to disembark and were greeted with a lilting Indian melody sung by young, colorfully dressed people. They walked between the rows of chanters, some anxious, some smiling, all surprised.

"Welcome to San Francisco," I thought.

Then the swami was there, walking slowly toward us and beaming. With him was a teenage boy in a tie and business suit, an acquaintance made on the plane I assumed, to whom he talked animatedly. Janaki and I – the only initiated devotees in the crowd – bowed down when we caught sight of the swami, and the others followed suit, touching their foreheads to the terminal floor. The swami slowed down and smiled even more at this unusual greeting. Streams of passengers flowed past him as he slowed to an easy stroll, taking in the spectacle of the strangers who had come to greet him in this city he had never seen.

As the swami passed between the two rows of young chanters, each person offered him the flower they had brought with them.

*The swami, greeted by poet Allen Ginsberg (eyeglasses), upon arrival
at San Francisco Airport*

Soon his arms were overflowing with long-stemmed blooms, and
he began handing them back one-by-one to each person who had
come to greet him. Smiling and in no hurry, he made direct eye
contact with each person, and a feeling of familiarity enveloped the
gathering, despite the fact the swami was a stranger to them, and
they to him.

At the end of the aisle of people stood Allen Ginsberg, who
handed the swami his armful of yellow roses.

"Oh, you're here too!" exclaimed the swami, smiling broadly.
Ginsberg nodded and walked with the swami to the airport exit
with the greeting party which followed eight abreast. Dustin's collie, Ralph, ran around excitedly, trying to get the attention of his
master. As we headed for the parking lot, I realized we'd forgotten
something: what about the swami's luggage? I looked around for
someone to ask and found that the boy who got off the plane with
the swami was walking behind me.

"Hey," I said. "Did you meet the swami on the plane?"

He laughed. "No," he said. "I've been going to the New York

Ranchor accompanied the swami on the swami's first journey in an airplane.

temple for a while. My name's Ranchor. I thought I'd travel out here with the swami to check out the scene in California."

"Oh, OK, great, you might know then. Doesn't the swami have any luggage?"

"Uh-uh. He just brought that little suitcase he's carrying," Ranchor said. "I've got some stuff to pick up, but I was going to go back in and get it once the swami had left."

Relieved, I ran ahead to make sure that the swami's car was in the designated place. I didn't want anything to go wrong, plus I hoped that if I were there at the car I'd get to ride with the swami back to his new apartment. In the parking lot, as arranged, Harvey Corbett stood in a chauffer's uniform waiting beside a 1949 black Cadillac limousine he'd hired for the occasion.

When the swami reached the car I spontaneously embraced him. I was so happy – just overjoyed – to see him again. The swami didn't respond; he felt frozen and I felt like I'd done something wrong, but things were moving too fast for me to dwell on it at this point.

I opened the back door of the car for the swami and climbed in myself after him. Allen Ginsberg got in on the other side. As he was getting seated, the swami caught sight of Harvey.

"It's *you!*" he said, surprised. "When did you get here?"

"About two weeks ago," Harvey said. "Mukunda asked me to come down to help out with the artwork for the concert."

"What are you doing?" the swami asked.

"I'm painting in Mendocino."

"Where is that?"

"Just near San Francisco, about a hundred and twenty-five miles north."

"I see." The swami nodded.

"It was my first time in airplane," he said after some time.

"What did you think of it?" Ginsberg asked.

"Everything looked so small," the swami said. "The houses looked like match boxes. Just imagine how Krishna sees things." He returned to chanting on his beads and looked out the window attentively at the houses and hills.

"There was a blockade in my ears," he said.

"A blockage?" Ginsberg asked.

"Yes."

"San Francisco's architecture is very white," I said, trying to start a conversation. "Not like New York."

He nodded, and rode silently for the rest of the journey except for his barely audible chanting. As we approached Haight-Ashbury I asked him if he would like to look at the temple.

"Yes," he said. "I would like."

"Your apartment is very close, like in New York," I said. "Actually, it's in the same building."

When we arrived on Frederick Street, I opened the car door for him. He stood on the sidewalk and beamed when he saw the title above the window.

"Very nice," he said, turning to Harvey. "Did you do?"

"No, Swami, but I painted one of the paintings inside." The four of us entered the temple and Harvey pointed out the large painting of Krishna he had done after he'd finished the Mantra-Rock Dance poster.

The swami smiled as he looked around, taking in the altar, the rug, the musical instruments and the flowers scenting the room.

"Yes," he said. "Very nice."

"Your apartment is through the main entrance of the building," I said. I led him to the elevator and unlocked the door to his apartment. The rooms were sparsely furnished, but he seemed happy. He sat down on the edge of the bed we'd brought and placed his small suitcase beside the table we'd found in a thrift shop. Mrs. Dethridge's rocking chair sat in the corner of his main room, which was otherwise bare apart from another small table without a chair that we thought he could use as a desk.

"Now I will rest for some time," he said. "Thank you very much."

That afternoon, after the swami's short nap, reporters and photographers from the two major daily San Francisco newspapers, the *Chronicle* and the *Examiner*, came to interview and photograph him.

The next day the *Examiner* featured a photo of the swami sitting on the edge of his mattress using the small table in his room as his main desk. Above it was a picture of us at the airport. The journalist Harry Bergman called the swami "a lanky Master of the Faith" and quoted him as saying that his movement was about "the Science of God." He also referred to the swami's "square values."

I was excited when I saw the article and bought a copy to show the swami.

"Swami, there's an article in the newspaper about your arrival." I handed it to him and he read it carefully from top to bottom.

"What is the meaning of this word *lanky*?" he asked.

"Um, it means 'tall' or 'thin,'" I said.

"Why have they said this?"

"I really don't know," I answered. "Maybe he saw you sitting so upright at your desk that he thought you were very tall. He didn't see you standing."

That evening the swami held his first program in the San Francisco temple. It was filled to capacity with lots of young hippies and a handful of people in their thirties. The swami led the chanting for half an hour, followed by a short lecture and another chanting session, just like in New York. At the end of the program he took a single apple and cut it into thin slices, put them on a plate and gave the plate to Janaki, who passed it around to each guest.

The evening programs were immediately instituted on Mondays, Wednesdays and Fridays, just as we'd hoped, and there were programs every morning, regardless of the day of the week. About a week before the Mantra-Rock Dance, the swami officiated as Dustin and Melody were initiated and married. Their new names were Shyamasundar Das Adhikari and Malati Devi Dasi. A few weeks after the Mantra-Rock Dance, at another ceremony, the swami married and initiated Jim and Joan, giving them the names Gurudas and Yamuna Devi Dasi.

The swami presides over a fire sacrifice in the San Francisco temple, February, 1967.

Mantra-Rock Dance

Our publicity worked. At 7:45 on show night the Avalon was filled to capacity.

I was at the top of the staircase above the front door taking tickets for the first hour. From the top of the long red carpeted stairway that led up to the hall from the entrance, I could see the line of colorful late arrivals waiting to get in to the Avalon. We'd stuck with our "first-come-first-served" policy in selling tickets, so late-comers were out of luck. Specially deputed agents of the San Francisco Fire Department stood outside at the hall's main entrance, monitoring the number of people inside. When someone came out, they'd let someone in, although that wasn't happening much, because those inside really wanted to hold onto their places.

Chet poked his head out of his office door and yelled to me.

"Looks like a sell-out," he said. "You don't usually get the place full before the show starts. And this is a Sunday!"

"Yeah, it's great," I said, feeling excited. "Thanks for letting us do this here." As I scanned the crowd, I spotted Timothy Leary and Augustus Owsley heading up the stairs toward me. As I took their tickets, I was surprised to note the strong smell of alcohol wafting around Leary.

"That's weird," I thought. "Leary's so anti-establishment, but getting drunk is the 'establishment' way of getting high. Shouldn't he of all people be high on LSD?" I took the ticket from him, and he proceeded to a nearby phone booth where he sat talking on the phone for the rest of my ticket shift.

Finally, at 9:00 PM, Malati came to relieve me of my ticket duties so I could get back to managing the show. Inside the ballroom devotees were handing out thousands of orange wedges to the crowd. I pushed my way through the crush and up the stairs to the balcony to check on how Ben and Roger were doing with their light show.

"Hey, how's it going?" I asked.

"Yeah, great, man. We're all ready to go here," Roger said. "Hey, we just brewed some tea – really nice stuff. You want some?"

"Nope, it's OK," I said. "I'd better get back out there."

"Hey, no, come on," Ben said. "Have some. It'll relax you. You look like you need it."

I hesitated. "Well, OK, just a small cup." Roger grabbed a little Japanese-style cup without a handle and poured me some of the liquid from a blue ceramic teapot. I took a couple of sips to be polite. It had a bitter undertone.

"Thanks a lot. I've really got to get going." They waved to me, smiling, and as I headed down the stairs to the dance floor, I realized that the tea had been spiked with acid. "No wonder it tasted bitter," I thought, my head spinning.

It was time to start the show, so in my mildly altered state I did my best to round up the devotees for the opening act – a sort of overture – an Indian-style chant that we hoped would set a mystical, spiritual atmosphere for the evening. We'd managed to get exotic clothing to wear on stage – Merlin gowns for the men and saris for the women – and when we came on the stage, the crowd began to cheer. We sat on brightly colored cushions in front of microphones and began to sing a mellow Krishna mantra with *tamboura*, harmonium, hand cymbals and drums.

As we sang, I looked out into the crowd. Everyone appeared to be high on something – mostly pot and acid, I thought. Many people had brought their own cushions – tasseled, jeweled, patchworked and embroidered – and they sat on these during our chanting, closing their eyes or joining in with their own wooden flutes or bells. Some stayed standing and swayed in time to the music. A few cried, whether because they were moved by the chanting or simply high I couldn't tell. What I hoped was that the swami's chanting and presence would – in the jargon of the Haight – "lift everyone to a higher level of consciousness," not through drugs but through genuine spiritual experience.

After our serene opening, Moby Grape took the stage and the crowd went wild. Malati was right – they were fantastic. The ballroom shook with their amplification, and the crowd gyrated in time with Ben and Roger's strobe lights and their multi-colored oil shapes projected onto the walls. The colors bounced, cascaded, broke into beads, morphed together and separated, jumping to the beat. The music was deafening, the light show mesmerizing.

Things seemed to be going fine, so I headed backstage to the readying room, where Big Brother was tuning up for their performance. With a can of Jim Beam in her hand, Janis Joplin turned away from her mirror as I entered the room.

"Hey, you're one of the Krishnas, right?" she asked. I nodded. "Why do you feel you have to chant that mantra?" She sounded challenging, if not a bit hostile.

"Because it makes you feel good," I said moving quickly out of the room. I didn't want to get into *that* discussion now. I'd seen her three days earlier walking two large Dobermans down Haight Street holding a half-finished pint of Smirnoff.

When Moby Grape finished playing their hour-long set, fifteen of us stepped onto the stage in preparation for the swami's appearance. Allen Ginsberg came into the hall and joined us on stage to the accompaniment of loud applause. Finally the swami entered the Avalon through the main door, followed by Ranchor and another New York devotee named Kirtanananda, whom I'd met briefly before we'd come to California. The stage was about five feet above the dance floor, so I had a good view of the swami as he made his way across the length of the ballroom toward the stage, walking slowly with his wooden cane. The crowd grew quiet as he walked and parted to allow him to pass through. The hush was broken by a few isolated cheers and some scattered applause. It was a bit like the greeting the swami got at San Francisco Airport, only this was bigger – much bigger.

When the swami reached the stage, he stopped for a moment and glanced around; then he saw a small stairway to his right, which he climbed slowly as if he were deep in thought. Ginsberg greeted him with folded palms when he reached the top.

"Welcome, Swami," he said. "Let's sit." He gestured toward two large fluffy yellow throw cushions at the front of the stage. They made a funny pair, Ginsberg with his bushy beard and slightly rumpled brown suit with a white T-shirt underneath, and the swami with his clean-shaven head looking regal in his soft saffron robes as he sat cross-legged, his cane resting across his lap. The hall was quiet except for a few muffled voices and the sounds of some people I didn't know in khakis who were rushing around the stage positioning microphones in front of Ginsberg and the swami.

The hall darkened and the crowd sat down. I started playing the droning *tamboura* just as color slides of Krishna began appearing on the walls. Up on the mezzanine, Ben and Roger projected the sixteen-word Hare Krishna mantra on the wall behind the stage and focused spotlights onto Ginsberg and the swami. Ginsberg said something into the swami's ear, and the swami nodded. Ginsberg moved closer to the microphone.

"When I was in India," he said, "I got enthralled with the mantra we're going to sing. I'd like you to sing loud with me. It's meditation that's musical. It'll take you into another dimension, like it does for me every time.

He paused and squinted through the spotlight.

"The mantra is called the *maha-mantra*. In Sanskrit, the word *maha* means 'large' or 'great,' and *man* means 'mind.' *Tra* means 'that which delivers.' So the word mantra literally means 'mind deliverance.'

"Sometimes you can have a bad acid trip, and I want you to know that if you ever do, you can stabilize yourself on re-entry by chanting this mantra." He looked earnest and serious, like he was discussing literature with a group of poets at a university.

"Now," Ginsberg continued, "I want to introduce you to Swami Bhaktivedanta, who brought this mantra to the place where it was probably most needed, to New York's Lower East Side – to the dispossessed, to the homeless, the lost, the anarchists, the seekers."

The crowd applauded and cheered.

"He left India, where life is peaceful, where he could have remained happily chanting in a holy village where people never heard of war and violence, where life is slow and meaningful. But instead, he's here with us tonight, his first time in this city, his first time in America, and he's come to share with us something precious, something to treasure, something serene."

Ginsberg gestured to the swami to speak. The swami's countenance was bright as he responded to the invitation. He spoke slowly, and his ageing voice exuded confidence.

"Thank you for inviting me to your beautiful city of San Francisco to speak here," he said. "This chant comes from India. It will lead us to the spiritual world. You may begin tonight or any time. The mantra is not only for Indians. Hare Krishna chanting is for all people, because Krishna is everyone's father. We should not think that Krishna is Hindu god or is for the Indians and not others. He is for everyone." I was excited to hear him as he looked admirably around at the rapt audience. "If He were not, how could He be God? God cannot be God simply for a particular type of man or for a particular section of society.

"God is God for all human beings, beasts, aquatics, insects, trees, plants – all varieties. That is God. The words of this chanting are *Hare Krishna Hare Krishna Krishna Krishna Hare Hare, Hare Rama Hare Rama Rama Rama Hare Hare.*" Ben or Roger bounced the words on the wall behind the swami. "These words are a transcendental sound incarnation of the Absolute Truth. Incarnation means … the Sanskrit word is *avatar,* and that is translated into English as 'incarnation.' The root meaning of *avatar* is 'which descends or comes from the transcendental sky,' the spiritual sky to the material sky. Or His bona fide representative comes from that sky to this material plane. That is called avatar."

A female voice at the other end of ballroom yelled, "Yeah!" Another voice somewhere in the hall yelled out, "I'm God!"

The swami continued unfazed. "So this sound is the sound representation of the Supreme Lord. Material or spiritual, whatever we have got experience, nothing is separated from the Supreme Absolute Truth. Nothing is separated. Everything has emanated from the Absolute Truth. Just like earth. Earth, then from earth, you have got wood, fuel. From fuel, when you get fire, first of all there is smoke. Then, after smoke, there is fire.

"Similarly, there is a link. The whole material cosmic situation, manifestation, what we see, it is just like the smoke. The fire is behind it. That is spiritual sky. But still, in the smoke, you can feel some heat also.

"So similarly, this sound vibration of the spiritual world is here, so that even in this material world, where there is a scarcity of that spiritual fire, we can appreciate, we can feel the warmth of that fire.

"So I wish to thank Mr. Jinsberg and all of you for participating. Now Mr. Jinsberg will chant. Thank you very much."

The audience burst into applause that lasted nearly a minute. Some people stood up and a few whistled and many banged the floor with their hands. A trumpet sounded from the back of the room.

"Thank you, Swami," Ginsberg said. "So I'm going to chant the mantra. These are the words," he said, glancing behind him. "They're on the wall behind me for you to follow. I'll chant the whole thing once and then you repeat it. I'm going to sing a melody I learned when I was in Rishikesh in the Himalayas." He paused. "Everyone sing loud! And dance if you feel like too!"

Ginsberg began to sing, and all the devotees on the stage sang the repeat of the mantra. Everyone began playing their instruments after the first few mantras, except for me; I had to quickly re-tune the *tamboura* to be in tune with Ginsberg. Fortunately, he stayed in the same key throughout his chant.

The audience caught on quickly. Encouraged by the fact that the mantra was being sung by one of their icons, the crowd responded enthusiastically. Everyone sang along, and most people stood up and began to sway with the beat. As the tempo began to pick up, Ben and Roger made sure the oil pulsations were in time with the beat. The chanting reached a fast tempo quickly; Ginsberg and the few devotees who were keeping time with the instruments had to start everything over again. The audience still stood, waiting.

This time Ginsberg started the chanting slowly and kept the tempo constant. The audience's response singing was a roar that echoed through the ballroom.

Suddenly and unexpectedly, the swami stood up from his cushion and raised his arms, gesturing for everyone to do the same. All the devotees on the stage exchanged surprised looks. Janaki and I had seen the swami dance once before at Dr. Mishra's *ashram* in upstate New York, but no one else had seen him do this before. And none of us had expected it tonight.

The few still sitting now stood up, and the whole audience danced as one body in one giant motion: left foot over right, right foot over left, left over right, just like the swami was doing. Thousands of arms waved like willows in a grove, fluid, silky and hypnotic. It was rhythmic, yet languid and ballet-like. Everyone, including the snack sellers and bouncers, were swaying back and forth and singing. Only a few stood motionless at the periphery of the ballroom, excluded from the dancing probably because they were too high to take part. Their mouths hung open as they stared at the spectacle and drooled.

Ginsberg removed his microphone from its stand and unwound the cord so that he could hand it to the swami. For a few minutes the swami led the chanting. As he did so, musicians from the bands joined us on the stage with their instruments. Don Stevenson from Moby Grape sat down behind his set of drums, which was still on stage from their set, Phil Lesh and Pig Pen from The Grateful Dead plugged their guitars into amplifiers, and Peter Albin and Sam Andrew from Big Brother started plucking the strings of their guitars. They all began by caressing their instruments as only musicians do, testing the sound levels cautiously, tuning the strings and adjusting the tones and levels, experimenting as to how they could best accompany and augment the chanting.

As they began to play, the devotees gave up trying to keep the tempo and decibel level of the chanting constant. Even though the musicians played their instruments so as to augment the chanting rather than dominate it, this chanting session was taking on a life of its own, and the few devotees could no longer control it. It had turned into a spiritual jam session, and the audience screamed their approval as the celebrity musicians took their places behind the swami and the devotees. The stage was now packed with people: janitors, roadies, stage managers, security guards, firemen. Most of the audience danced serenely, but there were unusual spectacles as well from those who had taken too much acid. Some lay on the floor and squirmed like wounded snakes, while others shook, pranced, spun, shrieked, laughed and cried.

Briefly, the swami's voice singing could be heard above the instruments, but mostly the other sounds eclipsed his voice. He gave the microphone back to the now red-faced Ginsberg, who continued to chant energetically. Beads of perspiration appeared on the swami's face. His arms were upraised, and he moved left and right placing one leg in front of the other.

The oils were pulsing madly, faster and faster. The bright little circles of light danced across every surface in the ballroom – the ceiling, the floor, the walls and the bodies of the dancers. Incense billowed cumulus clouds of fragrant smoke from dozens of ceramic pots around the room.

I glanced back at all the musicians on the stage and caught sight of an angry face among them. It was Kirtanananda, who was standing at the back of the stage screaming something I couldn't make out.

"What?" I shouted. I had stopped playing my *tamboura* and was now playing large Indian cymbals, which were loud enough to be heard above the sound of the other instruments. I looked down; my fingers were bleeding.

I looked back at Kirtanananda, trying to lip-read what he was saying to me. "Stop!" He was pointing at the swami who was lost in the chanting, his face wet with sweat. I glanced back at Kirtanananda. "He's an old man!" he shouted to me, his face scarlet. "You've got to stop the chanting!"

"Maybe the physical exertion wouldn't be good for the swami," I thought. "After all, he is seventy-one years old." Even though I wasn't convinced, I felt like I had to defer to Kirtanananda. He was a confidant of the swami, plus his panic alarmed me. Maybe he knew something about the swami's health that I didn't.

I tried to gesture to the musicians on the stage that it was time to wrap things up. I made eye contact with Don Stevenson, Moby Grape's drummer, and drew one of my large cymbals across my throat, indicating "cut" in musician language. He shook his head; he and the other musicians were clearly having a great time. I tried to increase the tempo by playing my large cymbals as loudly as I could with the plan of stopping the chanting when it got too fast to keep up with. This worked, but the chanting started again as soon as it had stopped. I increased the tempo again, and finally, when the chanting stopped for the second time, I raised my arms into the air holding the still-ringing cymbals, and then quickly bowed down on the stage floor. All the other devotees did the same. Finally the musicians stopped.

The swami's deep voice echoed through the hall as he spoke a long Sanskrit invocation that sounded like a blessing or a prayer. When I stood up at the end of his prayer, I saw the disappointed and disgusted looks on the faces of the musicians. I was unsure that I'd done the right thing in bringing the chanting to an early close.

The swami walked down the small staircase to the left of the stage with Kirtanananda and Ranchor in tow. Once again the audience parted to make an aisle-way through which he could pass. A few clapped, but most of the ballroom was hushed as the swami strolled through the crowd, the mirrored ball still beaming bright disks of light across the walls, and squeaking slightly now as it rotated. Ranchor opened the door for the swami, and the three of them walked out into the night.

Big Brother and the Holding Company took the stage. Their first number was Janis Joplin singing "House of the Rising Sun."

About half an hour after the swami left, I saw Ranchor back on the dance floor grooving to Big Brother. He was dancing enthusiastically with a teenage girl about his age with long blonde hair and a tie-dyed sequined miniskirt.

The Dance continued late into the night. Janis Joplin's performance had the crowd rocking, and afterward The Grateful Dead got the crowd even more excited.

The next day, Ranchor announced to a very disappointed-looking Swami that he would be heading back to New York the next day.

"What will you do there?" the swami asked Ranchor.

"Get a job, I guess. This San Francisco scene is kind of fun, but it isn't really right for me. I've seen what's going on out here, and I think I just want to do my own thing now, you know?"

"What about your Krishna consciousness?" the swami asked.

"I can take that wherever I go, can't I?" It was a rhetorical question that really didn't require an answer.

"Where you will stay?" the swami asked.

"I don't know yet, but it won't be a problem. I know lots of people in New York."

"When you will leave?"

"In a couple of days. I met a girl here – Michelle - and I want to see how things work out with her, see if she'll come to New York with me."

To me, the swami looked sad as he spoke to Ranchor, like a father who was losing a son.

A few weeks later, Moby Grape performed with The Doors at the Avalon and in the "First Love Circus" at the Winterland Arena. They were Moby Grape's first major professional gigs, and soon after this Columbia Records signed them up. Although her method was unorthodox, Malati had played a significant role in getting the unknown band their breakthrough in the music industry.

CHAPTER 16

Music Lessons

The week after the Mantra-Rock Dance I was hanging out at the Stanyan Street donut shop. I licked the chocolate icing off my fingers and scanned the newspaper headlines through the newspaper rack on the corner. "Rod Steiger Wins Top Oscar," the headline said. "So what," I thought. A multi-colored 1967 Ford convertible full of creatively dressed hippies cruised past, and I realized with a jolt how far I was from mainstream America – not in miles but in consciousness.

A delivery truck pulled up next to me as I popped the last bit of the sugary twisted donut into my mouth. "Hey buddy," the delivery guy said. "Do you know where the Hare Krishna temple is?"

"Just over there," I said pointing across the street.

"Thanks."

I watched him double park and unload a large wooden box. A guy named Murari, one of the new recently initiated San Francisco devotees, came outside to sign for the delivery, and I ran across the street, my interest piqued. The first thing I noticed was the Hindi writing on the sides of the box; other markings on the box indicated it had traveled from New York by train via Union Pacific.

"What is it?" Murari asked.

"I don't know," I said. "But I hope it's what I think it is! Let's get something to open this!"

Several devotees gathered around me on the sidewalk outside the temple while I pried open the top with a claw hammer. Inside, nestled in a bed of well-packed-in Indian newspapers, was the drum we'd been waiting for ever since the New York devotees had called us to tell us it had arrived in the States from India. It was the real thing at last!

Murari and I lifted the box inside the temple and unpacked the drum properly. It was cylindrical, sloping to a bulge near the middle, about three feet long, its beautiful, red-brown exterior covered with small reddish straps pulled tight around its circumference. One end was a lot larger than the other. The swami had told me that the drum was called *mrdanga* and that it was the forerunner of the *tabla*.

"If you cut a *mrdanga* in the middle," he had said, "and place each end upright, you have *tabla*." Now, as I saw my first real *mrdanga* before me, I saw that he was right.

I tried banging the leather heads a few times. They resounded loudly, the small end high and sharp, the large end rich and deep.

"Let's tell the swami it's here," Janaki suggested. "He should play it first."

Janaki and I went next door to 512 and took the elevator up to his fourth-floor apartment. We knocked.

"Yes?" he called through the door. "Come."

"Swami, the *mrdanga* has arrived," Janaki blurted out excitedly.

His eyes opened wide. "It is here?"

"Yes, in the temple. We unpacked it."

"I will come. One minute."

We took the elevator down so that we'd be back at the temple before he arrived, but as we were opening the old elevator's concertina door, we saw the swami already at the bottom of the stairs heading out to the temple.

"He really wants to see that *mrdanga*," I observed. Janaki nodded.

"Come on! Hurry up," she urged.

We followed him out into the sunny street and into the temple. I picked up the *mrdanga* and handed it to him. He smiled broadly and sat down on the ledge that ran along the large front windows.

The swami plays the first ISKCON mrdanga *in San Francisco, 1967.* Inset: *the "small" head of a* mrdanga

As he felt the drum all over, my mind flicked back to the way the musicians at the Mantra-Rock Dance had fondled their instruments – like a precious loved one, a priceless treasure, or the way a parent might hold their child.

Placing the drum in his lap, the swami played a few beats, delicately tapping the small end with the fingers on his right hand and striking the large end with his left palm. Then without saying a word he tore off a yard-long portion of his cotton *dhoti,* the lower single-cloth garment he wore around his waist. It was a substantial part of his *dhoti,* but not enough to expose his legs. This piece of cloth he wrapped tightly around the *mrdanga* so that the pointed ends of the cloth met in a hard knot over the bulge of the drum.

"This must never come off," he said. "Necessary to protect *mrdanga.* This drum is called *khole* in Bengali. It is made from earth. It will break very easy. Never remove this cloth."

We all nodded.

"This instrument I have played all my life," he said. "When I was a child my father insisted that I learn *mrdanga* from early age. He would have let me play all day, every day. Except for my mother, I would have missed school altogether."

He paused, striking the drum heads again and again.

"Bring water," he said.

"How much?" Janaki asked.

"Little."

Janaki went to the temple kitchen and came back with a Styrofoam cup half filled with water.

"That's sufficient," he said, reaching for the cup.

Holding it with his left hand, he dipped the ring finger of his right hand into the water.

"I will show you how to take care of this *mrdanga,*" he said, never lifting his eyes from the drum. He turned the *mrdanga* so that the large end was facing upward and was level with his chest. With the deftness of a life-long drummer, he ran his wet finger around the edge of the drumhead, dampening its small cream-colored margin.

"This you must do regularly," he said. "With little water like I am showing." He didn't explain why, but I assumed it was a maintenance technique to keep the application from eroding or cracking at its outer edges. Later, through following the swami's watering instructions, I also discovered that regular dampening helped to keep the heads taut.

The swami continued to test the sound of the drumheads, striking each end tentatively a few times while listening closely, his head cocked.

"Very good," he said after some time, and headed back up to his apartment. After a few minutes, I followed him. I found him writing at his makeshift desk.

"Swami, would you teach me to play the *mrdanga*?"

He looked up from his work.

"Yes," he said. "When you want?

"Today?"

"Get it," he said. "Just bring it. I'll show you."

I ran down the stairs to the temple and carefully carried it to the elevator, not wanting to risk dropping it in the stairway. The afternoon sun bathed the swami's main room with golden light. He was waiting for me in his rocking chair, chanting on his beads.

"You sit here," he said, indicating the new rug on his floor. Janaki had found it on special at a bargain store in town and had bought a couple so the swami's rooms wouldn't be so bare. The drum sat in my lap. The swami put down his beads and sat opposite me cross-legged, close enough so that he could hit the drum too.

"Every sound, every beat on *mrdanga* has a mantra. Always you must say the words of the mantra. The sound of the drum should sound like the words."

"How can a drum sound like words?" I asked.

"Watch. You must strike the drum with a different portion of your hand for each beat. There is a special place on drum for each beat. Watch."

He hit the drum heads and spoke these sounds: "Kee-ta-ta, kee-ta-ta, kee-ta-ta, kee – ta." The small end he struck with his second finger, and his third, fourth and fifth fingers were locked together. The large end he hit with his four fingers held flat.

"You hear the sounds?" he asked me.

"I think so," I said. Did I, or was I just imagining it?

"Listen again. Watch. First, kee-ta-ta, kee-ta-ta, kee-ta-ta, kee – ta. Then, ghee-ta-ta, ghee-ta-ta, ghee-ta-ta, ghee – ta. You see?"

I nodded.

"Good. Now again." He repeated the two beats again and again. "Now you do," he said at last.

I tried to hit the drum and say the mantra, but it was hard to do it at the same time.

"You must strike in correct place," he said. "Otherwise 'kee' and 'ghee' are not sounding different."

I tried again. I glanced up to see his expression and lost my place.

"Concentrate," he said. "Do not speed up. Slow. Slow."

I played again, trying to make the sounds from my hands sound the same as the ones I was making with my mouth.

"Always say words," he said. "They must sound like drum. Rythm is the universal language." He stood up.

"Is that the end of the lesson?" I asked.

"No, you must keep playing," he said.

I closed my eyes and focused all my attention on playing correctly without speeding up. "Kee-ta-ta, kee-ta-ta, kee-ta-ta, kee – ta; ghee-ta-ta, ghee-ta-ta, ghee-ta-ta, ghee – ta," I murmured as my hands hit the drum. Like a clock, I thought. No hurry. Like waves lapping the shore, timeless, constant, steady, no speeding up. I lost track of time, felt like I was lost in the sound, became oblivious to all other external sounds except for the drum beat. I was doing it right, I was sure I was!

"Where is the swami?" I suddenly wondered. I kept playing, but my mind drifted away from the *mrdanga* beat and back to him. Had he gone back to his translating or letter writing or chanting? I dragged my mind back to what I was doing. I had to keep it up or at least maintain a modicum of concentration: "Kee-ta-ta, kee-ta-ta, kee-ta-ta, kee – ta; ghee-ta-ta, ghee-ta-ta, ghee-ta-ta, ghee – ta."

Curiosity overtook me. I kept playing slowly and steadily, but I opened my eyes a thin slit for an instant and closed them immediately again. His feet were still right next to me. I opened my eyes and looked up. His eyes were closed, his brows knitted with deep concentration, but there was an unmistakable hint of a smile and he was wobbling his head slowly back and forth in time with the beat. He didn't notice that I was looking up. I closed my eyes and kept playing.

"The swami is more than just a teacher," I thought as I played. "He is genuinely happy to be teaching me, giving his knowledge to me, even though I'm such a novice at this instrument he's been playing all his life." I was so taken by the fact he was still standing there listening, that in my heart I became determined to perfect that one beat. "If I can master this beat," I thought, "I can eventually learn more. And if I can become like the swami in his drum playing, maybe I can become more like him in other ways too. If I could learn to play even a little, maybe I could inspire people to chant the way he inspired me."

I went back down to the temple elated that I'd managed to play the simple beat well enough to satisfy the swami. I carried the *mrdanga* carefully, but almost dropped it as I set it down on the temple floor.

"Be careful!" Murari said, looking up from the book he was reading in the corner of the room.

"Yeah, god, I'd feel so terrible if I broke it," I said.

"It's really not safe for it to be just sitting around in here," Murari said. "Anyone could knock it over."

We decided then and there that the *mrdanga* needed a box of some sort so that it would be protected. It had come so far to be in our temple, and I knew how much it would enhance our chanting, so we didn't want a tiny jolt to crack the delicate heads. Murari volunteered to construct a wooden box.

The following day he unveiled his creation. It had six panels made of sanded wood stained mahogany red-brown and covered with several coats of shellac and finished with a clear varnish. Every inside surface was lined with thick sponge rubber so that the *mrdanga* would be protected if the box ever fell over or was dropped. The top of the box had a brass handle, and it swung open on two shiny brass hinges. The box also had a metal fastener so that we could keep it locked. The whole structure resembled, I thought, a nineteenth-century coffin for a dwarf.

"I can't believe you built it in a day!" Janaki said.

"Yeah," Murari said modestly. "Well, I didn't want the drum to get broken."

"How did you to get the varnish and all that stuff to dry?"

"I rigged up photo lamps so that each coat of polish dried under the extra heat."

"Wow!"

Murari smiled. "Anyway, I made some keys for the lock," he said handing two to me. "One for the swami, one for you, and I'll keep one just in case."

I picked up the *mrdanga* box and carried it around the temple to try it out. I felt like one of the Haight-Ashbury musician who carried their guitars around, or like a Mafioso who, it was rumored, carried their machine guns in violin cases.

The next day, the regulars at the morning program waited in eager anticipation to hear the swami's drum playing. Murari carefully lifted the drum out of its box and passed it to him. The swami handled it carefully, gently trying out a few beats and listening intently like a father listening to his baby's first words.

Then the swami began to play in earnest; the rhythm was slow, the deeper notes blending with his deep voice. How could drumming sound sweet? The drum *did* add another dimension to the chanting as the swami carefully controlled the pace.

Its distinctive sound had a special effect for me, because the night before I'd done some reading about how such drums were used in kirtans in the past. I'd read about how important *mrdangas* were in the sixteenth century in India, when Lord Chaitanya Mahaprabhu was present. Many of his followers were known for their singing, dancing and playing of Indian instruments. During those days, singers sang melodies that were appropriate to particular times of the day. Each twenty-four hour period was divided into six four-hour segments, each of which was associated with a particular *raga*, or melody. And the drummers knew hundreds of different beats. Even the dancing followed defined conventions, although all of the regulations allowed for many varieties and embellishments within fixed patterns.

As I listened to the swami play, I imagined Lord Chaitanya's kirtans, and for the first time I felt I glimpsed what congregational chanting was all about, what it had been in the past and how it was supposed to be in the present.

I practiced and practiced my *mrdanga* beats until I could play them with other instruments in the temple kirtans. It took a lot of effort because my musical expertise lay in piano rather than percussion. We didn't have a piano at the temple, but we did acquire an old harmonium – a small hand-pumped organ with a keyboard that you played sitting on the floor. Someone had found it at an import store and donated it to the temple thinking that it would add a nice sound to the chanting. I often fiddled around with the harmonium, picking out some old jazz melodies and singing Hare Krishna to the tunes. I disengaged two of the metal levers inside the harmonium so that two keys would stay down, producing a drone effect that we used to start singing our mantras. One afternoon in February Murari interrupted my playing.

"The swami told me he knows how to play the harmonium," he said.

"Really?" I asked. "I've never heard him play. What did it sound like?"

"I haven't heard him play," Murari answered. "But he told me that they use harmoniums lots in India. And he said he's been playing for years."

I clipped the harmonium bellows shut. "I'm going to ask him about it," I said. "Maybe he'll teach me some Indian melodies. It'll be easier for me than the *mrdanga*."

"I don't think he's there now," Murari said.

I headed out the temple door just as a yellow taxi pulled up at the curb. The driver looked super straight – short hair, old-fashioned slacks and a plain cream-colored T-shirt. He bounded over to me.

"Hare Krishna," he said, putting out his hand. "My name's Jim."

"How you doin', man?" I asked surprised someone that looked so conservative would greet me like this.

"Hey, you got any more of those *Back to Godhead* magazines?" he asked. "My riders read them and I ran out."

"I think there's some inside."

When I got back with a stack of ten, he was back in the driver's seat with the engine idling.

"I gotta pick up a fare at the airport," he said. He reached out with both hands for the small pile. "Thanks a lot."

A little bit annoyed at being detained from seeing the swami, I bounded upstairs and knocked on the door.

"Come," the swami called out. He *was* there after all!

"Murari said you know how to play harmonium. Could you teach me some melodies?"

"Yes. Bring. I will show."

"When?"

"When you want?"

"Now?"

"Just bring."

I went down to the temple to get the instrument. It was an awkward shape to carry – a bulky rectangular box with small brass handles on the side that cut into my hands as I headed upstairs. We sat down in the same place on the rug in the middle of the room, the swami in front of the keyboard and me at his left side.

"So I will teach 'Govinda jaya jaya.' You know it?"

I shook my head.

"The words?"

"No. I don't think I've ever heard it."

"Listen. First I will teach words and melody. Then I will teach on harmonium."

He sang, "Govinda jaya jaya, Gopala jaya jaya, Radha-Ramana Hari, Govinda jaya jaya." The melody had a happy-sad sound and I could hear that it was in a minor key. He paused. "Now you sing." I tried, but didn't get it quite right.

"So, this song glorifies Krishna," he said. "Govinda, Gopala and Radha-Ramana are names of Krishna. Now watch. I will play the melody. It is in bhairavi raga. This raga is sung early in the morning."

He played the melody and sang at the same time. I thought that bhairavi raga was roughly equivalent to B-flat minor in Western notation. He sang the original melody a few times through and then slightly altered the chant: "Govinda jaya jaya, Gopala jaya jaya, Govinda jaya jaya, Gopala jaya jaya."

He stopped. "Now," he said, "you play harmonium and I will sing the melody." He slid the harmonium to me. I groped the keys, picking out a little bit of the melody, but I couldn't play it the whole way through.

The swami pulled the harmonium back. "Watch," he said. He played the melody again several times and slid it back to me. This time I got most of the melody, but it was still haltingly played, my jerky ramblings breaking the swami's attempts to sing along with my playing.

"We will play together," he said. He slid the harmonium over so that it was now between us. "You can watch me and play what I play." I pumped the harmonium and played the melody on the low notes while the swami played on the high notes. My eyes were glued to the keyboard. He sang the mantra over and over again, and his playing helped me to keep up. Whenever I got lost I watched his fingers on the higher register and mimicked their movement on the lower keys.

I had played the melody through on my own several times. "Enough for now."

I didn't want to forget how to play the mantra, so I went straight down to the temple to keep practicing on my own.

Murari was still in the temple talking to two teenage guys I hadn't met before. "Was the swami there?" he asked.

"He taught me a new mantra," I said. "I'll show you."

A woman plays a harmonium in Alachua, Florida.
Inset: a harmonium in a Hare Krishna temple

I sat down in front of the harmonium and played: "*Govinda jaya jaya, Gopala jaya jaya, Radha-Ramana Hari, Govinda jaya jaya.*" At first, I just sang it over and over again, not expecting anyone to respond. But soon the other three spontaneously started singing too: "*Govinda jaya jaya, Gopala jaya jaya, Radha-Ramana Hari, Govinda jaya jaya.*" We chanted the new mantra for two hours.

Three days later, Jim the taxi driver reappeared at the temple door. I saw him peering through the glass door, his right hand in his beige corduroy pants pocket with the thumb sticking out.

I opened the door. "Hey Jim, you want more magazines?" I asked.

"Well, actually, you know I was wondering what you guys do in here," he said, running his hand nervously through his crew-cut brown hair.

"Well, we chant a lot," I said. "And we have evening programs three days a week when the swami's here. Hey, he's here now. Why don't you go up and meet him?"

Jayananda chanting in Golden Gate Park in San Francisco

"You mean Bhaktivedanta Swami?" he asked. "I've read the stuff he wrote in the magazines. Can I go and meet him just like that? I mean, just walk in?"

"Sure. He doesn't mind. How old are you anyway?"

"Twenty-eight," he answered.

"Wow!" I said without thinking. "That makes you about the oldest person I ever met who was into Krishna consciousness!" The words sounded a bit coarse as they left my mouth, but he didn't seem to mind. "Look, the swami's apartment is right upstairs. I'll show you where it is and you can go and talk to him."

"OK," he said.

A week later, Jim moved into the temple and was initiated. The swami gave him the name Jayananda Das. He kept driving his taxi, and his salary became one of the temple's main sources of income. Soon he offered to be the temple president and took responsibility not only for earning money but also for the temple's daily maintenance and the welfare of the many devotees living there.

CHAPTER 17

Life with the Swami in New Jagannatha Puri

Although we knew the swami wouldn't stay in San Francisco forever, we hoped that he wouldn't go back to New York too soon, and when he did, we hoped that he'd split his time evenly between New York and San Francisco. As the weeks rolled by, our life with the swami in San Francisco began to acquire its own rhythm and schedule. We saw him each day at the morning programs, which would begin at six o'clock. We would all chant on our beads, chant as a group with instruments and hear him lecture, often from his translations of *The Bhagavad-gita As It Is* and his *Srimad-Bhagavatam*. His evening programs were also growing in popularity to the point that it was sometimes hard to get a seat in the room. More and more young people were beginning to take seriously the things he was saying. I could tell by the increased numbers at the morning programs. When the swami first arrived, there had been just the six of us, plus a handful of others, but now there was a regular congregation that faithfully appeared every morning.

Much of the new interest stemmed from the free daily lunches we began serving. This addition to our schedule was the swami's idea.

"There are so many here," he said. "Why not feed them? You cook simple preparations offered to Krishna and distribute. Everyone will take."

Dishes to be served out in the San Francisco temple in 1967

The swami was right about that. Soon we were serving two hundred people lunch seven days a week. Many were in pretty bad shape from taking too many drugs; sometimes the temple food would be the first square meal they had eaten in several days. Malati took it upon herself to form relationships with the local shopkeepers, especially in the fruit and vegetable stores, many of whom generously donated to what they saw as a charitable outreach to those in need. Malati would turn up each afternoon with a carload of supplies – rice, split peas, potatoes, sugar, bananas, or whatever was cheap or free – and we'd unload it and drag it into the small room at the end of the temple that had become a makeshift kitchen, complete with a six-burner industrial gas stove, donated to feed the masses.

The temple building itself received some modifications and important additions during the swami's first weeks with us. Most significantly, we got a deity of Krishna. Someone purchased Him for twenty-five dollars from the same import store that the harmonium came from. He turned up at the temple unannounced, a three-foot-high blue plaster deity with His hand on His hip and His head inclined in a vaguely mischievous manner. We found a white fluted column for Him to stand on, which we placed on the raised area at the back of the temple where the swami sat.

"We will call him Kartama-sayi," the swami said. "This means 'the Boss.'"

Kartama-sayi stood upon the column surrounded by flowers and various paintings of Krishna and Lord Chaitanya that we had acquired, including some Brijbasi prints of Radha and Krishna we had ordered from India. Shyamasundar fashioned an altar next to Kartama-sayi, behind which there hung a large oil painting of Lord Chaitanya leading a chanting party of twenty devotees, all of whom played *mrdangas* or cymbals or carried colorful flags. Harvey had painted it at the swami's request. The swami's emerald colored seat – his *vyasasana*, we called it in Sanskrit – was relocated from next to Kartama-sayi to the east side of the temple.

The same month that Kartama-sayi came to our temple, Malati also found a three-inch miniature form with a black face and big eyes that changed our temple forever. She brought it to show the swami one afternoon when I was in his apartment.

"I found this, Swami," she said, placing the tiny figure on his desk. He opened his eyes wide and immediately bowed down on the floor before it.

"Jaya Jagannatha!" he said.

"Who is it?" she asked.

"Lord Jagannatha," he said, rising from the floor. "This is the deity of Krishna loved by Lord Chaitanya. He is worshiped in Puri – Jagannatha Puri. Have you heard of it?"

"No."

"Where did you buy?" he asked.

"Actually, I didn't buy it," she confessed flushing deeply. "I liked it, and I didn't have any money with me, so I just took it."

"Were there any other deities with Him?"

"Yes," Malati confirmed excitedly. "There were two others."

"You must go and buy them," the swami said. "They are Baladeva and Subhadra, the brother and sister of Krishna. We must have all three."

Malati went back, and fortunately the other two figures were

Brijbasi print

still there. When Shyamasundar saw the three figures he told the
swami that he could carve larger-size versions.

"That would be very nice," the swami said. "The San Francisco
temple shall be called 'New Jagannatha Puri.' Jagannatha Puri is
also on the shore of the ocean – Indian Ocean. It is good name for
the San Francisco center."

Within a few weeks, the deities graced the altar above Kartama-
sayi, sitting on a redwood plank that Shyamasundar and I had
found at a wrecking site on Masonic Street. Three feet tall with
large eyes and brightly colored faces, they were an arresting sight.
The swami told everyone that they should bring a small offering to
Lord Jagannatha each time they visited the temple.

"It doesn't need to be expensive," he said. "Just a small flower or
piece of fruit. Whatever you have."

The temple's regular visitors took this to heart and always
brought something for the deities. During the evening programs,
Lord Jagannatha would stand smiling in a sea of flowers and pieces

Deities and painting on the main altar at the San Francisco temple

of fresh fruit and an array of other offerings: loaves of bread, a can of baked beans, feathers, incense sticks and sometimes even articles of clothing.

The swami seemed very pleased with the altar arrangement. He also liked the wall decorations, particularly one of the Brijbasi prints which featured a sixteen-year-old Krishna smiling a Mona-Lisa smile and holding His flute to his mouth. He wore a bright yellow *dhoti* and a glittering golden helmet, His back to a group of trees with a small waterfall to His left. I had hung the lacquered print of this opposite the swami's lecturing dais so that he could see it as he spoke.

The morning after I hung the poster, the swami, looking intently at it, recited a Sanskrit verse before he gave his lecture.

"This verse," he said, "was composed by Rupa Goswami, one of the principle followers of Lord Chaitanya. He was a great poet, great philosopher and playwright. The translation is as follows: 'If you still want to enjoy society, friendship and love, then don't go to the banks of the Yamuna River where that boy named Govinda is standing in His lovely three-curved pose. He is smiling and playing on His flute very beautifully, and His lips are brightened by the full moonshine.'"

I raised my hand, and the swami nodded in my direction.

"I could write the verse in Sanskrit, if you want. We could hang it under the poster."

The swami nodded but said nothing. He commenced his lecture.

Later in the morning, I went to his apartment and asked him if he could show me the verse to copy.

"Yes, I have," he said. He disappeared into his bedroom for a few minutes and came back with an ancient-looking brown hardback book.

"You can borrow it," he said, handing the book to me. "Don't let anyone else touch. I must have it tomorrow. It is only copy. This is verse."

"I'll do it today, right now," I assured him.

I went into town to an art shop and bought a thin white piece of cardboard to write the caption on, and some blue ink and a special calligraphy pen. In my apartment I carefully copied the Sanskrit letters, penning each about an inch high. My plan was to take the Brijbasi poster off the temple wall and glue it and the caption onto a large sheet of cardboard that I would hang so the swami would see it the next time he lectured.

I thought the whole thing looked pretty effective on the wall. The letters were large enough to see from the other side of the room, and the blue ink happened to be approximately the same shade as Krishna's skin. The next morning, I sat under the poster listening, hoping that the swami would notice the caption. As he concluded his lecture, he narrowed his eyes and studied the inscription.

स्मेरां भङ्गीत्रयपरिचितां साचिविस्तीर्णदृष्टिं
वंशीन्यस्ताधरकिशलयाम् उज्ज्वलां चन्द्रकेण ।
गोविन्दाख्यां हरितनुम् इत केशितीथोपन्कण्ठे
मा प्रेक्षिष्ठास् तव यदि सखे बन्धुसन्गो ऽस्ति रङ्ग ॥ *

"There is mistake," he said, shifting his gaze a few inches down from the caption to my face. "You have made mistake."

"I *did*?" I couldn't believe it; I had been so careful! I glanced around the room. Shyamasundar shook his head and Malati smirked. Janaki looked embarrassed on my behalf.

"Yes. It is incorrect."

The wrong inscription remained on the wall for two days. I was too lazy and ashamed to ask the swami for the verse again. On the third day, I took down the poster and gave it to Yamuna, who was a much better calligrapher than I was. She asked the swami for the verse and did a beautiful job of copying the Devanagari script. The poster went back on the wall and remained there with her caption.

———

In addition to our other programs, we started having a Love Feast at the temple on Sunday afternoon. This was similar to the evening programs in almost every respect except that it was a day-time event and included a large free meal that would be cooked by a team of people on Sunday morning. Word quickly spread about the Love Feast. Not only was it free, but the food was great: vegetable dishes, rice with green peas, deep-fried rissoles and buttery semolina pudding with raisins and lemon peel among our weekly delicacies.

To advertise the Love Feast, we started going to chant in Sharon Meadow, opposite the newly named Hippie Hill in Golden Gate Park, about ten minutes walk from the temple. Large gatherings of people were taking place on Hippie Hill that March, a kind of

---

* A mistake in this Devanagari passage is intentional

Chanting in Golden Gate Park at the foot of Hippy Hill in San Francisco

prologue to the Summer of Love that would take root a few months later when one hundred thousand people would converge there to explore the possibilities of political and cultural rebellion, free love, anarchy and adventure. Most of those on Hippie Hill were doing either LSD, marijuana, liquor or various combinations of mind-altering drugs.

We all felt that the Meadow was the perfect place to go and chant, because there were lots of young people there, most of whom were interested in spirituality and getting beyond materialism. It was also an aesthetically pleasant place, green and spiced with a pungent eucalyptus smell. The park chants were a prelude to the Love Feast, an event that started the festivities and collected a bunch of hungry and curious guests. We sat down in the park with our assortment of instruments and started chanting, and quickly a crowd gathered.

We made four large silk banners, which we affixed to ten-foot-high aluminum conduit pipes. The banners were designed to announce diversity and global spirituality. One was a pale blue Jewish star on a white background, another was a Christian cross painted on white silk, a third was a black Mohammedan star and crescent on bright red cloth, and the fourth was a red *Om* sign in Sanskrit painted on a yellow background. We pushed the poles into the soft sward, and the flags fluttered in the breeze.

A few of the devotees wore traditional Indian attire – the women in saris and the men in *dhotis* – but for the most part, we looked like everyone else there on the Hill. I always wore my large red initiation beads looped around my neck. I felt a bit self-conscious at first, but after a while I got used to chanting in the park; I even got up and danced with the other devotees a few times.

We were never sure whether or not the swami would turn up at our Sunday chanting sessions. We always anticipated his coming, but his appearances were unscheduled. When he came, he appeared in the middle of the chanting circle and we would immediately have him sit at the center so that he could lead. Sometimes he played hand cymbals while he chanted, and once he played the *mrdanga*.

The swami was an exotic spectacle in the park. He was always the oldest person there, and he shone radiantly in his flowing saffron robes. When he chanted, the crowd always responded enthusiastically. Many got up and danced with the devotees, holding hands to form concentric circles, which whirled around the chanting party. The dancing often took on bizarre forms, with people writhing on the ground or assuming different love postures. It was like a low-key version of the Mantra-Rock Dance, except outside in the open air and the sunshine.

We'd been going to the park for a couple of weeks when a jazz group started turning up to compete with us. They had a whole set of drums, a big stand-up double bass, a trumpet, a saxophone, congas and a heavy wooden upright piano. They set up only a hundred feet away from us and completely drowned out our sound.

"How did they get that piano down here?" Shyamasundar wondered when we got back to the temple. "That thing must weigh a ton."

"If they turn up again, we're going to have to move," I said.

"There really isn't anywhere quite as good as Hippie Hill, though," Shyamasundar said. "What if we got some kind of amplification? We could mike the lead singer's voice so at least people would be hearing the words of the mantra even if the jazz guys were there."

"It's a good idea," I said. "But it might be kind of expensive. I mean, we'll need a microphone and an amplifier and a generator to power it all."

"We've already got a microphone," Shyamasundar pointed out. "The one the swami uses here at the temple. And can't you just look into the other stuff? We've got a little bit of money, and I'm sure you can find something through your music contacts."

I knew a guy named Frank who ran a musical instrument store on upper Market Street, so I decided to start with him. He agreed to loan us a large speaker with a built-in amplifier on Sundays, because his store was closed that day. After a lot of research, I decided that the best way to power the amplifier was to get a gasoline generator. The one we bought was very small – only about a foot across – and it rested on a small base so it could stand up in the park. Relatively inexpensive but very powerful, it was called Tiny Tiger and was, appropriately, yellow with black stripes.

What we didn't foresee was that in addition to being compact, Tiny Tiger was very stinky and had a roar that was surprisingly loud for such a small creature. When Shyamasundar pulled the cord that started it up inside the temple's back room, the Tiny Tiger belched big white puffs of carbon monoxide fumes that threatened to fill the temple and asphyxiate us then and there. Its roar was just a shade or two softer than a jet engine.

"Well," said Shyamasundar, quickly turning off the generator. "I guess we won't have to worry about the jazz guys drowning us out. Tiny Tiger will do that all on its own."

"Plus it's going to kill us with monoxide smoke," I said. "What we need to do is get it away from where we all are. What if we got a really long electrical cord so that we could hook up the amplifier to it? We could put the generator far away in some bushes or in a hole in the ground or something. What do you think? Then all we'd hear is a purr instead of a roar."

"That could work," Shyamasundar said. "It would also fix the problem of the fumes. It needs to breathe, though – it's got to have air to function – so we couldn't really bury it in the ground. I think we should just put it in the bushes."

I went out and bought three seventy-foot cords, which we connected all together and dragged from the Tiny Tiger across the Meadow to the microphone amp. That afternoon our chanting was

The author (with beard) chanting with the swami in Golden Gate Park

beautifully amplified. The crowd gathered five deep to watch us chant, and there was only the faintest whiff of gasoline in the air. You could barely hear the Tiny Tiger in the distance.

I thought this was the end of our problems. The following Sunday afternoon I led the chanting, holding the temple microphone in one hand and tapping my knee in time to the music with the other. I closed my eyes and tried to absorb myself in the sound of the mantra. I felt the hot sun on my face and felt that this was the absolute best place I could be. Civilians were burning to death in Vietnam, and I believed that conventional politics wouldn't be able to solve the problems of the world. I had been an advocate of peace, but now I was bringing the swami's spiritual alternative to the people of my country.

Then someone punched me in the face. I reeled and dropped the microphone, holding my jaw in agony. My eyes snapped open, and I saw a woman in a white tennis outfit inches from my face. She looked mad as a hornet.

"What do you think you're doing?" she shrieked. She was holding her knuckles and wincing. "We're trying to play a game over there, and your stupid noise is driving us crazy!"

My eyes were watering with pain, but I could vaguely make out a tennis court in the distance. It was on the other side of the Meadow, through a grove of juniper bushes, and I doubted our sound system could really be causing a disturbance from so far away.

I looked around at the other devotees. They and the crowd were frozen with expectation.

"We have a permit to be here," I said coolly.

"With a loudspeaker?"

"Yes." I tried to be as casual as possible, hoping that she would just drop it and go away.

"I doubt that," she snapped. "I'm going to the Parks Department right now to complain." She stomped off racket in hand, shaking her bruised fist.

"It's OK," Janaki said, squatting down beside me. "There won't be anyone working in the Parks Department on Sunday."

I nodded and began chanting again, this time keeping my eyes open just in case. After a few moments of hesitancy, the crowd relaxed and joined in. Unfortunately, the woman returned twenty minutes later with a uniformed park official. The tennis woman looked confident and defiant, but the Parks woman looked like she'd rather not have to deal with the issue.

I stopped the chanting, and again the crowd moved in to listen.

"Do you have a permit to be doing this, sir?" the Parks official asked me.

I hated that – when people called you "sir" but you knew it was totally meaningless, sarcastic or official.

"Yes, I do," I said.

"He doesn't," the tennis player said to her.

"Can I see it, please?"

Suppressing a smile, I reached into my pocket and pulled out the permit. Luckily, I'd obtained a letter from the San Francisco Park and Recreation Commission permitting us to electronically amplify one voice on Sunday from 3-5 PM at our location in the

The swami in Golden Gate Park with Jagannatha deity to his right:
February, 1967

park. I carried it in my pocket just for moments like this. I unfolded
it and handed it to her. She read it carefully, while the tennis player
glared at me and sucked on the knuckles of her right hand.

"Well, this looks fine to me," the Parks official said, not raising
her eyes from the paper. "I think he's all right."

"What?" said the tennis player. "What do you mean, 'all right'?"

The Parks official handed her the permit. "I can't do anything,
ma'am. I'm sorry."

The tennis player looked defeated. "Nothing?"

"Well, do you think you can sing a bit quieter?" the Parks official asked us.

"Sure," I said trying to sound nonchalant. "I'll give it a try."

The following Sunday we decided to bring our Jagannatha deity
to the park. He stood in all His colorful glory in the middle of the
chanting circle, adding to the visual spectacle of our party. When
the swami joined us that afternoon, he sat next to the deity and led
the chanting for over an hour.

A group of about twenty people walked back to the temple with the swami that afternoon, including ten-year-old Star Dethridge, the daughter of the apartment managers.

"I take ballet lessons," she informed the swami loudly as we walked out of the park and through a short tunnel onto Stanyan Street.

The author behind the swami in Golden Gate Park

"Oh, yes?" he said.

"Yes. When I practice ballet, I always get tired, but when I dance with you, I *never* get tired."

The swami laughed. "Very good," he said.

"My mother likes you," she said. "She keeps a scrap-book with all the newspaper stories about you and the Krishnas."

"That is very good also," he said. He turned his attention toward me. "It is best," he said, "if the deity of Krishna stays in the temple."

"Oh, so we shouldn't have brought Jagannatha down to the park?" I asked.

"Actually, Lord Jagannatha is very merciful," the swami said. "Once a year He comes out from His temple to give His *darshan* – His audience – to the people. You must have this festival – Rathayatra – later. It is in June or July, I am thinking. But only on this day should He leave temple."

I nodded. "OK," I said.

"Also, deity should never sit on bare ground. Always He should have a nice sitting place, at least some cloth."

The next morning I found the swami looking down at the street though his apartment's south-facing windows. He turned around as I entered his main room.

"Mukunda," he said, "I have been watching traffic."

"Yeah, it's pretty busy here," I said. "Sorry we couldn't get you a quieter apartment."

"Apartment is fine," he said. "I have been watching trucks. You know, this kind of truck with – how do you say? – platform behind the driver."

"Like a flatbed truck?" I asked. "The kind with a long open platform?"

"Yes," the swami said. "Flatbed truck. I am thinking this vehicle would make good Rathayatra cart."

"You mean for the outside Jagannatha festival you were talking about yesterday?" I asked.

"Yes. I have made drawing. You please look here." On a lined pad of paper he had made an ink drawing of a flatbed truck with a four-pillar canopy positioned at the street end of the platform. Between the pillars he had drawn what looked like flat boards with dimensions written along each plane. Every part of the structure was numbered, and below the drawing the swami had composed a legend that described each numbered item. It was almost like a contractor's blueprint. A flag on a post jutted upward from the point at the top of the canopy. It looked kind of like an Arabian Nights tent, but without sides.

"So, this canopy will be made of cloth," the swami was saying. "And deities of Jagannatha, Baladeva and Subhadra will sit below the canopy. They will be tied to these boards," he said, pointing his pen at the wooden boards between the pillars. "Baladeva will face left side, Subhadra will face behind, and Jagannatha will face right side. In this way you may convert this flatbed truck into deity cart for festival."

"What about the space between the canopy and the driver's cab?" I asked. "What will go there?"

"There devotees may ride with the deity," he said. "There must always be kirtan with the festival."

"Maybe we could put a speaker there so the chanting can be loud," I suggested.

"Yes," he said. "That is good idea. There should be big kirtan with flags and banners. The deity car should drive slowly, and everyone should follow chanting beside. We will have big festival and feast. There should seven days feasting for Rathayatra festival."

"And where will we drive the truck?" I asked.

"It should ride to San Francisco beach, just like Rathayatra chariots in India. Every year there Jagannatha goes to seashore and remains there for week of festivities, but we will keep our deities at beach only one day. Then grand parade returns the deities to the temple. Here our temple is by the sea just as in Puri, so we should do. It will be very nice."

"OK," I said. "Should we try to arrange it soon?"

"No, wait until proper Rathayatra time," he said. "It should happen here exactly when festival is held in India. We can consult Vedic calendar for date."

Later that morning, as I contemplated the swami's proposed festival, I went to Frank's store to return his speaker. I noticed he had a foot-adjustable kettledrum in his store, which stood on a platform in the front window, its brass underside glittering in the sunshine.

"Hey, can we borrow that?" I asked. "It would really help our chants in the park."

"Yeah. Until somebody wants it you can hang onto it," he said.

"So, we won't have to collect and return it like the speaker system every Monday?" I asked.

"Nope, you can keep it at the temple," he said. "But you have to pay for any damage."

"OK. Thanks. That's great!"

The huge drum added another dimension to the chants in the park. Like the hand cymbals, it could be heard from far away, plus it was visually dramatic to see such a large musical instrument in a field of grass. I'd never seen one outside a concert hall, so I was pretty pleased Frank had been so generous as to loan it to us for free. I learned how to use the pedal to play the simple four-note Hare Krishna chant that we usually sang in the park. This was the original tune the swami had taught us. Its thunderous sound echoed throughout the park, drawing curious onlookers to the swami and his chanting party. I imagined how spectacular it would look by the

The author playing the kettle drum in San Francisco, flanked
by the swami and Gaurasundara

sea during the Rathayatra festival in July, and I hoped no one would want to buy it before then.

—

Most of my days were taken up doing errands or secretarial work for the swami. Each morning after the program, I went up to his apartment to ask him if he needed anything done that day. Sometimes he asked me to drive him somewhere, and other times he dictated letters to me. One Monday morning in February he asked me if I would buy him some milk.

"I will eat at eleven today," he said.

"OK, do you want the milk by then?" I asked.

"Yes," he replied. "I will have hot milk and *rasagula*. That's all. And later I will have lunch *prasada*. Maybe at three."

There was a loud knock at the door, and before I could open it, Mitchell Brown, a good friend of Janaki's, burst into the room with a copy of the *San Francisco Examiner* in his hand.

"Swami, Swami, your prime minister's been stoned!" he exclaimed loudly. "A mob in Bombay threw rocks and almost killed her! Look at this."

He handed the newspaper to the swami. In his excitement he'd forgotten to remove his Converse All-Star shoes at the door, and their laces were dragging on the floor. Mitchell was a nice guy, I thought, intelligent and young with large round glasses. Nevertheless, he was a little strange. His ambition was to travel round the world in a balloon.

The swami looked surprised but accepted the newspaper from Mitchell. Standing behind him, I read the headline: "Behind Her Sari Are Stone Wounds." While the swami read the article, Mitchell filled me in on its contents.

"There's a drought in Maharashtra," he explained, calming down somewhat as he spoke. "For some reason, the people there tried to kill her when she was there. I thought I'd come and tell the swami right away."

"Why would they want to kill her because of the drought?" I asked. "It's not her fault."

Mitchell shrugged, an intense look on his sallow face, while the swami read. "Don't know," he said.

The swami turned the newspaper page and scanned the stories on pages two and three. Then he looked up and smiled at Mitchell.

"This is very good, very good," he said, moving his head from side to side.

"Very good?" Mitchell looked bewildered. "How do you figure? They tried to kill her. How could it be good?"

"In our Indian tradition," the swami explained matter-of-factly, "the people looked to the king or leader to protect. They took it that the king was responsible even for weather. They were feeling always dependent on king. Kings were pious. They protected the subjects – women, children, old people. So if the people in Maharashtra remember their tradition, that is good. That is culture. Their simple feeling is good. They hold leaders responsible for anything wrong. That means even drought. Of course, no rains means no crops, and that is regrettable."

"But they almost killed her."

"They were angry. And no crops. Yes, they were angry upon her because they blamed her. That is natural. She is leader, and they are subjects."

Mitchell shook his head. "So they think she caused the drought?"

"They think it is because of higher powers – demigods, powers that can't be controlled. And because she is president, or, I mean to say, prime minister, she is representative of God. In India, king or prime minister is still worshipped as God. So they think she could have prevented, because they think she is representative of God. It is duty of the parent, king, teacher to protect dependents. All natural disturbances – flooding, storm, earthquake – they had power to stop. They know this." He sounded unflustered, like a teacher who had a job to do irrespective of what might be going on.

"The people still think like that?" Mitchell asked.

"Like what?"

"That she should have protected their crops?"

"They are mostly innocent," the swami said. "They are village people. And they are hungry. So they blame her. They know she is leader. Kings like Yudhisthira five thousand years ago, they were always feeling weight of their subjects, and their pains. It was their duty to protect against all disturbances."

"So that's good?" Mitchell asked.

"Their action to the prime minister shows they are feeling dependent," the swami said. "That is indirect show of God consciousness." The swami put the paper down on his desk and I quickly picked it up to read the article for myself. It said that an American ship, the Manhattan, had arrived in India with enough wheat to feed three million people for six weeks. Mrs. Gandhi was on her way to the capital of Bihar and was "as tough as ever," according to the article.

"So, I better go," Mitchell was saying.

"You have engagement?" the swami asked.

"Engagement?"

"You have to go somewhere?"

"I have to meet a relative at eleven thirty." Mitchell stood up. "I'll see you tonight. We're still going to the beach, right?"

The swami looked over at me, and I nodded in affirmation.

I didn't think he bore any ill feeling toward Mrs. Gandhi, but he also understood the inner motivations of the protestors. Years later, he met with Mrs. Gandhi and discussed the Hare Krishna movement, and once she even led an official government ceremony celebrating Lord Chaitanya's birth. The events in Mitchell's article were undoubtedly tragic, but the swami had shed a completely new light on the article for me. His perspective never failed to astound me, never failed to open up a whole new way of looking at the world.

Later that day, just before sundown, we piled into the Krishna car and drove three miles west to the beach. We'd recently started going out there to have kirtans on the nights that we didn't have programs in the temple. Because it was winter, there were never any people on the beach; it was always chilly and blustery, but we usually built a big, blazing fire and we'd warm up pretty quick.

This afternoon Shyamasundar was driving the Krishna car; the swami sat in the front seat, wearing a thick black and white hound's tooth coat. Murari, Janaki, Malati and I squashed into the back seat, and a couple of other cars followed us in a convoy.

We parked about half a mile south of San Francisco's Cliff House Restaurant and went down to the strip of beach below the promenade. As usual, there was a brisk wind lifting the dried sand and flinging handfuls of it in our faces. We quickly gathered up some drift wood and lit a fire. The swami stood looking out toward the sea, the rays of the sinking sun on his face. He wasn't wearing a hat, and I wondered if he was cold. Once the fire was burning, Janaki and I wrapped potatoes in tin foil and placed them in the ashes to roast. In a plastic container in her bag was a large block of butter and a red plastic salt shaker.

I started the kirtan as the wind whipped at our clothes and hair. We sat around the fire, chanting with our eyes closed, marshmallows on sticks toasting in the flames. With faces lit up by the firelight and the orange rays of the setting sun, some people raised their hands above their heads. The sticks in their hands made them look like animated scarecrows. A few people got up and danced in the sunset, the spray from the big, churning waves dampening their faces. I glanced around and thought how surreal we'd look if anyone had observed us from a distance – strange figures marooned on a vacant strip of beach taking part in a cold, windy picnic in the dusky light.

In any case, there wasn't anyone around to observe anything; we were the only ones brave enough to take to the beach at this time of year. We chanted for an hour and then ate our hot buttered potatoes and gooey marshmallows. A few months later, we collectively renounced marshmallows forever after someone found out they contained gelatin, but for now we ate dozens unaware.

That evening after our bonfire *prasadam* we all walked along the beach at the wind-swept end of Golden Gate Park, which ended at the promenade that ran along the waterfront.

"What is that?" the swami asked, pointing his cane toward something in the distance.

It was almost dark, and difficult to make out what he was pointing at, but I had seen the structure before.

"It's just an old windmill, Swami," I said. "Dutch-style. It's really run down."

"We can see closer?" the swami asked.

"Sure," I answered. "Let's take a look."

We walked up to the shabby windmill. It was more dilapidated than I remembered. The non-descript grayish-blue paint was peeling, and the main column had toppled, probably because it was rotten, I guessed. The four latticed blades that once caught the westerly wind from the ocean lay on the ground as if in defeat.

"Why was this built here?" the swami asked.

"I don't really know," Shyamasundar said. "Maybe the San Francisco local government built it as some kind of tribute. Or maybe it was donated by someone from Holland. Or maybe it's just a nice thing to have in the park."

"Anyway, no one seems to really care about it," I said.

The swami looked thoughtful. "Why don't you tell the government we can repair that windmill for them, and they can let us build temple?"

"OK," I said immediately. "Do you mean that we could restore the windmill and in exchange they'd let us built a temple in the park?"

The swami smiled. "That would be very nice."

"Oh, I see, OK," I said. "I'll see what they say." I thought back to the New York Con Edison episode when I'd tried to get the electricity connected for free. Like that scheme, I was pretty sure that I wouldn't be able to get the windmill project off the ground. In saying OK to the swami, I kind of felt like I was humoring him.

Years later, the windmill was restored, but not by the swami or his followers. When I saw how beautiful it looked I imagined what could have been if I'd taken a chance and not just considered the swami's proposal only a flight of fancy. I imagined a temple adjacent

Sign in Golden Gate Park designating windmill renovation project

The renovated windmill in San Francisco's Golden Gate Park

to the windmill, its blades revolving in the breeze, and I imagined that it would have been a tribute to my faith in the swami's dreams. Unfortunately, I didn't see things the way he did.

———

"Are you Allen Ginsberg's guru?" It was the first question after the swami's evening program and was totally unrelated to anything

The swami and Allen Ginsberg

the swami had spoken about. The guy was in his mid-thirties and was leaning against the wall with his hands in his pockets. He narrowed his eyes as he spoke, an expression that gave him a distinctly challenging air.

"I am *nobody's* guru," the swami declared instantly, looking directly at the man. He paused and said in a quieter voice, "I am everybody's servant." It sounded almost as if he were rebuking the man for asking such a silly question.

The swami paused and lowered his head. I was sitting close to him and heard him say almost to himself, "Actually I am not even a servant; a servant of God is no ordinary thing." He looked up. "We shall have kirtan now."

Janaki and I walked the swami back to his apartment after the kirtan and then retired for the night ourselves. A few short hours later, I was woken by a knocking sound and someone insistently calling my name.

"Mukunda! Mukunda!"

I rolled over and groped for my alarm clock. 2:05 AM. What was going on?

"Mukunda! Mukunda." There were three sharp raps on the door. Then three more.

I sat up, trying to get my bearings.

"Mukunda! Mukunda!" It was the swami's voice! I bounded out of bed.

"Janaki!" I called out. "Something's happened. It's the swami!"

I groped around for the light and staggered into the living room half dressed. Barely awake, I opened the door, blinking. There was the swami in his saffron robes. And standing a short distance behind him was a teenage girl with long brown hair hanging to her waist. She was dressed like she was about to go on a picnic: bright clothes, sleeveless blouse and sandals. I looked more closely at her face and saw that her pupils were dilated and she was staring at me in a creepy way.

"What's going on?" I asked the swami. "Are you OK?"

"This girl woke me up," the swami said, looking worried. "She said she wanted to talk. So I let her in and she sat."

The girl stood completely still as the swami spoke. She glared at me.

"So I said to her, 'What you are wanting?' " the swami continued. "And she looked at me and did not say anything. So then I asked her 'Do you want to say something?' She was silent."

So far it didn't sound terribly bad to me. At least the swami was OK. Janaki appeared at my side, a bathrobe thrown over her nightgown.

"This girl sat in my room but did not speak," he said again, as if he were repeating for Janaki what had happened. "So I told her she must go out so I could sleep, but she sat there only. She would not move. So I came to get you and somehow the door closed behind me, and I am locked outside my room."

"Oh yes, your apartment has a self-locking door like this one," I said, indicating our front door.

"Yes," the swami said. "So now I wish to get back, but I cannot, because it is locked and my only key is inside. So I came to get you."

Janaki seemed much more awake than I, and she immediately took the situation in hand. She pushed past me and started talking to the girl. Slowly the girl started nodding and showing some signs of life.

"You wait here, OK?" she said to the girl. She turned to me. "I'm going to get a key from the Dethridges," she said.

The swami and I watched her disappear down the hallway. The deranged-looking girl was leaning on the wall, but when Janaki left she pulled herself up and lurched toward the swami, shaking her head swiftly back and forth. With her hands on her hips she leaned forward and leered at him. "You're not ready!" she screamed. Before I could act, she turned and disappeared down the stairway.

"Swami, come in until Janaki comes back," I said, shaken by the whole affair. The swami looked surprisingly calm but agreed to come in. Janaki returned within a couple of minutes with a key.

"I woke up a couple of the men sleeping in the temple." I must have looked puzzled. "Just in case there was trouble," she explained.

"You have the key?" the swami asked.

"Yes. Here it is," said Janaki, handing it to him. "We will walk you back to your apartment."

We unlocked his door and accompanied him into his front room.

"You can sit," the swami said. He sat down himself. "When I opened the door to let the girl out, she followed me out of my apartment. She came out behind me and closed the door. So it locks automatically from within?"

"Yes, it has a catch that needs to be up, otherwise it locks," I said.

"She knocked on my door and woke me," he said. "I answered, and she said she must talk to me. So I let her in and sat down. She was sitting on the floor, but she would not say anything. So I waited. And then ..." He opened his eyes wide, raised his hands, and with palms out next to his ears he mimicked her. "She said, '*Maha-Buddha! Maha-Buddha!*' " He paused. "She said it again, '*Maha-Buddha!*'" I had never seen the swami so animated.

I shook my head. "I'm so sorry. We'll think of something so that this doesn't happen again."

The swami wagged his head back and forth. "Now I will take rest," he said.

"I can show you the lock again before we go," I said. I showed him how to fix it open so that it would not lock automatically when closed. "And you can use this chain when you are inside in case you don't know who it is," I said. "It allows you to open the door just a crack, see?"

"And here," Janaki said. "Here's an extra key. You can keep it with you always, just in case."

"Thank you very much," he said.

Janaki and I walked back to our apartment. "Why should an elderly man like him be awakened and subjected to such madness in the middle of the night?" I asked. "We have to stop this."

"Maybe we should get someone to stay with him at night," Janaki suggested. "Like a bodyguard or a bouncer or something."

The next morning at the program the young girl turned up in the temple. The glazed look had disappeared from her eyes and she looked normal. After the swami's lecture she approached me on the sidewalk outside the temple.

"Hi. Can I say something?" she asked.

"Yeah, sure," I said.

"I'm really sorry about last night … um … I mean earlier today," she said. "I didn't know what I was doing. I took too much acid."

"Don't worry. It happens. Just forget it."

"Can I stay in the temple for a couple more hours?"

"Make yourself at home."

From that day onward, the swami always had a male assistant stay with him in the apartment. His first full-time assistant was a new young devotee named Upendra. He slept at the swami's apartment at night and was available to him during the days also. We implemented a system so that whenever the swami needed something during the day he could push a button and a buzzer would go off at the back of the temple, alerting Upendra. As for the girl, she hung around the temple for a few weeks and then disappeared. Later I learned from Janaki that what she had really been saying to the swami was "Baha'u'llah," the name of the founder of the Baha'i faith.

CHAPTER 18

On Air

In between my secretarial work for the swami, I had been working on making contacts and getting public exposure for the new temple. In March I found out that we could speak on an AM radio station called KFRC. It played the top hits over and over and was fronted by a hyped-up set of high-powered disc jockeys. I knew how popular the station was and how many people would be listening if we managed to get on a show, so I was eager to get us some air time.

The station said that we could appear on the "Derry Haven Show," which started at ten in the morning right after the breakfast show. We were scheduled to meet him at ten, but we were a little early for our appointment, so we waited around in the radio station lobby, which was decked out in ugly mustard vinyl furnishings. Shyamasundar, Malati, Yamuna and I waited while one of the tube lights flickered overhead, threatening to give me a headache. The radio station's music played through speakers, and when the DJ came on-air a large illuminated sign over the studio door lit up. It said, "DO NOT ENTER WHEN RED LIGHT IS ON." A young unshaven guy in faded jeans finally showed us into the studio, a stifling hot and stuffy room only about ten feet square lit by blindingly fluorescent lights. I could see right now I wasn't going to make it out of this experience headache-free.

Derry Haven was perched behind a desk crowded with turntables, behind which was a wall of blinking lights. He had a crew cut and his sleeves were rolled up, giving him an air of military efficiency, but he seemed nervous and was chain smoking. I thought he looked like a forty-year-old race-car driver who had lost too many races.

"Hey, Krishnas," he said, one eye on a spinning turntable that was playing a Petula Clark song. "Hang on and I'll get you guys some chairs." He picked up the phone. "Hey, Harry, we need four chairs in here right away. Four Krishnas are here and they're gonna say something on the air." The guy who showed us in brought in four metal chairs with green back cushions. He carried them one at a time but rushed in and out, smashing each one against the door in the small studio.

Haven groaned each time Harry banged the door shut. He turned his attention toward us. "So what do you guys wanna say? You know it's all got to happen in three minutes. You know that, right? So be concise, OK? You know what I mean by concise? You have exactly three minutes. That's it."

Four heads nodded.

"And no talking when that red light up there is on." He pointed to a sign on the wall. "Not even whispering. OK?"

Four heads nodded again.

He glanced at the spinning turntable and put his cigarette down on the table so he could rifle through a file cabinet containing records. He selected a vinyl disc and put it down on another turntable. He was like a machine, so practiced and professional at what he was doing. He flicked a switch, put on some headphones, and put the stylus arm on the start of the record, spun it forward and then half a turn backwards, flicked another switch and leaned back in his chair. He took a few big drags on his cigarette and exhaled the smoke through his nose.

The song playing ended, and he swung his big microphone close to his face. A large red light on the wall flashed, and the sign below it illuminated:

"ON AIR."

"'Sign of the Times,' Petula Clark," Haven said, his face lighting up as he spoke. Suddenly he looked ten years younger. Without missing a beat he rotated another turntable of car sounds and simultaneously spoke into the microphone. "And if you want a *new* color on your short, Bart Leandro has it today," he said, reading from a stack of papers on his desk. "520 Valencia for a fine finish in cherry-pie red, blazing blue or shiny silver. Pin stripes and flames to order. Only forty-two ninety-five till the end of March. In at ten thirty, out by four thirty, same-day delivery. Bart Leandro, 520 Valencia, open through Saturday."

Quickly and quietly, he flicked to another page and continued smoothly. "And if you're looking for something to wear, check out Garcy's at 1334 Union Square. Boys and girls skirts, shirts, jackets, pants, everything you need for the weekend." His tone sounded like he'd just seen a flying saucer. "Kashmir sweaters, Levi jeans, Houston shirts, and every kind of print you ever wanted." He turned a dial and held back a turntable from spinning. "Don't delay, get to Garcy's today. Be there or be square." He waited two seconds and then let the record spin. Lee Dorsey's voice rang out, and the red light on the wall went out.

Haven's face dropped to the floor. He spat his cigarette out and stomped on it while he lit up another. He was forty again, and he spoke in a lower, more lethargic tone than his on-air voice.

"So, you guys can sit around that other mike over there." He pointed to the other side of the tiny room. "Do your thing when this record's over. Which one of you wants to do the talking?"

He scanned our blank faces. We shifted nervously in our seats and looked at each other.

"OK, I'll do it," I said, feigning confidence.

We all moved our chairs over to the microphone. I sat right in front of it, its spongy blue covering only an inch from my face.

"I'll give you a signal to start," he said. "I'll just point at you, OK? Oh hey, what's your name?"

"Mukunda."

"Muk-hundha. Did I say that right?"

"Sounds OK," I said. He scribbled on a pad.

The record ended. " 'Working in a Coal Mine' – Lee Dorsey," Haven said. "And now members from the Hare Krishna temple in San Francisco would like to tell you something. Their spokesman, Muk-hundha, has the scoop. Muk-hundha?"

He pointed and looked at me, widening his eyes.

Feeling nervous, I looked at my notes and spoke in what I hoped was a professional-sounding radio voice. "The Radha-Krishna temple at 518 Frederick Street is open every day from five in the morning to ten at night, and everyone is invited to come and chant with us." My voice felt quivery. "On Sunday at four in the afternoon we have a free Love Feast and lots of good vegetarian food. More than you can eat, actually, and at Golden Gate Park on Sundays at Hippie Hill you can come and chant with us. You might remember us from the Mantra-Rock Dance at the Avalon Ballroom a few weeks back."

I paused to try to catch my breath, then rushed on feeling more confident.

"Our spiritual master, Bhaktivedanta Swami, was there with Allen Ginsberg. The Grateful Dead, Big Brother and the Holding Company and Moby Grape were also there. The mantra we chant is *Hare Krishna Hare Krishna Krishna Krishna Hare Hare, Hare Rama Hare Rama Rama Rama Hare Hare.* Anyone can do it regardless of age or religion. It's a transcendental sound vibration that gets you to the spiritual platform instantaneously. You don't have to do any difficult austerities, like emptying your mind or sitting on ice in the winter or around fires in the summer. It's a sound anyone can make. So you don't need a ticket or invitation, just come to 518 Frederick Street and see it for yourself. If ..."

I felt a hand tapping my left shoulder. I glanced back. Malati was pointing her chin at the microphone letting me know she wanted to say something.

"... if you're looking for something to do on the weekend just drop by the Radha-Krishna temple. It's right next to Kezar Stadium. Malati has something she wants to say. Here she is."

I got up fast, and she slid right into my chair so as not to miss a second. Sounding all out of breath, like she'd just won an Olympics 100-meter race, she said, "And I can tell you myself ... uh ... that dancing is where it's at," she giggled nervously. "You can just lose yourself in the sound of the mantra. You can jump and twirl, and no one will care. I mean you can be really uninhibited. It's a way you can, you know, really express yourself and no one will tell you not to."

I cringed. Was she for real?

"And the temple's not too far away," she went on. "If you get as far as Haight and Ashbury, it's only a few blocks away. You head down Haight toward the park, turn left at Stanyan, go a couple of blocks to Frederick, turn right, and you're there."

I cringed again. Giving street directions was the last thing we needed to be using our radio time for.

"And there's always food, even on weekdays at one o'clock in the afternoon, you can come and get a lunch for free."

She nodded, indicating she was done. My eyes were glued to the second hand on the clock. It looked like we had fifteen seconds left, so I slipped back into the microphone seat. This time I was more nervous, and I really didn't know how to follow Malati's act.

"Uh, thanks Malati," I said. "Uh … and every Sunday I want to remind you that at one o'clock, just at the entrance of Golden Gate Park, we'll be there chanting, so please join us. Then we can walk over to the temple for more chanting and the Love Feast."

Haven shook his head up and down rapidly. Our time was up. "Hare Krishna," I concluded.

"And they all look pretty straight to me … well almost," Haven joked flirtatiously as if he was wooing his microphone. "Anyway, it sounds like something worth checking out. Here's The Doors."

———

Shortly after our radio stint, we secured a recording opportunity. Several months before, Hayagriva – the English professor from New York – had written a song about Narada Muni, the sage from the *Srimad-Bhagavatam* who travels the universe chanting the glories to Lord Krishna. He had given me the lyrics, and I had set them to music and had the whole thing copyrighted. It was called "Narada Muni – the Eternal Spaceman" and was, at best, a mediocre song. We decided to try to record it anyway, partly because I had always wanted to make a record and partly because we knew lots of contacts from the music industry and thought it would be a good way to get some more exposure and to make some money for the temple.

As I was investigating our recording options, an eighteen-year-old musician named Jerry Maytern turned up at the temple. He was the lead singer of a band called Moon and Beyond, which had made a successful recording in England four months before. Now he'd gone AWOL from the US Army and had stumbled into the Haight scene and our temple. When Shyamasundar and I talked to him about our idea to record the Narada Muni song, his brown eyes shone with enthusiasm.

"Sounds good," he said. "Probably best to record it as a forty-five and maybe make the flip side a Hare Krishna mantra track. I'd love to help out. I could sing or play guitar or whatever you want."

I arranged some studio time in a recording studio across the Bay in Oakland. It was owned by Dick LeMonte, who liked the Krishnas and agreed to donate the studio time to us. He wasn't sure he could be there to engineer it, and he gave us keys to the studio just in case he didn't get around to showing up.

Sure enough, on the night we recorded, Dick didn't show, so Shyamasundar and I did the best we could with operating the control board ourselves. The studio had its own organ, which I played, and a set of drums, which a friend of mine played. Jerry played guitar and contributed some special effects, while others played our standard temple kirtan instruments – cymbals and *mrdanga*. Our plan was to make the Narada Muni song sound something like a Krishna version of a Rolling Stones hit, so in my best Mick Jagger impersonation I crooned into the microphone:

Oh Narada Muni eternal spaceman
Can travel much further than spaceships can
Sending sounds of love and joy vibrations
To all the cosmic super-stations
For the song he always shouts
Sends the planets flipping out
He sings to Cancer and the Pleiades
For he can travel where he pleases
But I'll tell you before you think me loony
That I'm talking about Narada Muni

Although it was recorded professionally on an eight-track system, the finished product sounded peculiar. The Narada Muni song was unlike any song I'd ever heard, and the flip side was an unusual

Hare Krishna mantra melody that we recorded with *tamboura*, *mrdanga* and cymbals. A friend of mine named Billy played cascading embellishments on the sitar for the mantra.

When the recording, mixing and printing were done, we dashed up to see the swami to play the Narada Muni song for him on a battery-run, portable record player. He listened carefully but was completely expressionless throughout. I couldn't tell whether he really liked it or not, but when the song faded out he smiled.

"Very good!" he exclaimed. "It is done in your country's tune. Immediately print a thousand copies."

We didn't have enough money to print a thousand copies. We made a hundred copies that sold within a few days. I later realized that we probably could have borrowed a little money and easily sold a thousand copies in the area, at least as a novelty. Once again, I found myself regretting my failure to take the swami's practical financial advice. He was wise and worldly as well as having great spiritual depth.

CHAPTER 19

Psychedelia's Pseudo-spiritualists

One afternoon in March a group of five orange-clad Indian men appeared at the door of the temple. I'd been reading a lot about India, and I thought that these new swamis looked Bengali, like our Swami. Their saffron robes reached to their ankles, and they were much younger than the swami – probably only around thirty years old. Instead of having shaved heads, they all had wavy jet-black hair.

My first instinct was to greet them as brothers of the same Vaishnava culture. But one thing held me back: the chubbiest swami cradled a young manicured black poodle in his left arm, and he entered the temple with the dog. It wasn't so much that he had a pet; it was more that being from India he should have known not to bring an animal into the temple. Immediately I was skeptical about these Indian mendicants.

"Hare Krishna," I said, putting aside the no-dogs-in-the-temple rule for the moment. "Welcome to the Radha-Krishna temple."

"Thank you," said the man holding the puppy. "I am Subal. And this is Kardama, Nitin, Subhag and Guddhi. Hare Krishna."

"Please come and sit down," I said, indicating the ledge in the front window. They sat down. The dog was fidgety; it wanted to get down and explore.

"You're from India?" I asked.

"Bengal! We heard about your temple, and we decided to come

and see it. We play at Fillmore next week, sponsored by Albert Grossman. You know him? He is Bob Dylan's manager."

"I've heard of him. What is your group's name?"

"We are Bauls," he said, switching the dog to his other arm. The animal squealed. When he told me they were Bauls, I realized I'd heard recordings made by them and had thought their sound was pretty ordinary. Subal noticed me looking at the puppy. "Is it wrong to have a dog in temple?"

"Actually, the swami doesn't let dogs in," I said.

"Should I take her out?"

"Well, it's OK this time," I said. The dog didn't have a leash or collar, and even if it did, it was so small it could have easily gotten stepped on out on the sidewalk.

He smiled. "I'll hold her. I promise," he said. "She won't touch floor. She is baby."

I decided to ask the swami about the Bauls. Something about them didn't seem right to me, but I couldn't quite put my finger on what it was.

Subal reached into his pocket. "Here are two tickets to Fillmore Saturday. A gift. We thought you would like." He handed me two royal purple tickets.

"OK. Thanks. Thanks a lot."

"You are Vaishnavas? Worshipers of Visnu?" Subal asked.

"Yes," I said. "We worship Radha and Krishna. The swami – Bhaktivedanta Swami – is from Bengal too."

They walked around the temple room, looked at the altar and the paintings and then headed on their way.

Shyamasundar and I went to the Fillmore on Saturday night to see the Bauls' performance. A group called Canned Heat was also performing that night. I got caught up in watching them, and then we had to leave before we saw the Bauls.

I thought that was the last of them, but Subal appeared a week later in the Straight Theater, where we'd been invited to chant the following Saturday night. We were billed as the main feature of the evening. The Straight Theater was the perfect place for chanting. Someone had bought the ailing movie house and had removed all the seats, leaving a large open space. We sat down cross-legged on the floor, and the two hundred hippies that comprised the audience followed suit. There were lots of familiar faces in the crowd, people who had been at the Avalon or who were now frequenting the temple programs. Soon everyone was chanting with us, and within fifteen minutes the whole room got up and danced, swaying to the beat of the *mrdanga*. It was like the chanting at the Avalon, but with a sense of intimacy that could be achieved only in a small venue like the Straight Theater.

As the chanting got louder and faster, Subal suddenly made his entrance, bounding into the middle of the circle in his orange robes, his arms raised and his eyes cast upwards. His dancing was graceful, but it looked choreographed to me. He skipped, bounced and frolicked around the hall with abandon, presenting a spectacular performance. The eyes of the crowd were on him – the young Indian swami – as he spun and swirled around with his eyes half closed.

The Haight Theatre that became known as "The Straight Theatre"

When the chant ended, all the devotees bowed and touched their heads to the floor. The crowd did likewise. Subal stopped dancing and quickly lay face down on the floor, arms stretched out in front of him, his legs straight back and spread out. I said a brief version of the spoken prayer the swami chanted after kirtan, after which we all stood up, exhilarated, and got ready to leave the theater. Subal stayed on the ground, prostrated and unmoving. Several people tried to rouse him, but no one could make him move.

"I think he's faking," I whispered to Shaymasundara. "He wants everyone to think he's fainted in spiritual ecstasy. He wants to show he's a spiritually advanced person."

"I think so too," he said. "But everyone seems to think he's having a mystic swoon."

People were crowded around Subal's frozen form, looking either worried or impressed or a bit of both. A Hindi proverb spoken by the swami passed through my mind: "If you tell lies, you can illusion an entire planet; if you speak the truth, people will throw rocks at you." I didn't want any proverbial rocks thrown at me, so Shyamasundar and I left the theater and headed home. It didn't seem like an issue important enough to make a big deal out of.

The next morning we reported back to the swami about our theater chanting event.

"That is wonderful," he said when we told him about the crowd dancing.

"Also, Swami," Murari said, "there was this young Bengali swami who came. He was dancing in ecstasy like Lord Chaitanya, and at the end he lay on the ground in a mystic swoon."

The swami raised his eyebrows.

"Actually, I don't think it was ecstasy," I said. "I thought he was just trying to attract attention with his dancing."

"Oh?" the swami said like he wanted to hear more.

"They came to the temple a few days ago," I said. "They are from Bengal and they sang at the Fillmore. Said they were Bauls. What is that all about?"

"The Bauls are a Vaishnava sect from Bengal," the swami said. "Pseudo-Vaishnavas, like Sahajiyas and Smartas."

"One of them, Subal, carried a small dog when he first came," I said. "I think last night he was imitating Lord Chaitanya. He was dancing and twirling while we chanted. At the end of the kirtan he lay on the floor with his face down and his arms out and didn't or wouldn't get up." I kind of felt like I was tattling on someone I didn't like.

The swami said musically, "You should have said to him, 'My dear Chaitanya ...' " He paused and suddenly looked stern. "And you should have kicked on his face with boots. That's all." He kicked his right foot out towards the doorway and laughed. The swami's words drew the sting from my anger. I felt vindicated, but I also saw that there was not an ounce of anger in the swami.

———

Part of the reason the Bauls were able to make such an impression was the same reason our Swami was able to: America was overflowing with interest in all things "mystical" or "spiritual" or "alternative." There were numerous stores in the Haight area that were dedicated to marketing merchandise on this theme: arrays of roach clips, water pipes, cigarette papers, paintings, drawings, clothing, hand-made pottery, tie-dyed T-shirts, dresses and trousers, sculpted candles, incense, wooden flutes and various hand-crafted items.

One of the most prominent stores was the Psychedelic Shop on Haight Street, which was run by Jay and Ron Thelin, two brothers who were friends of ours. In addition to all their drug paraphernalia and "headware," they sold our Krishna posters and frequently sent curious people and seekers to the temple. The store had a meditation room at the back where the brothers held a program every Saturday night. They had invited the swami to attend several times, but we always declined because we wanted to spare the swami from that kind of setting as far as possible. It constantly played the music that was part of the rock revolt and was always full of the spirit of giddy wild alternative consumerism. It smelled like a combination of musk, marijuana, incense, scented candles, essential oils, perfume, whiskey, beer, wine and dirty human bodies.

Still, we knew we couldn't keep refusing the Thelin brothers. We decided to accept one of their many invitations to come to the Psychedelic Shop on a Saturday night, but we told them we wanted to leave early, by nine at the latest.

It was a warm cloudless evening in late March when six of us set out to the Psychedelic Shop with the swami. The smell of marijuana and incense wafted through the warm air. On weekend evenings Haight Street had acquired a perpetual background soundtrack of guitars, bells, bongos, recorders, flutes, seaweed horns and rock music that pounded from storefronts and handheld blasters. Many were smoking pot and hashish or were drinking Olympia beer out of brown stubbies, sharing Gallo wine or swigging Johnny Walker out of big bottles in brown paper sacks. Others with packs and sleeping bags on their backs strummed on guitars, singing as they walked. Dozens of boys and girls and same-sex couples walked past holding hands or arm in arm. Some embraced and kissed, leaning against storefront windows. Cross-dressers lounged in doorways. People wearing flowers and feathers in their hair set up stalls against the building walls and decorated the sidewalk with multi-colored chalk drawings while they sat waiting for customers. It was like a hippy flea-market, a bizarre open-air psychedelic mall.

I walked in silence next to the swami, while Shyamasundar trailed behind with four of the new San Francisco devotees: Chidananda, Sankarshana, Lilavati and Gaurasundara. It was seven o'clock. I thought the whole scene before us must appear very decadent to the swami, and I didn't know what to say about it to him.

Finally, I said, "It's a beautiful night."

The swami scrutinized the street sellers, looked at passing smokers and bongo players, people with painted faces and wild, brightly colored costumes. He appeared to smell the air, taking in the burning odor of marijuana and the sharp putrid stench of alcohol, which was tempered by the fragrance of roses and carnations. He turned, smiling, and said, "*Everything* is beautiful."

I was surprised because I thought the swami would perceive this streetscape as being debauched and disgusting. But as we walked in companionable silence, I realized that the swami actually liked to be surrounded by people; after all, he had grown up in India, one of the most densely populated countries in the world. More than this, though, I thought that the swami perceived Krishna in this place. Many of these people were genuine seekers, eager for knowledge, ripe and ready for Krishna consciousness. I remembered the swami saying earlier in his San Francisco visit that hippies embraced detachment, and that *that* was their qualification. There was no good or bad from the pure angle of vision – everything and everyone in every part of creation was Krishna's energy, and because the swami was in touch with that energy, he saw this beauty. The people were beautiful because they were all potential devotees. Everything was beautiful because everything was connected to Krishna.

His remark was more an instruction than a casual comment. I realized the vast difference between him and the young Bauls who we had met the previous week. The Bengalis were really a group of performers who were playing the Eastern spirituality card as a way of coming to America and becoming famous. To the American public they were as unusual as our swami was, but I didn't think they were driven by a desire to present genuine Vaishnava philosophy. I suddenly realized how America's current interest in spirituality left people wide open to be exploited by those offering some flavor of Eastern culture with a personal motive attached – be that fame, power or wealth. I knew from my own observation of our swami that he was not after any of these things; he was driven by a desire to fulfill the wishes of his spiritual master, and I felt immensely grateful to have found him in the great mystical melting pot that was America's alternative culture.

The swami was still smiling as we reached the Psychedelic Shop. Ron and Jay greeted our little group with folded palms at the front door.

"Hey, man!" Ron said to me.

"How ya doin', Ron?" I said. "Well, we finally made it."

"Yeah," Jay said. "Swami Bhaktivedanta! We thought you were *never* going to come." He held out his hand and the swami shook it. "We got the meditation room ready. There's people waiting for you."

"Oh. You are having meditation?" the swami asked.

"Every day," Jay said. "Every night. Saturday night especially. Full of people. They're waiting for you – really! It's great you came."

"What time does the program start?" I asked.

"It started already," Ron said. "But this is the *real* beginning, now that the swami's here."

"Come on in," Jay said. "We'll show you into the meditation room."

The small store was crowded with people. There were a few couples smooching in the corner and a group of young teenage boys watching the smooching couples while pretending to check out the

Haight-Ashbury Psychedelic Shop proprietors Ron (left) and Jay Thelin

boxes of roach clips, pipes and Riz-la papers that were spread out on the counter. Beside the counter sat a table filled with sculptures and trinkets – candle holders, beaded lamps and crystal balls filled with raindrop-shaped granules and white snowflakes.

"The meditation room is at the back," Jay said, ushering us through the crowd. The swami and I filed past a gaunt woman with knee-length hair who blew a perfect ring of marijuana smoke as she stared at us.

The meditation room was constructed of four India-patterned bedspreads hung at right angles to form four walls at the back of the store. Ron pulled back one of the walls. Through the thick smoke I could see five people sitting erect in lotus posture with their eyes closed, two young women who were lying on their backs passed out cold, and two huge black men lying on their sides puffing on large pipes of hash. The two men were both bearded and had scars on their faces, arms and hands.

"Just go in and start," Jay said. "They've been waiting for you." I thought this was something of a misnomer. The people in this quasi-opium den didn't look like they were waiting for *anyone*. But we went in and sat cross-legged on the stain-pocked carpet, the swami in the middle and the rest of us on either side of him. Those who were conscious looked at us hazily through half-closed eyes. The smoke was overwhelmingly strong, but the unmistakable stench of unwashed bodies remained like the active ingredient of some kind of obscene perfume. The meditators' clothes all looked unwashed, their hands and feet grimy, their hair greasy. I looked upward, trying to avoid eye contact, and saw the shop's black ceiling above us.

The swami took out his hand cymbals and began to chant. *"Hare Krishna Hare Krishna Krishna Krishna Hare Hare, Hare Rama Hare Rama Rama Rama Hare Hare."* He chanted for half an hour and everyone who was awake in the meditation room responded. The sound of the chanting drew more people into the meditation room, and soon the small space was packed. At the end of the chant the devotees bowed down on the floor while the swami said prayers in Sanskrit. No one else bowed down. I noticed cigarette burns in the carpet as I sat up.

"This movement is very important for all classes of men to follow," the swami began saying. "If you see another human being as American, Indian, black, white, male or female, this is skin disease. There are eight million four hundred thousand forms of life. In this human form, we have great responsibility. We have to inform others that there is no permanent situation here. We must experience old age and disease. No one can say, 'I'm young man; I'll not become old man.' No. It is impossible to say.

"Just like I am conscious throughout my body. If you pinch any part of my body, then I feel. That is my consciousness. So consciousness is spread, all over my body."

Ron came in and sat down, smiling at the swami.

"This is explained in *Bhagavad-gita*. That consciousness which is spread all over this body, that is eternal. But this body is perishable, but that consciousness is imperishable, eternal. And that consciousness, or the soul, is transmigrating from one body to another. Just like we are changing dress. I may have this dress. You may have another dress. I may exchange your dress with me. So this changing of dress is going on every moment.

"Medical science also says that every second we are changing blood corpuscles, and therefore change in the body is going on. So you say or I say that 'body is growing,' but in the Vedic language it is said that 'body is changing.' Just like a child is born so small from the mother's womb, and it changes body every second. Then he becomes a young child or a boy, then young man, then old man like me, and so on. In this way, this changing, body changing, is going on. And the final change is called death. Death means ... Just like the too much old garments cannot be used; similarly, this body is the garment of the soul. When it can no longer be used, we have to accept another body. This is called transmigration of the soul."

I couldn't believe the swami was continuing to speak in this setting. Around us, most of the people had either passed out or were sleeping. Only a few – those who had been awake to begin with – remained sitting erect. One of the black guys also listened from his reclining position.

"Human life is not in large quantity. Out of that there are very few Aryan families. The Aryan family – the Indo-European family, they are also Aryan – they are very few."

Hearing the word "Aryan," I immediately was on alert. Being Jewish, I'd grown up around those who had either been affected or were from families affected by Hitler's desire to establish a "pure" superior race. I knew that "Aryan" was a widely used Sanskrit word, but I'd never heard the swami use it before in a public lecture. I quickly looked at the black guys; one of them looked suddenly more attentive.

"The Europeans, they belong to the Indo-European group. The Americans, they also come from Europe. So this group of human society is very few. The Vedanta says, 'now you have got developed human form of life, civilized life, you have got nice arrangement for your comfortable life.' Especially in America, you have got all material comforts. You have got cars; you have got good road, nice food, nice building, nice dress, nice feature of your body. Everything God has given you very nice. The Vedanta advises, 'Now you talk about the inquiry of the Supreme.'"

The black man stared at the swami motionless. I couldn't really tell if he was processing what the swami was saying. Perhaps they were too high to grasp his points, or maybe they accepted that identification of the body was a false identification from the spiritual perspective, or maybe they understood that Hitler had misapplied the Vedic terminology. What I did know for certain was that San

Francisco was full of black supremacists and that many of them took Hitler's Aryan philosophy personally; and why wouldn't they when he supposedly considered everyone who was not blond and blue-eyed to be inferior?

The swami concluded his talk and the audience applauded. We stood up to leave.

"So, you want to come again next Saturday?" Ron asked.

"Well, we'll be here on Tuesday to give you some more posters for the store, so I'll let you know then," I said. I didn't think this was really the kind of place we would want to visit regularly.

"OK," Ron said. "Thanks for coming, Swami. You were great!"

The swami nodded and I shook hands with Ron. As we started to walk back to the temple, I looked over my shoulder to make sure the scarred men weren't following us. They looked like Dickensian convicts to me, and I was anxious that they might try to pick a fight once we were out of the laid-back atmosphere of the store.

"I was worried they were going to start a riot in there," I said to the swami. I glanced over my shoulder again. No one was following us.

"What is 'riot'?" he asked.

"It's like mass violence. Like the Hindu-Muslim riots in Calcutta," I said.

"Oh, yes," he said. "I am knowing this word. Why you think this?"

"Lots of people get upset about the word 'Aryan.' Especially black people and Jewish people."

"Oh? And why is that?" he asked.

"Well, because of Hitler," I said. "Adolf Hitler believed that the German people were a superior race and he called them Aryans. He killed Jews and Gypsies – anyone who wasn't pure German – because they were different."

"Oh," he said, looking straight ahead. "I am knowing about this. But not about word 'Aryan.' Hitler used this word?"

"Yes."

We walked a couple more blocks in silence, observing the swarms of people enjoying the warm evening on Haight Street.

Then, as we neared the temple, he looked at me out of the corner of his eye and smiled.

"It's a beautiful night," he said.

The author walks with the swami in San Francisco.

CHAPTER 20

A Date with the Indian Ambassador

On the Monday morning after Jay and Ron's program, I went up to the swami's apartment to see if he wanted me to do anything.

"Yes," he said. "Today I would like to visit Mr. B.K. Nehru. He is Indian Ambassador to the United States on short visit to San Francisco. You can drive me there?"

"Sure," I said. "Do you know where he's staying?"

"At St. Francis Hotel. You know it?"

"Yeah, I think so," I said. "I'll have to check the address, but we'll definitely be able to drive there. Do you have an appointment?"

"I have," the swami said. "It is at one o'clock."

"OK," I said. "I'll make sure no one is using the Krishna car around lunch time so that I can drive you there."

We drove into the heart of the city's business district and parked in the loading zone at the main entrance of the St. Francis. The hotel's large glass doors were manned by a doorman wearing a flat-topped hat and a knee-length dark blue coat with brass buttons. Several other porters and valets were busy opening the doors of expensive-looking cars – a Mercedes, a couple of Rolls-Royces and a limo – to welcome arriving guests. I felt out of place in my partially soiled green sports coat, slacks that didn't match and shabby uncut hair. I realized suddenly that I didn't know what to do in this environment and hadn't thought ahead. Where should we park? Would the valets open the door of the beat-up old Krishna car for the swami to get out? Would they let me go into the hotel wearing such clothes?

The uniformed doorman stared at me as I slammed the spray-painted car door and walked up to him.

"Good afternoon," I said, trying not to sound helpless and un-cultured. "The swami has an appointment with Mr. Nehru, the Ambassador of India. I was wondering if we could leave the car here with you if I give you the keys. We'll be about half an hour."

The doorman bent down a little so he could get a good look at the swami in the Krishna car. I knew how incongruous we looked together, the swami aristocratic and exotic in his saffron robes and me in my scruffy attire and decrepit vehicle. The traffic swept past the St. Francis, and I waited for him to ask me to leave the premises.

"Certainly, sir," he said. He held out his right palm for the keys, all the while watching the swami. "Go ahead, but don't be too long." He clenched his fingers over the keys and then dropped them in the deep pocket of his uniform.

"Phase One successfully completed," I thought. I opened the hotel door for the swami, and we walked to the big marble counter in the glittering lobby. My heart was pounding, and I straightened up, trying to look dignified.

"We have an appointment with Mr. Nehru," I said to the im-maculately clad man behind the counter.

"Certainly, sir," he said. "Top floor, Penthouse Suite." He ges-tured toward a bank of six elevators that stood on the other side of the lobby.

The elevator was paneled with mirrors and had a brass handle that ran around its circumference. I pressed the button marked "Penthouse," and up we went. The elevator door opened onto a marble tiled entrance way. There was only one large double door to knock on, and I realized that the penthouse suite must have oc-cupied the entire top floor of the hotel.

The door was answered by a tall, debonair-looking man with gray hair.

"Hello, Swami Bhaktivedanta," he said, holding out his hand. "I am Braj Kumar Nehru. Please come in." The swami shook his hand.

"Thank you," he said. "This is my assistant, Michael Grant." Nehru shook my hand too and led us down a cream colored hallway that was lit up by a large chandelier hanging from the ceiling. Nehru looked very Westernized in his dark-blue three-piece suit. I was surprised he had opened the door himself.

"Come into the living room and make yourselves comfortable," he said, opening the door for us. The living room was lavishly decorated with crystal chandeliers, thick carpets, and huge butter-yellow overstuffed chairs and sofas embossed with jacquard daffodils. Two of the room's walls were made of glass, and through them I could see the Golden Gate and Bay bridges.

The swami sat on the end of one of the couches and motioned for me to sit at the other end. Nehru sat opposite us in one of the overstuffed chairs. A small light-complexioned woman in a blue sari came into the living room, and Nehru stood to greet her.

"This is my wife, Shobha," he said. Mrs. Nehru looked kind, but tired and frail. She half-smiled at us and sat on the edge of a chair off to her husband's right.

As soon as everyone was seated, the conversation switched into Hindi, which I didn't understand. I could see they were all more comfortable speaking their own language, and I didn't really mind being excluded from the conversation. I was tired, and my mind began to wander. "Maybe it would look good to the Indian Ambassador that the swami has an American assistant," I thought. "Maybe that was why the swami introduced me by my legal name." I felt drowsy. I hadn't had enough sleep the previous night, and the drone of the foreign language lulled me into a kind of relaxation.

In the midst of his Hindi, the swami said my name and added in English, "my assistant." I snapped to attention and saw the Nehrus nod and smile. I tried to look attentive and hoped I at least looked like I understood what was being said. The swami's Hindi was peppered with English words: "childhood," "chemist" and "steamship." He looked imploring and earnest as he spoke. "But one word from you ..." he said to Nehru in English, and quickly resumed speaking Hindi.

I gathered that the swami was asking Nehru for a favor. I thought his use of the English sentence was tactical – he wanted me to know he was asking for something, and he wanted Mr. Nehru to know that I knew.

Nehru was a genial host, but he remained deadpan throughout

the swami's request. He said something in Hindi, and finally the swami stood. Mrs. Nehru and I stood as well, and her husband led us back to the front door.

"Thank you very much for coming," Nehru said. His wife said something to the swami in Hindi and handed him a golf-ball-sized object wrapped in aluminum foil. The swami held out his right hand to accept it.

"Thank you very much," he said to her, and dropped the object into his pocket.

We all shook hands.

"All the best," Nehru said.

"Very pleased to meet you," I said.

"And I you," the ambassador replied. "Goodbye."

We took the elevator down to the lobby and walked out into the cold San Francisco wind. The Krishna car was still parked in the loading zone beside a sign that said *No Parking or Waiting*.

The doorman handed me the keys. His eyes twinkled, but his mouth was firm. "You take it easy, now," he said.

"Thank you so much," I said. He continued to stand there, like he was waiting for me to say something. "Thanks again," I said. It was only as I drove away that I realized he had probably been waiting for a tip.

As we drove back to the temple I asked the swami about Mr. Nehru. He launched into a long, complicated explanation of how he was related to Jawaharlal Nehru, India's former prime minister. I didn't understand the family connection, and I asked him to explain it again. He did so in an even more convoluted way. Ambassador Nehru was apparently related to the late premier through a brother's wife's cousin's brother's daughter's uncle or something equally obscure. As the swami explained it, it seemed to me like everyone in India must be related in some way to everyone else.

"What were you asking him?" I asked.

"I want to purchase a building for temple in San Francisco," he said. "Mr. Nehru could help me."

"Do you think he'll help?"

"I don't think so," the swami answered. He seemed unconcerned with the outcome of the meeting, not disappointed or upset at all.

I didn't ask the exact nature of his request, and he didn't offer the information.

"Why was Mrs. Nehru so light-complexioned?" I asked. "Is she Indian? She looked Western to me."

"She is Parsee," he answered. "Originally they are from Persia but now live in India." He took the silver ball out of his pocket and unwrapped the gift Mrs. Nehru had given him. Inside was a date, the biggest I had ever seen. It looked delicious.

"Oh, very nice," the swami said. "It is *medjool* date." He took a bite out of it and handed it to me. I was surprised. No one had ever taken a bite out of a piece of fruit and given it to me. He didn't say, "Here, taste this. It's really good"; he acted as though giving me a half-eaten date was a completely natural thing to do.

I took the date because not taking it seemed a worse option. But as I held it, I realized I didn't really want it. The thought of another person's saliva made me shudder a bit, even though I used to drink out of other people's wine or whiskey bottles and even share soggy joints or water pipe hoses. Somehow I knew taking a bite was the right thing to do. Casting aside all thoughts of aversion, I bit into it, and it tasted great. I immediately forgot my initial hesitation.

There was still about a third of the date remaining, so, as I steered the car with my left hand, I held out the remaining part for the swami so he could finish it. He looked at it and shook his head coolly and distractedly. I'd made a cultural faux pas, but I wasn't sure what it was. I quickly ate the rest of the date and wound down the window so I could spit out the pit; I was careful not to let any spit blow back into the car.

We drove along in silence. I was tired.

"How many hours of sleep should I have?" I asked.

"You are feeling tired?" the swami asked with genuine interest.

"Sometimes," I said. He obviously hadn't noticed me drifting off on the ambassador's couch, and I was glad of that.

"How many hours you are having?" he asked.

"Usually five."

"You can sleep till you are refreshed. Somebody's refreshed by sleeping four hours. Somebody else is refreshed by sleeping ten hours."

"Some of the devotees say we should have only six hours or less," I said.

"Six is usually enough," he said.

When we arrived back at our apartments on Frederick Street, I saw the swami to his room and then went down to the temple to discuss the date incident with Shyamasundar.

"Oh, yeah," he said, when I'd told him what had happened. "I read in the *Srimad-Bhagavatam* that eating the remains of your spiritual master's food is good for spiritual advancement. I think the swami was giving you a gift – not just the other half of his date."

America's First Rathayatra

The payphone in the back room of the temple rang loudly one afternoon in the final week of March. I closed my book and stood up and stretched, half hoping it would stop ringing before I made it back there to answer.

"Hello, Radha-Krishna temple," I said.

"Is Swamiji there?" It was a voice I knew. I took a guess. "Gargamuni? Is that you?"

"Mukunda?"

"Yeah, it's me," I said. "How ya doin' over there?" Gargamuni had just started attending the swami's programs on Second Avenue when Janaki and I left New York. He was the brother of Bruce, now Brahmananda, the devotee who used to be a wrestler and who had helped raise funds to pay back Ginsberg the money he had loaned us for the swami's visa extension.

"It's going good in New York," he said. "What's going on there?"

"Well, we organized some good programs for the swami," I said. "I think he likes it here."

"Yeah, we heard all about your rock and roll dance," Gargamuni said. "Is that what you call a 'good program'?"

"Rock and roll dance?" I repeated. "Actually, it was called the Mantra-Rock Dance."

"Rock and roll," Gargamuni repeated, his disapproval radiating through the phone receiver. "How could you put him through that?"

"The swami loved it," I said. "He really did. He chanted, you know. *And* danced." All the devotees on the West Coast knew that the New York crowd thought we were too liberal, too far-out. They were skeptical about our hanging out with alternatives, our kirtans with the hippies in the park and our musical ventures.

"You guys really like that kind of music, doncha?"

"Whaddya mean?" I said.

"I mean hippy music. Rock and roll."

"Well, the swami said everything can be used in Krishna's service," I said.

"Maybe," Gargamuni said. "But better is to not be too radical. Like, we made a record here with the swami, but we kept it traditional. And people love it! We've sold tons of copies, and even the Beatles have ordered some – three hundred of them!" I'd heard the *Happening Album* Gargamuni was talking about and had to admit it was good – it had the swami chanting prayers to his spiritual master on one side and him singing the Hare Krishna mantra with the New York devotees on the other.

"Anyway, we don't really care what anyone thinks of what we're doing out here," I said. "Except the swami, of course, and he *loved* the Mantra-Rock Dance."

"Can I talk to him?" Gargamuni sounded impatient now.

"He's up in his room, and I don't think he'll want to come all the way down to talk on the phone," I said. "You could call back later."

"When's he coming back?" Gargamuni asked.

"You mean to the temple?"

ALLEN GINSBERG says: "It brings a state of ecstasy!"

Hare KRISHNA

Transcendental Sound Vibration

Here is a sublimely devotional experience offered for the first time on a 12-inch LP record! Swami Bhaktivedanta leads an authentic chanting of the Vedic Mantra HARE KRISHNA, sings 2 prayers and plays drum! *Now available at the Psychedelic Shop*

MAIL THIS COUPON TO KRISHNA RECORD 518 Frederick, San Francisco, Cal. 94117
Please send me the HARE KRISHNA Record. I enclose $3.00 for each record.
NAME
ADDRESS
CITY STATE
Number of records wanted Amount Enclosed
(Dealers please write for special wholesale price)

Newspaper advertisement for the Happening album 33 1/3 vinyl LP recording

"I mean to New York," he said. "We heard he was coming back in April."

"I don't know. I haven't heard that," I said. I felt my heart beat a bit faster. April was only a week away. "I can ask him if you want."

"Yeah, OK. But I'm pretty sure he's coming back next month."

"I'll ask him," I assured him. "I'll call you back when I talk to him."

"OK, thanks. Hare Krishna," he said.

This was the third call from the New York devotees asking the swami to go back east. Other people had always answered the phone, but now, when I'd spoken to a New York devotee myself, I could see how determined they were to get him back. I knew they had also been writing letters with the same message. Shyamasundar and I decided we had to discuss the situation with the swami.

The next day after the morning program, we headed up to the swami's apartment.

"Swami, Gargamuni called yesterday," I said. "He wants to know what your plans are."

"Yes, I have had letter from Gargamuni," the swami said. "I am thinking to go to New York on April 9th. He says he will send ticket."

We were both surprised. "So," I thought, "Gargamuni wasn't really calling to ask when the swami was coming back to New York. He was calling to finalize the swami's travel arrangements."

"We are planning to organize other programs here, though," I said. "Like the Rathayatra in July."

"And what if there is another chant at the ballroom?" Shyamasundar asked.

"I will not make definite plans until he sends ticket," the swami said. "But once ticket has come, I will go there."

"I think tickets can easily be changed," I said.

"In any case, I will go there by April," he said. "But I will come back to San Francisco when you call for me. Certainly for Rathayatra I will come."

"We can send you an airline ticket, or pay for it like we did last time," I suggested.

"That will be very convenient," he said.

"So, maybe after a few weeks you will come back to San Francisco?" Shyamasundar asked.

"Yes, maybe few weeks. Maybe few months."

On April 9th, thirty of us went to San Francisco Airport to bid the swami farewell. In the departure lounge the swami sat on a vinyl cushioned bench and we crowded around him. Everyone looked somber and subdued. People stared at us, but we didn't care.

"You all please maintain the center nicely," he said. "I will return to San Francisco for Rathayatra in July."

—•—

The swami did return to San Francisco in July, but it was under different circumstances than we had imagined. In the intervening months between the swami's departure and his anticipated return, we did our best to maintain the routine that had evolved during his stay with us. We continued to hold morning programs, the evening programs, the Sunday Love Feast and the park chanting. We tried as far as possible to continue as though he was still in San Francisco, all the while expecting his return in July.

Three devotees chant on San Francisco's Haight Street.

Then, on June 1st, we received a phone call from Gargamuni in New York informing us that the swami had suffered a stroke and was in critical condition in Beth Israel Hospital in Manhattan. His doctors told devotees to be prepared that he might not live through the night. I shut that possibility out of my mind.

"We're going to stay up all night tonight to chant," Gargamuni said to me. "We thought we should pray to Krishna to save him."

"We'll do that too, then," I said. "The swami's doing God's work. Why wouldn't he be saved?"

That night, thirty people gathered in the San Francisco temple room for the overnight vigil. Yamuna led the chanting for the first couple of hours, her distinctive voice blending with the tones of the harmonium. About ten o'clock I made my way upstairs to our apartment. I'd been up for eighteen hours doing preparation for the Rathayatra, plus attending to numerous other routine jobs. I had to sleep, and I knew the swami would understand.

When I went back down to the temple at six o'clock the next morning, Janaki met me on the sidewalk.

"Did you stay all night, then?" I asked her.

"Yeah," she said. "I started feeling really tired about two in the morning, but at that time a few of us felt a change in the air, and I decided to stay."

San Francisco temple room, June, 1967

"What does that mean?" I asked. "A change in the air?"

"I don't know how to explain it," she said. "It's just that a few of us knew at that time that the swami had survived and that he was going to be OK."

"Well," I said a bit skeptically, "I'm sure Krishna's looking out for the swami."

"Yeah," Janaki said. "I'm going up to get some sleep now, but you should go into the temple."

"I will," I said.

We chanted until the phone at the back of the temple rang a couple of hours later. Everyone stopped chanting abruptly and tried to hear what Shyamasundar was saying into the phone receiver.

"That was Gargamuni," he said breathlessly a few minutes later. "It's OK. He made it through."

There was a collective sigh of relief. A few of the devotees had tears in their eyes.

"So is he back at the temple?" I asked.

"He's still in critical condition, but the doctors say he's made it through the worst. He'll be in the hospital for a while, but he wants Ayurvedic treatment. He's written to someone he knows in India to try to get some Ayurvedic medicine."

Over the next day, I thought about what we could do to help the swami recover. I decided we should make a recording of the San Francisco devotees chanting. The swami could listen to it while he was recovering in the hospital. The next day a group of about fifteen people gathered to sing for the swami's special recording. The finished product included a couple of Hare Krishna melodies, the "*Govinda jaya jaya*" song the swami had taught me and a new song called "*Sri Ram Jai Ram*," which I'd recently learned from a World Pacific record called *Hindu Chants*. We used *mrdanga*, small *karatala* hand cymbals, *tamboura* and two guitars for accompaniment. A couple of days later I sent the tape by airmail to New York.

Gargamuni and I spoke on the phone almost every day about the swami's health. One evening when I answered the phone he told me that our tape had arrived in New York.

"Has the swami heard it yet?" I asked.

"Yeah," Gargamuni said. "He loved it. In fact, he loved it so much that I thought maybe it would be worth seeing if a radio station wanted to play it on the air."

"Really?" I was incredulous because Gargamuni was so critical and right-wing about everything we did. "Was anyone interested?"

"Yes." He sounded a bit grudging, but I knew the swami's precarious condition had inspired us both to overlook our petty differences. "I took it to an FM station called WBAI. Do you know it?"

"I've heard of it," I said. "Owned by Pacifica Corporation. Kind of artsy for the intelligentsia."

"Yeah, that's right," he said. "Well, they liked it too, and they played it last night. They said they have up to thirty million listeners each evening."

"Wow – thanks, Gargamuni."

"That's OK," he said. "The swami was happy when I told him."

The following day an airmail letter arrived from the swami:

> My dear boys and girls,
>
> I am so much obliged to you for your prayers to Krishna to save my life. Due to your sincere and ardent prayer, Krishna has saved my life. I was to die on Tuesday certainly but because you prayed sincerely I am saved. Now I am improving gradually and coming to original condition. Now I can hope to meet you again and chant with you, Hare Krishna. I am so glad to receive the report of your progressive march and I hope there will be no difficulty in your understanding Krishna consciousness. My blessings are always with you and with confidence you go on with your chanting *Hare Krishna Hare Krishna Krishna Krishna Hare Hare, Hare Rama Hare Rama Rama Rama Hare Hare.*
>
> Thanking you once more,
>
> Your ever well-wisher,
>
> A.C. Bhaktivedanta Swami."

We were thrilled to hear this from him, but I was even more overjoyed the following day when a letter arrived addressed to me:

> My dear Mukunda,
>
> The record which you have sent singing '*Sri Ram Jaya*

Ram' and other kirtan is really a new turn and we have enjoyed the record so nicely. You should practice this kirtan more so that during your Rathayatra festival you can have this singing with the procession.

Please inform all the devotees, boys and girls, especially Janaki Devi, that I am progressing well. As soon as I get a little strength for traveling I shall come to San Francisco. In the meantime I shall be very glad to know what arrangements you are going to do for the Rathayatra festival. Make it a grand procession and unique introduction in the United States.

Most probably I will be able to come to S.F. by the 25th of this month.

Your ever well-wisher,

A.C. Bhaktivedanta Swami."

I couldn't believe the swami was thinking about the Rathayatra so soon after almost dying. This letter gave us all renewed enthusiasm for organizing the Rathayatra, which we had all but forgotten in the turmoil since the swami's stroke.

Jayananda and Shyamasundar became the driving force behind the festival. Shyamasundar contacted a carpenter friend of ours named Bob Simmons, who said he'd be happy to help with the construction of the truck-shrine the swami had drawn. The swami had said we should have several days of feasting at the temple for the festival, so Jayananda got donations of vegetables, grains and *dahl* from his numerous merchant-friends around the city. Others made bright triangular flags, which were affixed to doweling so that they could be carried in the procession. We also strung the flags side-by-side on long pieces of ribbon so that they could be hung from the deities' canopy.

I wanted to know more about the festival itself, so I spent a day in the library reading up about it. I found out that it had been held for thousands of years and that it was India's largest outdoor festival. Over a million people attended every year. Even though I knew ours would be tiny in comparison, I thought it was exciting to be involved in organizing America's first-ever Rathayatra.

Prior to the swami's return, Gargamuni made sure to impress

upon me his need for peace and quiet, so we decided to try to rent a place for him out of the central part of the city. We managed to find a beachfront house just north of a small town called Stinson Beach in Marin County across the Golden Gate Bridge in a locale known as Paradisio. Before the swami's arrival, we burned plenty of incense and decorated the place with vases of flowers and posters of Krishna.

The swami arrived a week or so before the Rathayatra was scheduled to take place. We knew he was weak, so a small group of only nine people met him at the airport. The devotees took him to the temple to see the deities for a few minutes and then drove him along the winding, mountainous road straight out to Stinson Beach, where Janaki and I were waiting to receive him. He walked up the two front steps with Hayagriva and Kirtanananda – two of the New York devotees – right behind him. We bowed down before him as a sign of respect, and when we stood up I saw that he looked smaller and frailer than I had ever seen him.

"Welcome, Swami," Janaki said. "We're so happy to see you."

"Thank you," he said. "Hare Krishna."

"Would you like to have a look around the house?" I asked.

He tilted his head in assent and followed us through the kitchen, the two bedrooms, the den and the living room.

"This is very nice place," he said, looking out the large living room windows toward the ocean. "What is the arrangement you have made for me to have such nice place?"

"Well," I said, "the place belongs to a Mr. and Mrs. Bodé. They agreed to sublet it to us for four weeks."

The swami raised his eyebrows in surprise. "They agreed to rent for so short time?" he asked.

"They wanted to rent it to us for a longer term," I said. "But I managed to negotiate with them so they'd give it to us for just a month."

"Where is the money coming from?" the swami asked.

"There are a few devotees working," I said. "Like, Jayananda drives his taxi and Shyamasundar has had a few carpentry jobs. The poster sales are going really well at the Psychedelic Shop. So there's enough to pay for the rent on this place for a month. Everyone's agreed to pitch in."

The swami smiled. "Thank you very much," he said.

The swami walked over to the spinet piano that sat in the corner of the living room. He lifted the lid and touched one of the keys.

"The piano is just like the harmonium," I said. "Except you get to play it with two hands." Janaki shot me a withering look as if to say "I think the swami's seen a piano before!"

I pulled out the piano stool for him. "You can sit here," I said.

He sat and with both hands began to play the keys, feeling out the instrument and testing its sound. Then he began to play a melody I didn't recognize.

"He plays beautifully, doesn't he?" Kirtanananda said, looking impressed.

I nodded, but as a pianist I thought that the swami's playing was more suited to a harmonium than a piano. He seemed intrigued by the fact that he could play with both hands; I thought maybe the only keyed instrument he had ever played was a harmonium.

Over the next week, the swami rested at Paradisio, spending most of his time chanting and writing. Hayagriva and Kirtanananda stayed in the house with him to cook and take care of his needs, but I also traveled out to Stinson Beach most days to do things for him and to report on the devotees' progress with the Rathayatra. I told him that everything had been left to the last minute, but it promised to be a great festival. We all hoped that he would be strong enough to come into Frisco for the parade, even if only for a few minutes.

On his second day there, I knocked on his door and sat down on the floor in front of the bed he was sitting on.

"How are you feeling, Swami?" I asked.

He continued to chant softly, gazing at the somewhat primitive painting of Radha and Krishna on the wall to his right painted by a devotee artist. I thought maybe he hadn't heard me, but after a few minutes he put down his beads and stood up.

"What is this body?" he said, making a gesture with his palms open and his arms outstretched. He looked almost disgusted to inhabit an ephemeral body and incredulous that I would be concerned to inquire about the state of something so fleeting. I realized that although I had read about the temporary nature of the body and the eternality of the spirit soul, he was actually living that philosophy.

For him the material world was not as important as the spiritual world, and he didn't really care about his body coming to an end.

I went back into the kitchen and told Hayagriva and Kirtanananda about what the swami had said and my impression of what he meant.

"He's not concerned about leaving his body for himself, because he'll go back to be with Krishna," Hayagriva said. "But what would happen to the movement if he was to die?"

"What?" My mouth hung open.

"All I'm saying is that he's going to leave his body some time," Hayagriva said. "Maybe you should ask him if someone should take over when he dies."

"Maybe *you* should ask him," I said. I thought he was being a bit too pragmatic about such a sensitive issue.

"No, it should be you," Hayagriva insisted. "You're the one he talked to about it."

"Well, actually, no, he didn't," I clarified. "I was the one who started thinking about this stuff because of his comment about his body."

"Whatever the case, we need to know how we should continue our Krishna consciousness education if he's not here, shouldn't we? And how we'd keep his movement alive, right?"

I thought for a few seconds. As blunt as Hayagriva was being about the issue, I had to admit that deep down I wanted to know the answers to these questions for myself too.

"OK, I'll ask him," I said. "I guess somebody has to ask about it eventually, and I guess it may as well be me."

I knocked on his door again.

"Yes?" the swami said from within.

"Swami, can I ask you a question?" I asked.

"Yes." He sat down on his bed again.

I took a deep breath.

"When you die, what will happen to the movement?" I asked. "Will you have a successor who will continue your work and look after our spiritual education?"

As I heard myself say the words, I realized it had been a mistake to ask this. I saw suddenly that I had been put forward to ask this delicate question on someone else's behalf. The swami sat silently, looking out the window at the sand dunes and the mountains. It was high tide and I could hear the waves pounding the beach. Gulls shrieked. I could feel two sets of ears straining from the kitchen to hear his answer.

The swami muttered something quietly.

"I couldn't hear what you said, Swami," I said carefully. "Can you repeat it?"

"Actually, it is an insult to the spiritual master," he said a little louder.

He turned away from the window and looked at me pensively, as if he was hurt by my question.

"I'm sorry, Swami," I said. I felt like shrinking into the carpet.

He closed his eyes. Outside a dog barked. A shallow stream of tears appeared below each of his eyes and flowed over his cheeks. He slowly wiped them away.

"My spiritual master ..." he said, and his voice choked to gravel.

I was stunned. What had I done?

The author (top), Hayagriva (left) and Gurudas near the front of the San Francisco temple, 1967

"My spiritual master," he said, "he was no ordinary spiritual master." He paused again, and then whispered falteringly, "He saved me."

"I'm sorry," I said. "I'll go now." I was too overcome myself to say more.

Hayagriva and Kirtanananda looked furtive when I came back into the kitchen. I pushed past them and went and sat out on the porch by myself. The swami's answer was crystal clear to me. There was no question of replacing the spiritual master. His potency to teach would not end with his death but would continue even in his physical absence. What struck me the most was the way the swami taught me this. He didn't just tell me with words; he showed me through his spiritual emotion toward his own spiritual master.

"The swami is no ordinary spiritual master," I thought to myself. "I must learn to love and serve my spiritual master unconditionally with the fidelity and loyalty with which he serves his."

I brushed a few grains of imaginary sand from my hands and went back into the house to talk to Kirtanananda and Hayagriva about the swami's instruction to us all.

———

Shyamasundar and Bob had rented a flatbed truck, which they parked in a Safeway parking lot while they worked on constructing the deities' canopy. I drove past on my way home one evening. Bob was holding up a pillar while Shyamasundar secured it to the back of the truck. I saw that the swami's sketch was tacked to the back of the driver's cabin so they could refer to it.

"Hey, Mukunda," Shyamasundar called as I got out of the car. "How's the swami feeling? You think he's going to be able to come for the parade?"

"I don't know," I said. "He seems a lot weaker than I expected. He's recovering kind of slowly."

"Well, if he can't come to the Rathayatra, we'll take the Rathayatra to him," Shyamasundar declared. "Jaya Jagannatha!"

"Hey, you know those big trucks called Juggernauts?" Bob said. "The ones with big trailers and everything? You know where the name for those things came from? From Jagannatha!"

"Really? It came from the Sanskrit," I asked.

"I guess so. Juggernaut, Jagannatha. They sure sound the same," Bob said.

"Doesn't the truck look great?" Shyamasundar asked.

"It really does," I said. "You guys nearly done?"

"Sure are," Bob said. "Did the whole thing in less than twenty-four hours."

I reported to the swami about Bob and Shyamasundar's amazing efficiency the following day while we walked along Stinson beach.

"It looks so great," I said to him. "They've made the canopy exactly according to your drawing."

"This is very nice," he replied.

"Do you think you will feel well enough to come?" I ventured.

"Actually, I am thinking not," he said. He walked silently for a moment. "I will return to India soon."

"To India?" This wasn't really a surprise, but I was disappointed nonetheless.

"Yes," he said. "For Ayurvedic treatment and rest. Now I will rest here. I will get strength for journey, then I will go."

"When?"

"Perhaps end of July," he answered. "We will see what Krishna desires."

We marched up the steps of the house and removed our shoes. I took the swami's hound's tooth coat and black hat and hung them on the row of coat hooks inside the front door. The swami went into the den and sat down in one of the beige armchairs.

"Mukunda, come," he called. He gestured toward the chair opposite him. "So," he said a little playfully, "what is your definition of Krishna?"

I was pleased, because a philosophical discussion meant he was feeling somewhat better.

"Krishna is God," I answered. "He is the Supreme Being, and our duty is to worship him." It wasn't exactly a philosophically penetrating answer, but he seemed happy with it. He looked hard at me for a long time.

"You must chant sixty-four rounds every day," he said finally.

I was shocked. He must not have liked my answer after all. "Chanting that much – eight hours every day – would be impossible," I thought. I wasn't sure if I was being singled out because of spiritual deficiency or if this was going to be a new requirement for everyone, but I knew it would be unattainable for me. I had enough problems just trying to get sixteen rounds done every day.

The swami saw my hesitancy. "Then you must chant at least thirty-two rounds," he said.

That was a consolation, but even thirty-two seemed like an awful lot. The swami stared hard at me.

"Well, OK," I mumbled, looking at the floor. There was a long pause.

"You must chant at least sixteen rounds a day," he said.

"Yes, Swami," I said loudly, looking up. I was so relieved! This I knew I could do, but I felt like I was reconfirming my earlier promise to him. I understood now that sixteen rounds was only a quarter of the ideal sixty-four. Even though I knew it was all I could handle for now, I rededicated myself to chanting at least sixteen rounds daily without fail.

———•———

Rathayatra day dawned overcast and blustery. The Summer of Love was at its peak and a festive feeling was in the air that Sunday morning, despite heavy winds. Shyamasundar parked the truck in front of the temple so the deities could be transferred from altar to mobile shrine. The canopy looked glorious, decorated with multi-colored flags, strings of bells and long loops of marigold and carnation flower garlands.

Everyone assembled at the temple for the start of the parade dressed in their best, the men in jeans and nice shirts and the women in bright colored saris that they'd managed to organize for this special occasion. Shyamasundar, Gurudas and I decided to wear our white-and-brown Merlin regalia so that we would stand out from the crowd. We still didn't know for sure if the swami would show up.

"Hey, Mukunda," Shyamasundar said. "Why don't you go and call Paradisio and see what the story is?"

The temple room was gradually filling up with festival goers, but I weaved my way through the kirtan to get to the phone at the back of the temple.

The phone rang ten times before Hayagriva answered it.

"It's Mukunda," I said. "Can I talk to the swami?"

"He's resting now," Hayagriva said.

"So does that mean he's not going to be able to come for the Rathayatra?" I asked.

"Yeah, he's not going to be able to come," he said. "He's just not well enough."

I felt downcast. "Well, can you tell him that we wish he could be here but that we'll make sure the parade's amazing even if he can't come," I said. "We've got a huge feast ready here at the temple for after the parade, and we'll report back everything that happens."

"OK, sounds good," Hayagriva said.

Outside, the deities were now on the truck ready to go, Subhadra looking straight out back, Jagannatha and Baladeva facing either side. About ten people sat on the flatbed, their legs dangling off the edges of the truck holding handfuls of smoking incense. A large kirtan party with *karatalas*, drums, tambourines and flutes chanted beside the stationary truck. The speaker system we used in Golden Gate Park was fixed to the back of the truck, the large speakers positioned between the canopy and the driver's cabin. The amplifier was powered by the Tiny Tiger, which sat next to the devotees on the wooden truck bed.

Shyamasundar sat in the driver's seat with the engine idling.

"So, is he coming?" he asked.

"No, he's not strong enough," I said. "But let's do the parade for him! He's the energy behind it."

Someone made a space for me on the flatbed, and I jumped up just as Shyamasundar pulled away from the curb. I started up the Tiny Tiger and plugged in the temple microphone and began to lead the chanting. Immediately I saw the problem: the generator was going to drown out the singing and every other sound as well.

I turned it off and got Shyamasundar to stop the truck so we could discuss how to amplify the kirtan.

"We could put the Tiger in a car and get someone to drive a hundred feet or so behind us," I said.

"That would mean running an electrical cord between the truck and the car. That's too dangerous," Shyamasundar said. "We'll just have to put the thing in here with me and roll up the windows to muffle the sound."

"That'll be too much for you," I said. "The fumes'll kill you! And if they don't, the roar'll make you deaf by the end of the parade."

"It'll be OK," Shyamasundar said. "I don't think it'll be that bad. It's not like I'd be inhaling smoke."

The parade moved forward once again with the generator roaring away on the floor of the truck. I climbed on the flatbed again and began to lead the chanting. The truck drove slowly down the street and the devotees walked beside it, chanting and smiling and waving to onlookers. Two barefoot young women I'd never seen before danced along the street in front of the truck, twirling and clapping with their eyes closed. The sound of my voice wafted over the buildings, "*Hare Krishna Hare Krishna Krishna Krishna Hare Hare, Hare Rama Hare Rama Rama Rama Hare Hare.*"

The whole time I was leading I was worried about Shyamasundaradas, and after half an hour I asked a devotee named Jivananda to sing so that I could see how he was doing and if I could help in any way. I opened the passenger door of the moving truck and the smell hit me.

"God, it's like a torture chamber in here," I shouted over the deafening sound of the Tiger. Shyamasundar grinned hazily at me

First Rathayatra *procession gets underway in San Francisco*

through the thick smoke as I jumped in beside him.

"We gotta get the windows down here," I shouted. "We're going to suffocate! Roll down your window!"

"But it ruins the sound," he screamed, smiling.

"OK, just roll them down for a minute, and then we'll roll them up for a minute, then down, then up!"

Fresh air flooded the driver's cab. We rolled the windows up and I held my breath for as long as I could, and then rolled the windows down again. I could see the headlines: "Krishnas suffocate to death as chant delights crowds." The insane hilarity of the situation struck me and before long Shyamasundar and I were in fits of laughter. Everyone was having a good time, the parade was a success, and we were somehow managing to tolerate the poisonous carbon monoxide!

The swami said the parade must be unhurried, so we moved westward toward the beach slowly. We came to a slight grade in the road and the engine stalled. The vehicle rolled backwards about six feet while Shyamasundar was frantically trying to start it and braking intermittently. It felt like there was a boulder or lump under the wheels.

"Surely we haven't hit someone," I thought frantically, jumping out of the truck. It was just a pothole! Shyamasundar jammed his foot on the brakes, pulled up the handbrake, and got the truck started. Everyone cheered.

We pulled into Irving Street, a nice wide road with plenty of room for the parade participants to dance and twirl. There were lots of Sunday shoppers, and despite the meager publicity we mustered, a lot of people saw the festival.

Once we were into the rhythm of opening and closing the truck windows, I got Murari to take my place. I felt very sick because of the smoke and didn't think I'd be able to make it to see the swami that night. We were halfway to the ocean, but I turned around and headed back to our apartment to sleep.

That afternoon, the festival participants returned to the temple for a huge feast in honor of America's first Rathayatra festival. I staggered down to the temple. When everyone had eaten their fill, nineteen devotees jumped onto the back of the flatbed truck with the deities and Shyamasundar drove them out to see the swami.

The next day, they told me that it had been dark and cold and windy and there was nothing to hold onto on the flatbed. Somehow Shyamasundar negotiated the sharp curves on the narrow roadway, causing the devotees to scream in excitement and fear. The slope down to Stinson Beach and Paradisio was precipitous, but everyone was so eager to tell the swami about the Rathayatra that they didn't mind much.

Hayagriva greeted everyone on the front steps.

"Come in," he said. "The swami wants to hear all about it!"

They carried the deities inside and placed them on the spinet piano. The swami bowed down before them and sat down in his chair, smiling broadly at everyone.

"We had the parade, and so many people saw it!" Shyama-sundaradas said.

"Everyone was chanting and dancing in front of the truck," Malati said. "We walked all the way to the beach, and then every-one went back to the temple for a big feast!"

"At one point we thought the truck was going to roll backwards over the crowd," Gurudas said. "The engine stalled."

The swami opened his eyes wide. "Yes, this is also happening in Puri," he said. "Lord Jagannatha's cart sometimes stops and even rolls backwards! So this stoppage was the Lord's mercy. This first American Rathayatra was real Rathayatra, just as in Puri."

———

The morning I drove the swami to San Francisco Airport had a bittersweet quality. We were happy that he was now well enough to make the journey back to India, and I was glad that he would have the chance to recover there where he would be comfortable and would have access to Ayurvedic treatment. But we were also downcast because he was leaving and we didn't know if he would ever return to America.

At the airport the swami sat on one of the ugly vinyl chairs in the departure lounge surrounded by the twenty people who had come to bid him farewell. Most of the devotees were exuberant, talking and laughing among themselves, but the swami sat quietly, soberly. Shyamasundar came forward to tell him the news he and Malati had received the day before.

"Swami, we won't see you for a while now, maybe not even when you come back to America," he said.

"Oh? Why is that?" the swami asked.

"Me and Malati, we have to go to jail."

The swami looked a little surprised, but he gave a small smile. "That's all right," he said. "Krishna was born in jail! His uncle Kamsa imprisoned his mother and father." He paused. "Why?" he asked. "What did you do?"

"Well, it was before we were devotees," Shyamasundar said. "We were selling some drugs and we got caught. Drug dealing."

"Never mind, I was also drug dealer," the swami said. He chuckled softly.

"Yes, but these drugs weren't legal pharmaceuticals like yours," Malati said, laughing in spite of herself.

"You must chant Hare Krishna as much as possible while you are there," he instructed.

They nodded. "We will."

"I read in the paper that there have been riots in Delhi," I said. "The report said seven hundred people were arrested yesterday."

"There were riots?" the swami asked. "What riots?"

"Racial ones," I said.

"Skin disease," the swami said. "This is based on body only."

From where she stood behind the swami's seat, Janaki reached over his shoulder and gleefully snatched his ticket and passport from him.

"Now you *have* to stay here," she said. "You can't go without these!"

"They'll let me in anyway. It is my country," he said, smiling at her joke.

"Do you promise to come back to San Francisco?" Janaki asked. "When you come back to America, will you come here first?"

The swami nodded. "Yes. If Krishna allows I will come," he said.

He stood and looked straight ahead to his departure gate. We accompanied him as far as we were allowed and then watched him pace down the telescoping walkway to the Boeing 707. Everyone stayed until the plane had disappeared into the clouds.

Welcome back, Swami!

Over the four months that the swami was away, our congregation increased and our programs got bigger. We had long energetic kirtans four nights a week, which were attended by musicians, meditators and other spiritual seekers. The *mrdanga* retained its place of supreme importance in the kirtan, but its rhythm was supplemented by numerous other musical instruments, especially the few pairs of *karatala* cymbals which we had acquired from India.

Because the temple was growing, I decided it would be a good idea to have some *karatalas* made. Importing them was a headache, and I figured it couldn't be that hard to make a few pairs of hand cymbals. The swami said *karatalas* were made from "gun metal," but I had no idea what that was.

I grabbed a copy of the yellow pages, found a metallurgy lab and walked over to see about getting the *karatalas*' metallic content analyzed. The coolie-hat-shaped *karatalas* clanged together in my pocket as I walked.

The metallurgy guy drilled out small shavings from the underside of one *karatala*.

"I'll do a quick spectro-analysis of these shavings," he said. "Then I'll be able to tell you what's in them."

He came back ten minutes later carrying a printout, which he handed to me.

"It looks like the cymbals are mostly brass," he said. I glanced

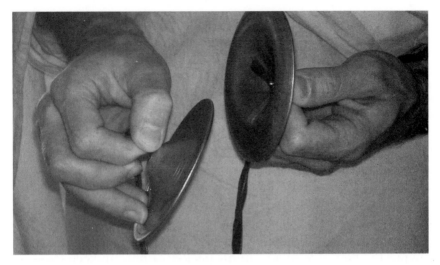

Karatalas *held by a devotee*

down at the printout: eighty percent brass, seventeen percent tin and the remainder a mixture of zinc, mercury, lead and manganese." So *that* was gunmetal.

"Do you think we could make something like them?" I asked. "You know, buy the metal and then cast, mold or forge them or whatever you do?"

"Sure," he said. "There's lots of places that would do it, especially if you find the stuff yourself."

I did some research and found out that buying brass and tin was expensive, so we scoured scrap yards for old brass ship valves and used refrigerator tin coils. Gurudas and I loaded everything into the trunk of Shyamasundar's green 1952 Chevrolet and drove it over to a foundry in South San Francisco operated by a Mexican guy named Godoy. The plant was a large hot Quonset hut with cauldrons of red-hot and white-hot molten metal.

Mr. Godoy was just the way I'd pictured him from his telephone voice: heavy-set, kind face and covered in soot.

"Hi, I'm Mukunda," I said, reluctantly shaking his filthy outstretched hand. "I called you about making the cymbals."

"Hi," he said in a thick Mexican accent. "Let's have a look at them then." I pulled the *karatalas* out of my pocket and handed them to him. He turned them over a few times and ran his stubby fingers over the surface as if he was trying to get to know them.

"Yep," he said. "I can do them."

"You can? That's great!"

"What kinda metal you got?" he asked.

"Um, well, it's all in the back of the car," Gurudas said. "You wanna see it?"

"Yep, and I wanna weigh it," he said. We transferred the metal to a giant scale piece by awkward piece. Godoy pulled a grime-streaked notebook out of the pocket of his overalls and made a few calculations.

"I figure you can get about a hundred pairs out of this," he said, gesturing toward the pile of twisted coils. "I cast them in sand." He put the pair of *karatalas* in his pocket. "I need to keep these to copy," he said.

I looked at Gurudas for confirmation. They were one of our best pairs. He shrugged. "OK," I said, "but please take care of them."

"You betcha," he said. "I'll make the mold and then you come back and see before I cast."

A week later, Gurudas and I returned to look at his mold. It looked like a waffle iron and could make three sets of *karatalas* at once. Godoy unhinged the shallow metal trays so we could see inside. The upper and lower trays were filled with hardened sand; the *karatalas* would be dropped out of the mold when the metal hardened.

When I collected the hundred sets of *karatalas* ten days later, I was a little bit disappointed in the way they looked. Each cymbal was a lot thicker than I would have liked, and the edges didn't taper to a thin edge like the ones from India. They also looked dingy. I sat in the car and tried out a pair. The sound wasn't exact but was OK.

Back at the temple, a few of us burnished the *karatalas* with commercial brass polish until they shone like gold. They looked so much better than when I picked them up that I decided then and there to show them to Jay and Ron from the Psychedelic Shop. They liked them and agreed to sell them on commission. For the sake of marketing, we found some white cardboard boxes, which we lined with white cotton padding. I bought a large piece of thin scarlet felt, which I cut into strips and used as a handle for each

Two devotee women (sitting) chant and play karatalas *on Haight Street.*

set of cymbals. The felt was soft against my fingers, and I knew it would make a comfortable handle with which to hold the *karatalas* as they were played. Finally I made an instruction manual printed on thick, textured paper of a light blue shade. The manual included an illustrated explanation of how to hold the *karatalas*, techniques for forming different sounds with them, music notation for percussion rhythm beats, and the words of the mantra.

Yamuna and Gurudas helped me fold the manuals and fit them inside the boxes. The *karatalas* fit perfectly in their white cotton beds with their deep-red handles; each polished set looked like jewelry. Ron and Jay said they would sell them at ten dollars a box and keep a dollar for each set. Not bad, considering the whole package of each unit – *karatalas*, felt, cotton, printed instructions and box – cost us only three dollars.

Sales were brisk. Within a month, the shop sold ninety sets. I kept a couple pairs for the temple and one pair to show the swami when he returned from India. I couldn't wait to present him with the first pair of American-made *karatalas*.

·——·

Although we did our best to maintain the temple as though the swami was still with us, we all missed him a lot and wondered if and when he'd ever return. Soon after he left us, we were surprised to receive a letter from him that said that he was missing us too:

> My dear students,
>
> Please accept my blessings. I am always thinking of you, and I am feeling separation. I wish to return at the earliest opportunity. I cannot stop my Western world activities and I have taken leave from you for only six months; and it may be that on or before I will come to you again. So continue your activities with great vigor. I shall always pray to Krishna for your steady advance, but try to follow the principles which are necessary to strengthen oneself in the matter of spiritual advance. Never think that I am absent from you. Physical presence is not essential; presence by message (or hearing) is real touch. Lord Krishna is present by His message which was delivered five thousand years ago. We feel always the presence of our past *acharyas* simply by their immutable instructions.

This letter cast a new light on the swami's apparent absence from our midst. He was present with us in his instructions, and we could be with him through hearing his message. Each time he wrote to one of us, he informed us that his health was improving, and each letter spoke of his intent to return to America soon. In October, the details of the swami's return began to become more concrete. He wrote to Janaki about his intention to honor her request that he return to San Francisco:

"I am trying to fulfill my promise," he wrote to her. "As you asked me to go to San Francisco while returning from India, I am thinking of going directly to San Francisco."

Finally, in the third week of November, a telegram arrived:

"Arriving San Francisco at 12:45 PM, December 14, flight PAA 846. More when we meet. ACB"

Fifty-five devotees drove out to San Francisco Airport to greet the swami that cold and windy but sunny Thursday. We were all excited, but I was also worried that the high winds could make it difficult for the plane to land. The plane circled the airport a couple of times before making a rocky landing on the runway. We pressed ourselves against the bullet-proof floor-to-ceiling glass that barricaded us from the customs arrival area. I was breathless with anticipation.

The passengers began to trickle out into the customs area – a tattered youth with a red bandana on his head, a woman in a maroon wool coat, a man in a suit carrying a briefcase, an exasperated-looking mother dragging two whining children by their hands. A few cleared customs quickly, and a few had to lift their luggage onto the white ceramic counters for inspection.

Then the swami was there. I felt a lump in my throat and my eyes blur with tears. Around me I heard gasps and cheers. The swami saw us immediately; he beamed and waved, and a muted cheer went up from the greeting throng. He looked fitter and thinner than I had ever seen him – happy, agile and sprightly, much younger than his seventy-two years. In his beige turtleneck sweater and saffron robes, he shone with radiance. As he got in line at the customs counter, I noticed that even his walk was animated.

Only a pane of glass separated us from him, but it was hard and sound-proof, so we couldn't hear what was going on inside. The customs officials rifled through the swami's hand luggage, where they found some small brown bottles, which I assumed were the swami's medicine. The customs inspector held a couple of bottles up to the light while he talked to the swami and then led him away from the counter. The swami looked back at us as he followed the official away; he nodded as if to say "This won't take long. Don't worry. Everything is all right."

After five minutes, I grew impatient, and some of the other devotees around me were getting angry.

"Why are they hassling him like this?" Murari asked. "God, it's just his medicine!"

"Maybe they want to analyze it," I said. "I mean, they don't know it's just Ayurvedic stuff. It could be anything." I was trying to be reasonable, but inside I was panicking. Drug abuse in the Haight was now a major social problem and had spread to the whole San Francisco area; barbiturate deaths and drug-related killings were increasing. What if they thought he was a smuggler in a clever disguise? What if they arrested him? Another five minutes went by. What if they confiscated his medicine and he had a relapse?

The swami bounded back into view, talking vivaciously to the customs agent. The official helped him reassemble his carry-on luggage; as he zipped up the swami's bag, he nodded and laughed at something he said. The swami accepted his arrival card back from the agent and handed it to a uniformed woman as he passed through the large automatic doors toward us. The devotees cheered.

"Welcome back, Swami," I said. "We have a car waiting for you." I pointed toward the exit doors, and everyone accompanied him to the parking lot before they made their way back to the temple in their own cars.

We drove the swami to Yamuna and Gurudas's three-room apartment on Willard Street about two blocks from the temple. They had volunteered to give the swami their home. Although it was up a steep hill, it had large windows and lots of light and was by far the nicest apartment that any of the devotees rented.

About twenty of us – all the devotees who had been around for the swami's first visit – crowded into his rooms. He set his suitcase down and sat beside it on a large patterned cushion in Yamuna's living room.

"I have gifts for you," he said, opening the brass clasps on his suitcase. "I want to give you each sari." He reached inside and pulled out a big colorful stack of folded cotton.

"Janaki, come," he said. She came forward and he gave her a forest green sari with a wide yellow border.

"Thank you," she said, looking overwhelmed. "Thank you."

"Harsharani, you are here?" he asked.

"Yes," she called from the back of the room. She was eighteen years old and had been initiated just before the swami had left San Francisco. She came forward to receive her pale blue sari. "Thank you, Swami," she said.

One by one, he called out the names of each woman and they each came forward to receive their gift. For most of them, these were the first real saris they had ever owned.

"Malati," the swami said. "Where is she?"

"They're still in jail," I said, a little too loudly.

The swami's look of happiness vanished like letters on a chalk board wiped away with a wet cloth.

"Oh, I remember …" he said quietly, looking down blankly at the pile of saris in his lap.

"I have a letter that Shyamasundar has written for you," Gurudas said. He handed the letter to the swami, who tore open the envelope and read it with a serious look on his face. Then he broke into a smile.

"He says his return to San Francisco will be like an 'arrow quivering in its target,' " he reported. "They are chanting whole day. This is very nice." He placed the letter beside him on the bed and turned his attention back to us.

"And you?" he asked. "You are all chanting? Murari, you are chanting sixteen rounds each day?"

"Yes, every day," he said.

"Jayananda? You are chanting sixteen rounds?"

"Yes, Swami, I am," he said.

The swami went around the room and asked each person this question. It was clear to me that this was the most important issue for him – whether or not we were chanting Hare Krishna. When he came to Annapurna, a seventeen-year-old from England, she turned bright red and was silent. The swami waited. Half a minute went by. She looked up at the light fixture in the ceiling and then back at the swami.

"I chant ..." She blushed, faltered, swallowed, paused and then tried again. "I chant ..." Her British accent and child-like tone made everyone giggle quietly. She pronounced "chant" so that it rhymed with the word "gaunt." She blinked her eyes rapidly and finally said "Sometimes I chant *more* than sixteen rounds." Her voice cracked on the word "more."

The swami gently said, "That's all right. Come, take this sari." He gave her the yellow sari on the top of the pile, and Annapurna looked self-consciously around the room and gave a sigh of relief.

I handed the swami the white box containing the *karatalas*.

"We made some *karatalas*," I said. He opened the box and held them by their soft red felt handles. "We made one hundred sets. We're selling them."

"Where they were made?" he asked.

"Right here. In South San Francisco."

He unfolded the blue instruction sheet and read it without expression. Then he clanged the *karatalas* together and listened to the sound, his head slightly cocked to one side. He rang them together again and looked beyond us into the dining room and listened until they stopped ringing. "Not so great," he said thoughtfully, gazing at me.

He reached into his bag and pulled out a small cloth bag containing a set of slightly larger *karatalas*. He then rang them together.

"*That* is great," he said, opening his eyes wide.

I was a bit disappointed, even though I knew from the beginning that our *karatalas* would never sound as good as genuine Indian ones.

"Now I will take some rest," the swami said.

A few days later, I picked up Shyamasundar and Malati from the airport. A mutual friend of ours had heard they were being released and called to let me know.

"How did you know we needed to be picked up?" Malati asked.

"Judy told me! It's great to see you guys," I said.

"This is all so amazing!" Shyamasundar exclaimed. "We both

got released just yesterday; I didn't know she was getting out, and she didn't know I was getting out, and we both ended up at Judy's house and now *you're* here!"

"And the swami's in San Francisco," I said, knowing this would be the icing on the cake for them both.

"I can't wait."

"Yeah. Staying at Gurudas and Yamuna's. Let's go see him. I know he'll want to see you."

On the way to the swami's apartment, Shyamasundar and Malati told me about their time in jail.

"It was a violent place," Shyamasundar said.

"Actually, it wasn't so bad where I was in the women's jail," Malati said. "But I just tried to keep to myself as much as possible."

"Yeah, and we both tried to chant as much as we could," Shyamasundar said. "The whole time I was in there, I was thinking about ways we could help the swami spread the word about Krishna consciousness. And I've got a great idea; it's fool-proof."

I was immediately wary. Shyamasundar's fool-proof ideas were inclined to be anything but. "Yeah?" I said. "What's your idea?"

"Well, I thought we should try to get famous people interested. Everyone pays attention to what they say, right?"

"I guess so," I answered.

"They do!" he insisted. "If famous people become devotees, Krishna consciousness will spread like wildfire." That was "Swami-speak," I knew. I'd heard the swami use the word "wildfire" in the same context a number of times, and I'd even found myself using it occasionally. "It'll spread when everyone sees them being devotees."

"Sounds great," I said sarcastically. "Now all you need is some famous people."

"I've thought of that," Shyamasundar said. "Who's more famous than anyone else, the most famous people in the world right now?"

Names and faces flashed through my mind. Lyndon Johnson? Frank Sinatra? The Pope?

"The Beatles!" Shyamasundar exclaimed triumphantly. "And the great thing is that they're already into mysticism and Indian stuff. We know that they know about our movement, because they ordered those three hundred copies of the New York devotees'

Happening Album. So they've already heard the swami chanting, and now all we have to do is go to England and meet them."

"It sounds like a bit of a pipedream," I said. "How many people arrive at London's airport every day hoping to catch a look at the Beatles? It's not like John Lennon's just sitting around waiting for people to turn up and make friends."

"We can do it," he said, undeterred by my negativity. "I'm sure we can. If Krishna wants it, it'll happen. I'm going to talk to the swami about it."

When we arrived at Yamuna's apartment, Malati stuck her head round the door to the swami's bedroom. The swami looked up and smiled broadly.

"Come in, come in," he said exuberantly. "I was thinking last night when you would come! And now you are here! Go to my suitcase. I have brought sari for you!" And he presented Malati with a beautiful rose-pink sari, which she wore until it was in shreds.

———

Within the first week of the swami's stay in San Francisco, we paid a visit to the US immigration office downtown to try to get him Permanent Residence status. He had been writing to me about this when he was in India and I'd made some initial investigations, but I thought if we went down there in person we might be able to make an impact and get the visa approved faster.

We took the elevator to the thirtieth floor of a big glass building. We were shown through to a small office by the young receptionist who greeted us at the front desk. Inside the office, a matronly woman with tired blue eyes and dyed blonde hair sat behind the desk as though she had been waiting for us. She gestured for us to sit in the two chairs opposite her.

"You are with Hare Krishnas?" She was polite, and even friendly, but in a distant business-like way.

"Yes," I said, nodding proudly.

"So what can I help you with?"

"We'd like to get a permanent visa for the swami," I said. "This is Swami Bhaktivedanta. He's just returned from India to continue with his mission to start an international spiritual movement."

"I can take your application," she said. "Do you have the forms?" She opened the filing cabinet to her left and flicked through the compartment tabs.

I had expected this kind of polite dismissal, so I had another tactic up my sleeve. "I heard there's a special type of visa for culture," I said. She paused, and then closed the filing cabinet drawer. "You know, for people who write books, paint, play instruments and sing or dance. Couldn't we apply for him in that category?"

"Has he won any prizes, like, you know, Pulitzer or anything like that?" she asked. I thought it was strange how she continued to address me rather than the swami, almost as though he wasn't there or couldn't understand what she was saying.

"Prizes?"

"Any kind of prize," she repeated. "Like a Pulitzer Prize or a Nobel Prize."

"Um, well, he presented his books to the Prime Minister of India. I have a photo of that," I said. I knew this was grasping at straws, but it was better than nothing.

"Any books on a best-seller list in this country?" she asked.

"I don't think so, but he's sold thousands." I thought that would count for something.

"Immigration and Naturalization would need to have certificates," she said. "I mean certificates for how many books have been sold."

"So can he apply under that category, using the photos?" I asked.

She glanced at the swami. "He can try," she said doubtfully. "But I can't promise anything."

The swami spoke for the first time. "I am here under visitor's visa," he said. "And it has been renewed two times. So now I want permanent visa. You can issue?"

"No. But I can take your application," she said congenially. We knew, of course, that she could take an application form. I felt like she was patronizing us.

"Why are there so many tall buildings if there are earthquakes here?" the swami asked. Why was he asking such a question now? "Oh, *this* building is earthquake-proof," she assured him. She absently shuffled a pile of typed documents on her desk and then looked up at the swami with an expression of curiosity on her face. "Isn't it hard to always remember Krishna?" she asked. Again I was surprised. I thought, "How does she know about Krishna and how important it is to try to think of Him?"

"It's just like you put clothes on in the morning," the swami said. "You would never go to work without clothes, isn't it?"

"No, never," she said.

"So it's natural, like getting dressed," he said. "You can also."

"Also what?" she asked.

"Remember Krishna always," he answered.

"I don't know," she said. She looked reflectively out the huge windows toward the building across the street and then opened the filing cabinet drawer and selected a form.

"Fill in your application completely," she said briskly, handing me the thick form. Looking at me again seriously she said, "Make sure you fill in all the spaces on the form so it won't get sent back."

I quickly scanned the form to see what was required. The swami leaned forward and read it with me.

"And be sure it's signed," she said, a note of finality in her voice. This was obviously the end of our interview.

"Is there anything else you want to say, Swamiji?" I asked. I'd heard other people call him that, using the suffix "ji" on the end of his name as a sign of affection. It was the first time I had ever addressed him in this way, and I felt a bit self-conscious about it. I glanced in the swami's direction and saw that his gaze was directed at her, not at me.

"Isn't there another kind of form we can take?" I asked.

"Here," she said, looking sorry for us. "Take one of these." I glanced down and saw it was the application for the special cultural visa.

"All right, let us go," the swami said to me. "Thank you very much," he said to the woman.

"You're welcome," she chimed. "Good luck."

We took the elevator down to the ground. As we walked toward the car, the swami pointed his cane toward a neon sign above a doorway across the street: "Cocktail Bar."

"What is this word 'cocktail'?" he asked.

"It's a drink of whiskey mixed with a soft drink," I said.

"What is soft drink?"

"It's a non-alcoholic drink that is usually carbonated," I said. "But in a cocktail it's mixed with alcohol."

He nodded, and we walked silently another half block. As we reached the Krishna car he said sarcastically, "There is no such thing as *earthquake-proof*!"

We pulled away from the immigration office. A block or so on we came upon a large group of shouting people outside a big Crown-Zellerbach building. They walked back and forth carrying signs that said "Stop Hiring Scabs," "Workers Wage Torture," and "Local Union Liars."

"What is this?" the swami asked.

"It's some kind of demonstration or protest," I said. I couldn't get a good look at the protestors, since I was driving, but I knew there were still a lot of draft protests. There were now major celebrities taking part in them, and some had even been arrested recently during a special nighttime march to the Pentagon.

"Always somebody is protesting," he murmured. He looked over

Demonstrations like this were common in San Francisco in 1966 and 1967.

at me. "You will come to help fill in this form tomorrow?"

"I can come after the morning program," I said.

"That will be very nice," the swami said.

The following morning, I went to the swami's apartment to fill in the papers with him as we'd arranged. I sat down on the woven square rug on the swami's living room to browse the forms and to figure out all the requirements.

"I think it's best if we apply under the 'ordinary' category," I said to him, flicking through the notes provided for applicants. "Without being a celebrity, the chances of getting residency under the 'special' category look pretty dim to me." I could see the permanent residency issue was not going to be solved any time soon. When I looked up at him for his approval I saw that the telephone wires outside were bobbing up and down. The windows began to rattle and I saw the floor tilt a few degrees. I froze in fear.

"What is this?" asked the swami.

"It's an earthquake," I said softly, my heart pounding like a jackhammer in my chest. The apartment was on a sharply rising street, and an earthquake could easily demolish the whole house and send us hurtling to the ground forty feet below.

The swami leaned back and broke out into a relaxed smile.

"This sound is similar like air-raid attack," he said. "I was in an underground bomb shelter in Calcutta in I think it was nineteen hundred and forty-two. There was an air attack."

The walls, floors and windows stopped shuddering. I sighed in relief, but the swami kept talking.

"Then I was thinking how nice it would be to die now while I'm thinking about Krishna," he said calmly, as if oblivious to the potential disaster that had just struck. I was amazed at the contrast between his sobriety and my fear. The disastrous San Francisco earthquake of the early twentieth century had shown the potential magnitude of earthquakes in this region; earthquakes equaled death, especially here, but the swami was not afraid. I was reminded of the North Vietnamese Buddhist monk who'd reached out to touch a live hand grenade and commented right before he died, "it feels hot."

"*Bhagavad-gita* says if one is situated in Krishna consciousness, even in the terrible situation, fearful situation, he is not afraid," the swami continued. "When everything is normal, we are not afraid of death. But as soon as we find there is earthquake, and we are afraid that this building may fall down, then we become very much disturbed."

"The swami really knows he's not his body," I thought to myself. "For me it's just a theory, but he really lives his life by this." The next day I found out that the earthquake registered 5.2 on the Richter scale and was the sharpest since the 5.3 quake in 1957. Apart from jolting my memory about the San Andreas Fault line, which we were all living on, the quake also gave me a glimpse into the swami's realized knowledge of the philosophy he was teaching.

CHAPTER 23

The Les Crane Show

When the temple pay phone rang three days after the earthquake, my first thought was "Gargamuni already? The swami just got here!" Expecting a long-distance showdown, I resignedly put my chanting beads down and answered the phone.

"Radha-Krishna temple."

"Hi. Can I speak to the swami?" It was a female voice.

"He's not here right now. Can I help you?" I said.

"I'm March Culbertson from *The Les Crane Show* in Los Angeles," she said. "We'd like to talk to the swami about being on the program."

I looked at my watch. 2:30: the swami's resting time.

"He's probably sleeping right now," I said. "Is there anything I can help you with?"

"I'd really need to talk to *him*," she insisted.

"I can get him."

"OK, I'll wait," she said.

"Well, it might take a few minutes," I said. "He's a couple of blocks away."

"Can I call him there?" she asked.

"No, there's no phone there."

"That's OK. I can wait." She sounded friendly, patient and cheerful. I wondered briefly what it must be like to work for a place where you could sit and silently wait on a long-distance call from Los Angeles to San Francisco. I let the handset down gently from its cord so it wouldn't bang against the wall. As I scurried out the front door, I paused briefly to tell the news to David, the only other devotee in the temple at the time.

"Wow! *The Les Crane Show*," David said. "What an opportunity! That's broadcast all over the country!"

"Hey, don't let anyone touch the phone, OK?" I said. "I don't want to lose the call."

"Sure, no problem. I guess I can watch the phone and chant at the same time."

Then I ran. I was breathless from the uphill sprint when I reached the swami's place; I bolted up the stairs two at a time and let myself into the apartment. White lace curtains hung inside the French doors that led to the swami's room; I couldn't see whether he was there, but I could make out the outline of his bed at the south end of the room. I knocked three times as gently as possible.

"Yes. What is it?"

I saw the outline of the swami's form rise to a sitting position in the bed. Now that I'd stopped running I realized my face was as hot as a firecracker. I took some deep breaths to try to slow my heart-rate.

"People from a Los Angeles television show want to speak with you," I gasped. "They're on the phone at the temple."

"Yes, yes, I'm coming." Through the curtains, I saw him stand and put on his clothes. "Just now. I'm coming." He opened the door and walked quickly down the hall toward the street. He walked fast and I struggled to keep up in my breathless state.

"I tried to speak with them, but they said they wanted to talk with *you*," I said. "I hope they're still waiting. I'm sorry I had to wake you up."

"That's all right," he said, without looking at me.

"It's really an important program. Millions of people see it!"

David stood by the phone at the back of the temple. I grabbed the handset, praying not to hear a dial tone or a mechanized voice saying "please hang up and try again."

"Hello," I said.

"Is this the swami?" She was still there!

"No. He's here. Just a minute." I handed the phone to the swami. "It's her. Her name is March."

The swami had looked intent and serious during our brisk walk to the temple. Now, as he took the telephone receiver from my hand, a transformation occurred in his face. There was a second of silence before he spoke, and then as he greeted her, his face broke into a wide grin as if he were opening the front door to meet her face-to-face. The only time I could remember seeing that expression on his face was when he was circulating the room with a pot of *prasadam* under his arm at the first Sunday Love Feast in New York nearly two years ago.

"Good afternoon," he said musically. He paused. "No, I have not seen your program, but I have heard it is very important." He spoke articulately, charmingly.

He listened intently.

"Yes, I can come then. Yes. Yes, I know it is long journey, but that is no problem." I could hear a faint echo of March's voice through the phone. "I am seventy-two years old ... yes ... from Calcutta ... I have been in America for almost three years ... In Calcutta we speak English. My school was Scottish Churches College, and we all spoke English, even in our mathematics classes ... Now I have many students, not only here but in New York, and India – many students."

March spoke again.

"So I should be there at seven o'clock?" the swami asked. "Yes, good. You can give the exact directions to my secretary, Mr. Michael." He handed the phone to me and stood beside me as I spoke to her.

"We want the swami to appear with one of his young followers, an American," March said. "Can you help us?"

"Sure, I can do it."

"How old are you?"

"Twenty-six."

"Have you seen *The Les Crane Show*?" she asked.

"I think I saw it once," I said. "But I know all about it."

"Where did you meet the swami?"

"In New York."

"What were the circumstances?" she asked.

"I heard from a friend of mine that he was lecturing," I said. "I liked what I heard, and I bought some books. I thought it was more interesting than Buddhism or Taoism, so I went back to hear him again. Then I started chanting. And I helped him start a temple here on the West Coast."

"Can you be in Los Angeles with the swami on the seventeenth of next month?"

"Yes."

"OK. We'll book for you and the swami," she said, sounding definitive. "You have to be here by seven o'clock on the dot for make-up and a warm-up. That's a Wednesday night. OK?"

"That's fine."

"Please phone me three days before and I'll give you the address to come to," she said. I wrote down her phone number. "You can call collect anytime and ask for March Culbertson, OK?"

"OK," I said and hung up the phone.

"So, when we shall go there?" the swami asked.

"Very soon," I said. "In a few weeks. I think I'll go before you to make arrangements for your stay in Los Angeles."

"Perhaps I would like to stay some time in Los Angeles," he said.

"Yes, I can arrange that," I promised.

I walked the swami back to his apartment and began planning the trip as I headed back down the hill to the temple. A few devotees had gone to Los Angeles to start a center there. Southern California, especially the land of Hollywood, was known for being liberal and open-minded to alternative lifestyles, so they'd been having some success. I knew they would be thrilled to have the swami visit their new storefront temple, and I knew they'd organize accommodation for him and for us. Janaki and I would drive down together in the Krishna car. We'd hardly seen each other at all lately.

The swami arrived in Los Angeles the day before the show and spent the afternoon recuperating from the flight in his apartment on Saturn Street. The following night, we headed down to the studios for our first television appearance. March met us at the door and led us through a warren of corridors to a small room.

"This is your preparation area," she said. "Do you need to prepare at all?"

"Um, no, I don't think so," I said. I hadn't expected this. Did they think we'd want to put on make-up or something? I suddenly felt shabby in my favorite sports jacket and green tie. I hoped that I looked respectable and not like some San Francisco hippie. To me, the swami looked as resplendent as always in his saffron robes.

"OK, follow me then," she said, and led us back out into the hall. "We're going to start with a warm-up interview so you get used to how the show is run." She opened the door to a larger room and motioned for us to go in.

There were already two other men sitting at a table inside the room – a bespectacled, white-haired man in his fifties wearing a plain gray business suit and dark blue tie, and a college student with blond hair and a crew cut. He looked tidy and presentable but a bit pimply in his suit and tie.

"This is Dr. Daniel Morgan," March said, indicating the older man. "He's the Campus Crusade for Christ leader here in LA. And this is one of his students, Joseph Shaw. They'll be going on the show with you."

"On the show with us?" I thought. No one had said anything to me about that. As the swami and I shook hands with them and introduced ourselves, I realized this wasn't going to be a simple, amiable interview with Les Crane. It was set up to be a televised confrontation between opposing theological parties. I hadn't bargained for this.

Enter Les Crane, suave, sophisticated and handsome. He had wavy brown hair, and a reddish brown tan. Over his dark-brown turtleneck he wore a gold pendant, a Hindu Om sign cast in Sanskrit letters. This glistening accoutrement immediately caught my attention and brought some familiarity into the strange environment. Maybe Crane would be on our side in this gladiatorial event.

After formally introducing all of us, the debonair host spent a few minutes with the Christian evangelists asking them questions like "What university do you work with, where do you live, what's your goal?" Then he pulled up a chair opposite the swami and me.

"So, you are from India?" he asked the swami.

"I was born in Calcutta and came to this country in 1965," the swami replied.

"You have followers in this country?"

"We have our temples in New York, San Francisco, and now Los Angeles."

"So what is the chant?" Crane asked. He was being very cordial to us; charisma oozed from his every pore.

Instead of giving a verbal reply, the swami pulled out his *karatalas* and, smiling all the while, began to sing the Hare Krishna mantra. I was surprised, but Crane appeared charmed and fascinated by this spontaneous performance of the mantra. He nodded his head in time to the tempo; grinning, he looked around the room and, still grinning, he glanced at the other television staff as if to affirm just how entertaining this Swami was. Crane had been buoyant from the start, but the chanting seemed to make him even more favorable.

The swami put down his *karatalas* after a few minutes and Crane beamed at him.

"That was really something," he said. "We're on in fifteen minutes. Follow me into the studio."

Inside the studio, the lights were bright and the three hundred tiered audience seats already full of chattering spectators, including twenty of the new Los Angeles devotees for whom March had managed to get seats. Crane seated the swami and me in swivel chairs next to the evangelists, Dr. Morgan and Joseph, on a round stage; he then busied himself with the cameramen and technicians. The swami and I sat silently as the flurry went on around us. I felt nervous, but the swami seemed composed. I leaned toward him, hoping that talking might help me to calm down.

"I was thinking about some things we could do to expand Krishna consciousness," I said. "What if we got a large hot-air balloon with 'Hare Krishna' painted on it? We could float it above LA or San Francisco and everyone would see it."

The swami nodded his head and closed his eyes briefly.

"I was reading the *Los Angeles Times* this morning," I continued, saying whatever came into my head. "There was this big headline that said 'End of Empire.' I guess it was about Britain's decline in power." I rattled on and on.

The swami nodded. "All right," he said, substituting these words for "enough is enough." I looked out into the audience and felt panicky, and decided I should just chant like the swami was doing.

As he stood, Les Crane shuffled a stack of papers around. A make-up artist ran onto the stage and patted Crane's face with powder. Then Crane held up a hand for silence. "It's one minute till we're taping," he said. He walked over to us and said, "When you see a red light on the camera, it'll be filming you."

"Just a minute, Les," someone called from the back of the studio. "We're getting some feedback sound back here. It's a weird buzzing that we need to figure out before we go on."

"OK, everyone just be patient," Crane said. "The show will be underway as soon as we get the sound problems worked out."

The swami and I continued chanting under our breath while sound engineers ran from speaker to speaker and adjusted everyone's microphones. Then Crane gave a loud laugh.

"That's it!" he exclaimed into his microphone. "The buzzing sound is these guys chanting!" The audience applauded as Crane put a hand over his microphone and spoke to the swami. "It's best you don't chant at all, not even quietly. When the red light's on, the cameras come on," he said. "That means we're taping. That's what'll be on the air. OK?"

"Yes," said the swami.

"OK, let's get started," Crane said with a grin to the cameramen. The head technician nodded, and the red lights came on.

"Welcome to *The Les Crane Show*," Crane said silkily. "I'm your host, Les Crane." A blue neon light flashed the word "APPLAUSE"; the audience did. "Tonight I have with me Swami Bhaktivedanta, the leader of the Hare Krishnas, a new spiritual movement which he brought to the United States from India about three years ago. Also with us is Dr. Daniel Morgan, the leader of Campus Crusade for Christ here in LA. Daniel and the swami have also brought along their students, Michael and Joseph."

As the audience clapped again, Crane stood and walked across the stage toward us, deftly stepping over the cord of the microphone he was carrying.

"Michael, why did you decide to join the Hare Krishna movement?" he asked me.

I was tense enough already without being the first to speak! I opened my mouth without knowing what to say.

"I offer my respectful obeisances unto my spiritual master, A.C. Bhaktivedanta Swami, who is very dear unto Lord Krishna, having taken shelter unto the Supreme Lord."

"And what is the purpose of that prayer?" Crane asked me.

I knew my opening was unconventional, so I tried to recover my profile in front of the audience. "This is something that we all say before speaking," I explained. "It's like a way of paying respect to your teacher and asking his blessing to speak."

"OK, that's nice," Crane said. "So, why did you join the Hare Krishnas?"

"I read some of the books the swami brought over from India, and they convinced me." I paused, getting ready to talk about the swami's lectures, but Crane had already moved on.

"What was your religion before?" he asked.

"I was brought up as a conservative Jew, but when I was seventeen, I'd become an agnostic."

"And what do you do?" Crane asked.

"Well, I'm a musician and I have been doing some importing for the swami," I said. "I'm trying to help out as much as I can so the swami's movement can grow and be spread around the world."

Crane walked toward the swami, once again adroitly avoiding the wires that writhed around the stage like reeds waiting to drag him down.

"And is the movement growing?" he asked the swami.

"Oh, yes," the swami answered. "I have many students now. They are chanting and feeling very happy."

"What is your outlook on life?"

"Krishna consciousness means that every living being is part and parcel of Krishna," the swami said. He spoke so confidently, I thought, completely different to the way I came across.

"What does that mean, I mean, being 'part and parcel,' and who is Krishna?" Crane asked.

"Krishna is God," the swami answered. "He has got many expansions. They are called personal expansions and separated expansions. So we are separated expansion, we are living entities, individuals, but we are part of the Lord. We are very intimately connected with Krishna, but somehow or other we are separated by connection with material nature. Krishna is God."

"Is there a devil?" Crane asked.

"Practically we have forgotten that we are part and parcel of God. That happens to everyone. Then we become demonic."

"So anyone can be the devil?" Crane looked a little confused.

"This Krishna consciousness movement means we are trying to realize original consciousness; that we belong to Krishna. In that way we become purified and our devilish tendencies become – I mean to say – swallowed up."

"When we were children, we were happy, right?" Crane said.

"The original consciousness is Krishna consciousness, not child consciousness," the swami answered. "Just like a man born in a wealthy family, he is rich man. But he sometimes forgets his own home, so sometimes he becomes a hippy. So our Vedic literature is meant for reviving our original consciousness."

Crane nodded at the swami and then redirected his attention toward the Christian evangelists.

"So, Dr. Morgan, what does the Campus Crusade for Christ say about original sin?"

"Everyone has to rid themselves of sin," the older slightly portly man said, pushing his glasses up on his nose. "Alcohol and narcotics are a problem for many college students."

"How would you correct these problems?"

"Biblical study and reading is recommended for every college student," Dr. Morgan said. "We have classrooms in schools all over the country, places where students can study and pray together. And sing."

"Wow! That's a lot of classrooms," Crane said. The audience laughed. "What do you do?" he asked the young evangelist, Joseph.

"I study mathematics at Stanford," Joseph answered.

"And you're the leader of the Campus Crusade for Christ ... at Stanford?"

"That's right. We have about twenty to fifty people in our group at Stanford – mostly freshmen. We meet three times a week."

Crane walked over to the swami and, thrusting a microphone at him, asked, "Do you think Jesus Christ can save souls?"

"Oh, yes, certainly," the swami answered. "Why not? He is son of God, isn't it?"

Walking quickly back to Dr. Morgan, Crane asked, "Do you think people can be saved by Krishna consciousness?"

"Jesus Christ walked a very narrow path," he answered. "He said we have to come to the Father through him."

"Are you saying then that people who take the swami's religious route can't be saved?" Crane persisted.

The CCC leader squirmed and frowned. "No, I didn't say that," he said. "It's just that we have a very narrow path to walk."

"Do you think someone can get to heaven by following scripture like theirs?" he asked. "The *Baha-gavad-gita*?" He turned and looked over his shoulder at the swami. "Did I say that right?"

The swami smiled and moved his head as if to say "Not really, but it's not important."

"Everybody who comes to our prayer meetings feels the presence of Christ and becomes transformed," the young Christian said. "I can vouch for that. I've been there." They were avoiding a direct answer to the question.

Crane spun around and, still gracefully wielding his microphone, bounced over to the swami.

"Do you think anyone can go to heaven through the Bible?" he asked.

"Yes," the swami answered immediately. "*Any* word of God."

"The Bible?"

"Yes."

The blue neon light above us came on: "FIVE SECONDS TO COMMERCIAL."

"We'll be right back with the swami and the Crusade for Christ," Crane said. "Don't go away."

It seemed like no time since the start of the program, but when I looked at my watch I saw that nearly fifteen minutes had already elapsed since the beginning of the interview. The devotees in the audience were talking excitedly among themselves and smiling at us.

"Your answers were very good," I said to the swami. "I think he likes you."

The swami looked ahead and nodded. "Let us see," he said.

"Millions of people will see this show." I was making small talk.

"Yes," he said. He opened his eyes slightly wider on hearing this but continued to sit silently watching the audience, most of which stared back.

The red camera lights flashed again and we were back on air. After a brief re-introduction, Crane continued where he had left off.

"So you approve of the Bible, then?" he asked the swami.

The swami nodded. "Of course."

The host quickly turned and walked up close to Dr. Morgan, shoving the microphone in his face. "But you don't approve of the *Baha-gavad-gita*. You wouldn't recommend it as the word of God?"

"No, I wouldn't," he said slowly and deliberately. He looked uncomfortable, trapped and unable to handle the situation.

Crane turned to the cameras. "It's time for our studio audience to ask questions." A technician in plimsolls and a blue shirt mounted the stage and pointed a microphone on a long, thin stick at the audience. It had a three-foot-long barrel that made it look like a rifle.

A man raised his hand. Crane said, "Yes. Stand up please."

The man stood, and I immediately saw that he was an actor planted there by the show's producers. He had lots of orange rouge on his face to make him look like the Native American Indian in *One Flew Over the Cuckoo's Nest*. The viewers at home probably wouldn't notice, but *I* could see it clearly. He wore a white broadbrimmed ten-gallon hat and long black braids that descended over his ears through two holes in the hat's brim. He pointed angrily at the Christian man.

"If your religion is so good, why did you slaughter a million of my people?" he shouted, looking defiant with his arms folded across his chest.

The CCC leader fidgeted and finally said, "I think you're mistaking US Union Army soldiers for Christians. It wasn't like that. I think you have gotten some of your facts wrong."

"I *know* they were Christians," the man said. "You can't say they weren't. And a lot of people died. A lot of women and children – *thousands*."

"I'm sorry, but they weren't followers of the Gospel," he insisted.

"That's your apology?" the pseudo American Indian scoffed.

"Please sit down and let someone else ask a question," Crane said, feigning surprise at the man's outburst.

A lady in a patterned green dress raised her hand.

"Please stand up, ma'am," Crane requested.

"I want to know is Krishna God to the swami?" she asked.

"He is our name for God. God has many names. Krishna is one of the many names of God. Chief name."

"Thank you," she said, and sat down.

A fat, red-faced man raised his hand. He was wearing jeans and a Hawaiian shirt.

"I want to ask the swami if this is yoga," he said.

"This is *bhakti-yoga*," the swami answered. Krishna says '*yoginam api sarvesham* – the best yoga is to meditate on Me.' This is meditation on the personality of God. You can do this anywhere."

A young-looking sandy-haired woman in a white dress stood and said, "I want to go to Stanford, or the University of San Francisco, and I'd like to know how I can pursue religion in college studies."

Crane looked at the Christian pair on the stage, and the Stanford student said, "If you go to Stanford you can apply Bible studies in your work. I believe the University of San Francisco is a Catholic College."

"Thank you," said the woman and sat down.

"OK," Crane said. "That's all the time we have tonight. Thank you to all our guests for being on the show with us tonight. Next week we're going to hear from a team of scientists who are researching chimpanzees in Tanzania. We hope to have your company again, and until then, goodnight."

The red camera lights died, and I breathed a sigh of relief. Crane came forward and shook all of our hands. He was cordial to each of us, but I thought there had been a distinctly anti-Christian agenda to the show. The Christians came off as old-fashioned, closed-minded, bigoted and unwilling to fully apologize to the native Americans, while the swami looked like a forward-thinking individual – progressive, ecumenical and accepting of everything, including Christianity. It had been a coup for the swami and his movement.

"When will it show in LA?" I asked Crane at the studio door.

"It'll be a week from today at eight o'clock in Los Angeles, Channel Four, and a week later in Frisco. I don't know about other places."

"New York?" I asked.

"Yep. Definitely," he said. "But I don't know when. But soon."

Outside the studio, audience members waited to shake the swami's hand. The man in the Hawaiian shirt gave the swami a strong slap on the back and said, "I'm a yogi too, Swami, a *karma* yogi." The swami kept walking but smiled at him and said, "Very good, very good!"

It was dark and warm outside in the parking lot, and the air smelled like grilled hot dogs and perfume. The swami walked toward the car with the devotees who had sat in the audience. I felt light-hearted knowing that the swami's message would reach millions of people. I was sure he was happy too, although he wasn't saying so. Sometimes when he was very happy he became very quiet.

The swami saw a sign that said *Men's Room*, and he gave me his chanting beads to hold and asked me to wait for him. Everyone stopped to wait for him with me.

"The Christians really got cleaned by that Indian guy in the audience," one of the devotees said.

"I think he was a plant," I said.

"Plant?"

"You know, an actor."

"You came off really good, I thought," he said, beaming. "And the swami was great. He had such elegance and dignity."

As we stood there chatting in the dark, the CCC student ran up to me. He had pockmarks on his cheeks, and his tie was fluttering in the breeze.

" 'Scuse me. How ya doin'?" he said. "Hey, I wanted to ask you how many members are in your organization?"

I looked over my shoulder. The older Christian man was walking slowly about a dozen paces behind us. Then the swami came out of the men's room and saw me talking with the Stanford student.

"About five thousand," I said. This was not true, but I thought it was justifiable hyperbole, given that this was our on-air adversary.

"Thanks," he said and dropped back.

"What did he say?" the swami asked as we continued toward the car. I gave him back his beads and he slipped his hand into his bead-bag.

"He wanted to know how many members we have."

"So you said?"

"Five thousand," I answered.

He was silent a moment. "They are worried about us," he said.

A week later, the show aired in Los Angeles. The day after, I was walking with the swami in a Los Angeles park when a Mexican man driving past slowed way down, leaned out the car window and waved at the swami. "Hiya, Swami!" he said cordially.

After waving back, the swami turned to me and said grinning, "He has seen me on the television."

⊷

As a result of *The Les Crane Show*, we were suddenly presented with other opportunities to appear in the media. A week after the show, we received a phone call from Peter Bergman's radio program, asking us to appear live the following week. Bergman was the driving force behind the Firesign Theatre, a group of comedic radio performers who had gained a bit of a cult following in California. He was also a part-time disc jockey at a nightclub in the San Fernando Valley. His program was broadcast live from the club every Saturday night. To me, the idea was an exciting prospect. Not only was I a Firesign Theater fan, but I also knew the radio program was broadcast all over the Los Angeles area and had a listening audience of millions.

The following Saturday evening, I drove the swami out to the Valley in the Krishna car, accompanied by the swami's assistant, Umapati, and Nandarani, one of the Los Angeles core devotees. We were followed by another carload of devotees who were going to act as the chorus when the swami chanted on air. I'd gotten in the habit of burning essential oils in the ashtray of the car to create a pleasant atmosphere. Malati's essential oil business had really taken off in San Francisco, so we had an abundance of high-grade essential oil, which Malati bought by the gallon from a firm called George Leuder & Company. I thought the swami would appreciate the aroma, so I fumbled around in the glove box until I found one of the small blue glass bottles that Malati packaged the oil in for resale. While we waited at a red light, I placed a small brick of charcoal in the ashtray and lit it with a lighter. When it was glowing, I placed a few drops of high-quality sandalwood oil on the charcoal.

The car quickly filled with fragrant white smoke. I re-corked the lid on the little bottle as I drove and took a deep breath. The smell was rich and invigorating, but I'd put a few too many drops of oil on the charcoal. Soon I was choking and could barely see the freeway through the clouds of smoke. I rolled my window down to let some of it out, but a lot of smoke stayed inside.

"Is it too much smoke?" I coughed at the swami.

He was watching the world whiz by from the passenger window, chanting quietly and apparently unbothered by the white billows.

"Smoke is nice," he said, sounding content. The sandalwood *did* smell good, even if it was in copious amounts. We rode the rest of the way in silence, mostly because it took all my concentration to navigate from inside our smoky bubble.

It was dark when we arrived at the club on Ventura Boulevard. Loud music pulsated from inside. Peter Bergman met us at the door all smiles, his glasses slipping down his nose.

"I'm really glad you could make it," he said. "Come on over to my corner; I've got all my stuff at the back down there."

At the back of the club was a tiny semi-circular stage two feet above the floor. The area was full of turntables and columns of electronic equipment with Vu-Meters and flashing green and red lights.

"Here," Bergman said. "Have a seat on the stage. Swami, you can sit in this chair here at the table." He pointed to a hard-looking chair at a round table. He sat in the chair opposite the swami, and the rest of us squeezed into the tiny space as best we could.

"OK. Everyone settled?" he asked, sounding a bit like a schoolteacher. I could see the record that was playing was just about done. "I want you all to sit here quietly while we're on the air. I'll introduce you, and then I'll give you a signal when I want you to start chanting."

The record came to an end, and Bergman said into his microphone, "Welcome to *The Peter Bergman Show*. Tonight we have with us Swami Bhaktivah-danta and his followers. We'll hear the swami speak, and his students will chant."

He looked at me, mouthed a big "Hare Krishna" and pointed to one microphone for us to sing into. I led the chanting, Nandarani played the *tamboura*, Umapati beat a drum and the others played their *karatalas*. Bergman tapped his foot and drummed the table with his fingers in time to the beat. We sang for fifteen minutes before he made a football "time-out" motion in the air indicating our time was up.

"Thank you," he said. "That was Swami Bhaktivah-danta and his followers singing their mantra. Swami Bhaktivah-danta is the leader of the Hare Krishna movement, and I'm going to be asking him some questions this evening so we can find out what it's all about."

He looked over at the swami and spoke in a serious tone. "Swami, just what *is* Krishna consciousness?"

I thought it was a pretty good first question, but then everything went into slow motion. The swami reached into an inner pocket, found his glasses and methodically placed them on over his eyes and ears. But for a few clinks of glasses at the bar, it was dead silent. I coughed self-consciously because I knew everything was going out live. The swami then reached in another pocket and pulled out some sheets of paper, which he unfolded and flattened on the table. The seconds ticked by. He cleared his throat.

"I think the swami is going to read something to us," said Bergman.

He read, "Krishna consciousness is not an artificial imposition on the mind."

He paused momentarily and looked for a second at Bergman who had shoved a table mike under the swami's mouth.

"This Krishna consciousness movement was started five hundred years before by Lord Chaitanya. This is not a new movement. Practically, it is as old as the creation of this world, but as things change in course of time, so it required rejuvenation. So this move-ment was rejuvenated about five hundred years ago.

"So, our problems of life, as it is stated in the *Bhagavad-gita,* is to solve these four things: no more birth, nor more death, no more disease, no more old age. Always remember that we are all eternal. Just like in this body, beginning from my mother's womb up to this old age, I am the same eternal soul, but my body is changing. So after changing this body also, I shall remain the same. Simply I shall have another body. This plain truth, there is no difficulty to understand. If I am eternal means no death, no birth, no disease, no old age. That is eternal. So if I am eternal, is it possible to get an eternal body or eternal happiness? That is the problem of human society. If you can solve that problem, then you can be proud of your civilization. Otherwise there is no difference between cats and dogs' civilization and your civilization, because you are simply try-ing to solve the problems of eating, sleeping, defending and mating, and these problems are already solved by nature's law."

He read slowly and clearly through his script for thirty minutes. The speech was heavy and was very long, and as he finished one page, he turned over the next page and continued. One by one, he read slowly through the pages.

"So our developed intelligence should be utilized for solving these problems by Krishna consciousness. We are presenting this movement before you, your country, because you are intelligent, you are materially advanced. You are greater than all other coun-tries. Therefore, I present this scientific movement before you. You just try to understand it. Lord Chaitanya's movement ..."

I felt my attention drifting and couldn't help thinking that the listeners must be wondering what was going on. I had no idea that the swami was going to read something. Except for me occasionally sniffing, the swami clearing his throat now and then and the rus-tling of the swami's papers, there was nothing to hear but a raspy voice. I cursed myself for smoking up the car so much when the swami was going to have to speak.

I couldn't tell if Bergman was either too interested or too po-lite to cut the swami off. Throughout the reading he interjected remarks: "Right," "I see," "OK," "I understand," "That's interesting," "Really?" "That makes sense." Maybe it was to let listeners know he was still there, or maybe it was to preserve some semblance of the interview format.

After twenty minutes Bergman started looking at his watch and glancing nervously at the stack of paper in front of the swami. But the swami persisted for a full half an hour until he had read to the end of his presentation. He folded the papers and put them back into his breast pocket.

"Well, I guess that about sums it up," Bergman said, trying to maintain the affability he had shown us at the beginning of his program. "Thank you for answering my question so thoroughly, Swami. And thanks to the chanters for being with us tonight. I

Devotee-produced leaflet, "Drown in the Ocean of Bliss,"
distributed in Haight-Ashbury

hope you can all join us again sometime. Can you chant some more before you go?"

I nodded and Bergman gave us a thumbs-up sign, signaling us to begin immediately. We chanted for another fifteen minutes, until he put on a record.

"Thanks again for coming in," he said to the swami. "I hope everything goes well for you while you're here in LA. Hang on and I'll just cue another record and then I'll walk you to your car." I was surprised Bergman didn't seem perturbed that his guest had given such a long answer to his one and only question.

On the drive home, I thought how determined the swami was to get his prepared message across in its entirety, despite the pressures, formalities and conventions of commercial radio. Although I had been uneasy throughout his talk, I knew that those who wanted to know about Krishna consciousness had gotten a comprehensive explanation. In a way it was good, because the swami didn't have to deal with the usual questions about his clothes or forehead markings. He didn't have to explain why lots of devotees shaved their heads, say what the musical instruments were called or explain how many had joined the Hare Krishna movement. He didn't have to talk about his itinerary. *The Les Crane Show* had been primarily visual and the swami's answers had to be short and incisive. But because radio was an aural medium, he could expound on the finer points of the philosophy, knowing that people would be *listening* and would be more attentive to spiritual concepts.

———

The next morning at 5:30 I spontaneously decided to take the swami for a drive in the Krishna car to Griffith Park. On the way, we passed a golf course where a few stalwart early-birds were playing. Trying to be observant and conversational, I said, "This is the king of frivolous sport." "Frivolous sports" was a term the swami had used several times in lectures. He nodded, and just kept chanting softly on his beads, observing things through the window.

When we reached the park, I noticed that the gate to the zoo was wide open. So I drove through.

"Let's walk through the zoo," I suggested. "We can park here. I don't see very many people around, but it looks like it's open already."

We chanted softly as we walked among the cages. When we reached the eagle cage, the swami stopped.

"Why your country has chosen this bird as its representative?" he asked.

"They probably thought the eagle was a sign of victory," I said eventually.

"Yes, even the animals, they are in modes of nature," the swami said. "These kinds of birds are in the mode of ignorance. In India, I have seen many vultures."

We walked around the bald eagle cage chanting. The eagle cocked his head as if he was listening to what we were saying.

"Birds like vultures are in *tamas*, the mode of ignorance," the swami said. "Swans and ducks are birds in *sattva*, mode of goodness." He paused. "In India we have the lion for national – what is called, symbol?"

"Mascot?" I didn't know if there was a proper term.

"Yes. So, animals are also affected by modes of material nature. Cows are in mode of goodness. In next life, cows generally are born as humans in *sattva*. Lions and tigers are in mode of passion and monkeys are in mode of ignorance. They become in next life humans in passion and ignorance."

We continued to chant through the park for another half an hour and then returned to the car to drive back to the temple. As we drove out through an open gate past a small sentry house, a frowning official in a blue uniform looked at our car.

"The zoo's closed," he said to me crossly. I apologized and was grateful he didn't push the issue any further.

In Transit
to England

August 1968

The Haight-Ashbury phenomenon came and went like a thunderstorm on a hot summer day. Shortly after the Summer of Love, the *Oracle* folded and there were drug-related murders, street rioting and subsequent police infiltration. It was as though the peace-and-love veneer of hippydom had been stripped away to reveal an ugly, festering underbelly of drug dealing, addiction and prostitution. The waves of spiritual seekers trickled out of the Haight to live on country communes or to submit to conventional lifestyles that they had so abhorred just a few short months earlier. Our temple continued to thrive, but the neighborhood began to resemble something suspiciously close to what it had been when I'd visited in 1962: an unexceptional part of a large Californian city populated by lots of Polish immigrants.

Shyamasundar continued to dream about going to London to meet the Beatles and start a center. The swami responded enthusiastically to his idea and suggested that he and Malati go there as soon as she recovered from delivering the child they were expecting:

"I am very much eager to open a center in London," he wrote. "As soon as it is possible then I may also go there for some time to meet with the Beatles. Any sincere person, never mind whether he is hippy or Beatle, if he is actually searching for something beyond this hackneyed material sense gratification, surely he will find the most comfortable shelter under the lotus feet of Lord Krishna."

Shyamasundar was pleased at the swami's endorsement and persisted in his attempts to convince me of the viability of his plan to give Krishna consciousness to the world's most famous band. His enthusiasm was infectious and gradually Janaki, Yamuna, Gurudas and I were converted to the idea of going to London. We were all keen to travel beyond the safety and boredom of the United States; even though we had almost no money, no winter clothes and no London contacts, we wanted to help the swami spread his mission. And for that we needed to go to a country where they spoke English, so England seemed the obvious choice. I secretly thought that our success with the Beatles was less likely than our success in opening a center. After all, we had all shared the experience of opening the temple in San Francisco. How much harder could it be to open one in England?

We were scheduled to leave for England toward the end of August, but first the six of us plus Shyamasundar and Malati's new baby girl, Saraswati, flew to Montreal to spend Janmashtami with the swami. We hoped to be able to meet with him for a final briefing before we set off on our big British adventure.

We arrived at the Montreal temple just after seven o'clock in the morning. The building had previously been a bowling alley, but the devotees had converted it into a temple. I double-checked the address on the crumpled piece of paper in my pocket and paid the cab driver.

"I guess this is the place," I said. "Let's hope the swami's speaking now – it's about the time for his morning talk."

We climbed the stairs to the second-floor temple room. Sure enough, the swami sat on a large maroon seat against one wall, speaking to a room full of devotees, almost none of whom we knew. We all bowed down as we had been taught and sat down to hear the swami's talk. The swami looked regal sitting on his seat. It sat five feet off the ground and had six white wooden stairs that the swami would have had to climb to sit on the padded cushions. The temple room was huge, with foot-high Jagannatha deities at the far end on a simple altar. I couldn't be sure that the swami had noticed us come in.

Toward the end of the class, the swami looked at us, sitting at the back of the room. "You have come here from San Francisco prepared to go to London, so my hearty welcome to you," he said. So he *had* noticed us! The other devotees turned around to get a look at who the swami was addressing. "Please do this missionary work very nicely and Krishna will be pleased upon you. It is said in the *Bhagavad-gita* that anyone who is trying to spread this Krishna consciousness movement is the most dear friend of Krishna. Krishna says that person is his most dear friend. 'Nobody is so dear to Me as such person who is trying to spread Krishna consciousness movement in the world.' So you are all pledged to satisfy Krishna. So if you take up this work seriously Krishna will be very much pleased upon you. Thank you very much."

We exchanged some happy looks as everyone in the temple bowed down, signaling that the morning program was now over.

"It's funny that he called us missionaries," I said to Shyamasundar as we walked back down the stairs. "I never really thought of us in that way."

"I know what you mean," he said. "It's not like being a missionary in the traditional sense of the word. It's more like a magic carpet ride!"

The swami was staying in an apartment building a few blocks from the temple. That afternoon, I decided to walk past the building; I knew the swami would want to see us eventually, so I thought at least one of us should know where it was. It was a hot, claustrophobic afternoon in Montreal, suffocating and without a breath of wind. I was tired and slightly headachy from the flight. Usually I loved the heat, but today it wasn't helping my fatigued condition. As I trudged down the street, I saw a knot of people outside a building, and as I got closer, I saw they were devotees. Well, that had to be the swami's building, I thought, and turned to walk back to the temple. I looked back at the group and, on second thought, decided to go and see what they were doing loitering around on the sidewalk.

There were four devotees, I saw as I approached, and in the center sat the swami perched on a chair on the sidewalk, soaking in the sunlight. I looked up at the building: no verandas, and this facade was facing south. This was obviously the place the swami came to get his daily sunshine.

"So, we can practice Krishna consciousness in any condition of life," the swami was saying. I sat down on the pavement next to one of the Canadian devotees and tried to look inconspicuous. This extemporaneous outdoor class was a bonus I hadn't counted on.

"Whether one is rich or poor, anyone can practice Krishna consciousness and perfect one's life." A short, dark-complexioned man – maybe Turkish or Italian, I thought – came up behind us and stood for a few moments by a car, taking in the unusual scene in front of him. Then he curled his legs under him and sat down on the sidewalk next to me.

"We must learn and always adhere to the teachings of the Vedic literature," the swami was saying. "There's difference between ignorance and innocence. Innocence means one is like a child. But ignorant means he has no knowledge; he is fool."

The man interrupted. "I think we have a lot to learn from children," he said.

It seemed a rather innocuous and innocent interruption to me. But the swami's response was abrupt. He didn't want to make small talk today – he wanted to teach.

"You can't learn anything from children. What can a child teach you?"

"What do you mean?" the man asked.

"Child has no knowledge," the swami said. "But we can learn from animals. Animals have much to teach us. We can learn faithfulness from the dog. Even if the master aims his gun at the dog's head and shoots him, the dog will remain faithful to the death."

I realized right away that the swami was playing a philosophical debating game with this man, as he often did with his students. The stranger seemed interested and listened for a while, but he didn't offer any further comment. The conversation veered in another direction, and after a few minutes the man got up and went on his way. It was almost as if the swami was aiming his discourse solely at the devotees.

It was still a couple of days until the Janmashtami festival, so the six of us busied ourselves with organizing the final details of our trip. We had booked the cheapest possible route to England, a convoluted journey with Loftleider, the Icelandic airline, which went from New York to Luxembourg via Reykjavik, the capital of Iceland. We discovered that in order to get into England each couple should have about four thousand pounds for maintenance.

There was no way each of us could come up with that kind of cash, but between us we could cover two people. So we came up with a plan where we would pool our money and travel one couple at a time to London; each couple would present the required amount at the border and then would wire the same money back to the next couple, who would repeat the process.

Over the next few days, I noticed a young Indian man who came to the temple punctually at noon to pay his respects to Krishna. Dressed in a dark business suit and tie, he bowed down and touched his forehead to the floor in front of the dozen or so paintings of Krishna on the wall. As he bowed, he said *"Om Krishna Om Krishna Krishna Krishna Om Om, Om Rama Om Rama Rama Rama Om Om."* His behavior struck me as eccentric, but it was obviously devotional. Watching him the day before Janmashtami, I realized we all have our own individual and personal relationship with God.

The morning of Janmashtami I was filled with nostalgia, remembering our first Janmashtami in New York two years earlier. As I sat and listened to the swami speak in the Montreal temple room, I looked around at all the new devotees' faces and thought how different this celebration was to that first festival. Not only were there more people; there were more *committed* people who were dedicated to helping the swami spread Krishna consciousness. I took in the paintings on the walls, the large temple room, and the swami's beautiful seat. This all served as evidence to me that the seeds the swami had planted were flowering. I knew, of course, that the movement had grown dramatically, but now I felt as if I was seeing it for myself. We were celebrating the birth of Lord Krishna in another country, but for me, this day was also about celebrating the swami's achievements.

The format of the Janmashtami observation was to be the same as the New York one had been: fasting all day, chanting with instruments, listening to the swami speak and chanting individually on our beads. This was to continue until midnight, when we would have a special *arati* ceremony for the deities, followed by a feast. And as in New York, there was an initiation ceremony with many new devotees receiving their beads and Sanskrit names from the swami. The six of us were awarded second initiation – Brahmin initiation – which I remembered the swami mentioning at my first initiation ceremony. He gave us a sacred mantra, which he called Gayatri and which he said we should memorize and chant three times a day at sunrise, noon and sunset.

The swami stayed in the temple room with everyone for a good part of the day, chanting with us and speaking about Krishna.

"God's senses, Krishna's senses, are not limited," he said. "Just like I can see with my eyes but Krishna can also eat with his eyes. He is within your heart, He is everywhere, so He can appear from everywhere. Just like the sun rises from the eastern side. It does not mean that eastern side is the mother of sun. We simply see that sun is rising from the eastern side. In this way, if we try to understand in truth, then we can understand what is God. Superficially, if we try to understand by our experimental knowledge, then it is not possible to understand God.

"Of course, this Janmashtami ceremony is observed by all Hindus. Irrespective of becoming Krishna follower or not, this ceremony is observed in India in every home. Just like in your Western countries the Christmas is observed in every home, similarly Janmashtami is observed in every home. Today is a great ceremonial day.

"So today we should offer prayers to Krishna. The other religious sects, just like the Christians, they offer prayer; the Mohammedans, they offer prayer. So prayer, offering prayer is also one of the items of *bhakti*, devotion.

"So, I shall invite all of you today to speak about Krishna," he said. My heart sunk. This was a trip down memory lane, and this time I was pretty sure I wouldn't be able to get out of it. The swami was looking around the room. "So I shall request Janardan to speak something about his realization of Krishna."

Inside I shut out whatever Janardan was saying so that I could mentally prepare my speech. Then I found an old receipt in my wallet and jotted down a few ideas with the leaky red pen that I found in my pocket. My face felt hot; I glanced over my shoulder and saw that the room was full of people: devotees, interested Canadian guests and many Indian-born Hindus.

"So we should try to chant Hare Krishna as much as we can," Janardan was concluding. "I guess that's my main realization. Hare Krishna."

The swami nodded at him and asked a young Texan devotee, Gaurasundara, to speak. Then Yamuna, then Janaki. The devotees spoke lofty philosophy, borrowing many of the swami's phrases. I was surprised that they sounded so elevated, so eloquent, so persuasive, despite being relative newcomers. I could imagine them speaking with any professor, any philosopher, any penetrating intellectual. My confidence was dwindling. Whatever I said was going to be redundant and anti-climactic.

"Let him speak," the swami said, turning in my direction. "Mukunda."

I cleared my throat and looked out at the darkening sky, my face burning. "Well …" I said. "I offer my respectful obeisances to our spiritual master, Bhaktivedanta Swami, who is very dear to Lord Krishna, having taken shelter unto His lotus feet." I swallowed hard and looked at the wall.

"The Krishna consciousness movement is intended to make a solution to our everyday problems," I said after a long pause. "It's not a kind of place where people just come because there's some religious rites being performed. Everyone in this age is thinking that 'I am free,' but actually I am not free. I am very bound up. We're strictly bound up by the stringent laws of nature. In every status of life I have to serve somebody or something or my own body. In every status of life I have to serve my wife or I have to serve my children, I have to serve my pet, I have to serve my work, my boss, my associates."

I heard myself repeating phrases I'd heard the swami use. *Bound up, stringent, status* and *serve* were not words that I used – not in public speaking, not in writing and certainly not in casual conversation.

"If I'm very wealthy, very elevated, or very beautiful physically," I continued, "even then I always have to serve somebody. If nothing else, one has to serve one's own stomach. I have to eat. I have to get food. I have to serve my stomach. So I am not free at all. I have to do these things. There's no way I can stop. If I don't eat, I will die.

"So our natural position as a living entity is that we have to serve something. That's our natural position. If something is wrong with my hand and I want to be cured, I don't grab onto some food-stuffs or some medicine, some herbs, and squeeze them with the hand and think that this hand is going to be nourished or cured. I take the medicine or the food through my mouth, and then it circulates through the digestive system and through the blood and finally comes to the hand. So the hand, unless it's serving its source, is useless. The servant must serve the master or the part must serve the whole. And our relationship with God is the same. Just like the hand is made out of mucus, bile and air, flesh and bone, as all the body is. It is just stool."

I liked this example, and it always made me laugh inside. "Bile," "stool" and "mucus" were terms I knew Ayurvedic medical practitioners used, words that the swami also used to describe human physiology. I'd never used the word "stool" before I met the swami except maybe in a doctor's office or in the word "stool-pigeon." I figured the Indians in the temple room might like this touch. I glanced back and saw the young suited man looking blankly toward me from the other end of the room.

"But we're made of spirit," I rushed on, promising myself that I wouldn't look back again. "Qualitatively we're the same as Krishna, but quantitatively we're many millions of times smaller. Qualitatively the same, quantitatively different. So if we're fragmental portions, separated parts and parcels, we can serve the source or the whole and we can be cured of this material disease which is rampant nowadays. And this is possible only by mercy."

I glanced over at the swami. His eyes were closed, his face expressionless. He looked to me like he was listening intently. I felt like I'd become a mouthpiece transmitting information rather than being any kind of original speaker.

"So, simply by hearing the message of *Srimad-Bhagavatam* and *Bhagavad-gita* we can immediately get some relief from this material existence. Just like when we were chanting here you could feel some ecstasy. Well, this ecstasy goes on unlimitedly and infinitely, eternally, if one takes to it. It's always eternal, ever increasing. Just like the relationship between ourselves and our spiritual master is eternal and ever increasing, our relationship with God is the same. So please try to realize that this is a very serious movement, and we're not asking you to sign up or pay us anything, but simply to sincerely try it, and you'll immediately feel some benefit."

I was done. I looked at the swami, but he was already scanning the room for his next speaker. I breathed a sigh of relief.

"Nanda Kishor," the swami was saying. "Say something about your realization of Krishna consciousness."

Nanda Kishor scrutinized his hands, turning them over as if examining them for forensic evidence. His orange T-shirt and yellow *dhoti* were splattered with cooking stains; I knew he'd been cooking a lot today ... every day. There was a long pause, and I thought perhaps he hadn't heard the swami – we had been fasting all day, so maybe he'd just zoned out. Then he glanced up at the swami.

"Well, I like to spend time doing service in the kitchen," he said in a voice so soft I could hardly hear him. "Especially rolling *chapattis*. For the guests that don't know, *chapattis* are round Indian pancakes made of wheat flour. I make them every day for the devotees instead of bread."

"This is really weird," I thought. "Why is he talking about food instead of philosophy?"

"We make them out of whole meal flour," he muttered, continuing his flat-bread soliloquy. "You roll them in a circle and then put them over a flame and they inflate like a balloon." There were a few giggles in the audience. "Anyway, if I have nothing else to do for the rest of my life, I would be happy to continue rolling *chapattis* for Krishna. Whatever we can do for Krishna, whatever talent we can offer, Krishna will accept that service and give us complete satisfaction."

I looked over at him; he looked like he was recalling the happiest moment of his life. *Chapatti* rolling suddenly took on a new meaning: the service he did – something I thought to be tedious – was his way of pleasing Krishna. I realized at that moment that devotional service could be varied; it wasn't limited to the front-line type of work I thought I was doing. Nanda Kishor was speaking philosophy after all! And his heartfelt talk made more of an impression upon me than any other speech that evening.

About ten o'clock, a stocky Indian man with white hair entered the temple and stood at the foyer at the top of the entry stairs. Under his suit the collar of his shirt was open, giving him a slovenly demeanor. The swami watched him as he walked toward the guests' shoes, which were lined up in pairs against the wall. He appeared to scan the pairs and then picked up the swami's white shoes that curled up a little at the toes. I was puzzled; what was he doing with the swami's shoes? Looking straight at the swami, he banged the shoes together sideways two or three times. A cloud of dust rose and formed a puffball and then faded into the air as it fell to the floor. The swami broke into a huge smile and nodded enthusiastically at the man who grinned toothlessly back at him. The man took off his own shoes and sat on the floor close to the swami's seat. And while everyone else silently watched, the swami and the man conversed in Hindi for a few minutes. I didn't understand what had just happened between them, but I assumed it involved something to do with Vedic etiquette of some kind. I knew that it was traditional for a holy man's shoes to be respected, and it was a gesture of humility to touch them, although I wouldn't have dared to.

Just before midnight, a group of Gujarati Indian women appeared carrying sticks and dressed identically in red sequined saris. I thought they looked like a soccer team.

"Who are they?" I asked a man standing next to me. "What are the sticks for?"

"They are dancers," he said. "They will dance the *rasa garbha* dance. You know it?" I shook my head. "Often it is performed on Janmashtami," he told me.

I wondered what the swami would have to say about choreographed dancing in the temple. In general he was very traditional, so I doubted he would approve. But when the swami saw them he beckoned for them to come forward. One woman plugged in a small cassette player and pressed the play button. A melodious Gujarati song rang out in the temple and the women began to dance in graceful, symmetrical movements, touching their sticks together as they whirled past one another. Their red skirts rustled as they rose and fell in small waves. The swami nodded to the beat of the music and smiled throughout the whole fifteen-minute performance.

"Very good! Thank you very much," he exclaimed at the end. The sequined women gathered around his seat, and they had an animated group conversation in Hindi until it was time for the midnight *arati* ceremony.

The room was filled to capacity, mostly by Indian guests dressed in all their finery: heavily jeweled saris, dripping gold jewelry and opulent Punjabi outfits. The singing of a hundred throats filled the candle-lit room as the deities' curtains opened for the *arati*. The swami stood before the altar to perform the ceremony. Holding three incense sticks in his right hand, he made big clockwise circles to offer the incense to the deities. In his left hand he rang a small silver bell. The swami offered other articles: a burning cotton wick dipped in clarified butter sitting in a small bronze holder, water in a conch shell, a handkerchief, fresh flowers, a yak-tail fan and a peacock feather fan – and then blew three long blasts on a conch shell to indicate the end of the ceremony.

Everyone took their places sitting in parallel lines on the temple floor. After a long day of fasting, it was finally time to serve the beautiful Janmashtami feast, which included Nanda Kishor's celebrated *chapattis*.

—

Three days later, it was time for us to return to the US to catch our flight to Europe. The six of us and the baby went up to the swami's apartment to bid him farewell and tell him about our plans for England.

"I am very pleased you are going to England," he said. "This is very nice service. You have some contact there?"

"Actually, no," Shyamasundar said. "I'm the only one who's been to London before, and I don't really know anyone there. I was only there for a little while."

"No matter," the swami said. "Krishna will help. When I came to America, I knew no one, and Krishna sent all of you to me." We all smiled, glowing inwardly. This was all we needed to hear before leaving.

"We're going to be going back to New York today," Janaki said. "Then we'll fly to Luxembourg and then take a train to London."

"Do you have any last instructions for us before we leave?" I asked. "Any instructions about how we can introduce Krishna consciousness there?"

"Drama will be important in England," he said. "It is land of Shakespeare." He was quiet for a moment, looking out the window thoughtfully. "When I was a child I saw a silent movie by comedian Max Linder. You are knowing him?"

We all shook our heads.

"In movie there is scene of people at outdoor ball dance. So the men were wearing – how do you say? – tuxedos. No, coat tails. And the women were dressed for evening enjoyment. Then some naughty boys were putting glue on the benches. So when a couple sat on the bench, the man would arise, but his trouser seat stuck to the glue, ripped off the coat tail, and exposed his thigh." He laughed. "Of course they were all drinking whiskey, so he did not realize. And the lady did not notice."

I looked from the corner of my eye at the others, bewildered why the swami was telling us about this.

"So, they danced, and all the other dancers looked at them. The men thought it was something new, so they also copied the style exactly, ripping off coat tails so their thighs showed. Then everybody was doing it." He laughed heartily at the memory. We laughed along with him at the story, even though it seemed an odd moment to recount something like that.

"Well, thank you," Malati said. "We have to go to the airport now."

We all bowed down.

"Thank you very much," the swami said.

As we walked back to the temple to our luggage and waiting car, I thought about the swami's story.

"Why do you think he told that story?" I asked Gurudas. "I mean, why bring it up?"

"I don't know," he said. "It didn't seem related at all to us going to London." We crossed a street, and suddenly it became clear to me.

"I know why he told it!" I exclaimed. "I asked him for ideas on how to introduce Krishna consciousness in London, right? And then he told us about doing plays and then launched into the sequence from that silent movie."

"And?"

"Well, the story about the film was his answer to my question about how to spread Krishna consciousness. The guy with the ripped coat tails in the film was a bit weird, but he was enthusiastic, so everyone else started copying him. So the swami was telling us to be enthusiastic, no matter how strange Krishna consciousness might seem at first."

"Yes," Janaki said. "That makes sense. When we do public chanting, people will definitely think we're weird, maybe amusing if we're lucky. But that's OK. If we're enthusiastic, people will join in, just like in the film!"

"First they ignore you, then they laugh at you, then debate you, then they accept you," Gurudas said, quoting the old dictum. We smiled at the swami's surprising way of giving us our last orders.

PART 3

LONDON

The Empire Strikes Back

A foggy day, in London town,
It had me low, and it had me down
I viewed the morning, with much alarm,
The British Museum, had lost its charm
How long I wondered, could this thing last,
But the age of miracles, it hadn't past
And suddenly, I saw you standing right there
And in foggy London town,
The sun was shining everywhere

—*George & Ira Gershwin*

London devotee pioneers, 1970
From left to right bottom row: Yamuna, Malati, Janaki
middle row: Kulashekhar, the author
top row: Gurudas, Shyamasundar

CHAPTER 25

The Streets of London

When Janaki and I arrived in Dover, the fog stroked us with its clammy hands like an unwelcoming, Hitchcocky host. The immigration official followed suit in her attitude.

"What's your purpose in coming here?" she demanded. Her dark hair was pulled into a severe knot at the nape of her neck.

"I write for a magazine called *Back to Godhead*," I said. "Do you want to see a copy?"

"Let me see." She sighed and held out her hand. She flicked through the pages in a distracted manner and looked us up and down. I glanced at Janaki's skirt and jacket. "She looks presentable and conventional," I thought, and I hoped I did too. I'd combed my hair before we'd gotten off the ferry.

"Are you with Scientology?"

"Who?"

"Scientology."

"I don't know what that is."

"Can I see proof of your funds?" she asked.

We showed her the bank bag of notes, which was by now a much more seasoned traveler than either of us.

She sighed again and brought down the stamp on my passport in a violent motion. Janaki handed over her passport and, without a word, the official repeated the thud of her stamp.

"Next!"

"Can we go?" I asked incredulous that that was all there was to it.

She nodded, now fixing her eye on the elderly Italian man behind us in the line.

We exited the ferry terminal and peered through the gloom to try to find a train station.

"Excuse me, could you tell me where we could get a train to London?" I asked a man holding an umbrella. He pointed right.

"Head that way about one hundred yards," he said. "The station is down there. You can't miss the sign."

"Thanks." It was such a relief to be in a country where we could understand the language. Our four days in Holland had been difficult, most people spoke some English, but we couldn't read signs or ingredients lists on packages – a very important part of being vegetarian.

We caught a train and then a bus to the three-room upstairs apartment that Shyamasundar and Malati had secured during their first few days in the country. It was in a south-London suburb called Herne Hill owned, they told us, by an Indian widow named Mrs. Kholi. When our taxi pulled up, the four of them tumbled down the stairs to greet us and help us drag our heavy suitcases up to our new home.

"We're all here now!" Shyamasundar exclaimed. "Finally, we're here in England! Can you believe it?"

"Actually, I'm so tired I'll believe anything right now," Janaki said.

"Yes, you need to rest," Yamuna said, still vaguely maternal toward her younger sister. "Why don't you have a shower and we'll cook something for you. Then you can sleep or unpack or whatever."

They showed us to our room and Janaki went to have a shower. I heard the water flowing, but then heard her shouting down the hall.

"Hey, Malati," she called. "What's going on with the water? It's freezing!" I went out into the hallway in time to see Malati heading toward the bathroom. Janaki's head was poking out the door.

"Here," Malati said, giving Janaki a fistful of change. "To get hot water you have to put coins into that metal box thing on the floor by the tub."

"Really? You're kidding!" Janaki looked dubious.

"I thought you just said you'd believe anything," Malati said.

•——•

Over the next few days we discussed our strategy for introducing Krishna consciousness in London. We decided that we'd begin here the same way we began in San Francisco: by finding young hippies, chanting with them and having regular programs. People would become interested, our numbers would grow and we'd start a temple – simple as that. The catch was that there didn't seem to be very many unconventional people around. In fact, in the first few days I was in London all I saw was tourists and men in suits. After spending more than two years in the American alternative scene, England seemed heavily controlled, conservative and undemocratic.

We did a bit of asking around and found out about a place called the Arts Lab on Drury Lane in Covent Garden. Shyamasundar was told that this was the London hub of the hippy movement, the main place where people into alternative living congregated. Top on our list of priorities was to visit the Arts Lab to make some contacts with the objective of hopefully having programs there.

One of the first things we decided we should do now that we were in England was dress in traditional Indian Vaishnava clothing; it seemed in keeping with the swami's suggestion to be enthusiastic and upfront about being devotees, especially because the Max Linder film story he told involved wearing unusual clothing. We men were more nervous about the clothing proposal than the women were. We quickly realized how many Indians and Muslims there were living in London, and many of the women wore saris or *burkas*. Even though Yamuna, Janaki and Malati might be the only Westerners around in saris, at least there were other women in London wearing similar garments. The Indian men in London, though, tended to dress like everyone else. They certainly didn't wear the white *dhoti* loincloth and shaved head of traditional Hindu monks. The British public might have been used to seeing Muslim men in their cotton robes or women in full *burka*, but I thought that a European man with a shaved head and wearing a piece of white cloth instead of pants might be another story altogether.

When the three of us emerged from the bathroom with our heads shaved clean but for the small tuft left at the crown by Vaishnava priests, we were greeted with cheers. I was attached to my hair and felt self-conscious, but Janaki gazed fondly at my bald white head.

"You look beautiful," she said, and I immediately felt better.

The next day, I embarked on my first journey as a full-fledged, out-in-the-open devotee. I was on my way to the Arts Lab in my *dhoti*, yellow turtleneck sweater, shaved head and blazing white *tilaka* mark on my forehead indicating, for anyone who cared to look, that my body was a temple of God.

As it turned out, a great many people looked. I was followed by stares as I walked to the bus stop, and a few people made double takes. I boarded the bus and made my way to the upper level with

Tilaka *markings worn by devotees of Krishna*

The "a" at the end of "tilaka" is usually not pronounced, and the word is generally pronounced in English as "tee-lock."
Inset: tilaka *more perfectly made*

the eyes of all the passengers on me. Most were too polite to stare, but they sneaked looks at me from behind their tabloids. My head was cold. I felt like I was performing an act of surrender mixed with a hint of exhibitionism.

Drury Lane turned out to be situated in the center of the London entertainment scene. The Arts Lab was run by a couple of American guys called Jim Haynes and Jack Moore, and it was neighbored by lots of theaters and opera houses. I intrigued Jack and Jim by the way I looked, and they quickly agreed to allow us to hold programs at the Arts Lab.

The Lab wasn't exactly a community, because no one lived on the premises, but it nevertheless served as a central gathering place for the increasingly large numbers of young Londoners interested in peace, justice, vegetarianism and left-wing political activism. The Arts Lab functioned as a center of music-making, as an art gallery and as a venue for the screening of alternative films. Occasionally, the Lab also allowed blue-film makers to shoot nudey films there; fence-sitters would be enticed to strip off for the shoot with ten pound notes, or a bit more if they were prepared to do "other things."

Later that week, the six of us piled into the red 1935 Ford Poplar pickup Shyamasundar had purchased for next to nothing. Its cab held only two people – him and Malati, plus Saraswati – so the rest of us sat cross-legged in the back on the truck's wooden floor. During a torrential downpour a few days earlier I had erected a wooden frame around the rear tray of the truck, over which I hung an olive-green tarpaulin. The covering hung down on the sides to protect us from the elements, but it had the effect of concentrating London's omnipresent diesel fumes. I could see that we were going to have to get used to the smell of diesel if we were going to continue traveling like this. Fortunately it was a short ride to the Arts Lab.

The place was full of people milling around the front counter and reading the large bulletin board that held announcements of gigs, gatherings and other events in the city. Someone was selling pottery, and someone else was giving a demonstration of some kind of New Age therapy. There was a book stall where people talked together and passed joints around. The air smelled musty like cigarette smoke, incense, pot and feet. The patrons looked pretty much like the alternatives in San Francisco, and they loved the chanting, even if they seemed a bit more reserved than their American brothers and sisters. On our first night there, Jim and Jack let us chant in the main hall, which was about half the size of a basketball court. There were lots of happy faces and people singing along that night, and several even took off their shoes and danced on the carpeted floor.

The author (playing mrdanga) *and Shyamasundar in London's Arts Lab*

London
Oct. 15, 1968

Dear Swamiji,

Please accept my humble obeisances. I am writing to you because within one week I have been influenced by Krishna Consciousness.

It started when I went to a rock 'n roll dance in London. I knew that the advertised "Radha Krishna Temple" was 6 devotees from the Temple in San Francisco, as I had read previously about it in the "New Yorker" magazine. Because of certain feelings, I did not join in— at first. However, I saw the devotees chanting, and those magic words, HARE KRISHNA HARE KRISHNA KRISHNA KRISHNA HARE HARE HARE RAMA HARE RAMA RAMA RAMA HARE HARE!! So I finally gave in, and joined them, repeating over and over again. It certainly felt good afterwards.

Two days later, I went to Kirtan, at the devotees' private house. This time it hit me! I was lost in bliss, divine bliss! Soon, I learned all the devotees' names, Mukunda, Janaki, Shyamsundar, Malati, Gurudas and Yamuna. They invited me back again and after only 4 days since I first experienced chanting, they invited me to perform with them. I was overwhelmed!

Now, Krishna Consciousness really had a hold on me, and I can't believe it's all happened so Fast! Tomorrow I am going to move in with them, as Mukunda told me, for someone just entering into Krishna Consciousness, association with devotees is very important. I have shaved my head, so I am complete with a sika, and I hope you can understand how happy I am feeling at this moment. Although I know very little about Krishna or His life, I am so eager to learn. Already names like Lord Chaitanya, or Bhagavad Gita are starting to mean something to me. I am determined to devote my whole being to Krishna, and although we have not met, I long for the day we do—because if it were not for your Divine Grace, I would not be writing this letter and I would not be so happy at this moment.

I chant every day, naturally, and I am concentrating hard on chanting 16 times round the beads in 2 hours. I have also given up stimulants (which played a considerable part in my previous life), swearing, pre-marital sex, in any way. I gave up meat eating, over 6 months ago, because, after I had thought very hard about it, I decided that eating meat was really eating a warmed up corpse! And I like to see animals free and alive and I don't want them to die for me, it is as simple as that.

I can honestly say that Krishna Consciousness is the light in my darkness...

I remain, influenced,
Mr. Andy Anderson

Stratford, England

My beloved God-brothers, Mukunda dasa, Shyamasundar dasa, and Gurudasa, and the Brahmachari (who was with us in the pick-up while going from Herne Hill to Drury Lane), and God-sisters.

I am grateful to you for giving me an opportunity to meet you on last Tuesday afternoon. I am impressed by your enthusiasm to spread Krishna's knowledge in this world, for which it will be indebted to you and in future you will be remembered as great pioneer-saints.

Success is yours; because Krishna dwells in your hearts and therefore His Shakti (power) is behind you. I look forward to the day when we shall have our own Krishna Temple in this city where we can chant His Holy Names, perform Puja (worship) and exchange our spiritual experiences.

Please do not think of me as a stranger. Ours is the only true relation—that of Krishna Consciousness. All others (worldly) are Mithya (imaginary). I should consider it a favour if you could kindly keep me informed of your activities. But when Swamiji's arrival date is fixed, please do let me know.

You are the real charmers; with Krishna's Names on your tongues you are performing the Wonder of Wonders—turning beastly humans into Godly saints, for which you deserve Krishna's special grace. As you are Jnanis (those who know), it is not for me to remind you that no service goes unrewarded by Krishna.

So, my beloved God-brothers and God-sisters, Godspeed to you,

Lakshmidasa

Parts & Parcels
**two letters
to the London
Hare Krishna temple**

*Letters to the London temple as printed in the
Back to Godhead magazine, October 15, 1968*

Our Arts Lab programs became a regular thing, our primary venue through which to get in touch with the British public. Three times a week we drove into the city and chanted with about a hundred people. After the first couple of weeks, the novelty of the programs wore off and Jim and Jack relegated us to the smaller room upstairs, which was painted all black and was used as the Lab's the-

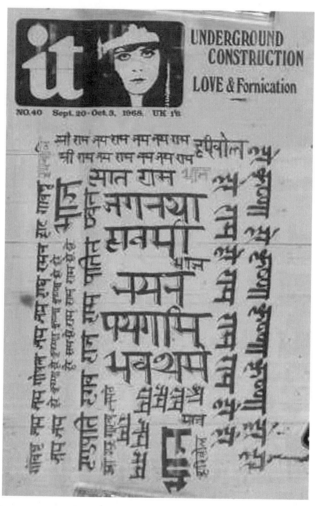

Cover of London's International Times, *October 1968, calligraphy by Yamuna*

ater. It was always covered in cigarette butts that we had to sweep up before each chanting session.

We wrote to the swami to inform him about our programs, hoping that he would respond positively. We knew our primary objective in London was to open a temple, but we were quickly realizing that things were different here than in America. The swami responded promptly to our letters, and when each letter arrived from him, the person to whom it was addressed read it aloud for everyone to hear.

"This is giving me so much pleasure to hear how nicely you are carrying on this movement in London," Malati read out loud in September. "It was originally my Guru Maharaja's desire that there should be a center established in London, and by his mercy, now you have successfully begun this mission; so please keep me informed how you are progressing there. I am very anxious to hear in each letter. You all three couples are expert in the matter of preaching Krishna consciousness, so I am sure by your combined effort in London, there will be a great successful center."

The matter of the center was always on our minds, but getting one started was a question of money and contacts. The swami wrote with some practical suggestions about how we could increase both: "Why don't you get *Back to Godhead* from New York?" he suggested. "Here in New York they are selling an average of one hundred copies of *Back to Godhead* each day. So try to get immediately copies from New York and try to sell them in large quantities. That is our backbone. Kirtan plus distribution of our books and literature is the basic principle of our success."

Here was a confirmation from the swami about how to spread his movement in London: distribution of spiritual literature and public chanting. And so it came to pass one cold and overcast morning that the six of us and Saraswati donned our best Vaishnava clothing, piled into the Ford pickup and headed out to have our first chant in the streets of London.

We decided to try Trafalgar Square first. It was always packed with tourists, and we thought that the statue of Lord Nelson atop his one-hundred-foot perch would be a fitting witness to our first public chanting foray in London. We parked the truck and filed into the square, cold and nervous, but exhilarated, our colorful clothing a stark contrast to the gray of the square. I started to play our only *mrdanga* while the others played their *karatalas*. The pigeons strutting about scavenging for crumbs took flight instantly at the sound of the cymbals. Our voices and instruments resounded around the sprawling cement plaza, attracting an immediate response. A crowd of tourists, shoppers and business people began to form around us. Some tapped their feet and smiled, but most stood statuesque in disbelief. To muster up courage, I pretended the swami was there in the crowd watching us.

Cars, lorries, taxis and bright red buses careened past us on four sides, and the square's fountains spewed water, but to anyone close enough our chanting drowned out every other sound: the traffic, the warbling of the birds and the spray of water cascading into the pools that surrounded the fountains.

"Nelson must get bored up there sometimes," I thought, as we began to sway in synchrony. "This will liven up his day." Gazing up at the larger-than-life statue of the admiral standing regally on top of his column, I felt my apprehensions scatter like the flock of pigeons had a few minutes earlier. That is, until I started to notice the startled eyes of the uniformed police who had begun to gather on the periphery of the crowd. I thought maybe I was being paranoid, but there did seem to be an awful lot of them – maybe thirty or more. They formed a little klatch about ten yards from the crowd; they huddled together and kept glancing back at us, as if developing some sort of strategy.

"Surely they can't arrest us," I thought. "We have Saraswati with us, and anyway we're not doing anything wrong. We're just enjoying ourselves and giving the lunchtime crowd some entertainment, and I don't see how they can think there is anything wrong with that. On the other hand, they might think we've been taking drugs or that we're carrying acid."

The crowd had grown to nearly a hundred, and I realized that we should have made a leaflet to explain who we were and what we were doing. I kept chanting, pounding my *mrdanga*. Finally, one of the bobbies emerged from their conference. He strode purposefully toward the center of the crowd and waited until I wasn't singing and the other five were responding to my lead. I tried to appear clam, but inside I felt shivery and my heart was thumping. Panic was setting in. My traumatic encounter with the police in Hurleyville was still fresh in my memory.

"May I speak with your leader, please?" He pitched his words carefully, his voice authoritative and loud.

I relaxed immediately. "He's gently inquisitive," I thought. "How quaint."

I'd expected an American response: "You guys gotta get outta here right now!" Or worse: "We're gonna search your bags." I kept playing my *mrdanga*, but a bit softer. I felt the crowd close in ever so slightly, their eyes sparkling with curiosity. A derelict carrying a big black sack staggered by a few feet in front of us, and the policeman was momentarily distracted.

"You can speak with me, if you like," I said over the sound of my *mrdanga*.

"Right," he said. "I'm afraid I have to inform you that it is illegal to play musical instruments in this square."

"What about singing?"

"Not in a group, I'm afraid." He sounded so regretful – Where were the handcuffs and the attitude?

"That's illegal too?"

"I'm afraid so. There may be other parks where you can sing with instruments. Maybe you should try somewhere else."

Gurudas heard the whole conversation and informed the others. The policeman continued to stand next to me akimbo, his colleagues watching from a distance. We kept chanting but conferred together and decided we'd better go somewhere else rather than risk getting arrested. The policeman's stare was turning into a glare, so I brought the chanting to a close. The crowd immediately dispersed.

"OK, we're going to leave, then," I said. "We don't want to cause any trouble."

"Right-o," he said and sauntered away.

The mist was thickening as we hurried back to the pickup more than a little disappointed in our less-than-sterling start. The fog was turning into drizzle.

"Maybe we should just go home," Malati said. "This weather is depressing, and we're all cold."

"I think we should try one more place," Gurudas said. "The swami wants us to do public chanting, and how're we gonna do that if we don't get us'ta being out in public?"

"Well, we *could* wait for a brighter day," I said.

"I think we'll be doing a lot of waiting, then," Shyamasundar said. "This is London, not California. We've got months of this ahead of us." We all looked downcast at these words. "You know," he said, "the nice thing about all this is that we're really not doing anything. We're just instruments in Krishna's hands."

We trudged along silently absorbing his words.

"You're right, you know. That's right," Janaki said, flicking a rain drop from the end of her nose. "We always think it's us who're making things happen or not happen, but really it's Krishna."

"That can make you feel kind of distant from the world, though," I said. "You know – if you feel like you're not the one who's making stuff happen in your life."

"That's only because it's bruising to the ego!" Shyamasundar said. "We always want to be the one who's controlling everything. But we're not. Krishna has brought us here, and it's in His hands if we succeed or not."

"Well, sure," I said sarcastically. "We'll just sit back and wait for Krishna to do it for us." I was wet and the wind was freezing.

"No, we still hafta try," Gurudas said. "I read this story about a bird in the swami's books. She laid her eggs on the beach, and the waves washed them out to sea. When she asked the ocean to return them, the ocean refused. So she decided to dry up the ocean by scooping up the water with her beak. Then Garuda, the bird king, hears about her determination, you know, and he threatens to dry up the whole ocean, so then the ocean gets scared and gives back the little bird's eggs. So I guess the moral is if we're determined, then we get reciprocation from Krishna."

I thought about what they were saying. Before we came to England I had become particularly enamored with myself: the way I did things, the way I thought, the way I looked, the way I succeeded, the way I appeared socially with an attractive wife, the way I convinced people to do some service for Krishna, the way I organized events, the way I got publicity for the movement, even the way I walked. I was basking in the feeling that *I* was making things happen – not the swami, not Krishna, but me. "I'll have to continue to contemplate this concept of who is behind everything," I thought. In a way, it would be a great relief to be able to see myself as an instrument in a greater plan, as a small part in a great undertaking led by the swami, who was its architect.

"OK," I said. "Let's look for one more place and then we can call it a day."

We drove west for about fifteen minutes through the agonizingly slow and reeking London traffic. We spotted a little place called Soho Square, a much smaller area than Trafalgar Square enclosed by a black wrought-iron fence and covered with sodden grass and a few small paved walkways. In the center was a tiny wooden gazebo, a Georgian-style shelter that was big enough for about four people to stand underneath. The rain was now thundering down and the square was deserted, as empty as a raided cookie jar.

"The swami would be proud of us," I thought to myself as we parked the truck. "He would want us to be determined, and continuing to chant in this weather really shows that we are." We hurried into the square, the rain stinging our faces as we ran. No police in sight – no one at all in sight, actually. "Still," I thought, "this is our London debut, and we are the swami's spiritual warriors. A little bit of rain can't dampen our spirits, even if we are getting soaked to the skin."

We started chanting again and noticed a few brave souls zipping through the small park, their umbrellas shielding them from the curtains of water that swept over the square. I felt my determination drowning, my enthusiasm from ten minutes earlier being swept away with the torrent flowing into the subterranean pipes through the street gratings. Who would be mad enough to stop and listen to a band of chanters like us in this weather?

Then I saw that one person had stopped. He was a middle-aged man in foggy round eyeglasses with a wet newspaper folded neatly under his arm. He was fastidiously dressed in a blue overcoat and bowler hat and was holding a small leather briefcase with belt clips. The rain drummed on his umbrella, but he seemed oblivious to the weather. His head was tilted in curiosity. This wasn't some fickle tourist, I thought. He's a true-blue Brit, a member of the establishment! We chanted for five more minutes and then decided that staying out any longer might give the baby pneumonia and damage the drum.

As we started to make our way across the square, our sole spectator came toward us.

"What's it in aid of?" he asked. Because of the unfamiliar intonation of his British accent, I had to ask him to repeat his question twice.

"This is the same singing that Chaitanya Mahaprabhu did in the sixteenth century in India," I explained once I'd figured out what he was asking. I hoped I was sounding authoritative to this English gentleman. "We're his followers, so we're doing the same thing."

He was listening intently. Rivulets of water flowed off my bare head and into my eyes. He tipped his umbrella toward me and moved closer so that I was sheltered from the deluge.

"The mantra you heard us singing was sung in public every day in West Bengal. And it's still sung in many parts of India today. The philosophy is based on the *Bhagavad-gita*. Have you heard of that?"

"Yes, I certainly have," he said. When he spoke his trimmed brown mustache moved in time with his words.

"The *Gita* was first written in Sanskrit five thousand years ago," I said. "It's a very old system of chanting, so what you just heard is something very ancient."

He nodded. "What is the location of your school in London?" he asked.

"We don't have one yet," I said. "We want to start a center, but we haven't found a place yet." I was delighted that someone so conservative-looking would have such genuine interest. I glanced at the others who were walking away toward the truck.

"I think we're gonna have to go now," I said. "It's really wet."

"Thank you very much for your time," he said politely. He tipped his hat at me and waved to the others. "Good luck," he shouted, as I walked away.

"Keep an eye out for us," I called, "because we'll be back."

I couldn't possibly have known then in 1968 that those words of mine would prove prophetic. Not only would our chanting parties be established as a daily event in London within a year, but less than a hundred feet from us in Soho Street lay the building that would become an ISKCON center in 1978, the permanent inner-city temple of the Hare Krishna movement in London.

CHAPTER 26

Alchemical Wedding
at the Albert Hall

In December we moved from our second apartment in Clapham to a more central location in Covent Garden, the London center of the wholesale fruit and vegetable trade. We hoped being more centrally located would help us in our endeavor to find a temple. The building we secured as our temporary residence was a four-story abandoned fruit warehouse on Betterton Street that was up for sale and was just a three-minute walk from the Arts Lab. Nigel Samuel, the owner of the building, agreed to let us stay there for free until it sold. We converted part of one of the floors into a crude temple room where we thought we could chant; Shyamasundar constructed a small altar for the six-inch high Jagannatha deities we had brought with us from the US. In the course of our public chanting and our Arts Lab appearances, we had collected a few young guys who were keen to know more about Krishna consciousness. One of them – Andy – stayed a few weeks with us in our south-London flat, but we'd asked him to move on when we found some lewd drawings that he'd done lying around. The others – Colin, Tim and Richard – all moved into the Covent Garden building with us. We made one floor the single men's *ashram*, and the rest of the building we couples occupied. It was an austere, Spartan abode with burlap floors, bare walls, no central heating and no bath or shower except for a wobbly makeshift shower jerry-built in the garage. But being located in the Covent Garden area gave our address a prestigious look and sound which we thought was important. In our corre-

311

spondence we all got a kick out of ending our address with "Covent Garden, London WC2."

The Arts Lab organizers, Jack and Jim, decided they would host a kind of British happening called the Alchemical Wedding. They hoped it would be a defining moment in British alterative history, a "be-in" where anyone and everyone interested in peace or New Age living could come and hang out. Hundreds of posters went up all over London advertising the event, and young people handed out fliers in the streets in hope of getting a big crowd. It was to be held at the Royal Albert Hall in Kensington Gore, across the street from Kensington Gardens, and would run from eight until late on December 18th. We all thought it was incredibly funny that the British alternative festival was to be held in one of the country's most prestigious concert halls, an ornately decorated amphitheater built in the reign of Queen Victoria and dedicated to her deceased husband Prince Albert. The event smacked of the mixing of the alternative and the establishment, which we were coming to see as characteristic of England. The schedule of entertainment was unclear from the advertisement. Word of mouth had it that there would be some music (though no one really knew who) and that you should bring your own smoke and come loaded for a good time. It was rumored that John Lennon and Yoko Ono would be attending.

This was the closest thing to the San Francisco be-in that we had come by in England, so we immediately decided we would go along and try to get some time on stage to chant. When we got to the Albert Hall on the night, there was no stage at all; instead all the organizers had arranged was a cloth-covered floor in the center of the hall. Seats rose in several tiers around the circumference of the auditorium, but most of the people were sitting in seats around the edges of the center oval. There seemed to be very little going on. With everyone just sitting and talking and smoking dope, this event teetered precariously on the verge of being a non-event. We assembled under the seats, backstage as it were, to talk to Jim and Jack about whether we could perform.

"Sure, you can chant if you want to," Jack said. "It's up to you, you know. The evening's gonna be pretty easy-going, so if you decide you want to, just go ahead. Go on out."

This all sounded a bit vague to me. "So you're sure you don't mind?" I persisted.

"Completely your choice," Jack affirmed. "If you want to chant, chant. No one's going to stop you."

Then, unexpectedly, he walked out into the middle of the oval of people and started pacing up and down a chalk line that someone had drawn across the oval's short axis. He didn't say a word but held his index finger over his lips indicating that everyone should stop talking. When it quieted down he raised his arms over his head and closed his eyes. The hall was cloaked in silence. Many people closed their eyes and swayed. I wasn't sure what they thought Jack was encouraging them to do. Maybe meditate, groove, observe, think or just be.

The silence was intimidating and put a handbrake on our intention to chant. With the possible exception of Gurudas we were all somewhat introverted by nature, and charging unannounced into the middle of a silent meditating crowd didn't seem like the right thing to do.

"What do you think we should do?" I whispered to Janaki. "Don't you think it would be rude to start playing the *mrdanga* now?"

"Yeah, I think so," she said. "I mean, even though Jack said we could, this thing he's started here – whatever it is – makes it really hard for us to start something loud."

"Maybe he doesn't really want us to chant after all," I said.

"Look," Gurudas interrupted. "What would the swami want us to do here? He wants everyone to hear the mantra, right?"

"Well, sure," I said. "But he also wouldn't want us to irritate people."

"Swamiji said that a devotee should be 'daring and active,'" Gurudas said. "And for the service of the Lord the devotee is always daring and active and is not influenced by attachment or aversion.'"

I thought this sounded like a verbatim quote he'd memorized from somewhere.

"OK, we know what you're voting for," I said to him. "What do the rest of us think?"

Malati sighed. "I feel a bit funny about it, but the swami really wouldn't want so many people to miss the opportunity of hearing Krishna's names," she said.

"Yes," Shyamasundar agreed. "I think we're just going to have to do it. Let's just be daring and enthusiastic and run out there."

I took a deep breath and started to play the *mrdanga*, singing the Hare Krishna mantra loudly. The others followed me into the center of the hall, swaying and twirling and chiming their *karatalas* in time to the beat. We ran right out to the middle of the hall. The deep bass rhythm of the *mrdanga* echoed through the cavernous chamber. As we chanted, my nervousness evaporated, and when I dared to look out at the audience, I saw smiles and swaying and clapping. At first we danced in a circle, and then formed a straight line and swayed in choreographed symmetry back and forth, right foot over left, left over right as the swami had shown us.

People began to pick up the words and sing along, and before we knew it we were not the only ones dancing to the mantra. The first man to join us ran down an aisle stairway and vaulted into the middle of the oval. His hair swung out around him in a wide arc and his arms flailed wildly as he gyrated to the beat like some kind of flower-child Rasputin. More people took his cue – a woman in a crimson crushed-velvet smock, a teenage boy with an Indian headband pulled low over his eyes, a man in ripped jeans with strands of wooden beads draped across his bare chest. Gurudas put down his *karatalas* and ran to retrieve his camera from backstage. He was a good photographer and had recently started to sell some of his shots to papers and other clients for some much-needed cash. He began snapping photos of the hippy dancers and of us against the grand backdrop of the Albert Hall. Soon forty revelers skipped and jumped to the pulse of the *mrdanga*, and the swami's words reverberated in my head: "Rhythm is the universal language."

As Gurudas snapped away, the five of us maintained our synchronous dancing and tried to keep the tempo of the kirtan under control. Out of the corner of my eye I saw a couple of blue-uniformed police officers talking to someone in a fur coat, way up in the upper tiers of the hall. However, as the dancers packed closely around us, this glimpse of possible trouble slipped from my attention, and I was swept up in the waves of the kirtan once again; it seemed to me as if the entire hub of the hall was moving in time with the chant. As the pace of the kirtan increased, more and more people poured down the stairways to join the central throng. Our dance steps quickened. We had no amplification, and I could feel my voice giving out. Blood trickled down my hands from having to play the *mrdanga* with such force.

After half an hour, we brought the kirtan to a close. Utterly exhausted, we stood for a moment in the center of the hall while the crowd whistled and applauded.

"More, more, more," a few voices cried out. We wanted to continue, but we were too fatigued, and we ran backstage where we were greeted with laughter and pats on the back.

"Wow. That was amazing!" Jack said. A lanky woman with glazed eyes was draped around his neck. "Yeah," she said. "Wow."

"Thanks," Jim said. "I'm real glad you decided to chant. It really took things to another level."

"Yeah, that's what chanting does," I said. "Takes things to a spiritual level."

"Well, that's what this evening's all about," Jim said. "You guys gonna hang around for the rest of it?"

"Yeah, we'll stay a while," I said, not wanting to seem rude.

We stayed long enough to see the evening revert to the surreal fogginess that had dominated before we started chanting.

"Let's get outta here," Gurudas said. "I want to take my photos down to Fleet Street to see if the papers want to buy any of them."

We trundled out to the truck, and Shyamasundar drove through the dark streets toward the headquarters of England's national daily papers. He pulled up outside the offices of the *Mirror*, one of the biggest British tabloids.

"I might be a while," Gurudas said. "You guys wanna come inside and sit in the lobby so at least you're not freezing to death out here?"

"No, I'm too tired," Janaki said. "I'll just wait here." There was a general chorus of concurrence.

"I'll come in with you," I said. "I'm tired, but I can't stand this cold anymore."

When we got inside, one of the *Mirror* photo editors took Gurudas's film from him.

"Why didn't anyone let us know it was happening?" he asked. "Was there any press coverage *at all* there?"

"Just me," Gurudas grinned. "John and Yoko were apparently there too."

"What? You saw them? Do you have a photo of them?"

"No," Gurudas answered. "I didn't see them actually, but someone told me they saw them." This wasn't exactly true, as far as I
knew, but I could see it would increase the likelihood of Gurudas's
sale.

The editor looked tired and internally exasperated. "OK, I'm going to develop this," he said. "Then we can take a look at the photos
and see if there's anything here that'll interest us."

When he spread the developed black and white negatives on
the light table a few minutes later, other photo editors crowded in
to view Gurudas's work. There were shots of long-haired hippies,
their arms raised, their mouths open. In one shot, the Rasputin
guy was slightly hunched over in a stance that made him look like
a cave-dweller. In another, a group of scantily clad young women
looked like a line of go-go dancers. Another showed a young woman with smoky eye make-up holding a cigarette in her outstretched
slender hand; she looked like a movie star, her pose decidedly
provocative.

"These are great," Gurudas's main contact said. There were
murmurs of agreement. "We'll give you eighty pounds."

"OK," Gurudas agreed immediately. "Thanks."

The next morning, a million copies of Gurudas's photos were
printed for all of London to see. The *Mirror* featured a collage of
photos alongside an article with the headline "Rave Up at Royal
Albert Hall." However, the photo that got the most publicity – the
one that appeared on newsstand posters and on the front page of
the paper – was a photo of a naked woman who was apparently at
the Alchemical Wedding. The shot was blurry, indicating that it had
been enlarged and that the woman had been in the background of
a photo of something else. "Police Called to a 'Happening' at Albert
Hall," the tabloid screamed. We bought a copy and read the article:

"Blonde Elizabeth Marsh sits serenely in the audience at Royal
Albert Hall ... without a stitch on.

"She stripped off her ankle-length black dress last night when
Indian music was played during a 'hippie happening' at the hall
called an 'Alchemical Wedding.'

"Then twenty-four-year-old Elizabeth, from Texas, sat completely naked in the third row while hall officials pleaded with her to get

dressed. Police, who were called to the hall, tried to approach her.

"But some of the 600-strong audience formed a human shield around Elizabeth – and started to take their clothes off as well. At least one man stripped off and stood naked for a while.

"After nearly half an hour Elizabeth was persuaded by the organizers to put a coat around her.

"She said later, 'I don't know why I did it now, but at the time I had some good reasons.'

"Her boyfriend, twenty-four-year-old Peter James, said, 'She must have got carried away.'

"After the stripping, police stayed on guard while Beatle John Lennon and his Japanese girlfriend, Yoko Ono, writhed inside a huge bag, as a man played the flute."

All of this was news to us, and we wondered if the tabloids had gotten their only information from the few words Gurudas had said the previous night and had made the rest up. I hadn't seen John Lennon in the crowd (what to speak of writhing inside a bag) and I certainly hadn't seen any naked people running around. Then I

Cover of the Daily Mirror

remembered the brief incident when I had caught sight of the police officers and the person in the fur coat on the upper tiers of the hall, and I realized that that could have been Elizabeth Marsh. The whole thing had obviously been taken care of in true British fashion: quietly, politely and with minimum resistance.

We were disappointed that the *Mirror*, much less than include a photo of us, had not even bothered to mention the fact that it was our music that the people were dancing to. The *International Times* ran an article on the event as well, and they mentioned us, albeit in a brief, sensationalized way.

"Hare and the Krishnas came forth playing their bells, bald and robed vegetarian loveliness; one could not dislike them even in their plunging to discorporation. They were joined by any number of dancers and children and musicians and suddenly the Valley was alive with enthusiasm and indeed a kind of silence was filled. It was a promise of better things to come."

We all agreed that this coverage was better than nothing. We had participated in a big, high-profile London event and hundreds of people – and maybe even John Lennon – had heard us chant. We hoped that the Alchemical Wedding would indeed be the promise of better things to come.

The International Times *December 19, 1968 covers the Alchemical Wedding.*

CHAPTER 27

Crashing Kensington Palace Gardens

After a couple of months in England, we started to realize that we needed to do more than chant with the tiny hippy community. This was the Old World, and we needed to make contacts within the establishment if we were ever going to be able to start a temple. It was becoming painfully obvious that the maxim "It's not what you know, it's who you know" had a lot of currency in England.

As Christmas approached, we heard that the High Commissioner for India was holding a reception for Indian sitar master Ravi Shankar at Kensington Palace Gardens, a private street on which numerous embassies were located. I had attended some *mrdanga* lessons at Ravi Shankar's Kinara School of Music in Los Angeles, and I'd even talked with him on a few occasions. I thought maybe he'd remember me and that this would be enough to get us invited to the embassy party. But when I couldn't contact him, I called Surya Kumari, the Indian dancer and actress I'd made friends with in New York. She was in London for a while, but when I finally managed to get her on the phone, she barely remembered me.

"Look, Mukunda," she said. "I'm not invited to this thing, so why would I be able to get you invitations?"

"I don't know," I said dejectedly. "I thought you might know someone who was going or could get us in."

"It doesn't sound like a party that will even be worth going to," she said as if to console me. "Embassy parties just aren't interesting."

When I reported my lack of success to the others, we all decided that we'd just have to turn up on the doorstep of the embassy and see what happened from there. All they could do was turn us away.

As we drove down the narrow streets on our way to the embassy a few nights later, I realized just how out of place we looked in our old pickup. Kensington Palace Gardens was a street that was lined with palatial residences and buildings that looked like they were probably full of people who drove Mercedes Benzes, Rolls-Royces and Jaguars, not fire-engine-red pickups without enough seats for all the passengers. A uniformed security guard at the entrance to the street came out of the tiny kiosk beside the black wrought iron-looking gate which stood between us and the world of the establishment. Shyamasundar rolled down his window, and I prayed the dark would soften the dilapidation of our vehicle.

"Where are you headed, sir?" I heard the guard ask. He looked sleepy and bored.

"Good evening," Shyamasundar said. "We're going to the party for Ravi Shankar at the Indian High Commission."

"Do you have an invitation?"

"Yes, we do," Shyamasundar said. "I think it's here somewhere." He and Malati made a show of rifling through the glove box and Saraswati's diaper bag.

"OK, it doesn't matter," the guard said. "I really should see the invitation, but I can see you are all dressed for the occasion." He eyed Malati's turquoise sari and Shyamasundar's bright blue Nehru jacket and *dhoti*.

"Actually, we always dress like this," Shyamasundar said, but the guard was already walking away and opening the gate. He waved us through.

"Indian High Commissioner's home is the third house on your left," he said.

One end of a convex driveway was crowded with dark-colored late-model cars. Shyamasundar found a place between a BMW and a Jag. The truck belched a final puff of exhaust, and we hopped down from under the tarpaulin and attempted to smooth the wrinkles out of our clothes in preparation for our entrance. Gurudas and I wore freshly pressed south Indian *dhotis* with colorful hems and embroidered *kurtas*. We had all had precision-painted *tilaka* marks on our foreheads and had shaved our heads especially for the occasion. Janaki, Malati and Yamuna had flowers in their hair, and even Saraswati looked festive with a ribbon tied in a bow around her head.

We climbed the wide flight of stairs to the front door and rang the bell. My heart was beating fast. An emaciated Indian official in a suit opened the door. He looked us up and down with half-closed eyes and a tight-lipped smile.

"Name, please?" he said in a clipped British accent.

There was a long, panicked pause. I knew how stupid we looked. How could we not know our own names?

Slowly and distinctly in a voice I hoped exuded authority, I finally said, "International Society for Krishna Consciousness." As the words left my lips I immediately felt more comfortable, more confident.

"Right this way," he said. He turned on his heels and headed across to the entranceway toward a pair of large double doors that I assumed led to wherever the party was being held. We scurried after him, trying to keep pace with his quick steps. Head back, chest out, he flung the door open for us, and we stepped over the threshold of a deeply carpeted regal lounge where clusters of people stood talking and drinking Martinis under a huge Austrian chandelier.

He raised his right hand. "International Society for Krishna Consciousness," he said in a loud projective voice. I couldn't believe we were being *announced*! A hush fell over the room and people interrupted their conversations to stare at us. Then Ravi Shankar, the guest of honor, raised his free hand high and waved to us as if we were old friends.

"Hi," he shouted, raising his glass. He motioned for us to join him at the center of what was obviously the key group in the room. The chatting resumed in the room. The Pandit had endorsed our presence.

Everyone in Shankar's group had already drunk enough to be relaxed, the alcohol blunting the sharp social awkwardness of the official event. Everyone was a lot older than us – forty at least. As we walked over to Shankar, he was saying to his group, "These are the Hare Krishnas. I know them from the States."

Speaking with sitar maestro Ravi Shankar in London

"I love what you're wearing," a blonde-haired woman with sapphire earrings said to Janaki. "These clothes – are they called saris?" Janaki nodded. "Yes, well, they're so colorful and different than the clothes you usually see around." She seemed genuinely dazzled by Janaki, who admittedly did look glamorous in her marigold-yellow garment.

No one seemed at all concerned with consulting the guest list. "Alcohol in the service of God," I thought. I wondered if we could get into other embassies the same way. Even if it was a bit under-handed, it was a great way to meet people.

A waiter approached with a tray of pre-mixed drinks.

"Beverage, sir?" he asked.

"Ah, no, thank you," Gurudas said. He glanced at the rest of us. I could tell he felt awkward.

"Actually, could we order some plain Seven-Ups?" I asked.

"Certainly, sir."

"We'll have six please," I said. He bobbed his head in a single nod.

"So you don't drink alcohol, then?" an elderly man behind Gurudas asked.

"Oh, no, strict Hindus never drink alcohol," Shankar said, as if he were our spokesperson.

"Why is that?"

Shankar gestured toward us to answer the man's question.

"Well, we follow four main principles," Malati explained. "Not taking any intoxicants is one of them. It helps us keep ourselves sober and pure for studying the Vedas."

"What are your other rules?" the blonde woman asked.

"We don't eat any meat or gamble or have illicit sex," I said.

"Goodness!" she responded. "What about fish?"

"Nope," I said. "Not even eggs." She blinked her eyes rapidly as though she couldn't quite believe what she was hearing.

"So, how are you doing in London?" Shankar asked. "Have you opened a temple here yet?" Here it was at last, I thought, our chance to introduce the swami's cause to important people who could actually help us. And as I opened my mouth to answer, a short white-haired Indian man in a gray three-piece suit came into our circle.

"The commissioner," the blonde woman whispered to me, and I noticed that the room had once again gone quiet. The commissioner said a few words to Shankar and the conversations in the room resumed. Then he strode toward the six of us, his right hand extended.

"You're wearing Eastern clothes and I'm wearing a Western suit," he said laughing and shaking my hand with vigor. "You're Hindus, but I'm Christian! We must discuss this paradox! My name's Dhavan. I'm the high commissioner. You must come for dinner with my wife and me."

"We would love to!" I said, and all the others nodded enthusiastically.

"Can you come a week or so after Christmas?" he asked. "If you do not have other engagements."

"No, we don't have anything else," I said. "We would be delighted to come."

"Excellent," he said, handing me his card. "Call my secretary to confirm the date."

We spent the rest of the evening milling with the other guests, flushed with the success of our just-turn-up plan. Driving back to our flat a few hours later, we all deemed the evening a grand success.

The next day, I telegrammed the swami: "Went to party at Indian ambassador's home. Met with Ravi Shankar. Having dinner with ambassador next week."

The swami responded enthusiastically to my telegram, and years later I learned that he wrote about the event in a letter to a Dr. Chaudhuri of San Francisco:

"You will be surprised to know that I have sent there [to London] for preaching work six boys and girls, married couples, and they are neither elderly nor very much conversant with Vedic philosophy. But still, by their character, behavior, and devotion, they are attracting many people in London, including the High Commissioner of India and others."

To Yamuna and Gurudas he wrote:

"By the grace of Krishna you are all six together doing very nice Krishna consciousness activities, and I am so much pleased. Everyone is appreciating your presentation. Please keep up this standard of behavior. Do not make any artificial discrepancies among yourselves because you are acting on a very responsible business."

We all felt happy that the swami had entrusted us with the responsibility of his mission, and particularly that he approved of us trying to contact people like the high commissioner. A week later, we took up Mr. Dhavan's invitation to have dinner with him and his wife. The Indian servants were amused by our appearance and kept making furtive peeks at us around the dining room doorway in between bringing out platters of richly prepared vegetarian fare. Our conversation that evening was engaging, friendly and informal, although the Dhavans couldn't seem to figure out how anyone from the West could be attracted to their traditional Eastern ways. Out of respect for us, though, they themselves adhered to Eastern tradition at least for that night and refrained from drinking alcohol.

CHAPTER 28

Guess Who's Coming to Dinner?

One of the first establishment contacts we made was a member of the House of Commons, the Labour MP for Barking, Tom Driberg, who was a friend of Allen Ginsberg. Previously a journalist, Driberg was known to be controversial and to have communist leanings. In the middle of October we received a letter from the swami passing on Ginsberg's suggestion that we contact Driberg.

"I have received one letter from Ginsberg," he wrote, "and he writes to say that he has some friend in England to help you. This friend he names Mr. Tom Driberg, MP. Ginsberg has written to him and he has promised to help you in a letter to Ginsberg. So you should contact him. He is a prominent member, and Ginsberg says that he can help you in all matters of official and legal implications."

We tried to get in touch with Driberg, but it proved difficult to make contact with members of Parliament. Finally, in November, we got a tip-off from someone in the Arts Lab that Driberg was temporarily in St. Bartholomew's Hospital recovering from an eye operation. This was our window, I thought, our chance to meet a Member of Parliament without having to get through the swaths of red tape that seemed to wreath anyone with any official position in England.

Yamuna, Shyamasundar and I drove out to the hospital on a drizzly Saturday afternoon. The receptionist at the front desk looked at us suspiciously as we entered through the large glass doors. Our shoes and clothing were wet, but Yamuna was holding a silver platter of sweets decorated with white and magenta orchids, so we hoped this made us look presentable.

"Are you friends of Mr. Driberg?" the receptionist asked us.

"Ah, we're friends of a friend," I said, glancing at the others.

She paused, as if thinking over what to do. Finally she said, "All right. He is in Radcliffe Ward. It's on the third floor. But don't take too long. Visiting hours end at four o'clock."

"Thank you very much," Yamuna said, and we scurried down the hall before she could change her mind.

"Friends of a friend?" Shyamasundar said sarcastically. "Ginsberg wouldn't remember you if he tripped over you."

"Well, OK, it was stretching the truth, but how else were we going to get to see him?" I asked rhetorically. "And Ginsberg wrote to him for us, so he's a kind of friend."

"Anyway, the point is we're in now," Yamuna cut in.

"That's right," I said. "I think you should be the first person to talk to him."

"Why me?" she asked.

"Because you're holding the sweets."

"Well, here, you hold them, then," she said.

"No, really Yamuna, *you* should talk first," I insisted. "He's an old guy, so he'll be flattered if a young woman is nice to him."

Inside Radcliffe Ward there were two white beds between which sat a thin, wizened-looking little man with his back to the wall. His eyes were closed, and his mouth was twitching like he was dreaming about something.

Yamuna ran up to him, plate in hand, and in a loud, throaty, sing-song voice said, "Good afternoon, Mr. Driberg. I really hope you'll try one of these sweets. I made them just for you."

The man's eyes flew up and he began shaking uncontrollably as if he was having a seizure of some kind. He fumbled for a cord, which hung beside the bed and repeatedly pushed a red button. We could hear the buzz of an alarm at the nurses' station out in the hallway.

The three of us hovered around the man, trying to calm him down. I glanced behind me in time to see someone roll over in the bed behind us. A long hand with swollen veins reached out and jabbed Yamuna hard in the back.

"*I'm* Mr. Driberg, young lady," said a grave, authoritative voice from the bed. He lifted his head from the puffy white pillow, and I saw that he wasn't particularly old after all – maybe in his late forties. He had a white pad taped over his right eye.

"Oh, I'm so sorry, sir," Yamuna exclaimed as the room filled with nurses to attend to the trembling old man in the chair. They adjusted a few of his tubes, spoke in soothing tones and managed to calm him down. Within minutes his eyes were closed again.

Once the dust had settled, Driberg asked us who we were and what we were doing in his hospital ward.

"My name's Yamuna, and this is Mukunda and Shyamasundar," Yamuna said. "We're friends of Allen Ginsberg."

"Oh, you're the people he wrote to me about a few months ago," Driberg said. "I'm very *devoted* to Allen."

"Maybe Driberg isn't the type of man to be flattered by a young woman's attention after all," I thought.

"Well, he's definitely a great poet," Shyamasundar said. "I really loved 'Howl.' And he's helped us out really a lot in the past few years."

"And who exactly is 'us'?" Driberg asked. "Allen said you were trying to start a center in London and that you would need help with some legal affairs, but he didn't tell me what you stood for."

"We're members of an organization called ISKCON, the International Society for Krishna Consciousness," I said. "Allen was a guest of honor at a function called the Mantra-Rock Dance that we held in Haight-Ashbury about a year and a half ago."

"Yeah, he's really into the chanting," Yamuna said.

"We've got centers in New York, San Francisco and Montreal, and a few others that are just getting started," Shyamasundar said.

"I see," he said, eyeing our Vaishnava dress and taking a sweet from the platter. "Well, your look is certainly novel. That will get people's attention."

We talked with Driberg for another half an hour. By the time we left, he had given us his card with his private telephone number and had said he would try to visit our temple sometime in the near future.

———•

Things were getting tough for us what with being so far away from the swami and all. Even though he wrote to us every week, it felt like eons since we had actually seen him.

"I wonder if we should all take a little vacation," Gurudas said. "We could go back to America one at a time or one couple at a time, and that way we'd all get to see the swami."

"I miss his voice," Yamuna said. Her comment sparked an idea for me.

"Why don't we ask him to send a taped message over," I suggested. "We could play it every morning. It would be like he was here."

"Or better still ..." Gurudas said slowly, "we could play it for other people to hear. Mukunda, that's it! Lots of people would like that, hearing his voice, hearing him speak. It would inspire them to help us, and we might get some donations. Brilliant idea! Why didn't I think of it before?"

"Because you're not brilliant, that's why."

"So why don't we throw a party, like maybe on New Year's Day or something?" Yamuna said excitedly. "We can have a get together – invite everyone we know – and the swami can speak to them."

"Hey, yeah," Shyamasundar said. "We can have a big elegant function and a banquet and give lectures and stuff. It'll have to be something real classy, something that'll impress important people."

"It'll be like the Mantra-Rock Dance," I said. "Except without rock and without dancing. Mantra-Rock Dance: The London Version!"

That afternoon we sat down and chalked out a plan. We'd start by greeting everyone at the door with a drink and an appetizer of some sort. Then we'd give short focused presentations. Shyamasundar would catalogue the advances the Hare Krishna movement had made over the years, Gurudas would talk about the swami and his start in the US, and I would speak about our present status in England. Finally we'd take everyone into a banquet hall where we'd have hired silver and linen and we'd serve them a vegetarian meal better than anything they'd ever tasted.

The next task was to figure out whom to invite. Our goal was to invite as many of London's heavy-hitters as possible so as to expose them to our presence and the swami's mission. At the top of the list was Tom Driberg, who we were pretty sure would come. We also invited a guy we had met recently named Barry Miles, who owned a bookstore called Indica, and a monk named Simon Tugwell from Blackfriars in Oxford. The other invitees were people we had heard of, maybe friends of friends or those reputed to be keen on India, but were not necessarily people we had met. We invited some members of the House of Lords, members of the clergy, a few actors and academics interested in religion, a writer or two, and some arbitrary titled people who had exotic-sounding names, like Countess Vanessa de Graff. And of course, we invited the Beatles.

I wrote to the swami to tell him about our idea and included the guest list so that he could see the kind of people we'd invited. He wrote back enthusiastically and immediately sent a tape recording made especially for the occasion:

"You have arranged for the convocation and I have seen the list of invitees," he wrote. "It is very encouraging. Please conduct this convocation carefully and try to recruit some sympathizers for our nice London center. There is a Bengali proverb, *sa bure meoya phale*. This means that fruits like chestnuts and pomegranates, or similar other valuable fruits and nuts take some time to be fructified. So any good thing comes in our possession after hard struggle and endeavor. Krishna consciousness is the greatest of all good fruits, so we must therefore have necessary endurance and enthusiasm to get the result. Anyway, your honest labor is now coming to be fructified. Always depend upon Krishna and go on working with enthusiasm, patience and conviction."

This letter encouraged us immensely; we hoped that the swami's words would come to pass and that this event would provide some fruit for our labor. Of course, we were painfully aware of the gap between the elegant party we wanted to throw and the reality of our dwelling. We decided to send out a quirky invitation that would encourage the British gentry to attend but would also be off-beat enough to not leave them completely stunned once they reached our modest premises. After all, when they arrived at 22 Betterton Street, Covent Garden, they would find an abandoned, slightly dilapidated fruit warehouse with a large *For Sale* notice displayed on the outside, and inside no elevator, no furniture and only rough sacking on the floors.

The invitation we designed was on a single sheet of inexpensive, plain white paper with a small line drawing of Radha and Krishna surrounded by a circle of lotus petals at the top. This drawing was the logo the swami used for the official ISKCON letterhead. Under the logo, I typed "Guess who's coming to dinner? Maybe nobody, but here's who's invited." Except for the small RSVP request at the bottom, the rest of the page was filled with the names of those who we hoped would come. I'd gotten the idea from the 1967 film called *Guess Who's Coming to Dinner?* starring Spencer Tracey, Katherine Hepburn and Sidney Poitier. We hoped that those who received the invitation would see the event as a Covent Garden New Year's dinner party thrown by unknown hosts to be attended by a potpourri of prominent people. We wanted it to be perceived as *the* thing to attend, especially for adventurous social climbers.

A few RSVPs rolled in over the next few weeks: Driberg responded to affirm he'd be present, and so did the bookshop owner Barry Miles. We didn't let the small number of responses hamper our momentum; we told each other that lots of people wouldn't get around to sending in the RSVP slip and would just turn up on the night.

The day before the event, we cleared the little furniture we had from the third floor of our building, cleaned the floor in meticulous detail and put up long red crepe paper streamers and white and gold balloons. At the other end of the room we set up a long table covered in an embroidered white tablecloth; this would hold the vegetarian buffet that we were cooking under Yamuna's direction. We had found a catering company nearby that rented white china plates and first-class silverware to us for a reasonable price because we were paying in American dollars. We had also convinced them to give us fifty cocktail glasses for the evening at no extra charge. The plates, silverware and napkins were arranged on their own special table adjacent to the buffet. When we stood back to survey our handiwork at the end of the day, we all agreed that the place looked pretty classy compared with what it had been. Betterton Street, as we called the premises, still looked bare and showed we were dirt poor, but we hoped our guests would perceive our place as a model of modern minimalist décor or as a kind of happy haunted house.

The evening arrived, and the six of us dressed in our best clothing and donned long flower garlands made of roses and carnations.

Yamuna, Malati and Janaki looked dazzling in their saris and with flowers in their hair, and I thought we men sparkled in our bright white robes and flowing Nehru coats. Our freshly shaven heads looked a little bit like we'd buffed them with a high-gloss furniture polish. At eight o'clock on New Year's Day, cars began to pull up outside our building. A few people turned up wearing casual jeans, but many were dressed in eveningwear, the men in formal suits and the women in ball gowns. A few wore animal furs draped around their necks or were adorned with heavy diamond bracelets and earrings. I greeted them at the door with as much cordiality as I could muster.

"Good evening, sir," I said to one of the first men who arrived with a woman in a green spangled dress. "We're so pleased you could come. What is your name?"

"I'm Lord Musgrove, and this is my wife Viola," the man said. I scanned the name badges on the table.

"Oh, sorry, we don't have a name tag for either of you," I said. "But that's OK, I'll make you one now." I wrote "Lord Musgrove" on a sticker that said "Hello, my name is ..." and put it on his lapel. "Can I get you a drink?" I asked, gesturing to the table up one flight of stairs. The table held the cocktail glasses, each with a small strawberry at the bottom.

"Yes, that would be lovely," he said. I scurried up the stairs in front of them and asked Malati for drinks for Lord and Lady Musgrove. I looked on as she poured their drinks over the strawberries and handed them the cocktail glasses. The punch was made out of orange, apple and strawberry juice and I hoped he wouldn't notice it wasn't fortified until he was into the swing of things.

The number of people who turned up – forty-five in total – surprised us. We had braced ourselves for the guests' shock at the state of our building, but most bore it with a classic British stiff upper lip. They stood around in small groups chatting and looking only a little alarmed while Malati and Janaki wended their way through the groups with small trays of lemon cracker appetizers and yogurt dip.

As I was about to go upstairs to get the program started, a telegram arrived. I tore it open and read it: "Thank you for the invitation. Regret unable to attend, but wish you well. George Harrison." I ran up the stairs.

"I can't believe it, Shyamasundar – read this!" I said.

He read it to himself, grinned broadly, and then read it out in a loud voice for everyone in the room to hear. Even though it was a rejection message, Harrison had responded to us and that was success enough in itself, even if the rest of the evening was less of a victory.

"Ladies and gentlemen, thank you for coming this evening," I announced. "We're going to start off by giving a few presentations to explain what we're all about and why we've invited you here. Then Bhaktivedanta Swami, the founder of our movement, is going to say a word or two." We had decided earlier that we would lead the audience on a bit, and make them believe the swami was actually going to appear to speak. "Finally, we'll be having a vegetarian banquet, which will be served at the table down the back there. Now, if you'd like to all take a seat closer to the front of the room, we'll start the presentations."

A few members of the audience looked around to see if someone was bringing chairs in for them to sit on. No one was, and we realized immediately our oversight. The younger guests knew it was fashionable to sit with crossed legs on the floor, but some just couldn't manage the posture. Many of the guests were a lot older than us, and they looked uncomfortable sitting on the floor in their finery. The Right Honorable Tom Driberg sat down awkwardly on the burlap and leaned against the wall, crossing and uncrossing his legs as if he wasn't quite sure what to do with them. He had been smiling ever since he arrived, but now his smile seemed to turn to a grimace. Barry Miles stood leaning against the wall, looking suave in his navy suit and his wide red tie, his long blond hair in his eyes.

Shyamasundar, Gurudas and I made our presentations succinct, seeing the discomfort of some of the audience. We had set up a large easel, and we wrote up important points in felt-tip pen on large sheets of paper. Shyamasundar even had a chart and a couple of graphs that he had prepared earlier to illustrate the growth of the movement in the years it had been in the West. We kept saying throughout that the swami would speak shortly.

I wrapped up my talk about our endeavors to open a London center by showing a short soundless eight-millimeter film of the swami walking in San Francisco. We wanted seeing him on film and hearing his speech to be the center point and denouement of the evening. At the end of the film I introduced the swami.

"So, once again, thank you all for being here with us tonight at our first London convocation. And now I'm honored to present to you Bhaktivedanta Swami." Gurudas pushed play on the tape recorder and the swami's voice rang out across the room. He sang the Hare Krishna mantra for a moment or two and then began to speak.

"Ladies and gentlemen," he said, "Please accept my greetings in the happy year of 1969, and blessings of Sri Krishna, the Supreme Personality of Godhead, for your kindly participating in this happy meeting of Krishna consciousness." His speech was around fifteen minutes long. I was sure that by the sound of his voice and by the photos on our wall and the film the guests would be able to perceive him as being scholarly, erudite and special. Many listened to the tape with closed eyes.

"So, in ancient times, sages would simply gather under trees and be Krishna conscious in this way," the swami was saying. "But now, in London, in big city, to assemble and sit together we require a place for congregation. Therefore, a temple of the Krishna consciousness movement is required to be established in various centers in the world, irrespective of the particular country's culture, philosophy and religion. Krishna consciousness is so universal and perfect that it can appeal to everyone, irrespective of his position. Therefore I fervently appeal to you all present in this meeting to extend your cooperation for the successful execution of this great movement. Thanking you once more."

His speech was powerful and heartfelt, I thought, perfect for inspiring this audience. It was undeniably an appeal, a plea for help, but no one seemed to mind. After the swami's talk, they all talked animatedly among themselves, and I hoped that this meant that the swami's audio presence had made the whole evening as memorable an event for them as it had been for us. I felt as though the swami had been there with us, and I thought some of them might have felt that way too.

The guests all stood up, some stretching painfully and looking wobbly. They all looked greatly relieved when we invited them to come to our smorgasbord for the banquet. Soon the room was full of loud, happy banter as everyone sampled the amazing fare that Yamuna had created with our help. The dishes were exotic and outclassed the best of London restaurant fare: *urad dahl* patties called *bharatas* smothered in sour cream, pea and potato pastries fried in golden *ghee*, cauliflower tempura *pakoras*, spicy apple chutney, several vegetable curries with innovative sauces and fancy rice laced with tiny pieces of *panir* cheese, all served on fine-looking silver or ceramic platters with stainless steel and silver flatware. We finished the meal with *kulfi* – a special Indian ice cream made of condensed milk, saffron and cardamom and studded with pieces of glace ginger. Everyone complimented the cooks, and several asked about ingredients and recipes. As I circulated the room refilling people's plates, I remembered the swami milling with his guests, a serving pot under his arm at the first Love Feast on the Bowery. I hoped I was being as gracious and lively a host as he had been to us that night.

No one magically came forward that night with donations or promises to secure a temple, but we were happy with the way things went. We had made some friends, further solidified some existing relationships, gotten a telegram from a celebrity, made our best presentation to date, and had introduced our guests to the swami via the tape and the film. Years later, in his book about the Sixties, Barry Miles referred to the evening as a ceremony in a "basement shrine" (even though it was three floors above the ground) in which London welcomed our guru, Swami A.C. Bhaktivedanta.

A couple of weeks later, a *Sunday Times* photographer and a reporter turned up unannounced on our doorstep to interview us. The *Sunday Times* published the article on January 12 under the headline "Atticus Feels the Benefit." It heralded our arrival in the UK as a benevolent missionary act and included a large photo of me, Malati, Yamuna, Gurudas, Shyamasundar and Saraswati, who sat in her father's lap chewing on the chanting beads that hung from his neck. In the article's words, we were "gentle, unworldly, but not at all naïve." Some months later someone discovered that the Associated Press had reprinted the article, entitling it "Krishna Chants Startles London." Somehow the swami got a copy of the article, which was published in an American newspaper. He carried it around with him for months, routinely showing it to people to prove that ISKCON was now in England and making an impact.

When we asked the *Sunday Times* reporter how he knew about us, he said, "I heard about you from a friend." We left it at that, but we all suspected that the friend might have been a guest at our "Guess Who's Coming to Dinner?" party.

London's Sunday Times "Atticus" article of January 12, 1969

CHAPTER 29

Here Comes the Sun

Although most of our energy was directed toward trying to establish a London center, Shyamasundar never let us forget the other goal he'd had, long before we arrived in England: to meet the Beatles. Since their fame and influence reached far beyond that of the people we had met so far, we reasoned that they would be able to provide us with more significant help in setting up a temple should they be so inclined.

One afternoon I bought an underground newspaper while I was waiting in the subway and by chance read an ad that said the Beatles were forming a charity to aid talented people who were trying to break their way into the music scene. We put together a tape recording of us chanting Hare Krishna and sent it to Apple Studios on Saville Row, hoping that the chanting would spark the memory of the *Happening Album* the Beatles had ordered from the New York devotees a couple of years before. The response we got was a form letter saying that the company was sorry but couldn't help us.

This response was pretty much what we had expected, but we couldn't help being disappointed. We wrote to the swami to tell him about our failure, but he didn't seem to be discouraged at all:

"I think it is not probable to meet George Harrison," he wrote to me. "It doesn't matter. Let us grow slowly but surely. Let us try our best to spread this Krishna consciousness movement with sincerity. And Krishna will give us all facilities. After all, it is Krishna's business. So don't be worried, do your best and success or failure does not matter. Krishna is absolute, so there is no such thing as success or failure in Krishna consciousness, or in other words, there is no question of failure in Krishna consciousness, whatever we do it is success."

The swami's unconditional encouragement inspired us to try another approach. We called Apple and, claiming friendship with Allen Ginsberg, we managed to get an appointment with a man named Peter Asher, Apple's Artists and Repertoire agent. Asher was a singer himself who with Gordon Waller had a number-one hit called "A World Without Love" a few years earlier. We pitched ourselves as being interested in doing a spoken-word record; this, we thought, was something a bit novel that might make us stand out from the crowd.

On a chilly afternoon in late January we piled into our red pickup and descended on Apple armed, as usual, with several platters of vegetarian treats. Apple Studios was a four-story building situated in a street of men's upper-class tailors. Painted bright white, it was a beacon of liberality in a street that was very conservative. We jogged up the five steps and past the modest brass plaque that announced its famous occupiers with nothing but the diminutive words "3 Saville Row." Everything in the lobby was white as well – the walls, the carpet, the drapes, the couches. The only splash of color was a framed painting of a green apple on the wall behind the receptionist.

"Can I help you?" she asked.

"We're here to see Peter Asher," Gurudas said.

The first thing that struck me about Asher was his hair. It was an unforgettable shade of bright red and hung thickly round his pale face. He shook our hands and led us to an elevator, which carried us to his small third-floor office. He sat down behind a brown desk and straightened his wide tie.

"So, I hear Ginsberg's a friend of yours," he said, taking a piece of orange cake from the tray Gurudas was holding.

"Yeah," I said. "He helped us out of some tight spots when we were first getting our movement started in the States." We rattled through our association with Ginsberg. The conversation felt like a repetition of the one we'd had earlier with Tom Driberg.

"So, anyway, we thought if we could make a spoken-word record about the chanting – and maybe a bit of us actually doing the chanting too – that would be a really good way of letting people know we are here in London," Shyamasundar said. "That's the first step in getting a center started."

Asher took another piece of cake. "This cake's great," he said, taking a big bite. "But I don't set up record deals. For that you'd have to meet with George."

"Well, we'd like to meet with him!" Shyamasundar said. "How do we do that?"

"It's not very likely you can do that," Asher said sharply. He sighed. "Look, I'll mention it to him and see if I can get you an appointment. I guess you guys know he's into Indian stuff, so you might have more of a chance than all the other people who come in here wanting to make an album." He brushed the cake crumbs from his hands and escorted us out.

We left Apple a bit downcast because what Asher had told us was what we'd feared all along: the Beatles were out of reach, existing in a famous people's parallel universe guarded by an army of receptionists and managers and agents and security personnel.

Then, a couple weeks later, some people we knew from Haight-Ashbury came to stay with us for a few days. The group included novelist Ken Kesey, several Hell's Angels and Rock Scully, the co-manager of The Grateful Dead, the acquaintance of Shyamasundar. It was on the basis of this relationship that we had managed to get the Dead to play at the Mantra-Rock Dance in San Francisco. When Rock told us that they had an appointment with the Beatles, we saw a small window of opportunity open. Once again, I thought, Rock was going to prove pivotal to our success.

On the morning of the Beatles meeting, Rock agreed to let Shyamasundar tag along. That afternoon, an elated Shyamasundar returned home, bursting with news.

"So, when we got there we had to wait around for ages," he said. "They put us in this big reception room. When George Harrison finally came in, he came straight over to me! He said he'd seen us chanting on the street lots of times here in London and had wanted to come over to us but couldn't – he was always in a car or with other people or something."

"You're kidding!" I exclaimed.

"Nope. He hardly paid any attention to Ken or Rock."

"So, what did you say?"

"Well, I can't remember everything, but basically I told him all about the swami and about him starting out in New York and us starting the Frisco temple. And I told him we wanted to start one here."

"You're kidding!" I repeated.

"Nope, I'm not. And here's the best part: he wants to come here and meet all of us and chant with us!"

And so it happened that one afternoon in early February, George Harrison came to our drafty makeshift temple on Betterton Street. Shyamasundar met him at the door and took him up the single flight of stairs to the temple room, where he bowed down before the Jagannatha deities on our little homemade altar. We wanted to keep things light and informal, so we planned to just have snacks and talk. We all sat down on the floor, and Janaki handed out potato-and-pea *samosas* while we introduced ourselves. When I said what my name was, George interrupted.

"Mukunda. Yes, I remember your name. Didn't you write me a letter once?" he asked.

George Harrison and Shyamasundar Das

"Uh, I think so, but it was over a year ago now," I said. Until he mentioned it, I'd forgotten the letter I'd written in response to his *Oracle* article about how mantras could be used to reach the essence of music. I couldn't believe he remembered my name.

"Yes, I remember that letter," he said. "I was intrigued by what you said in it, because you turned what I was thinking around – you said it was the essence of the mantra we should be seeking, not the essence of music."

We talked for a couple of hours about the swami's philosophy and about our hopes to establish a temple in London. George said he'd love to meet the swami and discuss Krishna consciousness with him further. And he said he had a five-story building in downtown London that would make a fabulous temple.

"It's on Baker Street," he said. "We bought it a while ago and painted the outside with psychedelic art. Then the council told us it was illegal and that we had to paint it gray. It's just sitting there now. I like what you're doing, and I think I'd like to help you get started here in England. But I'll have to discuss the building with everyone else at Apple, of course."

Before he left, he invited us to come to his home in Esher a few weeks later. We escorted him to the door and watched him drive away. Although I realized we'd just met one of the most influential men in England, this didn't have the impact on me that I'd expected. George was just a regular, down-to-earth guy, a spiritual seeker who, like many others, seemed to be impressed with the swami's philosophy.

That night Shyamasundar wrote the swami a detailed letter about our meeting with George Harrison. The reply came quickly:

"It is understood from your letter that Mr. George Harrison has a little sympathy for our movement. Somehow or other the Beatles have become the cynosure of the neighboring European countries and America also. He is attracted by our movement and if he takes the leading part in organizing a huge chanting party consisting of the Beatles and our members surely we shall change the face of the world. His proposal to offer us a five-story building is very welcome. I am always anxious to go to London and I am very much hopeful when you say in your closing line, 'soon we will have a temple, soon we will have a temple, soon we will have a temple.' Thank you very much."

On a bright, cold Sunday afternoon in late February, we drove out to George's place in Esher, Surrey. The house wasn't the palatial place I expected, but it was certainly a modern, comfortable home, its exterior painted in psychedelic colors, which were incongruous with the rural atmosphere. We enjoyed a huge meal with George and keyboardist Billy Preston, and eventually George suggested that we do some chanting. We all ignored the large sofas and chairs and sat on the floor so that I could show him some Hare Krishna melodies on the harmonium. I played the *mrdanga*, George played electric guitar and Billy played the synthesizer. Playing with amplified instruments meant I had to beat the *mrdanga* extra hard; the chanting went on for several hours, and the bone of my left hand was badly bruised by the time we wrapped things up.

"You've got to record the mantra," George said to me as we were packing the instruments to leave. "It's a great way to tell the world about what you're doing."

"Yeah, that was our original plan in approaching Apple," I said. "But I'm thinking now, you know, we're not professionals."

"You don't have to be!" he said. "We weren't professionals either to begin with."

George Harrison at his house in Esher, Surrey

"What about if you recorded it?" I suggested. "Either by your-self or with the other Beatles?"

"No, it has to come from you guys," George insisted. "I mean, you even dress the part!" He eyed my creased white *dhoti* and winked.

That night on the way home, the back tire of the truck blew. I crawled out from under the tarpaulin to help Shyamasundar change it. A biting wind had picked up, and it chewed at our necks and hands as we bent over the jack and eased the muddy tire from its hub. I thought how ironic it was that we had spent the evening in the warm home of a celebrity, and now here we were in the cold rain, changing the tire of a 1935 pickup on the shoulder of the dark A4 highway.

In late March, George offered to produce a forty-five of us chanting, and so we found ourselves at EMI's Abbey Road record-ing studios in the same place the Beatles had recorded so many of their songs. The high ceiling was paved with acoustical tiles and microphone cords criss-crossed over the floor. When we arrived George was behind a glass wall on the recording console in the control room with three sound engineers. He waved when he saw us and came out to show us where to sit.

"So, we thought you could all sit on the floor down there," he said, pointing across the room to the large woven rug that covered a good portion of the wooden floor. "Each of you will have a mike, and your instruments are going to be miked too. Who's going to be playing what?"

"We decided that Yamuna and I will lead," Shyamasundar said. "I'm going to play the *esraj*, which we thought would sound good 'cuz it has a real Indian flavor. Mukunda's going to play the *mrdan-ga*, and Malati, Janaki, Richard and Tim will play the cymbals. Oh, have you met Richard and Tim?" He laughed. "Well, this is them right here!"

"And everyone will be singing?" George asked.

"Yeah. We were kind of hoping you would sing too," Shyamasundar said.

"Yep, I'll be singing," he said. "But I won't be miked. I can't be mentioned as a musician on the record because of my contract with

EMI. I'm going to be playing that harmonium." He pointed to the instrument, which was off to one side of the woven rug. Painted with bright flowers, the harmonium still looked something like an old organ, one that was pumped by foot and could be played with both hands. Next to it sat a huge brass gong that hung from a frame and looked like a Chinese museum relic.

"We decided that we'll just sing that simple melody that the swami first taught us," I said.

"That's a good idea," George confirmed. "It's uncomplicated and catchy. Good that it's in a major key."

After an hour or so of sound testing, we did a four-minute take of the Hare Krishna mantra. I thought we sounded pretty good, but George didn't think so.

"The sound needs to be bigger, especially at the end," he said. "Shyamasundar and Yamuna, you guys sound good, but the response is a bit weak. We need more singers so that it sounds like a choir."

"We can probably round up some more people," I said. "But we'd need some time to find them. I mean, we'd have to come back another day to finish the record."

"No, we need to finish it today, because today's the only time I was able to book for us in the studio," George said. "Hang on. I'll find some people."

Ten minutes later he returned with thirty people in tow – secretaries, sound engineers, agents and janitors from the adjacent EMI offices.

"OK, let's get all these guys miked up and we'll do it again," George said.

With nearly forty people singing the response, the second take sounded great. Many of the members of the improvised choir closed their eyes and swayed as the sound of the mantra swelled to fill the studio: "*Hare Krishna Hare Krishna Krishna Krishna Hare Hare, Hare Rama Hare Rama Rama Rama Hare Hare.*" At the end of the take, Malati spontaneously picked up a mallet and, without looking back, struck the brass gong that sat behind her. As soon as the engineers gave the official indication that the take was over, everyone burst into surprised laughter.

"What was that about, Malati?" I asked.

"I don't know," she said. "Just kind of came to me that it might sound good."

"I thought it was a great touch," George said. "You never know; that may very well be the take we end up using, gong and all."

We did another couple of takes of the song and then spent the rest of the afternoon recording what would be the flip side of the forty-five – a track called "Prayers to the Spiritual Master." At one point I looked up from my concentrated *mrdanga* playing and saw through the control room's large glass window that Paul and Linda McCartney were talking to George.

At the end of the afternoon, George congratulated us on our performance. He said he planned to do a bit more dubbing, particularly on the "Hare Krishna Mantra" song, to which he would add a short guitar introduction using a tremolo effect with something he called a "Leslie speaker."

"When do you think you'll release it?" Janaki asked.

"Not for a few months," he said. "Probably not until August."

Even though that seemed like a long way away, the popularity of the mantra was already growing even without the record. We had become a regular sight around London, and it had gotten out that George Harrison was into chanting Hare Krishna. As we

Devotees prepare to cut the first take of the Hare Krishna mantra at Abbey Road with George Harrison.

A session with George Harrison at Abbey Road studios

*Devotees in recording studio with George Harrison
sitting at a flower-painted harmonium*

left the studio, we were greeted by a group of a dozen adolescent females singing the Hare Krishna mantra outside of Abbey Road studios, presumably hoping to catch sight of one Beatle or another.

"My god," I thought. "If it's like this now, what will it be like when the record comes out?"

The author talking with George Harrison about how mrdangas *sound*

Bury Place Temple

Although we were recording music at one of the world's best-known studios, we were still living in dire poverty. We didn't mind too much for ourselves, but we knew we couldn't house the London branch of an international society in an abandoned fruit and vegetable warehouse forever. We had high hopes for the five-story building that George had told us about in Baker Street, but when he presented the idea to Apple, the idea was rebuffed. Spring came – at least that's what the calendar indicated – but the rain and gloom continued as if it were still February. I felt like I was permanently on the streets, which meant that I was also permanently wet. If I wasn't chanting on Oxford Street with the others, I was walking for hours on end trying to locate an appropriate building to have as our center. Nigel Samuel, the owner of Betterton Street, had begun to let others live in the building and had asked us to confine ourselves to a couple of floors. The lack of space coupled with the austerity of living with strangers who regarded our practices as bizarre compelled me to increase my efforts to find a suitable building for a temple.

There were numerous buildings to rent in London, of course – multi-story places in office or residential districts with large *To Let* or *For Sale* signs displayed in their windows. I always carried a notebook with me to write down agents' phone numbers and the addresses of potential properties. Unfortunately, there was always at least one thing wrong with any property we looked at – stairways in strange places, no plumbing, ancient electrical wiring, no suitable place for a main temple room. Most of the buildings were dilapidated, and all required major modifications if they were to be used as a temple. Moreover, the rental properties usually required a large deposit, the signing of a long-term lease, and planning permission from the local council before any alterations could take place. Some of the buildings were zoned for office use only. And all of them, despite their dilapidation, were far beyond our price range even to rent.

Even though we didn't yet have a temple, the swami repeatedly wrote that he wanted to come immediately. He encouraged us not to wait for the goodwill of others but to secure a building at our own risk. "You have written that you are missing me, and similarly, I am sitting here anxious to meet you as soon as possible," he wrote to Gurudas. In the letter, he continued:

"I think that without depending on anyone, we should take the risk of renting a nice house for our temple immediately. If you think that my presence will accelerate matters, I am prepared to go immediately. I can start immediately and see the situation which is preventing the renting of a nice house. You write to say also that everyone is awaiting my arrival, and they ask 'When is Swamiji coming?' So far as I am concerned, I can go immediately because I have no serious engagements here now."

After Gurudas received this letter we had a conference about bringing the swami to London without delay. We decided that while we all desperately wanted to see the swami, it would be better to wait until we could receive him properly, and we couldn't do that until we had a temple where he could stay. We didn't want to be like the other small Hindu centers in London which had settled for grungy out-of-the-way suburban locations. We wanted something centrally located and impressive, something that would establish ISKCON's presence in London.

As the months rolled by, it became apparent to me that real estate – like everything in England – was controlled by a network of old boys. We had a contact on the inside, a property magnate named David Cocking who we had met in the States and who we knew had some sympathies for the swami's mission. Unfortunately, Gurudas had lost the piece of paper on which he'd scribbled Cocking's contact details as we were packing to fly to London, and all our efforts were futile in trying to locate either the piece of paper or Cocking himself.

Then, just as drizzly spring was giving way to what promised to be a suffocating summer, things suddenly took an auspicious turn. Gurudas burst through the door one afternoon puffing and smiling from ear to ear.

"OK," he said. "I'm standing in line at the bank, you know, just standing there waiting for the teller. Then I turn around and you'll never guess who was behind me."

"George?" Janaki asked.

"Nope."

"Tom Driberg?" I asked.

"No! It was David! David Cocking! Can you believe it? After all these months of looking for him, he just turns up behind me at the bank!"

"Really? Oh, god!" Shyamasundar exclaimed, rubbing his hands together and smacking him on the back.

"Yeah. He gives me a big hug like I'm like some long-lost friend or something."

"Well, what did he say?" Malati asked impatiently.

"I told him how we'd been looking for him and how we were so desperate to find a temple. And ..." Gurudas paused for effect, before shouting, "he's got a building for us, right in downtown London!"

A joyful pandemonium momentarily ensued before practical concerns crowded in on our excitement.

"But how will we afford it?" I asked. "Isn't there a deposit we'll have to pay?"

"David says we can move straight in, just like the States. All we have to do is pay the rent."

"How much is that?"

"Five hundred and fifty pounds a quarter," Gurudas replied. "That's about forty-two pounds a week."

"So about one hundred dollars a week," Yamuna said. "That seems like something we can do."

"Yeah. It does," Gurudas agreed. "The catch is that we have to pay in advance. So we've got to find five hundred and fifty pounds somewhere so that we can move in. But I think we can do that."

"Yeah? How?" I asked skeptically.

"Well, I don't have it all worked out yet," Gurudas said. "I know we don't have that kind of money, but we're just gonna have to figure it out. We *have* to!"

"What about planning permission and stuff?" Shyamasundar asked. "I'm sure we're going to have to modify it somehow. Don't we need that before we move in?"

"David says occupancy is nine tenths of the law in England," Gurudas said.

"What does that mean?" I asked.

"It means if we just move in … then we're *there*. And we can get the permission once we're already in there. He says it'll be more or less automatic."

I felt like it sounded good, and when we went into town the next day to see the building ourselves this feeling was reaffirmed. The vacant Bury Place building was perfect for our needs, centrally located on a quiet two-block street adjacent to council flats, a pub and a few shops just two blocks from the British Museum. The building displayed a large sign that read *Trinitarian Bible Society*, and when the estate agent showed us inside my heartbeat increased with excitement. It was five stories high – six if you counted the basement – and had space for a temple, a kitchen, a room for the swami and residences for ourselves and others. We unanimously agreed on the spot that we had to secure this building somehow.

Two days after Gurudas met David Cocking we managed to get the keys to Bury Place even though we had not formally taken possession of the property. We wanted to show our friends and contacts the building, and we also wanted to do some chanting there as a way of celebrating our miraculous find. Most of the few people we knew worked during the day, so we gathered in the evening with a *mrdanga* and a harmonium for an inaugural kirtan. We didn't worry too much about the impact of the noise on the neighbors, but as we left the building that night I saw the net curtains move in the front window across the street and I realized we were being watched.

Being a property owner, Cocking didn't manage all his own real estate but had an agency look after the day-to-day running of the properties. His agents at Stickley Kent informed us that in addition to the quarterly payment, they required a guarantor. They looked surprised when I returned some days later with a letter from George Harrison on Apple Records letterhead. The one hurdle that remained was the initial payment. Finally, after much discussion, we decided to ask the swami for a loan. We knew that his book fund was doing well in the States, and we knew how enthusiastic he was to have the London center established. He responded quickly and had the money wired to us. We employed the services of a law firm called Goodman and Derrick Solicitors – the same firm that represented Harold Wilson, the Prime Minister – who drew up the papers for our agreement with a Stickley and Kent lawyer named John Jay. Jay's office was only two blocks away. The Goodman and Derrick lawyers regarded the arrangement as "highly irregular" but drew up the papers anyway.

We were not legally allowed to do anything to the building or even to live in it until we had gained planning permission from the Camden Council, which had to approve all building modifications in the area. Their granting the permission was contingent upon the agreement of the neighbors who had to approve of what the building was being used for. Instinctively sure that our evening chanting had disturbed the other residents of Bury Place, Janaki and I decided we would knock on each door to introduce ourselves.

"Good afternoon. My name's Janaki and this is my husband Mukunda." Janaki looked light and summery in her pale blue cotton dress. The elderly woman who had answered the door was regarding her with suspicion.

"Hello," she said.

"What's your name?" Janaki asked.

"Alice Masters."

"We're very glad to meet you, Mrs. Masters," Janaki persisted. "We thought we'd come and say hello, because we're hoping to move into number seven a few doors down."

"Are you the people who were making all that noise last week?" she asked gruffly. "I didn't know you were Americans." A vague hint of distaste hung behind her neutral expression, as though being American was to be unwashed and perhaps inclined to thievery.

"Oh, did you hear our music?" Janaki asked smiling. "Well, yes, that was us. But we're not going to be noisy. We're actually hoping to start a yoga school in the building."

"Oh? Yoga's quiet?"

"Yes, it is," I assured her. "And we certainly won't be making any more noise than they make at the Bull and Mouth on the corner. But we plan to soundproof the walls anyway."

"Well, that pub's always been there," Mrs. Masters said. "We're used to it. Some of us go to it. There's a difference between that kind of noise and the noise you people were making."

"We want to assure you that we're not here to make noise or cause any trouble," I said. "We're part of an international movement that is all about peace and helping people."

"What do you mean 'helping people'?" Mrs. Masters asked. "Are you going to be exorcising people in that building or something?"

Janaki and I laughed, even though we knew she was only half joking. "No, of course not!" Janaki exclaimed. "We help young people get off drugs and get their lives together."

"Yes, I guess that's a good thing," she said.

"We're really just normal people who are doing whatever we can to make the world a better place," I said.

Mrs. Masters' features softened as she gave a small smile. "I know you're worried about the residents' vote," she said.

"Yes, we are," I admitted. "But that's not the only reason we came to meet you."

"Well," she said, "I have my reservations about you people, but I'm glad to have met the two of you. It was good of you to come."

Janaki and I headed down the steps as she closed the door.

"One down, forty to go," Janaki said.

———

One morning we received a box of the latest issue of *Back to Godhead* magazine sent from the States for us to sell. In it we found an article that corroborated rumors that had been drifting across the Atlantic for some months. The swami was no longer going to be called by this name or even by the name "Swamiji." He was now going to be addressed as "Shrila Prabhupada" or just "Prabhupada," a name that denoted both spiritual respect and affection on the part of the disciples. The article said:

"The word 'Prabhupada' is a term of the utmost reverence in Vedic religious circles, and it signifies a great saint even among saints. The word actually has two meanings: first, one at whose feet (*pada*) there are many *prabhus* (a term meaning 'master,' which the disciples of a guru use in addressing each other). The second meaning is one who is always found at the lotus feet of Krishna (the Supreme Master). In the line of disciplic succession through which Krishna consciousness is conveyed to mankind, there have been a number of figures of such spiritual importance as to be called Prabhupada ... Therefore we American and European humble servants of His Divine Grace, from all the different centers of the *sankirtan* movement prefer to address our spiritual master as Prabhupada, and he has kindly said 'yes.' "

It took some effort to break our three-year habit of calling him simply "the swami," but in the months we were waiting for the council to decide our fate, the name "Prabhupada" began to feel as natural for us as "the swami" had.

As news of our Apple recording contract spread throughout the small ISKCON world, I received an unexpected invitation from a devotee named Dinesh to participate in a long-playing record made by the students of the Ali Akbar College of Music in Berkeley, California. An all-expense-paid vacation to warm, sunny California seemed like the perfect respite from all the hard work I'd been doing in England for the past nine cold gray months, plus I would get to see Prabhupada too, since Dinesh had invited him to sing on some of the tracks. I immediately wrote an enthusiastic letter of acceptance.

Then, a few afternoons later, I came home to find a letter from Shrila Prabhupada waiting for me. I tore open the envelope in excitement, and then my heart sunk:

"I have seen your letter to Dinesh, dated 26th June 1969, and I am a little bit disturbed in my mind. This recording business is not our line, so you should not divert your attention for the time being for such things. After a great struggle, you have now got a nice place for the London temple, and if you leave now, your other co-workers, godbrothers and godsisters will be discouraged. I know you are a musician, and naturally you have got a tendency for musical entertainment, but at the present moment our main business is to push the *sankirtan* movement. Music is one of our items for chanting, but we are not musicians. We should always remember this fact. The best example is that we take advantage of the typewriting machine, but that does not mean we are professional typists. So I repeatedly request you not to divert your attention to this matter at the present moment."

Prabhupada's letter was like a punch in the face. I folded it carefully and put it back in the envelope, but my measured hand movements disguised the turmoil and disappointment that had risen like a squall inside me. In the few days since I'd received Dinesh's invitation, I had become attached to the prospect of getting out of England; now Prabhupada was telling me in unequivocal terms that leaving England wasn't an option. "I repeatedly request you not to divert your attention to this matter at the present moment." The sentence hammered through my head in a loop over the next twenty-four hours, methodically nailing closed the entrance to California.

The next afternoon, I trudged toward Bury Place through a nearby park, trying to reconcile myself with Prabhupada's request. It was obvious that he was asking me to stay in London because he was pleased with what we were accomplishing – the record with George Harrison and the Bury Place building were both major milestones in the project to establish Krishna consciousness in London. Hearing him say that my godbrothers and godsisters would be discouraged, even by such a short absence, also made me feel important. He wanted me to stay not only because I was needed but somehow because he considered me to be a positive influence on the others. My ego was flattered, and I realized that even though I was angry about not being able to escape this dreary island, deep down I really didn't want to let them or Prabhupada down, especially not now when we had just found a temple.

What affected me most, what had the most indelible ring of truth to it, was Prabhupada's metaphysical statement that "we take advantage of the typewriting machine, but that does not mean we are professional typists." I had done a lot of typing for Prabhupada but never thought of myself as a typist. I had tried to get donations for the temple but never thought of myself as a businessman or entrepreneur or fundraiser. I had always thought of myself as a musician, but now I knew with certainty that my deeper identity was as a servant of Krishna.

If I thought in these terms, Prabhupada's letter made sense. In his capacity as spiritual manager and devotional teacher, he was asking me to act in the interests of Krishna rather than in my own interest. Up until now I had always done more or less whatever felt good to me. I realized now that surrendering was much more than being a fair weather friend. It was about moving to the beat of Krishna and my spiritual master. Somewhere in the distance I could hear someone banging something, and I walked in time to the thuds as though the sound was the beat of Prabhupada's *mrdanga*. I felt peaceful, serene even, as I turned into Bury Place.

The closer I got to the temple room, the louder the thuds became and by the time I was there, my tranquility gave way to alarm. The banging was coming from inside the temple building! I opened the front door and found Shyamasundar and Tim, sledgehammers in hand and covered in brick dust. We had already discussed the way we would renovate the building: the kitchen would be in the basement, the upper floors would be residences and the first floor would be the temple room. The temple-room-to-be was divided into two rooms by a brick wall and it was at this wall that Shyamasundar now swung his hammer.

"What are you doing?" I asked, panicked. "We don't have the planning permission yet!"

"Yeah, but if we're going to get this temple open soon, we've got to get started on it," Shyamasundar said. "Anyway, David said we'd get the planning permission without any problems, remember?" He sounded annoyed.

"I'm not so sure," I shot back. "Some of the neighbors haven't exactly been forthcoming with friendship, especially Mr. French next door. What're the Stickley people gonna say if we don't get the permission and you've taken down half of this wall?"

"We'll get the permission," Shyamasundar said belligerently.

A few days later, two inspectors from the Ministry of Public Buildings and Works turned up on our doorstep on what they claimed was an extemporaneous visit. I thought the neighbors had probably heard the thuds of the heavy construction work and had alerted the council. The inspectors – named, incredibly, Mr. Black and Mr. Savage – impassively surveyed Shyamasundar's handiwork.

"You are obviously unaware that it is illegal to alter a building without permission," one of them said in a bit of a Cockney accent.

"No, actually, we know," Shyamasundar said. "But we're hoping to get the permission any day, and we just thought we might get the work started. There's really a lot to do."

"Yes, well, I'm afraid that's a breach of the law."

"I guess we just thought the permission would come any day," Shyamasundar repeated. "The owner of the building said it'd be easy to get."

"The issue of the law is actually the least of your worries here," the other inspector said. "The more pressing matter is that this wall is a supporting wall and it is extremely dangerous to have it weakened in any way, not to speak of removed. The floor of the upper level is at risk of collapsing."

Shyamasundar looked dejected and angry.

"We are going to report that we asked you to stop renovations until permission is granted," the first inspector said.

"What should we do in the meantime about the wall and the upstairs floor?" I asked.

"That's not our problem," he said.

After they left, Shyamasundar spent the rest of the afternoon taking his frustration out by preparing a challenge to the Buildings and Works directive. The following day, he dragged me with him to meet the inspectors' boss, Mr. Wallace, who was a construction engineer at the Ministry head office.

Wallace was a poster-boy for the establishment. In a dark blue suit with combed back white hair, he sat behind a large desk that was empty except for an ink blotter and three framed photos of a woman and two young children. Although he seemed surprised that his pre-lunch meeting should turn out to be with shaven-headed Californian monks, he took the situation in stride and offered us a seat in true British fashion.

"And what can I do for you?" he asked.

"I'm here about our building," Shyamasundar said. "Seven Bury Place. We've got a wall half torn down, and these two guys come over, said they're from the Ministry and told us to stop."

"Is it your building?"

"We've been in there for a few weeks already and paid the rent," he said.

"What's the address again?"

"Seven Bury Place," Shyamasundar repeated.

"Let me see."

Wallace swiveled around in his chair, pulled opened a file drawer and lifted out a folder. He turned around, opening the brown manila envelope on his desk.

"Seven Bury Place," he said. "Right. Well, yes, you don't have permission to do any alterations. You can't do anything without planning permission from the local council. That's Camden. You know that?"

Shyamasundar shrugged and glanced at the framed pictures on Wallace's desk.

"What if your kids started using drugs?" he asked.

Wallace looked bewildered. "I'm sorry?"

"What if your kids started using drugs?"

"Well I suppose I'd tell them to stop. But what has that to do with ...?"

"Well, I've dedicated my life to helping kids get off drugs, Mr. Wallace, and that's what our society is doing." Shyamasundar segued into a pleading tone. "When they grow up, unless there's a viable alternative, there's every chance they'll use drugs. It's endemic of today's culture. This temple will be an oasis for such kids. The Mayor of New York praised our work with young people and our lifestyles as being a great example for today's youth."

He theatrically dropped a copy of a letter of appreciation from John Lindsay, the New York Mayor, on Wallace's desk. Mr. Wallace glanced over the letter.

"At least can you tell us what to do so the ceiling doesn't cave in?" I asked.

Wallace paused for a long moment.

"What kind of outer walls are on the first floor at Bury Place?" he asked finally.

"They look like regular brick walls."

"Apply straight away for planning permits – do it today – for what you want to do to the building," he said.

"We've already done that," I said. "We're just waiting on the results."

"OK, so what you need to do in the interim is you need to insert an 'I' beam into the brickwork at the ceiling level where the wall is. I'll draw you a picture. Understand?"

"I think so," Shyamasundar said. "How do I get it up to the ceiling level?"

"Jacks."

"I see." Shyamasundar hunched in to watch Wallace's quick, precise drawing.

"That's the only way that floor above is going to be safe." He pushed the paper over to Shyamasundar.

Realizing we'd succeeded in getting help with the dilemma, Shyamasundar quickly folded the paper twice and stuck it in his breast pocket, thanking Wallace as we left the room.

Wallace called after him, "You have to get that beam in straight away, or that floor could fall in. OK? Do it today! And don't do anything else to that building until you get permission!"

I looked over my shoulder briefly as we hurried out and thought I could detect the faintest glimmer of a smile on Wallace's face.

CHAPTER 31

A Dream Come True

August came and went, and still the planning permission did not come. The temple property was unlivable, Betterton Street had long since been sold and we were all living in scattered apartments as close as we could to Bury Place. When we received indication from Shrila Prabhupada that it was better if we all lived together, Shyamasundar found us an unexpected source of temporary accommodation – John Lennon and Yoko Ono's estate, Tittenhurst – an eighty-five-acre property near Ascot race-course that had previously belonged to the chocolate baron Cadbury family. The arrangement was that we could live in the servants' quarters free of charge in exchange for doing renovation work on the estate – peeling off paint, varnishing wood, cleaning up the grounds and weeding the fields and gardens. Prior to our arrival, the work had been done by John's American friends, a couple named Dan and Jill, who now took on the role of supervising us in addition to working themselves. Presumably this living arrangement had more than a little to do with the fact we were now Apple recording artists.

Our forty-five was released in the first week of September, just ten days before Shrila Prabhupada was finally going to be arriving in London. The sleeve featured a photo of us with our musical instruments, and said "Radha-Krishna Temple" in large letters across the bottom. Although we hadn't planned it, we quickly became called the Radha-Krishna Temple band. Described as "Indian Gospel" by the *New Musical Express*, the record hit the British charts almost immediately and climbed to number eleven. In other countries – reportedly in Japan and Yugoslavia – it reached number one.

Front cover of the Radha-Krishna temple's
"Hare Krishna Mantra" 45 rpm record

Consequently, when we finally welcomed Shrila Prabhupada to England on September 11, we did so in a way that was grander than we had ever imagined. Generations of *Gaudiya* Vaishnavas had dreamed of presenting Krishna consciousness in English, and for them that had meant bringing it to England, the center of the empire of which India was a colony. Prabhupada's own spiritual master had requested many of his disciples to speak and write

Flip side of Hare Krishna mantra vinyl disc

about Krishna in English, and his father, Bhaktivinoda Thakur had sent literature to libraries in England. Now, as Prabhupada touched down at London's Heathrow Airport, the Hare Krishna mantra was being played and sung all over the country and the faces of Krishna devotees were plastered across walls of the London Underground train system. Krishna consciousness had truly arrived in England.

Things were gaining serious momentum in the UK, and several devotees had come to England from the States to help us, so we were able to greet Prabhupada with a large party of devotees, Apple officials and media personnel. As the 707's door opened and Prabhupada made his way down the portable stairway, a few men ran out onto the slick macadam and bowed down before him in the

Apple 15

Radha Krishna Temple (London)

Side One
HARE KRISHNA MANTRA

HARE KRISHNA, HARE KRISHNA, KRISHNA, KRISHNA, HARE HARE
HARE RAMA, HARE RAMA, RAMA RAMA, HARE, HARE

Side Two
PRAYER TO THE SPIRITUAL MASTERS

NAMAH OM VISHNUPADAYA KRISHNA PRESTHAYA BHUTALE
SRIMATE BHAKTIVEDANTA SWAMIN ITI NAMINE.

SRI KRISHNA CHAITANYA PRABHU NITYANANDA SRI ADWAITA GADADHAR
SRI VASADI GOUR BHAKTAVRINDAM.

BANDE RUPA SANATANA RAGHUNATH SRI JIVA GOPALA KO.

ON CHANTING THE HARE KRISHNA MANTRA
by A. C. Bhaktivedanta Swami

The transcendental vibration established by the chanting of HARE KRISHNA, HARE KRISHNA, KRISHNA KRISHNA, HARE HARE/HARE RAMA, HARE RAMA, RAMA RAMA, HARA HARE is the sublime method for reviving our transcendental consciousness. As living spiritual souls, we are all originally Krishna conscious entities, but due to our association with matter from time immemorial, our consciousness is now adulterated by the material atmosphere. The material atmosphere, in which we are now living, is called Maya, or Illusion. Maya means that which is not. And what is this Illusion? The illusion is that we are all trying to be lords of material Nature, while actually we are under the grip of her stringent laws. When a servant artificially tries to imitate the all-powerful master, it is called illusion. We are trying to exploit the resources of material Nature, but actually we are becoming more and more entangled in her complexities. Therefore, although we are engaged in a hard struggle to conquer Nature, we are ever more dependent on her. This illusory struggle against material Nature can be stopped at once by revival of our eternal Krishna consciousness.
Hare Krishna, Hare Krishna, Krishna Krishna, Hare Hare is the transcendental process for reviving this original pure consciousness. By chanting this transcendental vibration, we can cleanse away all misgivings within our hearts. The basic principle of all such misgivings is the false consciousness that I am the lord of all I survey.

This (front side) was inserted along with the 7-inch disk.

puddles. The rest of us watched from behind a wall of glass that was fogged with condensation from our breathing. The uniformed police escort waiting for Prabhupada at the bottom of the stairway stared impassively at the muddy imprints and small pieces of gravel that studded the devotees' otherwise spotlessly white robes.

While the other passengers were herded away to buses bound for the immigration hall, Prabhupada was greeted by a plump, smiling immigration officer who took him aside and stamped his passport, thereby sparing him from the long lines. Finally, flanked by the official and the police escort, he walked through the glass door

Krishna consciousness is not an artificial imposition on the mind. This consciousness is the original natural energy of the living entity. When we hear the transcendental vibration, this consciousness is revived. This simplest method is recommended for this age. By practical experience also, one can perceive that by the chanting of this Maha Mantra, or the Great Chanting for Deliverance, one can at once feel a transcendental ecstasy coming through from the spiritual stratum. In the material concept of life we are busy in the matter of sense gratification as if we were in the lower animal stage. A little elevated from this status of sense gratification, one is engaged in mental speculation for the purpose of getting out of the material clutches. A little elevated from this speculative status, when one is intelligent enough, one tries to find out the Supreme Cause of all causes—within and without. And when one is factually on the plane of spiritual understanding, surpassing the stages of sense, mind and intelligence, he is then on the transcendental plane. This chanting of the Hare Krishna Mantra is enacted from the spiritual platform, and thus this sound vibration surpasses all lower strata of consciousness—namely sensual, mental, and intellectual. _There is no need, therefore, to understand the language of the Mantra, nor is there any need for mental speculation, nor any intellectual adjustment for chanting this Maha Mantra._ It is automatic, from the spiritual platform, and as such anyone can take part in vibrating this transcendental sound without any previous qualifications. In a more advanced stage, of course, one is not expected to commit offences on grounds of material understandings.

In the beginning, there may not be the presence of all transcendental ecstasies, which are eight in number. These are: 1) Being stopped as though dumb; 2) perspiration; 3) standing up of the hairs on the body; 4) dislocation of voice; 5) trembling; 6) fading of the body; 7) crying in ecstasy; and 8) trance. But there is no doubt that chanting for a while takes one immediately to the spiritual platform, and one shows the first symptom of this in the urge to dance along with the chanting of the Mantra. We have seen this practically. Even a child can take part in the chanting and dancing. Of course, for one who is too entangled in material life, it takes a little more time to come to the spiritual platform very quickly. When it is chanted by a pure devotee of the Lord in love, it has the greatest efficacy on hearers, and as such this chanting should be heard from the lips of a pure devotee of the Lord, so that immediate effects can be achieved. As far as possible, chanting from the lips of non-devotees should be avoided. Milk touched by the lips of a serpent has poisonous effects.

The word "Hare" is the form of addressing the energy of the Lord, and the words "Krishna" and "Rama" are forms of addressing the Lord Himself. Both Krishna and Rama mean the Supreme Pleasure, and Hara is the Supreme Pleasure-Energy of the Lord. The Supreme Pleasure Energy of the Lord helps us to reach the Lord.

The material energy, called Maya, is also one of the multi-energies of the Lord. And we the living entities are also the energy—marginal energy—of the Lord. The living entities are described as superior to material energy. When the superior energy is in contact with the inferior energy, an incompatible situation arises; but when the superior marginal energy is in contact with the Superior Energy, called Hara, it is established in its happy, normal condition.

These three words, namely Hara, Krishna and Rama, are the transcendental seeds of the Maha Mantra. The chanting is a spiritual call for the Lord and His Energy, to give protection to the conditioned soul. This chanting is exactly like the genuine cry of a child for its mother's presence. Mother Hara helps the devotee to achieve the Lord Father's Grace, and the Lord reveals Himself to the devotee who chants this Mantra sincerely.

No other means of spiritual realization is as effective in this age of quarrel and hypocrisy as is the Maha Mantra.

Hare Krishna, Hare Krishna, Krishna Krishna, Hare Hare
Hare Rama, Hare Rama, Rama Rama, Hare Hare.

This (back side) was inserted along with the 7-inch disk.

and into our midst. Our faces smudged the heavy gray carpet as we bowed down to offer our respects. When I stood up, Prabhupada was grinning widely, looking into the face of each devotee who had come to greet him.

"Where is Gurudas?" he asked as someone placed a fluffy carnation garland around his neck.

"Waiting for you at John Lennon's," I said. "We'll be staying there for the next few weeks."

"This John Lennon, he is George Harrison's friend?" Prabhupada asked.

GEORGE HARRISON (in black) amid the singers on " Hare Krishna Mantra "

Beatle George does an Eastern Ono band

RADHA KRISHNA TEMPLE (London). ✱ Hare Krishna Mantra (Apple).

IN case these label credits present something of a mystery to you (which means you haven't been reading the NME news pages). let me explain that this is George Harrison's attempt to do a Plastic Ono. And knowing George's musical leanings, you won't be surprised to learn that this has an Eastern flavour

Best described as Indian gospel, if I may mix my religions! Consists of little more than the title phrase being chanted over and over ("Hare," by the way, is pronounced "Harry") to a backing of hand-claps and Indian instrumentation.

The melody is tantamount to a

THE HOOK: In The Beginning (UNI). ● A heavy, hard-driving soul sound

it has the same insidious hypnotism as "Give Peace A Chance"

SIR DOUGLAS QUINTET tDynamite Woman (Mercury).

● For a change a vocal disc from the Sir Douglas Quintet — who dispense such a full and vigorous sound that they could almost be a full orchestra.

This is a rollicking slap happy item, in which the fiddles and jigging beat create an atmosphere of a hillbilly barn-dance — although the spirited vocal is strictly in the

New Musical Express, *1969 article*

"Yes."

Apple personnel ushered us to the large VIP room where they had arranged a reception and press conference. Prabhupada was directed to sit on a small cushion next to a tall brass vase of flowers holding a large bouquet of orange, red, pink and yellow blooms – lilies, delphiniums and roses. The devotees stood watching, slightly bewildered, while a pack of photographers in dark suits and ties clustered at the back of the room and circled in for the killer shot. The photographers were accompanied by a gang of reporters, Fleet Street hacks after hard-hitting, sensational news and photos.

Prabhupada reached into his bag, retrieved his *karatala* hand cymbals and began to sing the Hare Krishna mantra in the same simple melody that we sang on our forty-five. The lounge came alive as the devotees sang the response and some stood to dance and began to sway to the rhythm of Prabhupada's chiming *karatalas*. A group of middle-aged Indian female airport workers in Punjabi suits poked their heads around the corner of the door, smiled and chattered excitedly to one another. Even a few of the Fleet Street crowd managed to smile. Having Prabhupada here at last made all the wet, dismal days worth the trouble. Flash bulbs popped, and I saw fuzzy bright spots wherever I looked.

The chant ended and the reporters converged on Prabhupada, shoving us out of the way.

"Is this your first time to England?" one of them asked.

"Yes," Prabhupada answered. "First time."

"What have you come here to try to teach?" another asked. His voice was insolent and challenging.

"I am trying to teach what you have all forgotten," Prabhupada said.

"And what is that?"

"That is *God*," Prabhupada said in a loud, bold voice, his statement laced with the conviction of a life-long devotee.

There was a short pause. It was the first time I'd seen a reporter look stumped. Prabhupada – one; Fleet Street – nil.

"Some of you are saying there is no God," Prabhupada continued. "Some of you are saying God is dead, and some of you are saying God is impersonal or void. Any nonsense can come to me, I shall prove that there is *God*. It is a challenge to the atheistic people. There is God. As we are sitting here face to face, you can see God face to face."

"Do you plan to meet with George Harrison while you're here in England?"

"Yes, if he would like, I will meet with him," Prabhupada said. "I can meet with anyone who is interested in serving Krishna."

"Are you his guru?"

"I am no one's guru. I am servant, not master."

Again the reporters looked disconcerted. The movement had spread dramatically in the past twelve months, and Prabhupada was now often interviewed by reporters. He had visited New York, Montreal, West Virginia, Seattle, San Francisco, New Mexico, Los Angeles, Hawaii, Buffalo, Boston, Columbus and Hamburg. Temples were being established in France, Italy, Holland, Malaysia, Australia, New Zealand, India, Costa Rica, Brazil, Argentina and many Indian cities. Numerous media interviews lay ahead, and I could see Shrila Prabhupada's expertise in dealing with reporters. He possessed deftness without a hint of artifice.

When the press conference concluded, Prabhupada was driven in a white Rolls-Royce to Tittenhurst. We had set up the best part of the servants' quarters for him, a relatively large, warm room with a small south-facing window that would provide some natural light for him to work on his translating during the day. We planned that he would stay there with Purushottama, his assistant who had come with him from the States. Shyamasundar and I followed behind in the red pickup and immediately joined Gurudas in Prabhupada's room to explain how we had come to stay at John Lennon's place.

"And John Lennon organized this airport meeting?" Prabhupada asked after we explained the arrangement of our lodging at Tittenhurst.

"Not him personally," I said. "The Beatles' company, Apple, arranged everything. It's part of the promotion for the record."

"I see," Prabhupada said. "How is it selling, the record?"

"Well, it sold seventy thousand today," I answered.

Prabhupada opened his eyes wide in astonishment. "Oh, *very* big business!" he exclaimed.

"Yes, but we don't get very much money from it," Gurudas said. "Our contract is set up so most of the money goes to Apple. But whatever we get we will put into the new temple."

"Now one of you must go to Oxford," Prabhupada said. The room went silent. It had taken a year to bring him here and he was sending a third of our team away on the very day he arrived. I imagined Janaki and me living alone in Oxford – no income, no temple, no deities, no devotees, no Prabhupada, only the drizzly, gray streets of a conservative English university town populated by intellectuals who wouldn't take us seriously.

Prabhupada continued to smile. The conversation veered away from Oxford, but the venerable name hung in the air like a challenge from an erudite philosopher.

"Prabhupada is a dreamer," I thought to myself, "but his dreams are coming true." I thought of the dilapidated windmill in San Francisco and wondered what would have happened if I'd tried to pursue that dream. I thought of the first Rathayatra in the States and how it happened only because the swami had dreamed of it taking place outside of India. Prabhupada was obviously not going to let us rest on our laurels in London, and though I knew I wasn't up to starting a temple in Oxford, I could see that his mission would not be complete without a center in the English-speaking world's most prestigious institution of higher learning.

Oxford Town Hall program

Prabhupada raises his arms at Oxford Town Hall.

Prabhupada leads kirtan at Oxford Town Hall as the author plays the drum to accompany him.

CHAPTER 32

Tittenhurst Times

At Tittenhurst, Prabhupada immediately took up the same routine he always followed wherever he went: rising early in the morning to translate, chanting, lecturing, taking a morning walk and maintaining his global movement through letters. He continued to spread Krishna consciousness in the modest, methodical way he had done ever since I had known him. Each morning, we walked with him through the eucalyptus trees and California redwoods – some a hundred feet tall – that had been planted around the Tittenhurst estate. As the mild September weather gave way to genuine autumn, Prabhupada donned a heavy coat, black Russian hat and Wellington boots to protect him from the rainy, windy climate. We strolled through fields of long grass in the wee hours of the morning and along the meandering pathways that ran away from the main house. We never bumped into John and Yoko, who I figured were probably sound asleep at that hour.

Prabhupada's airport reception was covered by a number of high-profile newspapers, including the *Sun* and the *Daily Sketch*, each of which had large photographs accompanying their news articles. Beneath the headline "Enter His Divine Grace A.C. Bhaktivedanta Swami," the *Sketch* featured a two-page photo of Prabhupada playing the *karatalas* and chanting with his eyes closed. The *Sun's* back page showed a half-page photograph of all the devotees bowing down, and the headline read "Happiness is Hare Krishna."

Prabhupada's London arrival recorded in the Daily Sketch

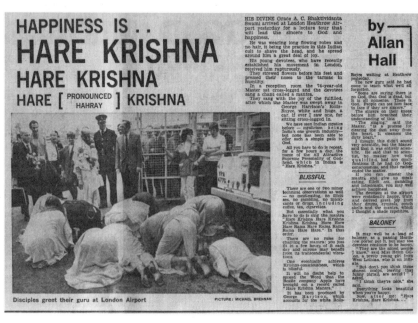

The Sun article

When I showed Prabhupada the newspapers the morning after his arrival, he smiled broadly.

"This photo," he said indicating the one of him with closed eyes, "This photo is very nice. I am thinking we should send it to Jadurani in America to paint."

"Yes, it is a great shot," I agreed.

"I was in ecstasy," Prabhupada said. Usually he just glanced at newspaper photos of himself without much comment, if any, but this photographer had captured the mood of that very special airport reception.

"While I am here in London," Prabhupada said looking up from the newspaper, "I am wanting to give lectures to the public."

"OK, we can probably arrange something," I said.

"You *must* arrange," he insisted. "I have many public engagements in America, and if I have none here then I must return to America soon."

"I'll talk to Gurudas and Shyamasundar about it when they get back from Bury Place tonight," I said. "Maybe we can rent a hall or something."

"That would be very nice," Prabhupada said. "Somewhere in center of London perhaps."

That evening the three of us agreed that we couldn't let Prabhupada leave London only because we hadn't managed to organize any worthwhile public programs. It was our goal to keep him with us for at least three months, so Gurudas suggested that we arrange a series of thirteen lectures that would be delivered once a week by Prabhupada to an audience that we would recruit via advertising. The next morning, Gurudas presented the proposal to Prabhupada and handed him a type-written list of the lectures we were suggesting he give;"Teachings of the Vedas," "The Golden Avatar," "The Song of God," and others. Prabhupada scrutinized the list.

"So I start on 28th September?" he asked.

We exchanged excited looks. "Yes, that's what we're thinking, Shrila Prabhupada," Shyamasundar said.

"That is OK," he said.

Overjoyed at our success in securing his presence until December, we quickly hired a place called Conway Hall, an austere but well-kept auditorium opposite a park called Red Lion Square, only five blocks from Bury Place. Inside, the six hundred audience seats were bolted to the floor and the wood panels on the walls looked as if they had all been cut from the same tree. With a stage, curtains, a sound-system and a mezzanine balcony on three sides, the hall had everything we needed, plus it had the added bonus of being inexpensive.

A few days before the first lecture, Prabhupada suggested some ideas for how we should position ourselves on the stage.

"This is London," he said. "It is important that we are looking nice." He took a piece of paper from the stack on his desk and began to sketch. The drawing looked something like the game strategy diagrams football coaches draw on boards in locker rooms.

"Top of page is edge of stage and bottom of page is backside," he said. "And these are tables." He indicated two horizontal rectangles in the middle of the page. "You can use tables from here – tables we use for *prasadam*." He drew a small rectangle between the large ones. "This is harmonium. Yamuna will sit here for singing. I will sit on left table and my Radha-Krishna deities will sit on right. You understand?"

I nodded.

He drew two columns along the left and right margins of the page. "This is where you all will be. Is that all right?"

"Yes," I said. "So you mean that the other devotees will sit and chant along each side of the stage?"

"Yes," he replied. "You will chant, dance, play *mrdanga, karatalas,* clap hands. And during lecture, you will sit in same way to listen."

"What if we sat in curved lines instead of straight ones?" I suggested. "That way the audience could see all the devotees."

"Oh, yes," Prabhupada said. "That will be very good." He drew curved lines over the straight ones and handed me the sheet of paper.

We figured it would take a lot of publicity to fill the hall, so we made a big push to advertise the lectures by distributing thousands of handbills on Oxford Street. Our efforts paid off. The first evening saw about four hundred people in the audience, each of whom paid ten shillings at the door. I thought the stage setup looked very pro-

Conway Hall program

fessional. Being three feet above the stage floor on the cushioned tables, Prabhupada and the deities were clearly visible even from the back of the room. I'd found an archaic-looking music stand that was just the right height for Prabhupada to use as a bookstand. And we had made a fifteen-foot purple cloth banner with the mantra on it in large yellow letters. This banner was the backdrop.

The evening opened with Yamuna leading a gentle kirtan for which we all stood in formation and danced as we played our motley collection of instruments – *karatalas*, *tamboura*, *mrdanga* and even trumpet. Yamuna then played the harmonium to accompany Prabhupada's pre-lecture kirtan. I watched the audience as Prabhupada sang and then lectured, and I could see that many were listening intently. When he asked for questions, a middle-aged man stood up.

"Why have you come all the way to London?" he asked in a booming voice. He spoke with impeccable Oxbridge English. "Why not focus on the Indian people and stay in your own country? You could influence the important politicians there."

"You are a great politician," Prabhupada instantly answered. "Therefore I have approached you."

The man blinked. "Thank you," he said quietly and sat down.

From her place behind the harmonium, Yamuna let out a loud "Ha-haw!" which echoed through the silent hall. The other devotees giggled at the sound as she covered her mouth with her right hand and looked around embarrassed. Prabhupada indicated she should lead another kirtan, so she began to sing and the rest of us danced in clockwise circles around Prabhupada and the deities as we played our instruments.

We were thrilled with the success of our opening night, but after the first few lectures the size of the audience began to dwindle. We didn't have enough money to keep producing the number of handbills we'd distributed for the first lecture. I did some research on advertising in the daily paper, but this proved far beyond our means. Getting Prabhupada from Tittenhurst to London was also more expensive than we had anticipated – twenty-five pounds round trip – and we found ourselves dipping into the Conway Hall entrance takings. We printed a few handbills each week, but we never managed to regain the size of the original crowds.

Nevertheless, the Conway Hall lectures proved an important body of knowledge and an inspiration for the devotees around the world who eagerly awaited recordings of each one. One of the lectures, "Wisdom of the Vedas," became the introduction to Prabhupada's book *Sri Isopanishad*. And a profile photo of Prabhupada taken at Conway Hall became part of the banner logo on the cover of *Back to Godhead* magazine.

———

Every morning during our two months at Tittenhurst while the Bury Place premises was under renovation, we had a program in a small building called the conservatory which had been used for chamber music recitals in days now long gone. Although it had good acoustics for kirtan, it was always icy, particularly at four in the morning, which was when our morning program began. We erected a simple altar for our Jagannatha deities at one end of the conservatory and an elevated seat on the right wall, from which Prabhupada spoke each morning. Before the early-morning *arati* ceremony, I made my shivery way to the conservatory to sweep the floor and turn on the kerosene burners to take the edge off the

Yamuna and Prabhupada approach the conservatory at Tittenhurst.

room's chill. Still, it was barely warmer in the conservatory than it was outside in the frost, and the cold got into my bones. It was like listening to Shrila Prabhupada lecture inside an industrial walk-in fridge.

There were very few of us staying at Tittenhurst, and the intimate atmosphere allowed us to ask Prabhupada lots of questions. One morning I went to where he was sitting and asked him about the way kirtans were performed historically.

"How did Lord Chaitanya do kirtan in the sixteenth century?" I asked, my breath making small clouds as I spoke. "What did the chanting parties look like in those days?"

"Yes," he paused, smiling like he was pleased with my question. He leaned forward as though he was revealing something very private. "Krishnadasa Kaviraja Goswami writes of this in his *Chaitanya-caritamrita*. There were two *mrdanga* players, two dancers and seven *karatalas*. Other people would join, but the main ones – the *mrdangas*, *karatala* men and the dancers – they were the center." He spoke quietly as if telling me a secret.

"The *mrdanga* players, they would inspire the dancers," he continued. "And the dancers, they would inspire *mrdangas*. One person would lead, and the rest, they would respond. Like we do here in temple – lead and respond." He paused. "In this way, they created ecstatic feelings by chanting the holy names very expertly.

"When leader chanted, drums and cymbals would play quiet so everyone could hear. Then when everyone sang, drums and *karatalas* played loud. And when leader sang again, they would play soft again. So soft and loud, they would go on in that way, and repeat."

Later that morning, I pulled on my green sports jacket and walked out to the gate to wait for the number seven Green Line bus. I had a busy day ahead of me. Prabhupada wanted larger premises for the temple, so I was going to view a couple of potential properties. I also had to meet with a few wealthy donors for the new temple, and I was capitalizing on our position in the music charts by organizing a weekend engagement for the "band" to earn some extra money for the temple. Instead of thinking about practical matters, though, I mused about how we could implement the kirtan techniques that Prabhupada had spoken about earlier that morning. The bus arrived, and as it crawled through the traffic, I decided it would be practically impossible to orchestrate that kind of kirtan in a temple, because of the spontaneous nature of such a setting. You never knew who exactly would be there and how long they would stay. It would be possible, I thought, only in a more controlled setting with participants who had a degree of musical sophistication. Prabhupada often spoke about his "long-cherished idea" for a World *Sankirtan* Party of twenty-five or so devotees who would travel the world performing kirtan at prestigious venues. I wondered if our being in the charts might assist us in forming the kind of party Prabhupada envisioned.

Thoughts of Lord Chaitanya's kirtan party stayed with me for the rest of the day as I made my way through my to-do list. When I arrived back at Tittenhurst that evening exhausted from meeting with potential donors, I found that another of our donors – a good friend – had called at the estate to meet with Prabhupada. Mr. Parikh was a slight bespectacled man of Gujarati origin who had come to England via Kenya, where he had been a schoolmaster. He was an influential member of the Indian community and had helped us in numerous ways. Several months before, he had sponsored and accompanied us to Leeds in Yorkshire, where we performed kirtan in a Hindu hall to an enthusiastic crowd of about five hundred people. Parikh was so enchanted with our performance that he started calling us "the real Hindus."

When I pushed open the door that evening, Gurudas was waiting for me in the hallway.

"Purushottama didn't let Mr. Parikh see Prabhupada," he exclaimed.

"Mr. Parikh was here?" I asked.

"Yeah. He came by bus," Gurudas said. "It took him four hours and he had to change buses six times. Prabhupada was resting when he got here, and Purushottama wouldn't wake him up."

"Did you tell him that they'd written letters to each other?" I asked. "And that Prabhupada would *want* to see Mr. Parikh?"

"I couldn't tell him anything," Gurudas said, exasperated. "We were out working on the main house, and when I got back Mr. Parikh was gone."

"How long did he wait?"

"Two hours," Gurudas said. "He left and didn't see Prabhupada."

I groaned. "Oh, man!" I was appalled that an elderly man who was such a good friend would have made the arduous journey for nothing.

"Prabhupada's angry at Purushottama. He said he doesn't know how to conduct himself in England."

"Can we make it up to Mr. Parikh?" I wondered aloud.

"I'm sure Prabhupada'll wanna to see him again," Gurudas said.

I thought that Prabhupada would remain unhappy with Purushottama for quite a while, given the magnitude of his blunder. But the next day when I entered his room before heading off to London for the day, I was surprised to see them interacting as though nothing had happened. Prabhupada looked over at me as I sat down before his desk.

"Your coat is a little soiled?" he asked.

I looked down at my sports jacket. "Yeah, I guess it is," I admitted. Prabhupada often said "cleanliness is next to godliness," and I thought that I was pretty clean in general. But now I saw my favorite sports coat with new eyes. It wasn't just a little soiled – it was stained and just plain dirty.

"In London, you dress then address. Dress, then *a-ddress*," he said. "Do you understand? You should have a nice new suit – like Purushottama." He nodded toward his assistant, who was now sitting in the corner of the room. Purushottama was wearing a dark blue pinstriped three-piece suit, beaming from ear to ear, obviously relieved to be vindicated from his gaffe with Parikh.

"OK," I said. "I'll buy a suit too. That'll make me look more official."

Prabhupada nodded and I left the room and sought out Janaki.

"Prabhupada wants me to get a suit like Purushottama's," I told her. "He said here in London we should look nice."

Janaki took it in stride. "I'll come with you," she offered. "We should go to Austin Reed. They've got nice stuff in there."

Riding the bus into London, I realized that many of the London business people I was dealing with recently had indeed looked me up and down when they'd first met me. I didn't want to look like a grungy American. At Austin Reed we found a well-cut dark-blue three-piece suit; Janaki also convinced me to buy a dark-blue wool overcoat. I wore everything out of the shop and around London for my errands, careful to hold an umbrella over my head to prevent my new clothes from getting damp.

When we arrived back at Tittenhurst at the end of the day, I planned to show Prabhupada my purchases. Janaki and I were making our way down the gravel path toward our rooms when we saw Prabhupada and Purushottama walking toward us. I prepared to offer my respects by bowing down before him, but as I bent my legs, I realized how muddy the narrow gravel path was. I remembered the devotees who had run out onto the tarmac a few weeks earlier and had bowed down before Prabhupada, unconcerned with the puddles and dirt that had stained their cotton robes. But there seemed to be a big difference between dirtying a piece of cotton cloth and soaking a three-piece suit in mud, and anyway, Prabhupada had rebuked me just this morning for wearing dirty clothes. I straightened up, and then changed my mind again and prepared to bow down, then saw the mud and straightened up once again. By the time Prabhupada reached us, he was laughing out loud.

"Prabhupada, I want to bow down, but then I thought ..."

"That's all right," he said, chuckling, and I knew he understood my predicament and was happy I hadn't dirtied my new suit and coat. He was obviously less concerned with my observing Vedic etiquette than he was that I be appropriately dressed to talk to people in London.

That night I thought about the Parikh incident and about my suit and tried to assimilate the inner meaning of the events. Just before Prabhupada had arrived in London, I had received a letter from him in which he had said, "I am so proud of having beautiful disciples like you who understand the inner meaning of my mission." I was struck by the phrase "inner meaning" and had thought about the significance of finding the inner meaning of things ever since. I realized that while regulations were essential for progress in spiritual life, I had to remember that pleasing Krishna and the spiritual master was not a simple matter of following rules. On the contrary, in special circumstances it was the right thing to violate custom for a higher purpose – to wake the spiritual master from his sleep to see an important guest, or to not bow down in order to preserve an expensive suit. Some years later I even heard that one devotee had complained that he wouldn't be able to open a temple in a communist country because there was no vegetarian food to eat. Prabhupada's response was, "Then eat meat, but spread Krishna consciousness like anything."

The art of being "tuned in" to the spiritual master preoccupied my thoughts all evening. My conclusion that night was that it takes time to learn to love someone and even more time to know what they want most.

———

During our stay at Tittenhurst, Janaki, Malati and Yamuna befriended a red-haired Scottish woman named Mrs. McDougal who was living in a small Georgian house on the property. Her husband was a bricklayer who was working on the estate and whom the Lennons were happy to accommodate in addition to paying him. Howard McDougal, the bricklayer, was a very quiet man.

One evening Janaki told me that Mrs. McDougal had confided in her that she and her husband were being kept awake at night by strange noises coming from the top floor of their house. They were afraid they were going to lose their home and employment because Mr. McDougal had to sleep during the day and wasn't getting enough work done on the Lennon property.

"They're convinced it's a ghost," Janaki said. "She said she thinks it's the work of the 'deil.' I think that's Scottish for devil. She asked me if I thought she was crazy, and I said no, that the Vedas say it's possible for a soul to be in a ghost body, I mean a subtle body, but no material body and senses."

"Maybe they should tell John and Yoko," I suggested.

"I said the same thing," Janaki said. "She said they'd told them, and Yoko hired an exorcist to get rid of it, but he couldn't do anything about it. He said the ghost was too powerful."

"What kind of sounds do they hear?" I asked.

"She said they hear heavy chains rattling and something being dragged across the floor."

"Like what?"

"She said it sounded like a body being dragged, or like boots."

"Chains and dragged bodies sounds pretty cliché to me," I said. I had always been skeptical about ghosts and supernatural beings, but when I met Prabhupada, I'd discovered that ghosts appear in many of the scriptures of India. Although the Vedas supported the idea of some ghosts being friendly, most of them seemed to be malevolent because they were frustrated. According to the Vedas, ghosts still had minds and desired food, sex and other sensory pleasures, but they could not fulfill these desires because they had no sense organs. Prabhupada said it was possible for a disembodied being to continue to reside in a particular house because of excessive attachment to the dwelling. He also said some powerful ghosts had the ability to possess others' bodies to gratify their desires, especially the bodies of those who had taken alcohol or drugs or were in some kind of vulnerable state.

"They're really upset about it. Can we ask Prabhupada what we should do?"

"I think so," I said.

When I told Prabhupada about the situation, his response was direct.

"Drive it out," he said gravely.

"How?" I asked. "They hired an exorcist and even he couldn't help!"

The author speaking with Prabhupada at Tittenhurst

"Yes, but Krishna can!" Prabhupada insisted. "On a cloudy day, ask the people to leave the house. Then you have loud kirtan. Use *mrdanga, karatalas* and keep blowing conch shell. Sprinkle water offered to Krishna on floor. Burn lots of incense. You must chant Hare Krishna in the house all day."

"You think that will drive away the ghost?" I asked a little doubtfully.

"Yes," he said with certainty. "A ghost cannot remain in presence of Krishna's name."

A couple of days later, twenty devotees gathered in the McDougals' home for a spirited Hare Krishna chanting session.

"We're gonna be a few hours," Janaki said to Mrs. McDougal. "Why don't you take a walk?"

"Well, there's a wee bit of rain, but we can take our brollies," Mrs. McDougal agreed.

The kirtan lasted five hours. We threaded our way through all the rooms of the small house, singing and playing our instruments loudly. At three o'clock we finally concluded our "exorcism" and I scuffed out across the sodden park to find the McDougals. I found them sitting on a damp bench among the rhododendron bushes.

"The coast's clear," I said. "You can go home now and, I hope, get a good night's sleep tonight."

The next morning, Mrs. McDougal reported that they had slept peacefully throughout the night without any disturbance coming from the attic. For the months that we stayed at Tittenhurst, the sounds were not heard again. The McDougals were immensely grateful to us and to Prabhupada for saving their sanity and their livelihood. This experience was something of a first for me, but I took it in my stride and reasoned that this was a demonstration of how Krishna conscious philosophy solved people's real-life problems in a practical way. I'd seen Krishna consciousness help improve people's health through vegetarianism, and I'd seen drug addicts come clean through practicing the philosophy that Prabhupada expounded. Now I could add to that list that I'd seen a home exorcised through the chanting of Hare Krishna.

Daily Sketch *article of 10 October, 1969 shows devotees taking prasadam at Tittenhurst.*

Prabhupada himself seemed quite taken by the incident. At Conway Hall a few nights later I was busy organizing something and wasn't paying much attention to Prabhupada's lecture. Then I heard him say, "We drove the ghost from John Lennon's house." I couldn't help smiling at the fact he'd told his audience about this in the middle of a lecture on Vedic philosophy.

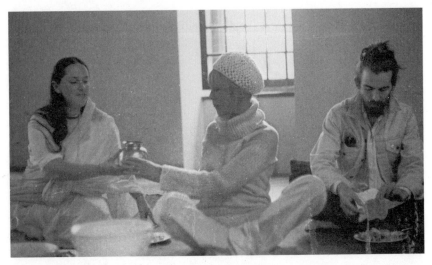

From left to right: Yamuna, Patti Boyd, George Harrison

John Lennon, Yoko Ono, and Janaki inside the temple room at Tittenhurst

John Lennon and Yoko Ono with George Harrison
outside the conservatory temple at Tittenhurst

CHAPTER 33

"London is Hell"

A dark-green twelve-seat van marked "BBC" pulled up in front of the Tittenhurst conservatory on a dry, cold evening in early October. The uniformed driver jumped out of his seat to open the van doors for us as though we were celebrities. The directors of one of the BBC's most popular programs, *Late Night Line-Up*, had invited Prabhupada and six of his American disciples to appear on the show.

The Shepherd's Bush studios were about an hour and a half drive from Tittenhurst. We entered the slick studio at 10:30 PM, and the warm air hit us in a wave, a tropical contrast to the chill of the parking lot we had just walked across. A young man in a suit escorted us up an elevator and into a plush room that was furnished with large taupe lounge chairs. There were already a number of well-dressed people chatting and drinking cocktails and generally making the most of the open bar at the far end of the room.

"This is our main guest lounge," the man said. "Everyone here is waiting to be called into a studio. Just have a seat and someone will come and take you to make-up shortly."

I sized up the situation. "Prabhupada, maybe we should move over there and sit down." I pointed toward some empty chairs as far away from the bar as possible.

He nodded his assent and sat. We sat on the floor around him, chanting softly on our beads while we waited to be called. Fifteen minutes later, a member of the make-up team led us into a lavish make-up room that was as big as a men's barbershop and was occupied by an alarming number of women armed with sprays, gels and numerous odd-shaped brushes. With the swivel chairs and the wall-to-wall mirrors, this setup gave every indication that these women were intending to give us each a full makeover.

When the team gathered to survey us, there was a bit of muttering between them, a covert discussion and some worried looks.

"Is there something wrong?" Janaki asked.

"Uh ... we don't like the markings on some of your foreheads," one of them said. "They're rubbing off and look a bit unkempt, especially compared with his." She pointed to Prabhupada, who looked back at her impassively. "They're not going to look good on screen."

I glanced around the group and saw it was true. Apart from Prabhupada, only Yamuna had freshly applied and perfectly executed *tilaka*. We had some genuine *tilaka* clay from India back at Tittenhurst, but often we relied on something called Fuller's Earth – clay used to absorb grease or other impurities. None of the pharmacies that sold it would be open at this time of night.

"Do you really need to have the markings?" the make-up team leader asked.

"Well, I think we'd like to keep them on," I said. "They're part of our culture. They show that our bodies are temples of God."

"Yes, so you should have them," she said. "Also they're kind of your trademark – pardon the pun." I smiled obligingly at her little joke.

"What if we painted the marks on their foreheads?" one of the crew suggested. "I mean, just completely remove what's there now and repaint them with a brush and, say, acrylic paint."

"That could work," the team leader said. She looked over at me. "What do you think? There's going to be lots of close-ups of your faces, so it'd be good to have the marks looking tidy. Would it be OK to paint them, I mean, by your protocol?"

I looked at the others. "Um, give us a few minutes to talk about it," I said.

After they retreated, the six of us had a hurried conference while Prabhupada sat and chanted softly in the lounge.

"I think we should go ahead and let them do it," Janaki said.

"Me too," I agreed. "We look a bit ragged as we are. We don't want people who see the show to think we don't care how we look."

"But that's acrylic paint," Yamuna said. "You don't want to be putting that kind of thing on your skin. Does that stuff even come off?"

"It'll come off," Janaki said. "And anyway, you won't have to put it on *your* skin because your *tilaka* looks great."

"I don't think they'll be able to paint them right," Shyamasundar said. "Painted *tilaka* will look weird."

"It's not gonna look any weirder than real *tilaka* to people who don't know," Gurudas argued.

"Wouldn't it be against the Vedic tradition to paint it with acrylic paint?" Malati wondered. "Maybe we should just go without it completely."

"No, we can't do that," I said. "Look, this really isn't a big deal. Let's just let them do it. We've gotta have *tilaka*, and it should be neat and tidy. If anyone's got a better idea than acrylic paint, let's hear it." There was a long pause. "So shall we just go for it?"

There was a general concurrence, more reluctantly expressed by some than others.

"OK, you can paint them," I called out to the make-up leader.

"Great, follow me," she said, suppressing a smile and leading us deeper into the shiny room.

They seated us in the heavy swivel chairs and used wet washcloths to rub off the remainder of our old *tilaka* markings. The team-leader gave Yamuna a piece of lined paper and asked her to draw a prototype so they would know exactly what they were trying to produce.

In my chair in front of the mirror, I watched as the make-up artist daubed a tiny brush into the white paint she'd squeezed from a tube.

"So, what's the mark mean?" she asked me in a northern English accent.

"It's to signify that we're Vaishnavas," I said. "Devotees of Krishna. In India millions of people mark their foreheads like this." I didn't say I'd never been to India and was telling her this completely on hearsay.

"Really?" she said. "I didn't know that." The room was full of sound as the make-up artists chattered to the devotees they were decorating. They asked questions about our clothes, our beliefs and our goals in England. Many of them had seen us chanting downtown. Yamuna kept running back and forth between one artist and the next showing her drawing and acting as a *tilaka* model herself. The result was six perfect *tilakas*, uniform to a degree I wasn't used to. I thought we looked great and that maybe we should adopt this *tilaka*-application method again for important functions.

When we walked into the studio, Shrila Prabhupada smiled up at us from the large orange cushion on which he was comfortably seated. Six other cushions were arranged in a semi-circle on the carpeted studio floor. The host, Tony Bilbow, also sat on a cushion on the floor. He was open-minded and liberal, but I thought he looked a bit uncomfortable sitting cross-legged.

The cameras began rolling, and I felt nervous, knowing millions of people would be watching. Bilbow introduced us and scooted along the ground on his cushion to ask us each questions: How long have we been Hare Krishnas? Why did we wear these clothes? Where was our center in London? Everyone except Gurudas seemed a bit nervous in their answers. Unlike the rest of us, he was outgoing and in his element interacting with the media. A few weeks earlier, we'd been chanting along the Strand, a one-time fashionable street linking Trafalgar Square with Fleet Street, when an ITV crew approached us for an interview. We'd pushed Gurudas forward and he'd answered their questions in a confident voice loud enough that he could be heard over the traffic and the chanting that was going on behind him. When they'd asked him if the chanting got monotonous after a while, Gurudas gave a memorable answer that ended up as the interview sound bite on the news that night.

"What's nice about these words," he'd said, "is that you can chant them over and over again, and you'll never get tired of hearing it. But if you chant Queen Elizabeth, Queen Elizabeth, Queen Elizabeth, over and over again, you'll get disgusted!"

Now in the studio, Gurudas shone and the interviewer kept coming back to him. Finally, after asking the six of us many questions, Bilbow turned to Prabhupada, whom he'd been saving for last. He asked him many of the usual questions. Prabhupada answered them briefly and to the point. I was surprised how short his sentences were, and though I wasn't sure whether Prabhupada knew that TV interviewers preferred direct and informative answers, I was sure that his mode of delivery was perfect for the typical TV viewer's short attention span.

"Do you have a concept of hell in your religion?" Bilbow asked.

Prabhupada paused briefly. "*This* is hell," he said matter-of-factly. "London is hell. It's always cold, damp, rainy and cloudy. In India the sun always shines." He beamed at his questioner. I felt a laugh boiling up inside me.

The suave Bilbow was at a loss of words. A few seconds of silence went by as he struggled to regain his composure. It was clear to me that Prabhupada hadn't meant to make this man lose his cool with this answer. Obviously seeing Bilbow's discomfort, Prabhupada quickly added, "Of course it is a great credit to the British people for having built such a great civilization in this climate."

Bilbow smiled, relieved. "Yes, it *is* a great civilization," he agreed. The interview continued as if the momentary glitch hadn't occurred.

Back at Tittenhurst that night we tried to remove our acrylic *tilaka* without success. "The conservatives had a point after all," I thought. It took us five days to remove the paint.

Pop Idols

By early October our "Hare Krishna Mantra" forty-five had achieved global popularity. We faced a constant struggle not to be thought of as a pop group who had simply adopted a stage persona. Few music lovers were interested in spirituality. Wherever we went, people asked for our autographs – when we were chanting in central London, when we were on the subway or even in supermarkets and gas stations. Over the next year or so, this would become tedious and dull for us: the fans, the TV appearances and the gigs – some of them with bands like The Who and The Moody Blues who went on to be genuinely iconic – lost their glamour quickly. Other temple concerns eventually took precedence over our music publicity, but for now the music scene was fresh for us and we were eager to promote Prabhupada's movement in this way.

A few weeks into our stay at Tittenhurst, a Dutch television station invited us to do a performance in Amsterdam. They offered an all-expense-paid flight to the Netherlands and back on the same day for nine members of the Radha-Krishna Temple band. It was Gurudas's idea to ask Shrila Prabhupada to go with us as a member of the band. When I asked him, he agreed immediately, so the six of us plus him and a couple of others were driven in a large van from Tittenhurst to Heathrow Airport, where we boarded a KLM 707 for the one-hour flight to Amsterdam Airport Schiphol.

New Musical Express (England) top 30 tunes, showing the Hare Krishna Mantra in the number 11 position

The program was the Dutch counterpart of *American Bandstand* or the British show *Top of the Pops*. It was one of the most popular TV shows in the country because it featured the chart-topping rock groups of the day. We had all been excited to be appearing on such a trendy television program, but as soon as we arrived at the studio the inhospitable reception of the producers removed our sense of adventure.

We were greeted by a blond bearded man in his mid-twenties who was carrying a clipboard with a sticker on the back that said, "If God dropped acid would he see people?" He led us down a dark staircase and into an undecorated concrete basement without windows. The walls were lined with hard concrete benches.

"This is our green room," he said. "Except we call it the gray room." He gave a laugh that came out as an ugly snort.

"Isn't there some chairs or something?" Gurudas asked. "Even just one chair for the swami? He's over seventy."

"We don't have chairs," the boy said dismissively, heading for the door. "OK, I've got stuff to do, so you guys hang out here."

I was taken aback at his offhand manner toward Prabhupada. "Won't someone be coming to talk to us about the show?" I asked.

"Yeah, Karsten's going to come down sometime."

Karsten turned out to be a skinny dark-haired man not much older than the clipboard boy.

"Hi," he said. "Thanks for coming over from England."

"This is Bhaktivedanta Swami," I said, gesturing toward Prabhupada. "He's the founder of our movement and a really respected scholar."

"Hey, Swami," Karsten said, holding out a hand to shake. "We don't get many scholars on our show. I hope you like to groove!" He laughed loudly. His teeth were bright white under his mustache. Prabhupada shook his hand and nodded at him without saying anything.

Karsten went on to explain that we'd be miming our song while the original played in the background, because they wanted to be certain that their audiences heard exactly what they were used to hearing on the radio. He also hinted there were some copyright issues. Then he, too, headed out of the room without any indication how long we would have to wait in the stuffy windowless basement.

We waited for an hour, feeling bad that Prabhupada would have to tolerate such facilities. Finally, a denim-clad young woman led us to the backstage area of the dimly lit studio. Scantily clad male and female dancers jived and wiggled on bleachers at the back of the stage while a band I didn't know played a rock song I didn't recognize. I felt embarrassed that we had subjected Prabhupada to this rock studio atmosphere. I glanced over at him and saw that he was looking up at the ceiling, a dark maze of metal beams twenty-five feet above us slung with insulated wires, lights, suspended microphones and electronic boxes. Prabhupada pointed upward with his cane and said, "Some day this will all be piled up like garbage." He looked around the studio and at the dancers. "Just see," he said. "They're not even symmetrical." I grinned and felt a bit stupid. After all, what did I expect to find, a holy choir of sexless angels?

The song ended, and a crew ran onto the stage to prepare for our act. Three of them were pushing a huge fat seat on a platform, a kind of throne on wheels.

"OK, Krishnas," Karsten said. "You ready? We've got ten minutes to get you set up before the cameras roll. Just do what the crew tells you." He jumped down off the stage.

"Just a minute," I said. "What's that seat for?"

"The seat?" Karsten asked, turning back. "That's the throne for the guru. He's an old mystic guy, so we want him to look mystical. We saw photos of how he sits on big seats in your temples. But we're going to do it even better than you guys do." He pointed backstage where three people were pouring water over tubs of dry ice. "He's going to look incredible in that smoke."

"Uh-uh," I said as I watched the stage crew put the dry ice around the throne. "This really isn't appropriate."

"Not appropriate?" Karsten looked genuinely surprised. "But the seat will look like it's in a cloud! That's the effect we want."

Prabhupada exiting the Amsterdam TV studio, October 1969

The author and Prabhupada at Amsterdam's Schiphol Airport

"No," I said. "We're not here to make Prabhupada look comical. He isn't an actor. He's a spiritual teacher and he should be treated that way."

"But it'll look good!" Karsten insisted. "That's what the audience wants to see."

I thought for a minute and decided to try for a compromise.

"Prabhupada will sit on the chair, but no dry ice."

"But we got the dry ice in especially for this!" the producer protested. "Why don't you want it?"

*Prabhupada and his personal secretary waiting in line
at Schiphol Airport in Amsterdam*

"It's not right." I was adamant. "We can't have it. No." I knew they needed us more than we needed them.

Karsten looked more than a little piqued. Prabhupada consented a bit reluctantly to sit in the chair, and we dutifully mouthed the words to the mantra while our record played over the huge speakers. Even though we knew our performance was being watched by thousands or maybe millions, the whole scene had become distasteful.

As we drove back toward the airport in the van, Prabhupada turned to me.

"You should inquire little more about program next time," he said. "Ask them what they want of us for next TV appearance."

I had a flashback to the *Les Crane Show*, where I hadn't realized Prabhupada and I would be pitted against the fundamentalist Christians. I remembered how I'd vowed then that I'd get organized and be prepared for our TV performances. Now I promised myself that the minute we got back to London I'd get a notebook devoted specifically to documenting media information.

A few days later, the tabloids covered my conflict with the Dutch producers. "Radha-Krishna Temperamental" was one of the gossipy albeit rather clever headlines.

—

Soon after our Amsterdam TV appearance, an agent offered us a contract to play at four venues in Germany for which we would be paid the princely sum of five hundred pounds. Every professional engagement we did meant more money to put into the temple coffers. We immediately accepted the offer, even though it meant a week away from Shrila Prabhupada.

Janaki and I drove to Hamburg in a dark-green BMC van that we got on credit with some of the proceeds from the single. The van had the words "HARE KRISHNA" painted on the back in tall sans-serif white letters. With us was a group of ten people, some of them new English devotees, some who had come over to help out from the States, and one – a devotee named Suchandra – who spoke German.

The high point of our German tour took place in the northern coastal town of Bremen in a place called the Cougar Club. When we pulled up outside at seven o'clock in the evening, the blue neon cougar on a sign on top of a pole in the parking lot was flickering like it was on its last legs. The club was housed in an old theater from which the seats had been removed, but which retained the stage and curtains. We went inside and the proprietor came forward to greet us. A cigarette hung from her mouth, and she looked sleepy and hung over, her black hair scattered and her pink smock and floral printed slippers worn and haggard.

The song title "Flat Foot Floozy" zinged instantly through my brain.

"Calm in to da dance floor and zee da whole plaze," she said with a sweeping gesture. We followed her in and saw that the stage was scattered with cigarette butts and potato chip pieces. There was no amplification system for miking our voices or instruments.

"We'd like to be paid in advance," I said firmly. I was getting more used to dealing with those who held the purse strings in the entertainment industry. Usually I found that a firm, confident approach worked better than submission.

"Zat's not possible," she said. "You'll be paid in cash when you sing vor two hours. Zat's what contract says."

I opened my mouth to argue, but the look in her eyes told me this was going to be one battle I wasn't going to win with firmness.

We were all pretty convinced that no one would want to come to such a hell-hole, but by eight o'clock the Cougar Club had filled with three thousand teenagers. We waited skeptically on the stage behind the curtains. The decrepit theater was full of excited chattering and shrieking. I peeked out at the crowd from a slit in the musty stage drapes and could immediately sense the air of anticipation. Our single was high in the German charts, and these kids knew our song; they were here, they were high, and they were clearly excited about the prospect of seeing us, because for them our band was a pop sensation.

When the curtains parted, the crowd applauded and screamed and hundreds of young girls rushed to the edge of the stage. Even though we thought the kids would know the words to the song, we had decided in advance that Suchandra would take them through it before we started performing. He stepped forward and tried to speak over the screaming. Without a microphone it was hopeless, so he just stood there until they quieted down.

I couldn't understand most of what he was saying, but I could read the concentration on the faces of the teenagers. Even through their layers of intoxication, they seemed alert to his words. When he called out each word of the mantra, they repeated it back to him with an exactness I'd never heard before in a crowd. The same thing happened when he taught them how to dance. He swayed back and forth, crossing one leg over the other as Prabhupada had taught us, and they copied his movement with uncommon precision. When he clapped, they clapped, and when he put the chanting, dancing and clapping together, they followed like an army division.

Because we didn't have any amplification, we had decided to play our instruments softly when Suchandra was leading the chanting, then loudly during the audience response. The audience caught on quickly to this soft-loud method and responded with an enthusiasm that was positively electric. With such a receptive crowd, I knew we would have to carefully control the speed of the kirtan. After all, we had to perform for two hours. Like a practiced choir, they responded in one voice. Chanting, dancing and clapping, they formed a perfectly regimented singing battalion.

Forty minutes into the chanting I began to play the *mrdanga* a little faster. I was startled by the way this audience didn't try to rush the beat. When the momentum finally became too quick, the symmetrical choreography turned into wild jumping and leaping, higher and higher, faster and faster. I brought the kirtan to a stop, and we started all over again. The audience quickly regained its original composure and followed Suchandra's slow-paced lead. By the time the kirtan sped up again, I felt such a warm rapport with the audience that I thought we should jump off the stage and into their ranks. I conferred with the others over the noise of the kirtan, and they agreed that we should stop being a spectacle and should participate with this audience the way Lord Chaitanya had kirtan. He was never on a stage; He was always in the midst of the chanters.

I looked at my watch. We had fifteen minutes to go.

When we jumped down and ran to the center of the floor, the audience looked startled but then joined in more enthusiastically than ever. Members of the audience swung their arms around our necks and shouted smiling comments in German. When I passed by Gurudas as we danced in concentric circles, he nodded at my clothes. I looked down and realized there were blotches of blood all over my white *dhoti*; my hands were bleeding from the vigorous drum playing. My watch told me that we had done our time and more, but the chanters were tireless and I could see it was going to be difficult for us to end this chanting session.

As we brought the kirtan to a close, I motioned to the devotees that they should all bow down to signal the finale of the chanting and to set the scene for a little philosophical talk to explain the significance of the chanting. I was surprised when every member of the audience also bowed down with us. After the short invocation, they all rose, shouting "Hare Krishna! Hare Krishna! Hare Krishna!"

We decided the only way for us to get out of the club was to make a run for it when the audience was bowing down. Suchandra led a quick five-minute kirtan and when the kids were bowing down, we exited backstage behind the now-closed curtain. As my eyes adjusted to the dim stage light, I noticed there was a sound system after all – an amp and a turntable on which was our forty-five! I wiped my bloody hands on my *dhoti*, which I was going to have to throw away anyway, and put on the record. We peeked covertly through the curtains and watched as the audience continued to dance in synchrony. When the gong sounded at the end of the song, they bowed down again and stood up chanting "Zugabe! Zugabe! Zugabe!"

"What does that mean?" Gurudas asked Suchandra.

"It means 'encore,'" he said. "They're really not giving up easily, are they?"

"I can't play anymore," I said, holding my palms out for them to see.

Suchandra parted the curtains and went back out onto the stage. The crowd cheered. Many rushed to the edge of the stage with pens and paper hoping to get his autograph. He began shouting in German, and when the noise subsided he spoke for a few minutes, I presumed to tell them about the mantra and to encourage them to visit our new center, which had recently opened in Hamburg. He folded his palms together in the traditional Indian way and said, "*Danke schoen.*"

We all spent a few minutes signing autographs from the stage. The matron of the Cougar Club crawled out from nowhere like a sleepy badger and counted us out five hundred pounds in Deutschmarks as everyone watched. In the van on the drive back to the Hamburg temple, Suchandra said, "Hey, you know, one kid asked me if there was a temple in Bremen, and when I said no, he asked if he could start one!"

———

In the months that followed, while Prabhupada was with us in London and after he left, we found ourselves embroiled in what was shaping up to be a young but serious relationship with the UK music industry. After the success of the "Hare Krishna Mantra" forty-five, George Harrison suggested that we put together a long-playing record, which we later called *The Radha-Krishna Temple*. In addition to other tracks, which we still needed to record, the album would feature the two songs from the single and should, he thought, also include a version of a tune called "Chintamani," which he'd heard us rehearsing at the Arts Lab one evening. The lyrics of the "Chintamani" song were two verses from a Vedic work called the *Brahma-samhita*. The song had become a staple in our public performances, and although it was a simple song, which we sang with just a pair of *karatalas* and *mrdanga*, George really liked it. On the evening he heard us play it he went home and developed a chord pattern, which he said he would like to use if we agreed to let him produce it.

A few weeks later, we found ourselves in Trident studios in St. Anne's Court in central London. Under George's direction, Yamuna sang the lead to "Chintamani" and Shyamasundar and I joined in on the chorus, "*Govindam adi-purusam, tam aham bhajami.*" In the song's finale, forty devotees sang the refrain. We were accompanied by our own *mrdanga* and *karatalas* – sealed off in a special soundproof room to avoid echoes – and an impressive array of instruments that George had organized: electric organ, electric bass, a Middle Eastern instrument called an *oud*, drums, and a mini-orchestra that included harp, flute, violins, violas, cellos, string basses, and orchestral bells.

The end result was a sophisticated piece of music that had a rock beat at its foundation but which had Eastern echoes as well. We decided to call it "Govinda," and it was soon released as a follow-up forty-five to the "Hare Krishna Mantra." It didn't climb as high on the charts as its predecessor – it made it to only number thirty-four – but that was high enough for us to sing it on "Top of the Pops."

Of course, for us, it was more important that Shrila Prabhupada appreciated our efforts than it was to win favor with the music industry. Prabhupada had left London by the time "Govinda" came out, so we sent a copy of it to him in Los Angeles. We heard there was some controversy about the record among some of the more conservative male members of that community who didn't think it was appropriate that a song led by a woman should be played in the temple. We thought this was absurd. Here was a recording of an ancient Vedic text, produced by one of the most popular musicians of our time and which was selling by the thousand all over the world. Eventually we heard that the liberals in the temple prevailed; they arranged that our song be played in the temple when the devotees greeted the deities as they did each morning. Prabhupada himself

Front side of the Govinda single

readily agreed to the proposal. As always, he was willing to take a risk and do something new.

The Los Angeles devotees later told us how events unfolded that morning. Hundreds were present in the temple, and as the altar's folding doors opened, "Govinda" surged forth over the big speaker system. Prabhupada bowed down before the altars and then made his way to his red velvet seat of honor, from where he was to give his morning lecture. Sitting there, he gazed at the deities, and then the devotees noticed tears gliding down his cheeks.

When we heard how Prabhupada had reacted to "Govinda," we knew that any controversy over the song was put to rest for-

Back side of the Govinda single

ever. We had been waiting to hear what he would say and how he would resolve the dispute, but he hadn't needed to say anything at all. Prabhupada later wrote in a letter that the song was "not ordinary singing. It [was] concert." I knew that Prabhupada wasn't concerned with the material categories the song fell into; he was interested only in the devotion with which the song was sung. Here was a beautiful piece of music, and since Krishna is understood in the Vedas to be the reservoir of all beauty, Prabhupada appreciated it, particularly because it glorified his Lord. I remembered reading in the *Bhagavad-gita* how Krishna is the ability in all people. Elsewhere, Prabhupada described ability as being great deeds, capacity, industriousness and the achievement of wonderful things. For him, all of these were part of Krishna, regardless of the gender or skin color or material condition of the person.

After that day in Los Angeles, Prabhupada requested that "Govinda" be played every morning in every temple when the deity altars were opened. We were overjoyed that he appreciated the song so deeply.

CHAPTER 35

Radha-Londonisvara Installed

During the months of Prabhupada's stay in London, we tried to limit our involvement in our music commitments in favor of trying to get the temple ready for opening. It was still many months before we would even think of recording "Govinda" or the long-playing record. For now we were still resident in a building with a half-demolished load-bearing wall and which Prabhupada wanted officially opened as the London ISKCON temple before he left in mid-December.

We were still waiting on the planning permission from the Camden Council so that we could begin (or rather, continue) with the necessary modifications. Prabhupada was of the opinion that we wouldn't get permission, but he encouraged us to continue trying, all the while hoping that we would chance upon a bigger and better building. By the time October rolled into view, I was desperate to get an outcome to the renovation conundrum. Prabhupada would be leaving us in just eight weeks, and we *had* to get the temple opened while he was still with us. I turned to Tom Driberg, the only member of the establishment I felt we could really count on.

"I'll write a letter for you," he said. "Perhaps that will help. I know some people involved in the building industry."

I was skeptical about this plan of action. Writing a letter seemed to me a typical non-committal British response that wouldn't yield much. I was wrong. Three days later, I flipped through our stack of

Inside the Bury Place temple shortly after it opened

mail and found a photocopy of a handwritten letter from Driberg to John Silken, the Minister of Public Building and Works. It began "Dear John" and said, "Friends of mine from America are occupying Seven Bury Place near the British Museum. I hope you will arrange for their convenient stay there." He signed it "Tom."

Planning permission followed quickly, though it was only a temporary permit, which was valid for three years. Although we would need to reapply eventually, this victory was more than enough for us. The race was on to prepare the temple for opening.

Shyamasundar and Tirthapada (formerly Tim) recommenced the temple-room renovations with fervor. Shyamasundar had a grand plan for how the temple room should look. For the altar, he managed to convince the musical group Rolling Stones to donate an opulent marble slab, which took six men to carry inside from the truck. He had already carved new large Jagannatha deities, who we all agreed would look spectacular. He procured stacks of imported wood – redwood mostly – and drew up an elaborate design for the temple room. His idea was to fashion a wooden ceiling that would

Prabhupada with guests in his room at the Bury Place temple

curve upwards from the walls to a point at the center of the room. The walls would also be wooden, constructed of columns, tongue and groove panels, and huge wooden beams that would run the entire length of the temple.

Not being a carpenter, I couldn't quite picture his idea, and it all sounded a bit ambitious and time-consuming to me. Sure enough, the temple room demanded Shyamasundar's entire attention over the weeks that followed. I wasn't alone in wishing he'd simplify the design, and even Shrila Prabhupada commented that it was unnecessarily complex.

While Shyamasundar fought to complete his self-imposed task on the first floor, other devotees worked to modify the upper floors of the building. The floor above the temple room was converted into a room for Prabhupada. We carpeted it with a thick oriental rug and painted it a light color so that it would feel bigger. Yamuna found a low glass-topped table to serve as a desk and a blue padded cushion for Prabhupada to sit on when he was translating or meeting with guests. She scattered a few additional cushions around the room for

While Prabhupada was in London, he was constantly looking for premises larger than 7 Bury Place.

others to sit on.

The basement was also being modified into a kitchen and dining room. We put in a sink and some shelves and stove, and carpeted the eating area so that the devotees wouldn't be cold sitting on the basement floor. Everything – the sink, the stove, the cushions, the wood – was donated.

The contacting of potential donors fell upon me. I found myself running around London trying to raise funds and secure useful building materials and paint and food supplies. I contacted the BBC so that we'd be sure to have some media coverage when the temple opened in December. And I was constantly looking for a larger premises because I knew Shrila Prabhupada wanted that, and also because looking at buildings had become a habit for me over the past year.

In addition to these temple-related tasks, I ran errands for Prabhupada. We continued to stay out at Tittenhurst, since the Bury Place temple was a construction site, and even if it weren't, we were supposed to have a maximum of only four people living on the premises at any one time. I traveled to London by bus from Tittenhurst, usually in the early morning when it was still dark, and I returned in the dark as well. Usually I chanted softly on the bus ride or read a book or sometimes an abandoned newspaper.

One morning, just as I was leaving for London, Prabhupada called me into his room and asked me to make a deposit of twenty-five pounds in his book trust account at the Long Acre branch of Lloyds Bank near the new temple.

"I don't think I can do it," I said.

"Why? You are doing many other things?" Prabhupada asked.

"Oh, no! I meant that I don't think you can make a deposit into an account unless it's your own account."

"That's all right," Prabhupada said. "I have written letter." He handed me a single sheet of paper, which read "My representative, Mr. Michael Grant, will make this deposit on my behalf." His signature flowed across the bottom of the page.

I finished my errands by early afternoon and stopped at Lloyds Bank on my way to the Ascot bus. I slipped my authorization letter and bankbook and the twenty-five pounds into the metal tray and slid them to the teller who looked bored behind his thick wall of glass. He read the note, put the money into a drawer and stamped the book with the amount and the date. I retrieved the book when the metal tray slid back to my side and made my way to the bus stop. Upon arriving at Tittenhurst, I went straight to Prabhupada's room to return the bankbook to him.

"Where is the receipt?" he asked, having opened the book to examine the stamp.

"Receipt?" I asked.

"The receipt. Do you not have it?"

"I thought the stamp in the bankbook was the receipt," I said.

"They did not give receipt?" he asked again.

"No."

"You did not ask for one?"

"No."

"They didn't offer one?"

I thought about the bank transaction, trying to remember if the teller had offered me a receipt during the exchange. But I clearly remembered that he hadn't said anything about one, or anything else for that matter.

"No," I said. "He just stamped the book. I thought that was the same as a receipt." Now I was beginning to feel uncomfortable like I had done something wrong.

"Do you know what this means?" Prabhupada asked.

I didn't know what to say. What did it mean? What was he getting at? I took a chance. "I was just careless, Prabhupada, I should have asked for a receipt."

"No, that's not what it means. What does it mean?"

"It means that he forgot to give me one," I said. If it wasn't my fault, it had to be his.

"No, that's not what it means," he insisted. "You do not know what it means."

There was a long pause. Prabhupada turned his head to the left and stared out the small window. He silently looked at the treetops and the clouds.

"Britain is finished," he said, shaking his head, still looking out the window. "The British Empire is finished."

It was an interesting comment, one that I would have liked to have heard more about, but my immediate concern was clearing up the bank fiasco. Prabhupada's British Empire comment seemed a little unrelated to the moment. He turned to me.

"After the second war there was a cartoon." His face broke into a smile and I felt relieved. "It was in the Indian newspapers. There was a lion that was supposed to be British. He was bandaged all over in a hospital bed and his legs and arms were hanging by ... what is the word? ... pulley."

"Tractions?" I suggested.

"Tractions, yes ... from the ceiling. Yes, tractions. So this was the condition after the war. Hitler ruined their empire, even though he was also ruined. The English policy of exploitation was not good."

He launched into a lengthy critique of England's policies of economic and political exploitation of her colonies. He spoke of how sometimes the British colonizers cut off the Indian weavers' thumbs because they produced cloth by hand that was equal or superior to that spun in Manchester cotton mills. "And there are many other things," he said. A member of a former colony and a one-time follower of Mahatma Gandhi's independence movement, Prabhupada said that Britain's decision to abandon India as a colony was deeply influenced by the militancy of Subash Chandra Bose's Indian National Army.

"Gandhi helped establish Indian people to no longer cooperate with Britishers," he said. "And Bose's show of army weakened Britishers' will." He paused and looked out the window again.

"This England," he said, "England today is deteriorated. Not like fifty years ago." I remembered driving around London with him a few weeks ago and how he'd commented on the run-down condition of many office buildings, on construction that was half-done and on dilapidated residential quarters. This was not the England he had heard so much about before the war.

"This land," he said, gesturing toward the expanses around him, "no one could afford to buy. So it is now owned by these young singers. This England is much deteriorated. Your country – America – is the best place for spreading Krishna consciousness. Once the sun used never to set on the British Empire, and now it never rises on it." He laughed. "Simply by testing one grain of rice, one can tell the situation in the whole cooking pot."

I pondered this cryptic concluding statement. I'd heard Prabhupada say this before, of course, but I wasn't sure how it related to the Lloyds situation and the fascinating if scathing dissertation about the decline of the British Empire. But then I realized that the bank's failure to issue a receipt indicated for Prabhupada a deeper malady. Just as it was possible to tell whether a whole pot of rice was cooked just by testing one grain, Prabhupada was saying that the bank's administrative failure was symptomatic of a wider breakdown. It was more than the fact the bank didn't think receipts were an important or necessary part of the deposit procedure for such small amounts. Whereas Britain once had the administrative ability to govern a worldwide empire, now Britain's empire and therefore its status as a superpower was history.

———

It was getting to be difficult staying at Tittenhurst, mainly because it was so far away. Prabhupada's room at the new temple was finished, but many of us didn't feel the Bury Place room would be appropriate accommodation for him, given the amount of noise that was going on in the building as devotees demolished walls, ripped up floor boards and brandished circular saws and sledgehammers. Prabhupada's room was right above the temple room, where most of the noise was coming from. I didn't think it was conducive for peaceful translating and writing.

Although there was plenty of opposition from devotees who felt he should stay in the temple, I managed to secure a three-room apartment about fifteen minutes away. Farleigh Court was situated across the street from Madame Tussaud's Wax Museum on Marylebone Road near Baker Street, and it had an elevator and a uniformed doorman. The apartment itself was clean and quiet with a large high-ceiling living room that was oddly shaped because it had five walls, one of which had a sash window. The view from the window was a redbrick wall about three feet away, a detail that I thought made the room seem like part of a comic film set. I signed a tenancy agreement for three months, hoping it would add impetus to the idea that Shrila Prabhupada could stay on in London a little longer. Prabhupada nipped this dream in the bud.

"Three-month agreement is too long," he said. "You should immediately cancel this agreement and make for one month only. I will stay that long."

Prabhupada stayed in the apartment alone except for Purushottama and spent most of his time translating sitting on a small flat cushion at his low desk. There was a *tamboura* in the room, and one day when I arrived to see him he surprised me by saying, "Teach me the art of playing the *tamboura*."

I was taken aback because it felt wrong for me to be teaching my spiritual master anything. I suspected that he was speaking more in fun or else was trying to encourage me in my music. He'd previously referred to me as a "music master," and I knew that he liked to tell others that I was a composer and had worked in New York as a professional musician.

I picked up the instrument and started to play it with my right hand; third finger across the first three strings, index finger across the fourth and last one. Before the next strum, I'd learned to let the last string ring twice as long as each of the other strings. Prabhupada watched for a few minutes as I swept my fingers across the strings, and listened as I explained the technique behind this kind of playing. Then I handed it to him and he began to play not exactly as I had showed him, but similarly. I didn't want to offend him but at the same time didn't want him to learn incorrectly, so I interceded and explained again the method for strumming the strings. He smiled and handed the instrument back to me, shaking his head as if to say that he wouldn't get it right and didn't really care. I remembered that my first words to him in the Bowery were, "I have a *tamboura*," and I wondered if he remembered asking me to bring it the next time I visited him.

The next morning, I was sitting in Prabhupada's room with Tamal Krishna, one of the American devotees who had recently arrived in London. Prabhupada informed us that his Omega watch had stopped running.

"I feel lost without a watch," he said to me. "Can you get this repaired?"

"Yes," I said.

"I need it back in two days," he said. "Can you do?"

"I can do it," I assured him, knowing that was what he wanted to hear but not knowing how I was going make it happen.

He slipped it off his wrist and handed it to me. I pulled up my sleeve and took off my own watch.

"Would you like to have mine?" I asked holding it out to him. "I mean, just while yours is getting fixed?"

There was a short pause. "Why not? Be practical," he said and put my watch on his wrist.

When we left the apartment, Tamal Krishna turned to me.

"I can't *believe* that you just gave him your watch!" he said in an accusing tone. "How could you do that?" Also I could sense he was holding back a laugh.

Later that day, I found myself at an office in a tall building in London's jewelry center, Hatton Garden. The man representing the watch department said it would take a minimum of a week to fix the watch.

"But the owner of the watch is leaving the country the day after tomorrow, so it's really urgent." I figured a white lie was appropriate in this case. "I'm pretty sure it only needs a battery replacement."

"OK," said the man. "We'll see what we can do."

"Then you can do it in two days?"

"I think so," he said.

Prabhupada was still wearing my watch when I returned late in the afternoon.

"Your watch will be ready in two days," I said, and he nodded. He seemed very pensive, like he was thinking about something else.

There was a pause. "I'm thinking about Vrindavana," he said at last. "When I look out this window at this brick wall, I think of my room in Vrindavana." I remembered him saying how he had stayed at a small temple in the holy city of Vrindavana from 1959 to 1965 and that it was from there that he had planned his journey to America. "I used to look through the window at the tomb of Rupa Goswami. It was too much ecstatic."

I couldn't see how this room could possibly remind anyone of India, much less Vrindavana, the village of Lord Krishna. But years later when I visited Radha-Damodara temple where Prabhupada had stayed, I saw that his eating room was the same size and shape as the sitting room in Farleigh Court. It had a high ceiling and five walls, one of which contained a single latticed window with no glass. This window looked out into the courtyard to the Rajastani-style tomb of Rupa Goswami, one of Lord Chaitanya's foremost associates. I had heard him say many times that he had prayed to Rupa Goswami for strength to take Krishna consciousness to the West.

Although Prabhupada had referred to his Farleigh Court apartment as a "fool's paradise," I now saw that he loved this room because the window and the bricks reminded him of Vrindvana, Krishna and Rupa Goswami.

———•

One of the tasks I was attending to for the temple opening was organizing Radha and Krishna deities for our altar. Janaki and I had had some eighteen-inch wooden deities in our home for some time, which had been carved by devotees named Gaurasundara and

Govinda from Texas. Rather than have these deities as the Lords of the London center, we had decided to investigate the possibility of getting the wooden deities cast in bronze. I'd already gotten an estimate and Prabhupada had approved it.

One morning only days before the opening, the phone rang. I jumped because I hadn't even known there was a phone in the apartment. When I answered it, the voice of an older Indian man drifted down the wire.

"This is Mr. Goyal of the East London Hindu Center," he said. "May I speak to the swami?"

"Just a minute," I said. "He's right here."

There ensued a long conversation in Hindi. When Prabhupada hung up he turned to me.

"You need to go now to Mr. Goyal's," he said. "He has Radha and Krishna deities he wishes to donate for the temple. I want you to go see them."

"Deities?" I asked, feeling resistant because I was attached to the bronze deities. "But Mr. Goyal has never wanted to give any donations before."

"You must go now," Prabhupada insisted.

I drove with Tamal Krishna, Yamuna and a devotee named Radharamana to an east-London residence to view the deities. They were on the floor covered with a sheet, and when Goyal whipped off the sheet, there was an audible gasp from all of us. The deities were three feet tall and intricately carved from white marble with black hair and clothes that were carved as part of the sculpture. Krishna wore a yellow *dhoti* and Radha wore a delicate sari. We had never seen deities this big, and certainly not this beautiful. When I looked closely at Krishna's face I saw subtle bluish striations on his forehead.

"There is some fault in Radharani's hand," Goyal said in English. "Some chipping occurred in transport. But we will repair before giving to you."

I realized that their "gift" was a way of giving away a deity that they deemed unsuitable for installation because it was against Hindu tradition to install a damaged deity in a temple. This cast a shadow over the whole proposal.

London's Radha and Krishna deities close-up

When I told Prabhupada about Radharani's chipped hand the next morning, he insisted on going to assess the damage for himself.

"We must go immediately," he said. "The damage is not great, and if he will give, we will have deities for our London center."

We were greeted by Goyal, his wife and several other members of the East London Hindu Center. Goyal escorted Prabhupada to a chair in the living area and sat down with his compatriots on the couches. We sat on the floor gazing at the sheet-shrouded forms that stood on the floor nearby.

"We represent the board of the Hindu Center," a Mr. Patel said. "We make the decisions on behalf of the temple managing committee." Prabhupada nodded. Goyal turned to me and said, "If you would like to remove the cloth so the swami can see the forms."

When I removed the covers, Prabhupada gazed on the deities expressionless. He began to speak in a serious tone in Hindi to Goyal and the others. The conversation was punctuated with English words "damage," "trouble," and "fixed up." I deduced that they were talking about getting Radharani's hand fixed before the temple opening.

After more than half an hour of trying to figure out what they were saying, the tenor of the conversation suddenly lightened. Prabhupada said something and his hosts began to laugh. Then Goyal said something in response and Prabhupada laughed, gesturing toward the deities with his right hand. The joviality continued for several minutes.

"We have a man," Prabhupada said in English. We snapped to attention, as he gestured toward Yamuna, a woman. The conversation lapsed back into Hindi, but then Prabhupada turned to Yamuna.

"Yamuna, she is expert," he said. "She can repair. Isn't it, Yamuna?"

It was a question, but he nodded to Yamuna as he spoke, and that made it sound more rhetorical, like a statement.

"Oh, yes," she answered enthusiastically, though I could see she wasn't entirely sure to what she was agreeing.

"Tamal Krishna, you can carry Krishna to the van?" Prabhupada asked. "See how heavy He is." Tamal Krishna put his left hand under the base of the Krishna deity and put his right arm around the back, lifting the deity off the covered carpet.

"Not too heavy, Prabhupada," he said, visibly straining.

"You can take Krishna out to the van with Radharamana," Prabhupada said. "Go ahead, take Him immediately." He turned back to his hosts, laughingly said something and continued talking in Hindi as if diverting them from the fact their deity was being carried out of the room. I heard the van door open and then a moment later close. Tamal Krishna and Radharamana then returned.

Prabhupada then beckoned Radharamana to come forward. "You can take Radharani," he said. "Go ahead. Take Her now. Mukunda will help you."

Carefully lifting Radharani, Radharamana and I carried Her to the van and placed Her on the back seat next to the deity of Krishna. When we returned, Prabhupada and his hosts were laughing and speaking animatedly in Hindi. Then Prabhupada stood and folded his palms in *pranam*. We all did likewise. I slowly started up the van and pulled away from the apartment building. The committee members waved goodbye as we went.

"Yamuna, you hold Her," Prabhupada said, turning around in the front seat and indicating Radharani. "Tamal, you hold Krishna. They must not fall." We rode in silence for some time.

Finally, I said, "Prabhupada, I think you just kidnapped Krishna."

He chuckled and was silent for a minute. "Once when I was in India, I presented an idea to my bank manager," he said. "He did not like. I wanted loan. He presented counter proposal. But I argued with him and foiled his scheme. So he said to me, 'Mr. De, you should have been a politician.'" His laughter was infectious and filled the van as we sped away, Yamuna and Tamal Krishna hugging our new deities close to them so the forms would not be damaged.

—

Sunday the 14th of December dawned sunny but bitterly cold. We had looked forward to this day for so long, but now I was panicked by the amount of things I had to organize. We had sent out hundreds of fancy invitation cards to everyone we knew, hoping that we would get a crowd. The temple room was finished in the nick of time. The walls were freshly varnished and adorned with paintings of Krishna; a thick maroon carpet stretched from wall to wall. A separate deity room had been built at one end of the room, divided from the main hall by a low balustrade and heavy blue drapes, and the temple's impressive curved ceiling looked like the hull of a boat turned upside down. When Prabhupada finally stood in the sparkling temple room he said to me, "You should install a brass plaque at the door that says 'This temple was built by the hard labor of effort of Shyamasundar Das Adhikari.'"

By noon, the temple was full of guests, most of them dressed up in suits and dresses or in their best saris. A BBC TV team arrived to film the occasion, and there was barely enough room in the temple for them to set up their cameras. The temperature climbed to what felt like at least ninety-five degrees Fahrenheit. Ventilation was not something any of us had even considered, and I could see this was going to a long, hot ceremony for the guests.

The deities were positioned on a low platform just outside the altar room. Prabhupada sat before them, surrounded by bowls of bathing substances: milk, yogurt, golden liquid *ghee* and rose-scented water.

Inside the London temple

"Thank you all for attending this most auspicious occasion," Shrila Prabhupada said in his short opening address. "This is most wonderful day for all of London, because Krishna is today appearing in this city. These deities will be called Radha-Londonisvara, meaning 'the controller of London.' "

He performed the installation ceremony by pouring ladles-full of the liquids over the deities. The milk, *ghee* and honey cascaded down their curved bodies, collecting momentarily in the ridges of their eyes and the folds of their carved clothing. Prabhupada then carefully bathed them in water, rubbing the milky film from their bodies with his hand. He dried them with soft green towels and requested that they be taken behind the blue curtains and into the altar room. Then he lit a small pile of wood that was stacked on a mound of soil in front of him, and ladling *ghee* over the sacrificial fire, he chanted prayers and invocations.

Then Yamuna, Gurudas, Tamal Krishna and I moved the deities behind the curtain and onto their marble plinth. Behind the closed curtain, the four of us began to prepare the deities and the altar for the first official presentation of Radha-Londonisvara. Then Prabhupada joined us, having finished the fire ceremony, and di-

Outside the London temple on Bury Place

rected Yamuna how to dress the deities in their new clothes. The rest of us were trying to position a purple silken canopy over the deities' altar. It was to rest upon four turned wooden columns that were painted silver. The problem was that the pillars slipped and slid all over the altar the minute we tried to place the canopy's aluminum frame on top of them. There was nothing holding the columns to the marble altar and nothing holding the canopy to the pillars.

Each time we put the canopy in position, the pillars skewed and the canopy careened toward the floor. The deities were dressed beautifully in their new silk clothing; gold crowns decorated their heads and Krishna wore a peacock feather. A raging kirtan was going on in the temple room as the visitors and devotees waited patiently to see London's new deities. Prabhupada's face was anxious, and perspiration streamed down his brow. We tried once again to place the canopy on the pillars, only to have it slip toward the deity of Krishna. Prabhupada sprang onto the marble altar and caught the cupola an instant before the aluminum frame crashed onto the deity's head. We all exchanged looks – standing on the altar was something none of us would dare to do, but the look on Prabhupada's face was that of someone rescuing his child from being crushed.

"Take it out," Prabhupada said to me, holding the frame in both hands. "Take this out."

He shook the canopy.

"Take it where?" I asked.

"Out. Take it out. Outside."

It wouldn't be easy maneuvering through that crowd especially with the canopy. I knew it would be almost impossible. I decided I would try to make it look like part of the ceremony. I emerged from the deity room being careful not to part the curtain and expose the deities to the crowd, and picked my way through the seated crowd, which grudgingly parted to let me pass. I tried to smile so I would

The author garlanding Prabhupada

look like I knew what I was doing; I felt like a geisha wobbling under a heavy load.

Outside, beyond the furnace that was the temple room, the cold air hit me like a welcome splash of ice water. I placed the canopy on the translucent glass squares between the black iron fence and the outer temple wall and breathed a cold sigh of relief.

I closed my eyes and nodded my head in time with the pulse of the *mrdanga*, remembering the first kirtan I went to in the swami's dusty, gloomy loft in the Bowery. A cheer rose from inside, and I quickly went back inside. From the back of the room I saw that the curtains had parted and Yamuna was twirling three smoking incense sticks the way Prabhupada had shown us in the first months we had known him. The *arati* ceremony progressed while Prabhupada stood with folded palms before his Lords. As the kirtan dipped and soared, he turned his face toward the crowd, and I could see by his broad smile that his spiritual master's dream for a London temple was now fulfilled. My own elation at his happiness was marred only by the remembrance that he would leave England in just two days, and the great empty thought that I might never see him again.

PART 4

EPILOGUE

From Then to Now

Death, be not proud, though some have called thee
Mighty and dreadful, for thou are not so;
For those whom thou think'st thou dost overthrow
Die not, poor death, nor yet canst thou kill me.
From rest and sleep, which but thy pictures be,
Much pleasure; then from thee much more must flow,
And soonest our best men with thee do go...

—*John Donne*

Epilogue

I did see Shrila Prabhupada again, of course, though as the International Society for Krishna Consciousness (ISKCON) continued to expand across the world, my time with him was never again as lengthy or as intimate as it had been in those first three and a half fledgling years in New York, San Francisco and London. Over the next seven years, the movement that Prabhupada had begun with a trunk of books in a dusty New York loft became a genuine international society just as he had envisioned when he asked me and Janaki to sign the incorporation papers in mid-1966. Temples, farming communities, restaurants and schools were established not only in the big American and European cities, but also in Australasia, South America, Africa, Asia and even in the Soviet Union and Eastern European countries, where devotees would, until the collapse of communism, take the risk of meeting secretly in their homes. With thousands of members contributing their undivided energy, the ISKCON's growth seemed unstoppable from the optimistic and exuberant perspective that most devotees possessed. In the mid-1970s, ISKCON's annual income was more than twenty million dollars, numerous books were being distributed and the monthly print run of *Back to Godhead* was over a million.

During this time, Shrila Prabhupada played the dual role of spiritual teacher and inspired chief executive of a global organization. The sheer size of the movement meant that rank-and-file devotees had less access to him, but his presence in their lives remained constant through his lectures, his books and his management of the society. Although he intended to give up the day-to-day running of the movement in favor of translating and writing, and although he established a Governing Body Commission whose function it was to lead and manage the movement, Prabhupada never gave up his hands-on concern with ISKCON. His senior disciples took on roles of major responsibility, but the ultimate managerial and spiritual authority continued to rest with Prabhupada, who was continually writing letters to all corners of the earth, offering spiritual instruction and giving savvy legal and financial advice to his young inexperienced managers. In the first eleven years of its existence, the movement seemed to go forward in leaps and bounds, with few apparent negative occurrences to hamper its momentum.

This was not to say that the movement was free of problems. Indeed, many of Prabhupada's leading disciples experienced personal and spiritual difficulties which, in many cases, increased in tandem with their power. Prabhupada was aware of these problems, but he pushed on like a general with wounded soldiers. During the 1980s, the movement was plagued with maladies, both internal and external. Externally, the movement faced challenges from various governments, some of which ransacked temples and imprisoned and even killed devotees. The anti-cult movement also struck ISKCON, fuelling a high-profile court case instigated by the parents of a former devotee, and in several instances kidnapping devotees to deprogram them. Internally, the movement suffered from the corrupt and errant leadership of some of Prabhupada's foremost disciples, a few of whom were involved in criminal activities. The children of Prabhupada's disciples suffered at the hands of unqualified, abusive teachers in the schools. In the 1990s, several apostasies appeared, and numerous disillusioned devotees abandoned the movement in favor of these breakaway groups.

The result of these difficulties has been an internal push for reform and maturation. ISKCON leaders and devotees in most cases sought to address historical problems legally, institutionally and holistically with the aim of never having them occur again. The twenty-first-century movement appears to have a slower growth rate, but has a much wider base than the movement of the 1960s or 1970s, when most devotees lived in the temples and distributed literature in the street. The movement has diversified its activities to include several higher educational institutions (including a center for Vaishnava studies in Oxford), a cow protection program, a few self-sufficient farming projects and one of the world's largest

London's first Rathayatra *festival in 1969, with author playing* mrdanga

The royal couple, the Queen and the Duke of Edinburgh, seem pleased with the touch of garlands that first touched Lord Kṛṣṇa. The Duke received his garland from Varsha Patel, the daughter of one of the Hare Kṛṣṇa movement's many life members in London.

"Hare Kṛṣṇa," said Bhaktimatī, greeting the Queen and the Duke with palms pressed together in the traditional *praṇāma* gesture.

"What did you say?" the Queen asked.

"Hare Kṛṣṇa," Bhaktimatī answered, nodding respectfully.

The Queen gave a gracious smile and bowed slightly to help the garland over the brim of her hat. Then Varsha offered a garland to the Duke.

Later, six-year-old Yamunā dāsī presented a garland to Prime Minister Margaret Thatcher. Yamunā was attired as Lord Kṛṣṇa, complete with bluish hue, peacock feather, glistening silk *dhoti*, and necklaces and bangles. The Prime Minister caught sight of Yamunā at a distance and walked directly up to her with hands folded in a gracious exchange of *praṇāmas*.

"Who are you?" the Prime Minister asked Yamunā.

"I am Kṛṣṇa."

"Then why are you blue?"

"Because Kṛṣṇa is blue."

The Prime Minister smiled and kindly accepted Lord Kṛṣṇa's garland. Then she gave Yamunā a big hug. (The next day the two were pictured together in the *Sun*, Britain's largest daily newspaper.)

Prime Minister Margaret Thatcher enjoys a few moments with Kṛṣṇa (portrayed by six-year-old Yamunā dāsī). "Why are you blue?" the Prime Minister asked.

Queen Elizabeth and then British Prime Minister Margaret Thatcher are garlanded at the "Year of the Child" event, 1983.

international vegetarian food-relief programs. By 2008, hundreds of initiated devotees had post-graduate degrees or were legally practicing medicine or law in their respective countries. Rather than existing outside of their local communities as was once the norm,

Above: Front page of The Guardian newspaper, July 9, 1973

Left: A Los Angeles Times front page photo and article from October, 1976 shows devotees picketing outside the home of a Pasadena, California family who deployed the services of deprogrammers to kidnap their daughter, Kulapriya.

the bulk of ISKCON's members are now people with families and careers who don't wear robes every day but who remain committed to Prabhupada and his teachings. As *Newsweek* reporter Michael Kress put it, "If you think that Hare Krishnas disappeared when the Age of Aquarius ended, look in the next cubicle – one may be working in your office, wearing a suit with a full head of hair."

Of course, all of this was decades away in December 1969 in London when I watched Shrila Prabhupada walk down the telescoping air bridge onto his flight to Boston. I couldn't imagine the successes and failures that lay ahead for the movement, but I knew that I wanted to continue on this journey that I had begun with him.

The six of us who initially brought Krishna consciousness to England remained on the front lines of the movement in London for another couple of years before we gradually began to drift toward America. For some of us the drift took longer than for others. Shyamasundar acted as the first Governing Body Commissioner (GBC) for England until 1971, when he, Malati and their daughter headed to India for a few years. They provided significant help to Shrila Prabhupada in establishing the big temples in India before they returned to the States.

Gurudas returned to America when his marriage to Yamuna began to disintegrate. She remained an active, highly visible member of the movement for many years and had traveled with Prabhupada in India as his cook.

As for me and Janaki, we stayed at the Bury Place temple until 1971, when she decided she wanted to take a step back from the movement. Her involvement had always followed along from mine, and at a certain point she began to question the strength of her own commitment. Wanting to keep our marriage together, I followed her back to Kelso, Washington, where we lived on the periphery of the movement for a couple of years. I tried to live a Krishna conscious lifestyle separate from the main body of devotees and made solo visits to the nearest temple in Portland, Oregon, but I always felt unfulfilled and strained, perhaps as she had when we had been in the thick of things in England.

Finally, in May 1973, she drove me to Portland's airport and I returned to London alone. I felt as if I was losing a part of myself, like my own arm or leg, but I couldn't renounce my commitment to

Enrico Berlinguer

society. In a restless and uncertain country, his contribution to the strengthening of the Communist Party was undeniable; thus his election as secretary-general at the party's 13th congress in Milan, when Longo was given the newly created role of party president, was no surprise.

After becoming "opposition leader," Berlinguer frequently declared his readiness to take an active part in government in what he termed a "historic compromise" between Christian Democrats and Communists. Such offers were rejected, but the June 1975 local elections clearly indicated that the general election of 1977 might give him that opportunity, one that the Italian Communist Party had long been striving for.

(FABIO GALVANO)

**Bhaktivedanta, A. C.,
Swami Prabhupāda**

In the period from October 1968 to November 1975, his divine grace Abhay Charanaravinda Bhaktivedanta, Swami Prabhupāda, astonished academic and literary communities worldwide by writing and publishing 52 books on the ancient Vedic culture. These

A. C. Bhaktivedanta, Swami Prabhupāda

BHAKTIVEDANTA BOOK TRUST

contained many original oil paintings reproduced in colour, translations from texts or *ślokas* printed in their original Sanskrit and Bengali alphabets, and detailed exegeses. His philosophical journal *Back to Godhead* had attained a monthly circulation of three million copies. These and other of his writings were being published throughout the world in 22 languages.

The International Society for Krishna Consciousness, which he had established in 1966, had expanded by the end of 1975 to 78 temples in five continents. By the late 1960s, as a direct result of his missionary activity, shaven-headed men and sari-clad women had become a familiar sight on the streets of the world's major cities as they performed *saṅkīrtana*, devotional chanting of and dancing to the *mahāmantra*: *Hare Kṛṣṇa Hare Kṛṣṇa Kṛṣṇa Kṛṣṇa Hare Hare, Hare Rāma Hare Rāma Rāma Rāma Hare Hare.*

A. C. Bhaktivedanta was 32nd in the spiritual succession, the *Gaudīya Vaiṣṇava Sampradāya.* Twenty-second in the line was Śrī Caitanya Mahāprabhu, who began the Saṅkīrtana movement in 15th-century India. Śrīla Bhaktisiddhānta Sarasvatī Ṭhākur, Bhaktivedanta's immediate predecessor and guru, had ordered him, as his foremost disciple, to disseminate Vedic literature in the English-speaking world. In 1965 Swami Prabhupāda sailed, with only 50 rupees, to Boston, Mass. His teachings were that the Vedic culture, when presented authoritatively and without personal motivation, would effect profound changes in the consciousness of a world afflicted with rampant materialism. Courses in Kṛṣṇa Consciousness were taught in institutions of higher education in many parts of the world, and the swami's books were in use as standard texts in numerous universities.

Born Abhay Charan De on Sept. 1, 1896, in Calcutta, India, A. C. Bhaktivedanta completed his B.A. studies at the University of Calcutta and in 1933 was formally initiated as a disciple of his spiritual master at Allahabad. (MUKUNDA DAS ADHIKARY)

Broadbent, (John) Edward

When David Lewis was defeated in a national election in July 1974, Ed Broadbent became interim parliamentary leader of the New Democratic Party in Canada's House of Commons. In January 1975 Broadbent announced that he would not seek the post of leader of the national NDP because it would not leave him enough time for himself and his family. Urging by important party officials and 10 of his 16 fellow NDP members of Parliament persuaded him, however, to run for the leadership post at the convention in Winnipeg in July 1975. Retiring leader Lewis, who had defeated Broadbent for the post at the 1971 convention, backed him, saying he "saw immense development in the man during the past year as parliamentary leader and given the opportunity he would make an effective leader."

At the convention Broadbent won on the fourth ballot, defeating Rosemary Brown who was supported by the feminist-socialist wing of the party. Backing by labour unions was important for his election. The New Democratic Party was formed in 1961 from the Co-operative Commonwealth Federation and the Canadian Labour Congress, and labour unions are entitled to almost half the votes at any convention. Broadbent, member of Parliament from the Oshawa-Whitby Riding in Ontario, a major auto centre, was backed by key Ontario unions.

John Edward Broadbent came from a working-class background. He was born in Oshawa, Ont., in 1936, the son of a clerk

for General Motors Corp. His brother [came an auto worker, but Ed attended (University of Toronto and received Ph.D. from the London School of Econom and Political Science. In 1968 he was tea ing political science at York University Toronto when he was asked to run for P liament. He won his first election by 15 vc and was reelected in 1972 and 1974.

A solid socialist, Broadbent hoped to velop a new economic plan for Canada 1977, using socialist experts in governm the universities, and the NDP. It wo focus on three major areas: housing, porate power, and resources. Housing, believed, should be removed from the vate sector and a ceiling put on mortg rates. He favoured selective nationaliza of industry, *e.g.,* those dealing with na resources, and believed that multinati companies should not have a voice in C ada's economic growth. What Broad wanted, he said, was an "independent (ada in which all men have the same direct or indirect, in running political economic institutions. (DIANE LOIS v

Brooks, Mel

For a funny man, Mel Brooks began t taken very seriously in 1975. He was filed in the prestigious *New York T Magazine* and analyzed in a *Newsweek* (story.

A onetime gag writer for Sid Ca television series "Your Show of Shows" an occasional performer himself, Brook reveling in the success of his fourth *Young Frankenstein.* This parody of h movies became the object of cultic a tion by young and antiestablishment It followed closely on the roughshod of *Blazing Saddles,* a gamey and prof satire that pricked the balloon of sacrosanct Westerns.

Brooks was born Melvin Kamins Brooklyn in about 1926. "Look at J history," he ordered one interviewer. relieved lamenting would be intolerabl for every ten Jews beating their b God designated one to be crazy and the breast-beaters. By the time I wa I knew I was that one."

At 17 he joined the Army and was : the Virginia Military Institute. "The us ride horses and cut down flags on ba poles. I was trained to become a Confe officer." Later, he fought in World V in the Battle of the Bulge. The war's sion from funny business over, he bec drummer in the Catskills, then filled a comic, and finally rose to the pinn Borscht Circuit success as social dire Grossinger's resort.

Soon he was hired at $50 a week t(jokes for Sid Caesar, who went on t as a television comedian. Then : teamed up with another writer in C stable, Carl Reiner, to invent "The Year-Old Man," a jaded kosher sag had seen everything and was nev pressed.

Later, with Buck Henry, Brook ceived "Get Smart," a television seri parodied the James Bond superspy fil won an Academy Award for his fi fort on film, a cartoon called *The* and then set out to write and direct length comedy, *The Producers.* The play for that movie brought him his Oscar. His other film credit was *The Chairs,* a critical success but not a one. He had achieved his own goal view of many observers: "To be the i has always been my aim," says Brook the most philosophical. Not the me found, but the funniest." (PHILIP)

Encyclopedia Britannica's Book of the Year, 1976 included a biography (written by the author) of Shrila Prabhupada.

On Janmashtami, 1976 the Los Angeles devotees made a one-ton cake for Krishna.

Krishna and Prabhupada. In 1975, at thirty-three years old, I began to wear orange robes, indicating that I had permanently given up the idea of ever re-partnering.

The flourishing ISKCON that I entered in London was bigger and more vibrant than the one I had left two years earlier. We retained the Bury Place temple as the inner-city center for several years until we began to have difficulties with our rental agreement. Prabhupada encouraged us to try to buy the property, but this proved impossible and we eventually relinquished our tenancy in 1978 in favor of a permanent building in Soho Street.

Meanwhile, George Harrison made a generous donation of a seventeen-acre property just outside of London in Hertfordshire's Green Belt. When we acquired the land it was called Piggot's Manor, but we changed the name to Bhaktivedanta Manor in honor of Shrila Prabhupada. I acted as the temple president of the Manor, all the while pursuing my growing interest in media and writing.

In 1976, I returned to live at the Los Angeles temple where ISCKON's Bhaktivedanta Book Trust published Prabhupada's books, where the international lecture and photo archives were housed, and where the devotees had film production and recording studios. In this environment, I reasoned, I could write and develop a much-needed media and public relations department for ISKCON. The deprogramming threat was already in full swing by then, so I became involved in dealing with the media on this and other issues.

Despite the fact that I saw Prabhupada for only short periods of time during these years, I never felt separated from him. I lived in a community of devotees that sustained me, confident that this was the life Prabhupada wanted for me. During the time I was living and working near Prabhupada, I got little direct praise from him, but he still always encouraged me by working with me in a way that seemed close and intimate to the point that he even appeared to depend on my advice. Now I felt that same intimacy, knowing that Prabhupada was satisfied with my life and my work, and, for the first time I began to comprehend the significance of the Sanskrit word *vani*, which literally means "instruction" but which is often used to denote love or service in separation. I had read in Prabhupada's books that even when the spiritual master is not physically present, his instructions or words are accepted as his presence. Living my life in accordance with Prabhupada's teachings, I felt him there with me. I began to realize that what I had heard from my spiritual master was that he himself, and the vibrations of his words, were alive. I genuinely felt Prabhupada's presence in his absence, and over the years, this sense of him being with me increased rather than decreased.

Inevitably, my conviction in Shrila Prabhupada's *vani* was tested. On Monday November 14, 1977, an announcement was made for all the Los Angeles devotees to gather in the temple room at 6:45 a.m. for an important meeting. It was on that morning that Ramesvara, the devotee in charge of the Los Angeles temple, told the three-hundred-strong audience the unthinkable news that Shrila Prabhupada had passed away owing to the devastating illness that had ravaged his body for several months. Later, devotees who had been at Prabhupada's bedside told us that he had continued translating *Srimad-Bhagavatam* into a dictation machine until just minutes before his departure. His lips barely moving, Prabhuapda had defied the pain that his doctors said a person of his condition would be in and, speaking softly into the microphone, he had dictated the translations and explanations of the verses of Chapter Thirteen, Canto Ten of his *Srimad-Bhagavatam*. At one point he had turned to the devotees close to him and said, "Don't think this won't happen to you." Mentally active and philosophically astute, Prabhupada had spoken and interacted with his disciples up until the moment when, suddenly rising into a half-sitting position, he had uttered "Hare K..." – and sunk backwards as he died. The sound of the devotees' chanting and crying had filled the room.

None of these details were yet known to me that morning as I rose blindly from the temple room and walked out into the early morning Los Angeles sunshine. Everything was too bright, like a plastic set from the huge Hollywood movie lots just a few blocks away. I scuffed north toward my office and apartment, my thoughts clambering to be noticed in the whirlwind that raged inside my head.

"Prabhupada, what was it like as you left your body?" I thought. "How can I make it without you? I don't even know what it means to say you are dead."

"Dead." The word sounded ridiculous in connection with Prabhupada. I knew, I had experienced, that even without being physically present, Prabhupada was always with me. Why, then, did I feel like this? Why couldn't I draw on my realization of Prabhupada's *vani* to overcome the grief that I felt engulfing me? The first understated line of Albert Camus' book, *L'Étranger* ran through my mind: "My mother died today." And then I remembered my conversation with Prabhupada at Paradisio when Hayagriva and Kirtanananda had pushed me forward to ask him what would happen to the movement when he died. I recalled the tears that Prabhupada himself had shed that day remembering his own spiritual master, and I realized that even though I would never be separated from Prabhupada – just as he was never separated from his spiritual master – I could still grieve for the terrible loss that had occurred that day.

I fumbled for my keys and heard the phone ringing inside my apartment. I got to it just in time.

"Hello?" I said.

"Is it true about Shrila Prabhupada?"

When I heard Shyamasundar's voice, my eyes flooded and I couldn't speak. Here he was on the phone, this person who was so dear to Prabhupada and who was so close to me, with whom I'd shared San Francisco and London, with whom I'd planned projects and with whom I'd excitedly torn open envelopes with "A.C. Bhaktivedanta Swami" written on the back. This, all of this, poured from my memory triggered by the sound of his voice. How could this be happening? How could Prabhupada be gone?

I gasped for breath. The voice on the other end of the phone was silent.

"Yes," I croaked at last. "It's true."

"When?"

"I don't really know many details yet," I said. Tears dripped from my chin, but I tried to control my voice. "A few hours ago, I guess. In India, but you know that."

"Were you at the temple?"

"Yes. Ramesvara made the announcement." I wondered why such details mattered now. Shyamasundar seemed to be waiting for me to say more, but I didn't know what else to say.

"I owed Prabhupada money," he said finally. "I hope I can clear up my financial situation soon, you know, make good on the debt I owed to him. Pay it back to the book trust."

"Yes."

"You want to go now?" he asked me.

"I guess so. But I don't know where or for what," I said.

"I know," he said, and we hung up.

I put my head in my hands and sobbed, thinking of the words of the sixteenth-century Bengali poet Narottama Das Thakur, who had written that being devoid of the association of Lord Chaitanya and His followers, all he could do was weep. Then I went into the bathroom and threw some cold water over my face. It trickled down my neck and over my crumpled clothes.

"I will go back to the temple to be with Prabhupada's disciples," I thought. "I will greet the deities that he installed because that's what he would want."

From the street I could hear that the deity greeting had already started. Yamuna's amplified voice rang out from the open doors: "*Govindam adi-purusam, tam aham bhajami.*" I remembered the happy moments making the record with her in London and how Prabhupada loved the way she sang about his Lord Govinda.

My thoughts were interrupted by a good-natured devotee named Gauranga who came up to me as I headed toward the temple. He didn't live in the community, but he came almost every day at some point or other.

"Hey, haribol Mukunda," he said, smiling as bright as ever. "Do you have any jumper cables? I'm having some car problems ... as usual, right?" He laughed. "That's what you get for buying a car for under five hundred dollars!"

His routine concerns took the wind out of me for a second, until it dawned on me that he hadn't heard yet. I opened my mouth to tell him, but he spoke again before I could form the sentences out loud.

"Mukunda. Are you OK?" he asked, and I nodded mutely. "The thing is I'm kind of in a hurry. Do you have any cables or not?"

Instead of telling him the news, I said simply that I could help. He was still unconsciously living in the old world where Shrila Prabhupada was physically present, and I didn't want to be the one who broke his last few precious moments in the safety of that world.

Shrila Prabhupada's obituary in the Los Angeles Times, *November, 1977*

ISKCON continued to grow and expand to many more cities and countries around the world after Shrila Prabhupada's passing. Above is the temple room of ISKCON Juhu Beach (Mumbai, India), circa 2002.

Photographic Credits

Torchlight Publishing would like to thank and acknowledge the following for permission to reproduce photos/pictures (All rights reserved. Used by permission and protected by the Copyright Laws of the United States):

New York Times 5, 107

Mukunda Goswami, 6, 41, 49, 79, 91, 94, 114, 126, 142, 147, 150, 163, 172, 177, 181, 186, 195, 196, 247, 279, 300

Village Voice, 22

New York Post, 73

Midnight, 77

Roger Siegel, 146, 175, 184, 187, 190, 197, 219, 242, 322, 339, 341, 344, 345, 346, 367, 368, 373, 375, 381, 383, 384, 393, 394, 406, 414, 417, 425

Harvey Cohen, 142

Krishnadas Bryant, 171

Bhaktivedanta Book Trust, 178, 302, 419

Oracle, 227

Malcolm Durny, 237

James Doody, 296

Back to Godhead Magazine, 303

International Times, 304, 318

Daily Mirror, 317

Sunday Times, 335

Apple Records/EMI, 360, 361, 362, 363, 401, 402

New Musical Express, 364, 391

The Sun, 370

Daily Sketch, 370, 382

Dennis Happerban, 404

Shirley Blimhost, 405

Violet Shonberger, 418

Christopher Michaels, 426

The Guardian, 427

Los Angeles Times, 427, 434

Encyclopedia Britannica, 429

Victor Hammer, 430

Namit Arora, shunya.net, 434

The publishers have made every effort to obtain permission for all of the photos/pictures and to credit all contributors. In the event of an omission or error, corrections will be made in subsequent editions.

The Author

MUKUNDA GOSWAMI, writer, editor, researcher, one
of the earliest members of the International Society
for Krishna Consciousness (ISKCON), and one of the
first western students of the movement's founder, A.C.
Bhaktivedanta Swami, has lectured in thirty-eight
countries, and published many newspaper and magazine articles. Author and co-author of several books, he
now resides in Australia, where he continues to write.